The history and antiquities of the city and suburbs of Worcester. ... By Valentine Green, ... Volume 1 of 2

Valentine Green

ECCO
PRINT EDITIONS

Eighteenth Century
Collections Online
Print Editions

Gale ECCO Print Editions

Relive history with *Eighteenth Century Collections Online*, now available in print for the independent historian and collector. This series includes the most significant English-language and foreign-language works printed in Great Britain during the eighteenth century, and is organized in seven different subject areas including literature and language; medicine, science, and technology; and religion and philosophy. The collection also includes thousands of important works from the Americas.

The eighteenth century has been called "The Age of Enlightenment." It was a period of rapid advance in print culture and publishing, in world exploration, and in the rapid growth of science and technology – all of which had a profound impact on the political and cultural landscape. At the end of the century the American Revolution, French Revolution and Industrial Revolution, perhaps three of the most significant events in modern history, set in motion developments that eventually dominated world political, economic, and social life.

In a groundbreaking effort, Gale initiated a revolution of its own: digitization of epic proportions to preserve these invaluable works in the largest online archive of its kind. Contributions from major world libraries constitute over 175,000 original printed works. Scanned images of the actual pages, rather than transcriptions, recreate the works *as they first appeared.*

Now for the first time, these high-quality digital scans of original works are available via print-on-demand, making them readily accessible to libraries, students, independent scholars, and readers of all ages.

For our initial release we have created seven robust collections to form one the world's most comprehensive catalogs of 18th century works.

Initial Gale ECCO Print Editions collections include:

History and Geography
Rich in titles on English life and social history, this collection spans the world as it was known to eighteenth-century historians and explorers. Titles include a wealth of travel accounts and diaries, histories of nations from throughout the world, and maps and charts of a world that was still being discovered. Students of the War of American Independence will find fascinating accounts from the British side of conflict.

Social Science
Delve into what it was like to live during the eighteenth century by reading the first-hand accounts of everyday people, including city dwellers and farmers, businessmen and bankers, artisans and merchants, artists and their patrons, politicians and their constituents. Original texts make the American, French, and Industrial revolutions vividly contemporary.

Medicine, Science and Technology
Medical theory and practice of the 1700s developed rapidly, as is evidenced by the extensive collection, which includes descriptions of diseases, their conditions, and treatments. Books on science and technology, agriculture, military technology, natural philosophy, even cookbooks, are all contained here.

Literature and Language
Western literary study flows out of eighteenth-century works by Alexander Pope, Daniel Defoe, Henry Fielding, Frances Burney, Denis Diderot, Johann Gottfried Herder, Johann Wolfgang von Goethe, and others. Experience the birth of the modern novel, or compare the development of language using dictionaries and grammar discourses.

Religion and Philosophy
The Age of Enlightenment profoundly enriched religious and philosophical understanding and continues to influence present-day thinking. Works collected here include masterpieces by David Hume, Immanuel Kant, and Jean-Jacques Rousseau, as well as religious sermons and moral debates on the issues of the day, such as the slave trade. The Age of Reason saw conflict between Protestantism and Catholicism transformed into one between faith and logic -- a debate that continues in the twenty-first century.

Law and Reference
This collection reveals the history of English common law and Empire law in a vastly changing world of British expansion. Dominating the legal field is the *Commentaries of the Law of England* by Sir William Blackstone, which first appeared in 1765. Reference works such as almanacs and catalogues continue to educate us by revealing the day-to-day workings of society.

Fine Arts
The eighteenth-century fascination with Greek and Roman antiquity followed the systematic excavation of the ruins at Pompeii and Herculaneum in southern Italy; and after 1750 a neoclassical style dominated all artistic fields. The titles here trace developments in mostly English-language works on painting, sculpture, architecture, music, theater, and other disciplines. Instructional works on musical instruments, catalogs of art objects, comic operas, and more are also included.

The BiblioLife Network

This project was made possible in part by the BiblioLife Network (BLN), a project aimed at addressing some of the huge challenges facing book preservationists around the world. The BLN includes libraries, library networks, archives, subject matter experts, online communities and library service providers. We believe every book ever published should be available as a high-quality print reproduction; printed on-demand anywhere in the world. This insures the ongoing accessibility of the content and helps generate sustainable revenue for the libraries and organizations that work to preserve these important materials.

The following book is in the "public domain" and represents an authentic reproduction of the text as printed by the original publisher. While we have attempted to accurately maintain the integrity of the original work, there are sometimes problems with the original work or the micro-film from which the books were digitized. This can result in minor errors in reproduction. Possible imperfections include missing and blurred pages, poor pictures, markings and other reproduction issues beyond our control. Because this work is culturally important, we have made it available as part of our commitment to protecting, preserving, and promoting the world's literature.

GUIDE TO FOLD-OUTS MAPS and OVERSIZED IMAGES

The book you are reading was digitized from microfilm captured over the past thirty to forty years. Years after the creation of the original microfilm, the book was converted to digital files and made available in an online database.

In an online database, page images do not need to conform to the size restrictions found in a printed book. When converting these images back into a printed bound book, the page sizes are standardized in ways that maintain the detail of the original. For large images, such as fold-out maps, the original page image is split into two or more pages

Guidelines used to determine how to split the page image follows:

• Some images are split vertically; large images require vertical and horizontal splits.
• For horizontal splits, the content is split left to right.
• For vertical splits, the content is split from top to bottom.
• For both vertical and horizontal splits, the image is processed from top left to bottom right.

THE

HISTORY AND ANTIQUITIES

OF THE

CITY AND SUBURBS

OF

WORCESTER.

VOL. I.

BY VALENTINE GREEN,

FELLOW OF THE SOCIETY OF ANTIQUARIES, LONDON.

LONDON:

PRINTED FOR THE AUTHOR BY W. BULMER AND CO. AND SOLD BY G NICOL, BOOKSELLER TO HIS MAJESTY,
EDWARDS, WHITE, CADELL, PAYNE, ROBSON, STOCKDALE, LEIGH AND SOTHEBY, EGERTON, HOOKHAM AND CARPENTER,
SHEPPERSON AND REYNOLDS, AND IN WORCESTER BY SMART, TYMBS, HILL, ANDREWS AND GAMIDGE, BOOKSELLERS.

MDCCXCVI

THE KING.

SIRE,

Modern WORCESTER *having had the distinguished honour of being known to your* MAJESTY, *that portion of its history, in the following Work, which treats of its present state, is so far anticipated in its purposes of information, that, in respect to your* MAJESTY, *it can only endeavour to discharge the humble duty of a mere reflecting mirror, producing objects already more correctly viewed, and better known, than by any representation it can pretend to offer.*

Ancient WORCESTER, *remarkable and important in its history, both ecclesiastical and civil, presents a feature in the national character of past ages not unworthy of minute contemplation : and the tracing of the steps by which a military station was improved into a metropolis, the feudal seat of a Saxon viceroy transformed into that of arts and opulence, will not, it is presumed, be found destitute of sufficient interest to merit attention.*

Its church, from the earliest times, has been one of the most renowned for its sanctity and discipline; its prelates revered for the extent of their learning and the eminency of their virtues ; its magistrates and citizens honoured for their probity and loyalty, and not less so for their upright administration of justice, and prompt obedience to the laws: zealous to dignify, by exemplary conduct, the character they respectively sustained, each has mutually assisted in elevating the name of their city to the most distinguished height of moral pre-eminence. Thus guided and guarded, by the firmest friends to its peace and its prosperity, WORCESTER *has become a complete illustration of the substantial good which results from a steady adherence to the principles*

a

of orderly government, supported by our glorious constitution ; under the benign auspices of which, rational liberty and social harmony, have not only been permanently secured to WORCESTER, *but to all the classes of a brave, a generous, and a free people, who have the happiness to share in the mild influences of your* MAJESTY's *beneficent reign.*

Such, SIRE, *is the object most graciously permitted me to lay at your* MAJESTY's *feet.   With talents less feeble, it would have been made more worthy of that honourable distinction ; with none could it have been prepared with a more ardent desire that it might become so : nor could it have occupied a mind capable of being more sensibly impressed with gratitude for the signal condescension, than that of*

SIRE,

Your MAJESTY's

most devoted,

most dutiful,

and faithful subject

and servant,

London,
April 23, 1796.

VALENTINE GREEN.

SUBSCRIBERS.

HIS MAJESTY.

His most Serene Highness the Elector Palatine, reigning Duke of Bavaria, &c. &c. &c.

Her most Serene Highness the Electress Palatine, &c. &c &c.

Abbott, L. F Esq. London.
Agg, Mr. Bookseller, Evesham, Worcestershire, 2 copies fine paper
Andrews, Mr Bookseller, Worcester, 4 copies.
Arrowsmith, Mr. Worcester
Astle, Thos. Esq F R. S. and S. A. London.
St. Aubyn, Sir John, Bart. M. P
Austin, Robert, Esq F S. A London.

Bacon, John, Esq R. A. and F. S A London
Barnes, Henry, Esq. Ombersley, Worcestershire.
Barr, Mr Martin, Worcester
Barry, Lieutenant Colonel.
Baty, Rev. Richard, Chancellor of the Diocese of Worcester
Beale, Rev. Mr Bengworth, fine paper.
Bedford, Rev Mr. Worcester
Bedford, Mr. William, Birmingham.
Beesley, Mr. Henry, Worcester
Berkley, Rowland, Esq. Cotheridge, near Worcester.
Berwick, Joseph, Esq. Hallow Park, near Worcester.
Berwick, Mrs. ditto
Bindley, James, Esq. F S. A. London.
Birmingham Library.
Bland, Robert, M. D. F. S. A. London.
Blayney, Thomas, Esq. Evesham
Bourne, Mrs. Worcester.
Bowyer, Robert, Esq. London.
Boydell, John, Esq. Alderman, London
Bright, Lowbridge, Esq. Bristol.
Bromley, Rev. Mr. London.
Bromley, Robert, Esq Abberley Lodge, near Worcester
Brookholding, Mr. Thomas, Worcester.
Brydon, Mr. John, London.
Bull, Mr. John, Worcester.
Bulstrode, G Gardiner, Esq. Worcester
Bund, Thomas, Esq Wyck, near Worcester
Burlingham, Mr Worcester
Byfield, George, Esq. London.

Cadell and Davies, Messrs. booksellers, London, 15 copies, 3 fine paper.
Calcott, Rev. William, Caynham Court, Shropshire.
Cameron, Dr. Worcester.
Carden, Thomas, Esq. Worcester.
Carr, Mr. London.
Carver, Rev. Dr. Archdeacon of Surrey, and Prebendary of Worcester.
Chapeau, Captain, Worcester.
Charlewood, Mr B. London.
Chelsum, Rev Dr Hants.
Claridge, John, Esq. London.
Clarke, Richard, Esq. Alderman, London.
Clarke, Richard, Esq Worcester, fine paper.
Clarke, jun Richard, Esq. ditto ditto.
Clifton, Mr. Deputy Register, Worcester.
Cochrane, the Hon. John.
Cole, Mr. London.
Collet, Samuel, Esq. Worcester, fine paper.
Combe, Charles, M. D. F. R. S. and S. A. London.
Combe, Mr. Thomas, London
Compton, Henry, Esq. London.
Connyngham, the Rt. Hon William Burton, Teller of the Exchequer, F. S. A. Ireland, fine paper.
Cooksey, Richard, Esq. Middle Temple.
Cosway, Richard, Esq. R. A. London.
Court, Mrs London.
Crane, Samuel, Esq Worcester.
Cribb, Mr. R. London
Cross, William, Esq. Worcester.

Dromore, the Rt. Rev. Thomas Lord Bishop of.
Downes, the Hon. Wm. one of the Judges of the Court of King's Bench, Ireland, fine paper.
Dolben, Sir William, Bart. M. P. London.
Dance, George, Esq R A. London.
Davenport, J. Esq Clapham.
Dimsdale, Richard Iles, Esq. London.

2 2

Dimsdale, Thomas, Esq London.
Dixon, Mr. John, London.
Dowdeswell, Captain, London.
Dowding, William, Esq. Worcester.
Downes, Dive, D. D. London, fine paper.
Downman, John, Esq London.
Duval, Rev Dr London.
Dudley, Book Society.

Ely, the Hon and Right Rev James Lord Bishop of
Eskgrove, the Right Hon Lord, Edinburgh, 3 copies.
Eades, Thomas Beach, Feckenham, Worcestershire.
Edwards, Mr Bookseller, London, 6 copies, 3 fine paper.
Egerton, Mr. Bookseller, London, 20 copies.
Eginton, Mr. Francis, Handsworth, near Birmingham
Eginton, Mr. John, Birmingham
Evans, Rev. Dr Archdeacon of Worcester, 2 copies, 1 fine paper.
Evans, Mr. W Gosport, Hants
Eyre, Mr. London

Farley, Mrs Henwick, near Worcester
Farington, J. Esq. R A London
Fittler, Mr. James, London.
Fletcher, Thomas, Esq Birmingham
Fletcher, William, Esq Birmingham.
Flight, Thomas, Esq Hackney, Middlesex.
Flight, Joseph Mr. London.
Forrest, Mr T Worcester.
Fountain, Rev. Thomas, Prebendary of Worcester.

Gamidge, Mrs. Bookseller, Worcester, 2 copies
Gem, Thomas, Esq Birmingham
Gisburne, Mrs Camberwell
Goodere, Mr. Ephraim, Worcester.
Gough, Richard, Esq F R S Director of the Society of Antiquaries, London
Gower, Charles, Esq Edmonton.
Grace, Mr Paddington
Graves, Walwyn, Esq
Gray, Rev William M A Christchurch College, Oxford.
Green, Mr Rupert, London, fine paper.
Green, Mr Worcester
Greenwood, Mr London.
Greville, Colonel
Griffin, Rev John, Worcester
Griffin, Mr Stephen, London

Griffiths, Captain, Paddington.
Grosse, Rev. Mr. F. S. A. Minister, Tower.
Gwinnell, Mr. Thomas, Worcester.

Harcourt, the Right Hon. Earl of.
Hurd, the Rev. Dr. Lord Bishop of Worcester, 2 copies
Hoare, Sir Richard Colt, Bart. F R. S. and S A. fine paper.
Hume, Sir Abraham, Bart.
Hacker, Mr Worcester.
Hamilton, the Rev. Anthony, D. D. F. R S. and S. A London.
Hall, William, Esq. Bevere, near Worcester
Hammersley, Tho. Esq F S A. London
Harrison, Hugh, Esq Hendon, Middlesex.
Hart, Henry, Esq London.
Harward, Rev. Mr.
Haynes, Mr Walter, Worcester.
Herald's College Library
Holl, Mr. Bookseller, Worcester, 25 copies.
Hookham and Carpenter, Messrs. Booksellers, London, 12 copies.
Hooper, Mrs. Mary.
Hooper, Miss
Hooper, Thomas, Esq Worcester
Hooper, Rev William, M. A University College, Oxford
Hopton, Mrs Worcester.
Howes, Miss Anne, Kensington.
Howe, Mr. James, Birmingham.
Hubbold, Mr C. Worcester

Ilchester, Right Hon Countess of.
Jacob, Mr London
James, John, Esq. London
Jennings, Rev Mr Evesham
Ingram, Richard, Esq Worcester
Johnson, Mrs Sarah, London
Johnson, Alexander, LL D London.
Johnson, Edward, Esq. London.
Johnson, Benjamin, Esq Worcester.
Johnson, Mr Thomas, Worcester
Johnstone, James, M D Worcester.
Johnstone, Dr John, Physician, Birmingham
Johnstone, Edward, M D. Birmingham
Jukes, Mr F London

Kendrick, Mr Joseph, London.
Kendrick, Mr Edward, London.
Kent, Nathaniel, Esq Fulham
Kilvert, Rev Richard, Prebendary of Worcester
Kitchen, Mr. Edward, Worcester.
Knapp, John Noel, Esq Powick

Knapp, M N. Esq. Henley, Bucks.
Knight, Edward. Esq. London, fine paper.

Leicester, Right Hon. Earl of, President of the Society of Antiquaries, F. R. S.
Lewes, Sir Watkin, Knt. Alderman, and M. P. London.
Lamb, Rev. Dr. Prebendary of Worcester
Lambert, Charles, Esq F. S. A. London.
Lane, John, Esq. fine paper, Lincoln's Inn
Layard, Rev Dr. F. R. S. and S. A. Prebendary of Worcester
Lea, Mr Jonathan, Worcester.
Lee and Sotheby, Messrs. Booksellers, London, 9 copies, 3 fine paper
Leycester, the Rev Mr. Cookham, Berks.
Lilly, John, Esq Merton College, Oxford.
Library, His Majesty's, fine paper.
Literary Society, Worcester.
Long, Miss, Worcester.
Lumley, Mr William, London
Lyttelton, Humphry, Esq Town Clerk, Worcester

Musgrave, Sir William, Bart. F R S. and S A London
Magdalen College Library, Oxford, 6 copies.
Martyn, Thomas, Esq London.
Mechel, Chr Basle, Switzerland.
Mellor, Charles, Esq Nottingham
Mence, R. M. Mr Worcester.
Meyrick, John, Esq F. S A London.
Millar, Dr John, London
More, Samuel, Esq Secretary to the Society for the Encouragement of Arts, Manufactures, and Commerce, London.

Nash, Rev. Treadway, D. D. F. S. A Bevere, near Worcester
Newton, Mr Greenwich
Nicol, Mr. Bookseller to his Majesty, London, 3 copies, 1 fine paper
Nicolson, Rev. Thos D D Newbold Pacy, Warwickshire.
Noel, J P Esq.

Onslow, Rev Arthur, D D Dean of Worcester
Oldnall, Rev Mr Worcester
Ord, Craven, Esq F R S and S A London
Osborn, Rev George, Worcester
Overton, Mr Samuel, Worcester

Paine, Mrs Mary, Worcester

Palk, Lawrence, Esq. M. P. London.
Palmer, J. F. M. D. Peterborough.
Paumier, jun. Mr. London.
Payne, Mr. Bookseller, London, 9 copies, 3 fine paper.
Pearkes, Martin, Esq. London
Penn, Grenville, Esq London.
Phillips, Mrs Evesham.
Phillips, Mr. Thomas, London
Pitt, Thomas, Mr. Worcester, 3 copies.
Plumptre, Rev. Mr. Prebendary of Worcester.
Pope, Mr London.
Porter, Miss A. 2 copies.
Poublon, Mr. Ghent
Pradoe, Samuel, Esq.
Price, Mr. Samuel, London.
Pyndar, Rev. Reginald, Hadsor, Worcestershire.

Radnor, Right Hon Jacob, Earl of, F S A.
Romney, Right Hon Lord, late President of the Society for the Encouragement of Arts, Manufactures, and Commerce.
Rous, Sir Charles William Boughton, Bart.
Ramsbottom, Richard, Esq. London.
Raymond, Mr London.
Raynsford, Rev Mr. C J Powick, near Worcester
Roberts, Rev Dr. Loughborough House
Roberts, Wilson Aylesbury, Esq Bewdley.
Robson, Mr. Bookseller, London, 6 copies.
Rogers, John, Esq Rickmansworth
Rogers, Mr Samuel, Hendon, Middlesex.
Ross, Mr. James, Worcester, 2 copies, fine paper.
Routh, Martin Joseph, D D. President of Magdalen College, Oxford
Russell, William, Esq Powick
Russell, Mr. London

Stamford, the Rt. Hon. the Earl of, F S A.
St John, the Hon and Rev Dr. late Dean of Worcester.
St John, St Andrew, Esq. Weasenham, Norfolk
St John, Henry, Esq Worcester.
St John, Rev J S Powick.
Sandford, Mr. Worcester
Savigny, Mr London
Sclater, Miss, Worcester
Selwyn, the Rev Charles Jasper, Blockley, Worcestershire
Sharpe, Edward, Esq. Temple

Shepperson and Reynolds, Booksellers, London, 3 copies, 1 fine paper.
Slade, Edmund, Mr. Southwark.
Smart, Mr. Bookseller, Worcester, 25 copies.
Smith, Mrs. Evesham.
Smith, Rev. Digby, Worcester.
Smith, Captain William, Evesham.
Smith, William, Esq Boston, Lincolnshire
Snape, Mr. John, Birmingham.
Spencer, Rev. Benjamin, Birmingham.
Spilsbury, Mr. London.
Spilsbury, Mr. Luke, Worcester.
Staples, Mr. Charles, Worcester.
Stephens, Francis, Esq. F. R. S. and S. A. London.
Stephens, Mr William, Worcester.
Stillingfleet, Rev. James, Prebendary of Worcester.
Stillingfleet, Rev Edward Helsield, Yorkshire.
Stockdale, Mr. Bookseller, London, 12 copies.
Strachey, the Rev John, D. D. Archdeacon of Suffolk, 2 copies.
Swift, Theophilus, Esq.

Thomson, Dr. Worcester.
Tighe Sterne, Esq. F. S. A fine paper.
Timings, Mr. J. Worcester
Topham, John, Esq F. R. S. and S. A.
Torkington, Rev Dr Prebendary of Worcester.
Townsend, Mr. F. London
Turner, Jacob, Esq Park Hall, Worcestershire.
Turner, Thomas, Esq. Coughley Place, Shropshire.
Turnor, Edmund, Esq. F. R. S. and S A.

Tymbs, Mr. Bookseller, Worcester, 12 copies.

University College, Oxford.
Withers, Sir Chas. Trubshaw, Knt Worcester.
Wakeman, Henry, Esq. Perdiswell, near Worcester.
Wakeman, Mr James, Worcester.
Wall, Dr. Martin, Oxford.
Wallis, Mr. London.
Weaver, William, Esq Tower.
Wells, Mr. Francis, Upton upon Severn, Worcestershire.
West, Benjamin, Esq. President of the Royal Academy, F. S. A. London.
White, Miss, London.
White, Messrs. Booksellers, London, 12 copies.
Whitefoord, Caleb, Esq. F R. S. and S. A. London.
Wickins, Mr. Thomas, Hoxton, Middlesex.
Wigley, Edmund, Esq M P. Worcester.
Willmott, J. Esq. M. P. London.
Winter, Robert, Esq. Clapham.
Wood, John, Esq. Worcester.
Woodhouse, J Esq London, fine paper.
Worcester College Library, Oxford.
Wyndham, Joseph, Esq London.

Yenn, John, Esq. R. A. and F. S. A. London, fine paper
Young, Mr. Constantine, Birmingham.
Young, Mr. George, Worcester.

Zachary, John, Esq. F. S. A.

CONTENTS.

VOL. I.

ERRATA.

Page 38, note (1) for *Preface*, read *Appendix*

Page 52, at the end of the last sentence in the second paragraph, dele the word *already*, and for *Preface*, read *Appendix*

For page 721, read 127.

Page 74, for *William* read *Wulstan de Braunsford*

VOL. II.

Page 31, the second article in the notes should have begun thus "According to Domesday Book," &c.

Page 108, in the list of the Saxon coins, after "No 1. Æthelstan," the following part of the inscription has been omitted "Rex To Br + Mondien Mon Veri"

Page 111, in the fifth text line from the bottom, after the word "nations," add, *of which*; and at the end of that paragraph insert, *is here given*.

APPENDIX.

Page xxiv, for Sect *VI* read Sect *VII*.

Page cxxv, cxxvi, cxxvii, cxxviii for Sect *XIX* read Sect *IV*

Page cxxxviii, in the running title, dele *XIX.* and insert *VI.*, and in the succeeding pages to p. cliv. after the word *Addenda*, insert *Sect VI*

PREFACE.

T_{HE} original " Survey of the City of Worcester," published in an octavo volume, with plates, in 1764, compiled during my residence there, forms the groundwork of " the History and Antiquities of the City and Suburbs of Worcester," contained in the following sheets. That publication was first intended as a mere abstract of its history, which had not before been attempted, to be united with that of its church, which had been drawn up and published by the Rev. Wm. Thomas, D. D. in 1736. But on a revisal of my manuscript by my late learned friend, the Rev Mr. Garbet, he suggested to me an extension of my plan ; and, in confirmation of his favourable opinion of the progress I had made in it, furnished me with the two first sections of it, and which, with very slight variations, now form the same portions of the present work, under the titles of " Worcester under the Romans and Saxons ;" the notes and illustrations which accompany them, are now first added. The accounts of the ancient castle, and of the Bishops of Worcester, from the Reformation to the year 1759, were assistances he also gave to the subject : to have the hand of one so able to lay the corner-stone of its foundation, was a distinction highly flattering to a juvenile attempt, in a department of literature not frequently essayed by youth. (1)

From those instances of his abilities (the only ones ever printed) it will readily be conceived the loss this undertaking sustains in being deprived of his further aid, and depending only on the vigilance I have myself been able to bestow upon it.

Collections for the history of the county, and much of what relates to the city of Worcester, were first made by Thomas Abingdon, Esq

---

(1) See Mr Gough's British Topography, vol II p 388, 389 ed. 2 1780, and Dr. Nash's Worcestershire, vol. II p 25 See also vol. II. Sect XXI. p 104, 105, of this work

b

between the years 1605 and 1647; an employment that occupied his leisure hours for near forty years. (1)   Those collections, transcribed and augmented by his son, were strongly recommended by Bishop Nicholson, in his Historical Library, to the revisal of Doctor William Hopkins, a prebendary of the church of Worcester, whose intimate knowledge of the subject, and extensive learning, peculiarly qualified him to undertake their publication   The task, however, was not entered upon ; and the papers soon afterwards luckily fell into the hands of Dr. Thomas, who, with an intention of giving them to the public, made many valuable additions to them from the registers he examined and transcribed, and from the remarks he made in his general visit to every church in the county ; a labour he actually performed, for the purpose of publishing them, but which his death prevented

The collection thus augmented, was purchased by the late Dr. Charles Lyttelton, Bishop of Carlisle, who also added many papers to them from the old Chapter-house, Westminster, the Tower Records, and other public offices   On the death of his lordship, in 1768, he bequeathed the whole to the Society of Antiquaries, London, of which he was president. In 1774, those papers were confided to the Rev. Treadway Nash, D D.; who, in 1782, having completed the arduous task of their revisal, and arrangement, published them with great additions and improvements, and with a splendid embellishment of plates, in two large volumes, folio, under the title of " *Collections for the History of Worcestershire*"

The Society of Antiquaries were afterwards pleased also to permit me to consult that collection of papers, and to make such extracts from them respecting the History of the City of Worcester, as might be found useful to the present work   in that research, however, I soon discovered that the industry of their learned editor had completely anticipated, in the above mentioned publication, every article of information that could have benefited me by the adoption.   It is, therefore, necessary here to premise, that many of those articles relative to the city of Worcester, derived from the collection for the

(1) See Sect. XX. vol II p 101

history of the county, and on which account Dr. Nash's work is often quoted, are principally such as are contained in Mr. Abingdon's manuscripts, unless where otherwise denoted to have been taken from the additions by the editor. The use Dr Nash has obligingly permitted me, of those parts of his own account of the city, in addition to the former collections, has enabled me to affix points of reference to authorities he has therein rendered easy and accessible, which otherwise must have been sought for in a labyrinth of voluminous papers, in which they could not have been traced but with extreme difficulty. It is here farther incumbent upon me to state, that Dr. Nash, previously knowing from me my intention to resume the subject of the " Survey of Worcester," has touched but slightly upon it, although it was indispensably necessary that that article should form a part of his work, and for which he was, doubtlessly, prepared. Concessions thus liberal and candid, merit the amplest acknowledgment and thanks.

In the archives of the Dean and Chapter of Worcester, many papers that relate to the ancient family possessions in the county, and in which are dispersed much matter of local information, remain still unexplored. Those, however, being generally foreign to the present subject, attention hath herein only been directed to what was found precisely to relate to its plan, and several curious articles have been obtained from that source.

The church of Worcester is already remarked to have been more fortunate than most others in preserving its charters and other instruments, relating to its state under the government of our Saxon kings; in which period it was considered one of the most flourishing in their land. Heming's Chartulary, Sir William Dugdale, Dr. Hickes, and Dr. Thomas, have preserved more of those ancient documents than almost any other church can produce. To those authorities, therefore, the curious are referred for further information respecting its original endowment

From the archives of the Corporation many articles have also been derived, useful to the more readily deducing from the ancient administration of the civil government of the city, the origin of its present form. But not to impede the course of the history with any of those records already published, and to be found in other authors, such as were absolutely indispensable, together with unpublished papers of that description, will be found arranged in the Appendix.

Information derived from official channels may be received with confidence. To decide upon the veracity of articles not clearly traceable to an authentic origin, forms the most irksome part of a compiler's duty ; posted between fact and fiction, to establish the first, and to prevent the approaches of the last, in the various disguises it puts on, is a service of real difficulty ; and from thence it arises, that after all the labours of elucidation, a degree of darkness will still be attendant on antiquity   On the present subject, all practicable means have been resorted to with a view to stamp the character of truth upon every representation offered to the notice of my readers, as well 'n the ancient as in the modern history of Worcester   And I trust it will operate to their satisfaction, when they are told, that in every instance of appeal for information respecting its early accounts, which has been made to those public and official sources from whence alone they can be gathered, full and complete returns have always been rendered, founded on evidence indisputably valid and authentic.   Actual and careful view constitutes the basis on which the representation of the present state of Worcester is raised.

Besides the stores of supply already noticed, other public depositories possessing materials for this work have also been visited ; but none with more success and attention, than that national ornament the British Museum ; from whence many interesting and curious particulars, transcribed from the original papers in that inexhaustible collection, have been obtained. To these I have yet to add the mention of a variety of other channels of useful and valuable information, which have been most readily and obligingly laid open to me, and for which I beg leave to offer my most respectful and grateful thanks to the following gentlemen ; namely, the Rev. Dr Evans, Archdeacon, and the Rev Mr Baty, Chancellor, of the diocese of Worcester ; Richard Clarke, Esq chapter-clerk, and steward to the dean and chapter ;

the Rev. Mr. John Griffin, head master of the King's school; Sir Charles
Trubshaw Withers, Knt; St Andrew St. John, Esq; Dr. Johnstone; Jo-
seph Berwick, Esq.; John Leonard Knapp, Esq.; Richard Ingram, Esq;
Thomas Carden, Esq; Humphrey Lyttelton, Esq. deputy town-clerk;
Mr F P Palmer; Mr. Thomas Pitt; Mr. E. Goodere; Mr. Tymbs; Mr.
Sheriff, and Mr James Ross; Worcester   The Rev Dr Routh, presi-
dent of Magdalen college, Oxford; Dr. Martin Wall, Oxford; Samuel
Tyssen, Esq. Norfolk; Edmund Turnor, Esq. Lincolnshire; Dr. Charles
Combe; Dr John Millar; Craven Ord, Esq; Joseph Planta, Esq. secre-
tary of the Royal Society; the Rev Mr. Brand, and the Rev. Mr Wrighte,
secretaries of the Society of Antiquaries; the Rev Mr. Ayscough, and the
Rev Mr. Penneck, of the British Museum, London

The present work hath farther been eminently honoured, as to its
embellishments, by the masterly engravings which have been presented to it.   It would be a gross affectation of humility, did I not appre-
ciate this munificent patronage at its true value, in considering it as a
public adoption of the subject, and as a distinction of which I may be
justly proud, should the discharge of my duty be found at all commensurate
to a support the more flattering, inasmuch as it hath been given wholly un-
solicited and unexpected   It is at this point, however, that I become most
feelingly alive to its defects, lest their nature and number should be such as
to prove that countenance to have been given *undeserved.*

Impressed with the profoundest gratitude, I embrace the present as the
most suitable medium of returning my humble thanks to the following

BENEFACTORS OF ENGRAVINGS TO THIS WORK.

	SUBJECTS.
The Right Rev. Richard, Lord Bishop of Worcester - - -	*View of Worcester Palace.*
The Honourable and Reverend the Dean, and the Reverend the Chapter of Worcester	*View of the Cathedral.*

SUBJECTS.

The Honourable and Reverend Dr. St. Andrew
St. John, Dean of Worcester   -   *View of Prince Arthur's Chapel.*

The Honourable and Right Reverend, James
Lord Bishop of Ely   - -   *Bishop Maddox's Monument.*

The Right. Honourable David Rae, of Esk-
grove, a Lord of the Session, &c. Scotland   *Mrs. Rae's Monument.*

Mrs. Sarah Johnson, sister of the late Bishop
Johnson   - - -   *Bishop Johnson's Monument.*

The Reverend Dr. Evans, Archdeacon of Wor- *Internal View of Prince Ar-*
cester   - - -   *thur's Chapel, Nov. 1788.*
     Ditto in its present state.

St. Andrew St. John, Esq.   -   *Internal View of the Cathedral.*

Richard Clarke, Esq.   - -   *Ditto of the Chapter-house.*

Sir Charles Trubshaw Withers, Knt.   *Monument of T. Withers, Esq.*
     and View of Sansom-fields.

Joseph Berwick, Esq.   - -   *Seals and Coins.*

Messrs. Joseph Flight, and Matthew Barr,
proprietors   - - -   *View of the Royal China Ma-*
The Right Worshipful Thomas Carden, Esq   *nufactory.* (1)
Mayor, 1790 ; (2) the Aldermen, and the

(1) I must express my regret that the arrangement of the engravings of the churches, having been carried into execution before the accounts of them had been written, they are thence not precisely placed in the order they occur in the parochial part of their history, which takes them up in a direct course of succession from the south to the north extremities of the city. The house of industry having been built after the plate was engraved, on which the infirmary and audit-hall are represented, the advantage was thereby lost, not only of having the two modern structures, devoted to charitable purposes, produced on the same plate, but also the two ancient edifices of Edgar's tower and the audit-hall, appendages to the cathedral, being given in the same order of conjunction.

(2) As the order of the chamber of Worcester for presenting those plates to the work, was made in the mayoralty of that gentleman, it is conceived most respectful to address that plate to the then presiding magistrate, and the other to the chief magistrate presiding at the date of its publication ; a measure, it is hoped, that will not give umbrage in having been adopted.

SUBJECTS.

In the history of the fabric of the cathedral, given in Section IV it will
be perceived, that entire new ground has been taken respecting the order
and progress of its erection.   Indeed one of the principal reasons which induced me not to abandon the revisal of this subject, but at some favourable
conjuncture to endeavour to render it more correct, was the dissatisfaction I
had continually felt on every recollection of that part of the first edition,
which treats of the building of the church ; and more especially from seeing
so many of its errors adopted into other publications.   And I was the

(1) The professional liberality of the three last-named gentlemen, have a peculiar claim to my thank-
ful acknowledgments but to Mr James Ross, of Worcester, whose sterling abilities as an artist, are
only equalled by his unaffected modesty, and by whose talents it will be found this work is enriched in a
manner highly honourable to his reputation, much more is owing than is *expressed on the title-page* By
his persevering and friendly attention to a variety of objects on which much of his time, and more of his
patience, hath been exercised, than any thing less than his attachment to the subject could have exacted,
my progress hath been much facilitated to the end of a labour difficult enough in every other point of
view, but rendered still more so on many occasions by my distance from the objects of investigation,
which, notwithstanding my having thrice visited Worcester, for the sole purpose of completing my in-
quiries respecting them, still required frequent recurrence to, and careful re-examination of ;—services
he has never ceased to render with equal promptitude and accuracy

more confirmed in that resolution by the observations Dr. Lyttelton, late
Bishop of Carlisle, had made on the subject, in his letter to Smarte Lethieullier, Esq. (1) and which his lordship was pleased to recommend to my attention, when I should undertake a future edition. The performance of this
duty, which I considered as an injunction, I have herein endeavoured to discharge with all the diligence and attention it was within the compass of my
ability to bestow upon the subject; in which, however, it will be found, I
have widely deviated from many of the most material points his lordship had
examined and discussed.

Attention hath also been paid to the internal order and arrangement
of our ancient churches, few of which were under stricter discipline, better provided, or more respectable than that of Worcester The accounts
of its ancient offices, and of its monuments, have also been reduced to
a regularity of representation, that has removed much of the obscurity
that heretofore pervaded them, by the immethodical and erroneous state-
ments of former compilers.

The learning of a new lesson may, indeed, be found irksome to those officers of the church, who for a length of time past may have been in the habit of detailing the traditional errors of its former history, and with whose
ill-informed predecessors, I am persuaded, originated, among many others,
the marvellous account I myself forty years ago heard a grave sexton retail,
whilst he was shewing the tomb of King John —" How that king had
been poisoned by two monks, who had administered it to him in vessels like
those they held in their hands, (which are censers ;) that to avoid detection
and punishment, they swallowed poison themselves ; and that the effects of
the destructive draughts first appeared upon the backs of their own and the
king's hands ;" the marks of which (where the jewels on the gloves of the
king, and of the two bishops, Oswald and Wulstan, had been set,) (2) he
did not fail to point out to his wondering auditory, in solemn confirmation of

(1) See Appendix, p cxli No. XLI   (2) See Sect VII p. 153 Art 25 vol I.

his narrative. This tale, and the equally absurd one of the Countess of Salisbury and her garter, (1) has not, however, been repeated there for some years since. Nor can there be a doubt, from a moral regard to truth, and a reverence of the place in which they are frequently called upon to render verbal accounts of various objects, and portions of the church, that the present officers will endeavour to supply the place of exploded fiction, by reports on which strangers who visit the cathedral may more safely depend, and by which its history, sufficiently abounding with real curiosity, may become better understood

The additions made to the history of the city, both ancient and modern, are numerous and extensive ; but to be fully informed of either, the Appendix, which is of considerable magnitude, must not be overlooked. The reader may form some idea of the necessity of adding to its modern history, and of the active exertions of the guardians of the interest and honour of Worcester, when he is told, that not one of the important additions and improvements mentioned in the subjoined note existed, or had taken place, when the first edition of this work appeared in 1764, (2) all of which are fully completed.

In the general course and progress of this work, many parts of the history of Worcester which no antiquary's torch had yet illumined, are brought to view ; it is presumed, that the inhabitant of that city, if he has not made antiquities his study, may find in it observations that are new to

---

(1) A *story* I was sorry to see retained in a very late publication, in other respects replete with entertaining anecdote.

(2) The infirmary begun in 1767, St Martin's church, 1768, the bridge, 1771, with the new streets, quays, roads, and avenues —The city water-works, 1772, the theatre, 1779; the old bridge taken down, 1781, the city new paved and lighted, 1783, the castle reformed and repaired, 1784, the city gaol repaired and enlarged, 1789, the new council chamber of the Guildhall reformed, 1791, and the house of industry built, 1793 the total expence of which, exclusive of the paving and lighting of the city, of carrying on the work of the new canal between Worcester and Birmingham, and of opening the new approach to the city from the London road, with a variety of lesser items, amounts to upwards of 65,000l.

c

him; discussions that are curious, if not satisfactory; and illustrations not fanciful, though in some instances not demonstrative. And that the stranger, whose curiosity cannot but be excited on his entrance into Worcester, may find no ordinary or inadequate guide to gratify it; but an intelligencer who has laboured to convey to him the exactest information, derived from the most authentic sources, and rendered with a faithfulness on which he may rely, although not dressed in a garb he may admire.

James Ross Seedon

Stulittle

WEST VIEW OF THE CITY OF WORCESTER

Subscribers to this Work this Plate is most Respectfully
in their most Devoted and Most humble

Valentine Gre

A Sparrow Sculp

ditted,

'll

THE

HISTORY AND ANTIQUITIES

OF THE

CITY AND SUBURBS

OF

WORCESTER.

―――――――――――――――――――――――

Worcester has a place among the most ancient and eminent cities of England. There are reckoned but five superior to it for extent and populousness Its situation is very pleasant. The principal part of the city occupies the most elevated ground from the north to the south, arising gradually from the eastern bank of the Severn. Abberley hills are seen towards the north-west; on the east side the view is finely terminated by several beautiful eminences tufted with trees: between the south and west, at the distance of about eight miles, the majestic and venerable piles of Malvern rise; useful in condensing mists in summer, but intercepting too soon in winter the evening sun. This mountain, which befriends its whole neighbourhood, is beneficial to Worcester by its salutary springs. The geographical situation of this city is in the latitude of 52 degrees 18 minutes, and longitude west 2 degrees and 15 minutes. Its remote antiquity has been generally allowed. But this is a point that deserves particular and attentive discussion.

―――――――――――

SECT. I.

OF WORCESTER UNDER THE ROMANS.

The origin of celebrated cities is not less obscure, than the first production of the rivers on which their commerce and splendour depend. And yet the antiquary, as well as the naturalist, will be warm and confident; the one, as if he had traced all the secret syphons that feed the fountain; the other,

B

as if he had turned up foundation-stones, inscribed with the name of the prince that laid them

Constantius Cæsar has been assigned for the founder of Worcester, on the credit of John Ross of Warwick, (a writer contemporary with King Edward IV.) who met with this anecdote in an old British chronicle, whose date being unknown, renders its authority dubious. It is uncertain too, which Constantius is meant, whether the son of Constantine the Great, Fl. Jul. Constantius, who died A. D. 361, who, as Ninnius pretends, built Caer Segeint (or Silchester), but more probably never was in this island; or Constantius Chlorus, the father of Constantine, who was declared Emperor, upon the resignation of Dioclesian and Maximilian, with the title of Cæsar. (1) We may allow that Britannia Romana owed many of its public works and ornaments to this prince his consort, the Empress Helena, (2) built more churches in the empire, than any nursing mother, imperial or royal, since her time · the public spirit of Constantius drew architects into Britain, whom, to gratify the people of Autun in Gaul, he was content to spare for the rebuilding that ancient city. (3)

There are writers, however, who hesitate whether the rise of Worcester should be ascribed to the Romans or the Saxons, by whom, about A D. 584, the kingdom of Mercia was founded, which soon reduced all the British settlements on the east of the Severn They surmise that this, and other places of strength on the eastern bank of that river, might be built and fortified by the Mercian princes, for curbing the independent tribes of Britons on the other side, and repelling their frequent invasions.

But Worcester, whether it owed its origin to the Romans or not, was

(1) While he served here under Aurelian, he married Helena, daughter of Coel, or Cœlius, a petty prince of Britain, by whom he had Constantine the Great, born in Britain • Fl Valerius Constantius, surnamed Chlorus, was eminent for his virtues, and for his profession of the Christian faith he resided several years in Britain, " called " as his panegyrist expresses himself, " by Heaven to the extremity of the world," † and dying at York, A D. 306, the year after his accession to the imperial dignity, he was deified, as appears by his coins ‡

(2) This is that Helena, who, in ancient inscriptions, is stiled " Venerabilis et Pientissima Augusta " Great honour has been done to her memory in this country, by inscribing many of its churches with her name, among which Worcester has an instance in the oldest of its parochial churches Morant, in his History of Colchester, of which town this princess was a native, has much curious information respecting her. (3) Eumenius in Panegyrico. VIII

• Gough's Camden, vol I p liv   † Eumenius, Paneg. ad Constantin. c. 7.   ‡ Camden in Yorkshire, Gough's Ed. vol. III. p. 10.

certainly of some note, and possessed by the Britons before the arrival of the Saxons (1) Gildas, who wrote in the middle of the sixth century, while the Mercian kingdom was not yet in being, speaks of Britain as adorned with twenty-eight cities. Bede, the father of Saxon history, treating of the pristine state of the island, says it was *viginti et octo nobilissimis civitatibus insignita* (2) Ninnius, an ancient British writer, has preserved the catalogue of them ; (3) in which the 14th city is Cair Guorangon ; and the 18th, Cair Guricon. In the last name we may plainly discern the Uriconium or Viriconium of the Romans ; and may safely follow the old historians, Alfred of Beverly, and Henry of Huntingdon, in admitting Guorangon to be Worcester, (4) which to this day retains that name in the British language. (5)

(1) Bishop Lyttelton, in a note on this text, says, " We have no just idea of British towns prior to the Roman invasion, either, therefore, Worcester was Roman or Saxon "

According to Cæsar, the strong towns or fortified places of the Britons were only thick woods, fenced with a ditch and a rampart, * by these they resisted the best troops under the command of the best officers in the world, and even gained from the greatest of the latter the repeated praise of excellent fortifications † Their towns, however, were not always scenes of either general or regular residence, they were often only their places of refuge amid the dangers of war, and not unfrequently like the " forest camp or fastness of Cassibeline, misnamed a town " ‡ The natural advantages of rivers, and the commodiousness of their banks, were as well understood by the Britons as by their successors, in as much as regarded their safety and convenience. Worcester, therefore, answering in every circumstance to the principles which were constantly attended to by the Britons in selecting a spot whereon to fix a residence, could not but become one of their favourite cities Situated on the border of an immense forest, on a knoll, on the margin of a great river, and at a fordable part of it, which must of necessity engage their strictest attention, whether in preventing the inroads of their opposite neighbour, or in availing themselves of opportunities of making incursions in turn upon them, its natural advantages were undoubtedly too apparent and too important to have been lost upon their observation.

It has not been unfrequently the practice of the Romans to unite the works which the Britons had prepared, with whatever mode of their own fortification they might adopt for the defence of those places from whence they had driven them, and as they extended their settlements in the island, they appear to have erected stations for themselves, and cities for the Britons Many instances are recorded of that practice, and also that it continued to be their custom in their progressive reduction of the island ‖ And thus Worcester, although it might not have had a Roman station fixed in it, might nevertheless become a very considerable and important British town under their protection and safeguard These instances of Romanized cities or towns so provided, are not to be confounded with those of which the Britons themselves were the constructors and inhabitants, prior to the Roman invasion

(2) Bede, Eccles Hist l 1 c 1 (3) Usseru Britann. Eccl Antiq. p 33, 34 Ed 2 (4) Britannis vel hodie Wigornienses dicuntur Gwyr changon, et corrupte Gwrangon [Baxter, Antiq Brit p 189]

(5) Worcester, anciently called *Branonium*, which the Welch corrupted in *Wrangon*, prefixing *Caer*, as was their method It signifies the city *ad frontem aquæ* [Stukeley's Itin Cur p 64] Caer Guorangon—*q d* a frontier town garrisoned with persons called by the Britons Barangi, or Guarangi, whence

* Cæsar, p 92. † Morant's Hist of Colchester, p 11 Ed 2 ‡ Ibid p 12. ‖ Tacitus Ann lib xiv. c 33, and lib. xii. c. 32 Richard, p 24 Stukeley's Itin Curios. p 195.

B 2

Worcester, then, was a city of the ancient Britons The other question recurs; whether it was Roman too? It was policy in the conquerors of Britain, for securing the obedience of very refractory provincials, to build forts adjacent to all the considerable towns of the Britons, for the reception of Roman garrisons; and to carry on a chain of military roads, through forests impervious before, for the more easy communication between these Castra Stativa, or stations. May we venture to suppose a Roman station of this sort at the British Guorangon? Let it pass, if the reader pleases, for a mere hypothesis. There are reasons, however, which may incline him to favour it.

I. Because it is not easy to conceive, that under a military government the Severn should be left unprovided of forts, (1) in the long tract of it from Uriconium (Wroxeter) to Glevum (Gloucester) Such fortifications might, after a few ages, be lost in a great town, as this, or even in Bridgnorth or Tewkesbury; but elsewhere, on a bank not crowded with buildings, nor loaded with rubbish, (from conflagrations, or other causes) their vestiges might be expected to appear.

II. At Worcester there is an important pass in the line of communication between two unquestionable Roman stations, Alcester and Kenchester, the river here being in most summers fordable, near the college especially; and a fort must have been necessary at the pass, for the reception of troops till they could wade, and for the protection of them in wading through the water when lowest, (as the Severn had no bridges in those days,) as well as for repelling the inroads of the Silures and Ordovices; the one remarkable for their ferocity, (2) the other for the extent of their territories, in the country west of that river.

the city itself had the name of Wrangon, Gorangus, Gerongus, Cuorongus, custos ostiarius According to Camden, Vortigern appeared a Guoroing, or Viceroy over the province of Kent [Camd Brit vol I. p. 210 Gough's Edit See also Spelman's Glossar v *Baro*, Barongus]

(1) Forts were actually built on this river by the Roman propraetor Ostorius. Ille (Ostorius) detrahere arma suspectis, cinctosque castris Antonam et Sabrinam fluvios cohibere parat [Tacit Ann l xii p 31] Dr Nash in his Preface, p iv says, " From this obscure passage some have inferred that the Romans were in possession of Worcestershire, but the country here described was probably near Tewkesbury, in Gloucestershire —That *cinctos* does not refer to the Britons, and that there is no mention of forts From this passage he therefore conjectures that the Britons were in possession of Worcestershire, and that Ostorius endeavoured to prevent their marching farther than Tewkesbury [See his " Worcestershire," vol 1]   (2) Siluras, super propriam ferociam, Caractaci viribus confisos.—Praecipua Silurum pervicacia [Tacit. Annal. l xii. 33 39]

III. The name given to this town by the Saxons, Weogorna Ceastre, implies, that they had found either a Roman camp or fort in this place; the addition of Ceastre or Chester being as sure an indication of a fortress in the Roman form, as that of Berig or Bury is of one in the Celtic or the Gothic. A camp it will be said might have been here, yet no station. Was it then a summer camp? The castra æstiva of the Romans were not certainly in low vallies, nor contiguous to towns. but eminences, that afforded extensive prospect, and the advantage of descrying distant motions of an enemy, were the proper situations for these. The camp at Guorangon, it will be replied, was for winter service. Now the point is conceded : for what were stations but quadrangular intrenchments with barracks, disposed at proper distances along the military ways, for the refreshment of the troops in their marches, and for the lodging of them, when they separated for cantonment during the winter?

IV There are found remains of Roman roads at no very great distance from Worcester, which point towards it, and seem to have intersected each other there I have heard of one, called the Ridgeway, to the north-east of Droitwich Take Mr. Salmon's account of the rest. "There is," says he, (1) " a raised way between Worcester and Aulcester, on the edge of the county called the Ridge-way. There is a paved way from Kenchester leading to a passage of the Lug, and so towards Ledbury, pointing to Worcester. (2) There is a way from Worcester (3) pointing towards Wrottesley (in Staffordshire) Another leads by Upton to Gloucester" If this account be true, Worcester was the centre to which several military roads were directed, and at which they crossed each other; the way from Glevum (Gloucester) on the south, to Mancunium (Manchester) in the north ; the way from Magnæ (Kenchester) on the west, to Alauna castra (Aulncester) on the east ; besides another way, which diverged from the same centre, to

(1) Salmon's New Survey of England, p. 686 699.

(2) On a little brook called the *Ine* stands *Ariconium*, from whence, after encompassing the walls of Hereford, it falls into the Wye Two great Roman roads here cross each other, the one called *Port way*, comes from *Bullæum*, now *Buelt*, in Brecknockshire, and passing eastwards by Kenchester through Stretton, to which it gives name, over the river Lug to Stretton Grantham, upon the Froome, *goes to Worcester* [Gough's Additions to Camden vol II. p 449 in Herefordshire]

(3) Mr Salmon inattentively says, that this military way crosses Shropshire It passes in a direction from south to north, touches the eastern border of that county near Abbots castle, leaves Chesterton on the left, and intersects the famous Watling-street in a heath b. E. of Newport.

Salinæ (Droitwich) on the north-east, and thence passed to Etocetum, near Litchfield. (1)

If the old parchment roll which Camden met with, might be depended on, there was formerly no want of Roman bricks in this city; *Romanis olim superba mœnibus.* (2) But I lay no stress on its authority If, as is most probable, the Norman castle, and the Cathedral church were built on the site of the old Roman fort; Urso d'Abitot, and Bishop Wulstan must have levelled with the ground the walls of that strong hold, many centuries ago.

But if Worcester be allowed a place among the Roman stations, the curious will be ready to inquire, what was its Roman name Camden flattered himself that he had found it in Antoninus's Itinerary, where the road from *Isca* (Caerleon) to *Uriconium is laid down*, and has these stages: 9 miles to Burrium (Uske), 12 more to Gobannium (Abergavenny), 22 more to Magnæ (3) (Kenchester), 24 thence to Bravonium, or Bravinium; from

(1) "No doubt," says Dr Stukeley, "but this (Worcester) was a Roman city, yet we could find no remains but a place in it called '*idbury*, which seems to retain from its name some memorial of that sort"

A Roman road goes hence along the river to *Upton*, where antiquities are dug up (I take it for *Ypocessa* of Ravennas), and so to Tewkesbury, where it meets with the Ricning-street way A little below Worcester, a river called *Teme* falls into the Severn, a river synonymous to the name of the *Thames*, which shews it a common name to rivers in the old Celtic language A river called Saltwarp falls into the Severn from Droitwich, a Roman town which occurs too in Ravennas, under the name of *Salinus*. [Itin Cur p 65]

Some of the military ways in this county are expressly mentioned in the Saxon charters A Folc Herpath, i e public military way, (from Here, which signifies army) occurs in the Saxon description of the boundaries of Grimley Another through a wood in the limits of Clopton, near the rivers Lawern and Temed Another called Salt-strete and Salt Herpath, in the boundaries of Wulfrington or Wulverton, a village not far from Spetchley to the east This seems to be the road to Dorchester, or to Verulam [See Heming Chartul p 148, 135, 349, 359, 417]

(2) Camden says, "Worcester was probably founded by the Romans when they built cities at proper intervals on the east side of the Severn, to check the Britons on the opposite shore. And formerly (as an old parchment MS has it) boasted Roman walls" [Gough's Camden, vol II. p 352]

There is an allusion made to those walls in a letter from the Rev Mr Carte of Leicester to Browne Willis, in which, in giving an account of the *Jewry Wall* there, by some supposed to have been a temple of Janus, he says, "It is difficult to judge now what the use of it was; but I am apt to think it was of the same nature with the *Werry Wall* at Lancaster, or the *old works at Worcester*" [Gough's Additions to Camden, in Leicestershire, p 208, and fig 1 in plate IV a view of the ruin]

On perusing the above account, a hope arose, that a vestige so important and curious might have escaped former research, and with the utmost diligence the ancient city walls were again retraced; but no discovery was made of any part of an arch or wall so constructed, so massive, or composed of such materials, as in the least could bear out the comparison made in the above-cited letter.

(3) Dea, I suppose, might be understood, the city of the great Goddess.

whence 27 miles complete the march, and terminate at Uriconium, which indisputably is the Wreocan Ceastre of the Saxons in Shropshire, now Wroxeter, famous for its Roman ruins. It is not in the least probable, that Worcester could be a station on this road Its line of direction runs very wide of Worcester, and the distances laid down in the Itinerary are irreconcileable with the supposition that *Bravinium* is here. (1) But if we look along the river Teme for the remains of that station; if we place Bravinium at Brandon near Lentwardine, where the Roman street crosses the Teme, and where square intrenchments, in appearance Roman, still remain : all difficulties then vanish ; the distances abovementioned are found just ; and the track of the military way, still visible near the Strettons in Shropshire, is regularly pursued. (2) The mistake, however, that Worcester was the

---

(1) It appears, however, that the direction of the routes in the Itinerary are far from being certain and correct. The military ways, and numbers of miles, with the measurement of the Roman mile, are also uncertain. In those parts of England where they were most to be depended on, is in the proportion of three computed English miles to four in the Itinerary of Antoninus. [Gough's Camden, vol. I. p 74 —And Talbot's Comm on Antoninus]

(2) As the opinions of many learned writers on the subject of the Roman roads in this county are given by Mr. Gough in his Additions to Camden, in Worcestershire, vol II p. 365, in which this passage is quoted, it may be most satisfactory to give the extract entire.

" From a view of the map formed upon Antoninus' Itinerary *one may venture to pronounce that the county of Worcester had no share in Roman transactions : consequently that its capital can hardly be Brunno-gemum,* which Ptolemy places among the Ordovices, but rather as Professor Ward inclines to place it with the Branonium,[*] or Bravinium of Antoninus at Ludlow,[†] where he finds traces of the second name in the river Onney [‡] Ravennas gives it the same name as Ptolemy. Mr Salmon, indeed, seems to make *Worcester the centre of four or five Roman roads,*[§] and Baxter has *no doubt of its being Brannogenium,* &c. But a later writer thinks it is to be sought for on the river Teme at Brandon near Lentwardine, where the Roman way crosses that river, and where square intrenchments still appear.[||] Dr Gale settles it at Rushbury in Shropshire, deriving it from the Welsh Brwyners, a rush [¶] There is no such name as Brannonium in Antoninus, but one MS. has Bravonio,[**] which probably misled Mr. Camden Burton disputes its title to Ninnius' name, Cair Guorangon.[††] Usher [‡‡] allows it to Caer Guarongon, but

---

[*] Quasi Barangonium, MS n Gale

[†] Horsley, p 365 Dr Horsley thinks Ludlow the Bravinium, or Bravonium of Antonine, and that part of its ancient name remains in that portion of the river Onney which runs into the Teme near Ludlow This, he says, is more remarkable if Bravonium, or Branonium be the true reading, as in the copy of the Itinerary prefixed to the Britannia, and in the book itself, p. 22 Brit Rom p 466.

[‡] Wesseling Antonin 460.   [§] P 686, 699.   [||] Green's Survey, p. 9.

[¶] P 127 At Rushbury in Shropshire, where Roman coins have been frequently found, Dr. Gale places the Bravonium of Antoninus, *by others supposed Worcester* The Doctor's only reason for this removal, is a fancied resemblance of brwynen, the British word for a bulrush, which suits with Rushbury, and its lying on the direct road from Magnis to Uriconium.

[**] Similes Wesseling.   [††] P 252.   [‡‡] Primord. c. 5.

Bravonium of that Itinerary, was much older than Mr. Camden's time.

transfers Caer Guercon to Warwick, or Wroxcester. Dr. Gale * translates the former name the City of Soldiers, by the Britons Barongs or Guarongs, and Camden in Kent mentions an officer called Gaorong.+ Dr Nash ‡ removes it beyond Ludlow

To the foregoing opinions I have yet to add others of a nature too curious, and of authority too respectable to be dispensed with.

" To speak my mind freely (says Mr Abingdon) I do not take Worcestershire to be any part of the Cornavii, but of the Dobuni nor do I think the city of Worcester had a being in the Roman times, for there are no footsteps of any Roman ways leading to this city, nor are their coins or antiquities found in any quantity All betwixt the Avon and the Severn was formerly thick and wild woodland. The Arden of Warwickshire, joined to that of Feckenham in this county, which with the forest of Ombersley, included all the north part of the county between the Stour and the Severn, quite down to Worcester, and the forest of Horewell southward, extended from Sudbury gate to within a mile of Tewkesbury.

" Some have imagined that the Romans would not neglect so fine a navigable river as the Severn, but would certainly follow the course of it from Gloucester, but at that time the Severn was not navigable about Worcester, it being used chiefly for fishing, there being, long after the time of the Romans, three wears within two miles of Worcester, Bevere, Barbone, and Timberdine " [See Abingdon's MS cited by Dr Nash, vol II p cvii article " Worcester "] In the same page the following observations of the late Bishop Lyttelton are also inserted

" I can by no means agree with those who think that Worcester was not a Roman city, though the true Roman name be lost, for as Camden in his account of Leicestershire § observes, ' Our ancestors never gave the name of Cester, but only to ancient cities or castles ,' and I believe there is not a single exception to this in the whole kingdom I must farther add, tnat Roman coins have been discovered here,|| but I lay little stress on that, as they are found more or less every where, and in greater abundance in the area of Roman camps, than in such cities which are universally allowed to have been first built by the Romans, as Exeter, Gloucester, &c And as to other remains of Roman antiquity, viz inscribed stones, mosaic pavements, sepulchral urns, Roman brick, &c. the many fires which have happened in Worcester which several times almost destroyed the whole city, have raised the ground so much that they seldom come to light, and this is the case in many other Roman towns throughout England With regard to Roman roads leading to and from Worcester, though it is asserted there are none, yet I f. cy on an exact search there would be found vestigia of them, though the plough may in this cultivated part of the country, during a course of so many ages, have almost quite levelled them If any credit may be given to an old writer, R Higden, cited in Gale's Essay on the Roman Roads,¶ the Ykenild-street passed through Worcester from Maridunum in South Wales to Droitwich, Edgbaston, Wall near Litchfield, Little Chester near Derby, and so on to Tinmouth in Northumberland, but though I cannot subscribe to this, as the Ykenild undoubtedly enters this county at Beoley in its course from Alcester in Warwickshire, and passes by Bordesley park in Alve-church, and so goes to Edgbaston and Wall, yet I have myself often observed a high raised road on the Lickey, pointing directly to Bromsgrove, from whence I make no doubt but it proceeded to Wich, the supposed Salinæ of Ravennas, and thence to Worcester Another

    * Ant. et aut ibi cit.   + P 352, note n.

‡ Pref p iii Worcestershire Dr. Nash further says, that he chooses rather to subscribe to the conjecture of Dr. Gale, or Mr Horsley, as above quoted, than to Camden, who thought it was the Branonium, or Bravinium mentioned by Antoninus, and the Brannogenium of Ptolemy, which was all one and the same place [Worcester, Appendix vol II p cvii]

§ Gibs edit p 530 1722 || See Dougharty's plan of this city, published 1741.

¶ Id Ibn vo VI j i ,

We find that one Senatus, a Benedictine of Worcester, in the twelfth century,

Roman road called the Port-way, and in Wulfrune's Saxon grant of Over Arley to the canons of Wulver-hampton,* denominated the *strete* or *street* (by which the Saxons generally meant the Roman street or highway), *lies now in the direct road between Worcester and Shrewsbury*, and I am persuaded was *the Roman road between Worcester and Wroxeter*, the town of Shrewsbury having risen out of the old ruins of Wroxeter.† A Roman road comes out of Salop or Staffordshire, and passes over the heath near Stour-bridge (where by a place called Green's Forge is a vast camp called the Churchyard, and mentioned by Dr Plott in his Natural History of Staffordshire), which proceeds through Hagley-common, and is known by the name of the King's Head-land; and not far distant is a great Roman camp on Wichbury-hill, and three lows or tumuli on the common very near it, and I suspect *this road also leads by Clent and Chaddesley towards Worcester*

" As to the argument against there being any Roman roads leading to Worcester, from the county being all a forest between the Severn, the Stour, and the Avon, including also the great forest of Arden in Warwickshire, I can see no force in it, since it is past a dispute that from Alcester to Edgbaston runs a Roman road, known at this day by the name of the Ickle or Ikenyld-street, and likewise the other road I metioned above, crossing the Lickey towards Bromsgrove, and the two last described, viz the Port-way in Over Arley, and the King's Head-land in Hagley, all which were within the ancient bounds either of the forests of Arden, Feckenham, or Kinvar; and to these I must add, a lane leading from the Lickey towards Tardebig and Alvechurch, commonly called Twatling-street, which no doubt is a corruption from Watling-street, a name common to Roman roads, as some writers have observed, there being one in Scotland, and two or three in England ‡

" The eastern suburb of this city is named Sudbury, and a huge tumulus or barrow, about a mile distant, called Cruckbarrow, still remains, both which it is probable derive their origin from the Romans; the former its name, and the latter its existence, the Saxons naming those places *burys* or *boroughs*, which had been fortified by the Romans; hence Woodbury-hill above Great Witley, Wichbury-hill in Hagley, Membury, near Dorchester, Woodbury-castle, near Exeter "

Andrew Yarranton,§ born in Astley parish in Worcestershire, published in two parts " England's Improvement by Sea and Land " The account given by Mr Yarranton, in the second part of that work, p 162, 163,‖ published in 1698, of his discovery of the hearth of a Roman foot-blast, and of the pot of Roman coin found by its side, near the walls of this city, merits more of credence than Dr Nash (who has quoted the narrative at length ¶) appears willing to allow to it Had, indeed, that hearth, the cinders, or even the coin, been the only instances of their kind he had ever met with, a doubt might have been raised on his competency of judgment respecting them. But of the first he was well acquainted, and enabled from his information (since he describes this to have been " firm and in order," for working) to give an opinion, by comparing it with others he had examined of the last I cannot suppose him so little informed of what nation the coin belonged to, as to hand many of them to Sir William Dugdale as Roman, without knowing them to have been such, that that learned antiquary, finding them of another nation, should have failed in undeceiving him, or that a portion of them would have been deposited in the king's closet under that description, had they been either known or found to have been of another. The coins still continuing to be found here may be considered as a sort of evidence less direct, yet the

* Dugd Mon tom 1 fol 988

† In Arley wood near this footway is a vast Roman camp, square and treble ditched, yet remaining.

‡ See the Index to Gibson's edit of Camden's Brit   § See a note in Gough's Add. to Camden, vol II p 357, in Worcestershire   ‖ See also the first part, p. 57, published 1677.

¶ See Appendix, vol II. p cviii, Worcester.

C

who wrote the lives of St. Oswald and St. Wulstan, stiled himself Bravonius upon this conceit. (1)

Brannogenium is another name that has been assigned for ancient Wor-

other proofs are strengthened by it   For an account of a considerable number found within these few years, see Sect XXII

I readily subscribe, however, to the opinion that although the exact spot has not been discovered where the mass of cinders Mr Yarranton speaks of is deposited, that it forms part of that rising ground seen on the north side of the city walls, including the Butts, and the eminence continued from thence to the west, and extending itself along that height to the site of the infirmary

On this subject I have been favoured with the following further information, communicated in a letter from Dr Johnson, an eminent physician in Worcester

" On the bank of the Severn, in Pitchcroft, and very near Worcester, a very considerable quantity of dross, such as remains after the melting of iron ore, is found   In one place it is called Cinder Point, and there some burnt bricks, appearing like the vestige of an iron furnace, are to be seen when the water is low   This dross or cinder is buried under the surface of Pitchcroft meadow, no where less than five feet, in some parts below Cinder Point, a foot or two more   and from these levels the dross is gradually washed from the bank, and falls down to the river   In destroying the old bridge, a structure which stood on the site of a former bridge of unknown antiquity, much of this dross was found in the foundation of the piers, and filled the old piers in the slovenly mode of ancient masonry   There is now no melting furnace near Worcester, nor is iron-stone, or any other mine of iron in the neighbourhood of it , none are known nearer than those of Dudley, Wednesbury, the Clee-hill, and Colebrook-dale

" In searching for the inducements for placing an iron melting furnace so far from its mines, we shall be led to circumstances, which in all probability discover the period of time, and the people by whom they were worked   The ancient Britons were undoubtedly acquainted with the method of converting iron ore into weapons of war, if not other utensils , but they could have no motive to reduce the ore at such distances from the mine   Such necessity seems peculiar to invaders and new settlers, before regular safe communications of a commercial kind were established , all carriage was liable to interruption from hostile attacks   From tradition, it seems probable the Romans first made their establishment at Worcester, in the time of Constantius Chlorus, father of Constantine the Great   This infant colony must be liable to be molested by the neighbouring hostile tribes , and from them the transportation of iron from other Roman settlements would be liable to interruption, along with every other kind of commerce.   But the carriage and transport of ore down the Severn from the iron mines of Colebrook-dale would be perfectly easy and safe   The Roman town of Uriconium which had been established in Shrop-shire, only a few miles from these copious iron mines, by Julius Agricola, must have been in the age of Constantius an old and strong colony   Iron ore could thence be easily conveyed by water to Worces-ter under the protection of the established colony, and timber, the other essential to the reduction of ore into iron, being then every where abundant, iron would be forged in sufficient quantity to supply the infant colony at Worcester, with greater facility than it could be conveyed to them at its first settlement. Hence, I conclude, that the cinder or dross found on this spot, is referable to iron furnaces worked by Roman settlers in the beginning of the fourth century, this is confirmed by the depth of soil in which it is buried, by the successive strata of mud left by the river breaking out on Pitchcroft, which is inundated by it in every wet year by the overflowing of the Severn, and also by specimens of pottery, apparently Roman, found mixed with this dross, a fragment of which I have in my possession   I send you a piece of the dross or scoria, which is in great abundance on the bed and bank of the river "

(1) He was well versed in the literature of those days, was esteemed an honour to his monastery, died, and was buried there, A D 1170   [Stevens's Monasticon, vol I p 202]

cester. Brannogenium occurs in Ptolemy, and is set down by him as one of the towns of the Ordovices. These were the old inhabitants of North Wales, and possessed also part of Shropshire to the west of the Severn : but whether that garden of nature, Herefordshire, or great part of it, were not included in their territory, is uncertain. Mr. Baxter is the only antiquary that brings Malvern hills within the southern limit of the Ordovices.

There is an old geographical manuscript, the work of Ricardus Corinensis, a learned English monk, which lay unnoticed many ages in the library at Copenhagen, and has lately been presented to the public by M. Bertram in Denmark. This curious compiler had copied into his work some Roman Itineraries, not less valuable than that which improperly bears Antoninus's name. In the tenth Iter that he gives through Britain, we find the station Brannogenium, and upon a road that points out Worcester as the place. From Etocetum in the way to Aquæ Solis (*i e.* from Wall near Litchfield in the road to Bath), the first stage, according to Ricardus, is Bremenium, (1) the next Salinæ; thence the road goes on through Brannogenium to Glebum, whence to Corinium Dobunorum is fourteen miles.

Corinium is well known to be Cirencester, the capital town of the Dobuni, or men of the vale; (2) Glebum is as certainly Gloucester; Salinæ, Droitwich, whose salt springs appear from this Itinerary to have been known to the Romans. And can any doubt remain, whether the station between Salinæ and Glebum be Worcester? (3)

Camden arraigns the negligence of Ptolemy's transcribers, by whom Brannogenium is classed under the Ordovices. He thinks it was a town of the Cornavii; whose principal settlements were Chester on the Dee, and Wroxeter on the Severn. But Worcester was separated from these by a prodigious tract of woodland; of which some remains only were seen in the last age, and called the forests of Wire and of Feckenham. This range of woods extended from the Clee hills in Shropshire to the neighbourhood of

(1) This seems to be Birmingham, which stands on the famous military way called Ikenild-street.

(2) From the British word Dwfn or Duvn, *i e* deep land

(3) Besides these main roads, Watling-street, Hermin-street, the Fosse, and Ikening, or Icknild street, it is certain that there have been a great many vicinal branches, and some which have crossed the principal ways at nearly right angles There have been also considerable military ways in Britain, on which no Iter has proceeded The first instance among many others is mentioned, Akeman-street, *leading from Alcbester (Alcester in Warwickshire) to Bath.* [Gough's Camden, vol. I. p 75. Antonini Iter Britannarum]

Worcester, (1) and took a vast compass eastward, extending, by the name of Ardene forest, over half of Warwickshire Hence, whatever tribe or clan of Britons possessed the city Wrangon, or Brannogenium, they were sepa rated by a natural barrier from the Cornavii on the north, and from the Coritani on the north-east ; but not so from the Ordovices, who might be settled along the fruitful banks of the Teme, down from Lentwardine to the junction of that river with the Severn in the neighbourhood of Worcester.

It must indeed be confessed, that the position of Brannogenium in Ptolemy's tables, with regard to its longitude and latitude, agrees better with Lentwardine (the old Bravinium) than with Worcester It is possible, that the Alexandrian geographer, or his transcribers, misled by the affinity of names, might have set down Brannogenium in his tables instead of Bravinium (2) If Cair Wrangon (ancient Worcester) did not belong to the Ordovices, it must have been a town of the Dobuni, who were masters of all that part of Gloucestershire which lies to the east of the Severn. (3)

SECT. II.

OF WORCESTER UNDER THE SAXONS.

It was long after the settlement of the Saxons in Britain, before they car ried their conquests as far as the Severn. Gloucester and Cirencester were not taken from the Britons till A. D. 577, and then were taken, not by

(1) Hendlip and Bradecote woods were branches of the king's forest when the Conqueror's survey was taken Ambersley was disforested by King Henry III

(2) M. Baxter shews plainly that Antoninu has corrupted Ptolemy's Brannogenium, which answers to Cair Gringon, or Worcester Glossar in voc [Gough's Add to Cam vol II p 411, in Shropshire]

( ) A late writer says, it cannot well be supposed that Worcester, situated on the east bank of the Severn, and so low down, could belong to the Ordovices If, however, Worcester was really a Roman town which is however probable, it seems to be that which Richard in his Chorography, assigns to the Dobuni, under the name of Brangenia, but which in his map, he calls Brangonium This last is evidently the same with the name Wrangon, given to Worcester by the Welch, whence the Saxons changed it to Wrangon ceaster, and thence by corruption comes its present name [See the late General Roy's

the Mercians, but by the King of Wessex, *i. e.* of Wiltshire, Berkshire, and Hampshire. The West Saxons, after this, turned their arms to the reduction of Somersetshire: it does not appear that they ever dispossessed the Britons of Worcester.

The kingdom of the Mercians was at first weak, and difficultly supported itself against the superiority of its southern neighbours. Penda, who began his reign in 625, was the first active and enterprising commander of these people; he made himself independent of the Kentish king, and extended his

---

Military Antiquities of the Romans in Britain, in Appendix, No I. p 173, published by the Society of Antiquaries, London, 1793]

From the foregoing opinions, it would seem that more pains had been taken to prove that none of the Roman ways, diverging or vicinal, had a direction from the r great roads towards this county, than that it would have been a policy too much unlike Roman for them to have suffered so considerable a tribe of Britons, over whom they had no control, to remain in possession of so large a tract of country on both sides of so important a river as the Severn, in the centre of a part of the island bounded by their stations, fortresses, and military strong holds, unknowing of, and unknown to them, notwithstanding they had been in possession of every other part of the island, and resident in it for upwards of four hundred years

It cannot fail to become apparent, that, from the difference of the opinions formed on the subject of the Romanity of Worcester, and which have been thus collected into one focus with a view to shew their agreement and disagreement, it has ever been considered as a point of great nicety on which to conclude. In a state of uncertainty, therefore, this question must still be left to individual judgment to determine, rendered perplexing from learned conjecture and fanciful interpretation, in which great reading and much ingenuity have undoubtedly been displayed, but in which, unfortunately, a tribe of Britons have been overlooked, and the Romans themselves so bewildered as, according to some, not one of their solitary footways have ventured to diverge from their great roads towards Worcester, whilst, according to others, it has been the centre from whence many of them have irradiated to various other places of consequence in this part of the island It is felt as a sufficient discharge of duty to have mingled an humble opinion with those of superior information, on a subject so ably discussed, and which, even if it be on the weakest side, has yet very powerful advocates to support it

Under the head of Roman antiquity, it may not be amiss to mention the crypts or artificial caverns under ground, which tradition attests to have been formerly discovered beneath a very populous part of this city, and to have been traced by some workmen quite from the College as far as a house called the Earl's Post, and that they are continued from then e to the nunnery of Whitstanes The use for which such subterraneous walks were made, is now impossible to be ascertained as for the ludicrous intention of them commonly assigned, it deserves not the least notice I shall content myself with observing, that some other Roman cities had the like galleries under ground Ranulf Cestrensis speaks of them at Chester, Giraldus at Caerleon Verulam (now St Alban's) had ranges of them extended to a prodigious length Abbat Ealdred, in the time of King Edgar, partly destroyed and partly filled up the vaults there, considering them as the coverts of impurity, the asylum of fugitives, and the dens of robbers And for the like reasons, they have been shut up ages ago, in other places [See Stevens's Monast. vol. 1 p 237]

territories westward to the Severn. In 628 he atttempted to take Cirencester from the West Saxons. (1)   The Britons were less capable of resist-
ing him ; Worcester, it is probable, fell into his hands about that time. The
Mercians were as yet pagans, and exterminated Christianity wherever they
prevailed.   If, as some old writers (2) pretend, this city was then the see of
a British bishop, suffragan to the metropolitan of Meneu (St. David's); the
bishop, as well as his clergy, had no choice at this juncture but death, or
flight; when all monuments of Christian piety were by these barbarous
conquerors destroyed.

Wulfere, the son of Penda, began his reign in 658, and was more victorious than his father. He had been converted to the Christian faith ; and
was zealous in propagating it, not only in his paternal territories, but in
those that he subdued. He made his brother Merwald his viceroy in Herefordshire ; who founded the monastery of Leominster. *Osric* (3) or Oshere,
another of his great men, he appointed to be viceroy of the Huiccii, or people
of Huicca province, under which name the Saxons comprehended the inhabitants of Worcestershire, and Gloucestershire, and of part of Warwickshire. The residence of this viceroy was doubtless at Wegerna or Wigornaceastre : so the Saxons called the city, which at present has the name of
Worcester.

The meaning of this name Huiccii or Wiccii, has exercised the skill of
etymologists   Dr. Thomas follows those who derive the word from Wic,
which, among other significations in Saxon, was used to express the creeks,
curvatures, or winding of river banks. But, besides that the Severn, in gliding
through Worcestershire and Gloucestershire, has fewer windings than most
rivers ; how unlikely is it that the eastern parts of Cotswold downs, near
Blockley and Iccumb, should have the name of Mons *Wiccisca* (4) (Wiccian
hill), from the meanders of a river which glide at so great a distance from it ;
yet so we find it named in a charter de Oswaldes lawe, ascribed to King
Edgar (5)

A learned writer, (6) who has sifted all remains of British antiquity with
great diligence, proposes another conjecture. He observes, that the vast

(1) Saxon Chron   (2) Roger de Hoveden, chaplain to King Henry II Walter de Coventry;
and John Bale   [See Usher Britann Eccl Antiq p 48 folio]   (3) *Wisber*, or *Osberus*, is
called the Duke of the Wiccians [Ab MS p 2]   (4) Wiccisia, orig Cott. libr Vit IX 2
(5) Heming Chart Hearne, p 520   (6) Carte

forests which spread themselves over the greatest part of Worcestershire, and ran far into the adjacent counties, were in those times useful, chiefly for the excellent pannage or mast they afforded for hogs . whence, as the wealth of the inhabitants consisted in droves of these animals, the province itself might have its name from them, and from Húkh (the British word for Porcus) be denominated Huicca, (1) or in Latin, Wiccia, and its people Wiccii.

The Huiccii of Bede, says Mr. Whitacre, are evidently the Jugantes of Tacitus, the appellation of the tribe being Huicc-ii and Guicc-ii, in the singular, or Jug-ant-es in the plural (2) And Brannogenium or Worcester seems to have been their capital The Ordovices, a distinct tribe from the Jugantes, (3) being masters of North Wales, Shropshire, Staffordshire, and East Cheshire, and becoming afterwards the conquerors of Worcestershire, Warwickshire, and North Gloucestershire, received the distinguishing title of Ord-uices, or Ordo-vices, the Great Huiccii, or honourable Vices. Their dominion was wide and extensive, but it did not long remain so. The combined forces of the Dobuni on the south, the Cornavii on the north, and the Silures, who penetrated into the centre of their possessions, put a final period to their empire (4)

After the expulsion of the Ordovices it appears that the Cornavii, with the auxiliary tribes of Britons, the Dobuni and Silures, became seated in the abovementioned counties, and in their turn were called the Wigantes, or Huiccii (5)

When the Britons were driven out by the Saxons, they retired beyond the Severn, and defended their new territories against the encroaching conquerors ; so that Worcestershire and the other counties bordering on that river were the frontier between the two people : hence it has been observed that most of the great cities on the east of the Severn and Dea were built by the Romans or Saxons, or both, against the Britons. (6)

The second part of the country of the Cornavii, now called Worcester-

(1) Huicca mægthe, i e Wicciorum provincia, occurs in a charter of Ethelbald, King of Mercia, in the Saxon language Heming p 45   (2) Ann lib. xii. c. 40. Bede, p 765.

(3) Ann lib xii c 40 and Agric Vit c 18

(4) Richard, p 24, 26 Whitacre's Hist of Manchester, vol I 8vo ed p. 202, 203, 204.

(5) Camden, Baxt Glossa p 88, 89, 90 Strutt's Chron. vol I p 243

(6) Twine's Breviarie of Britain, p 26 Gough's Add to Camd. in Worcestershire, vol. II. p. 356.

shire, was called by the Saxons Wire-ceaster-scyre, whose inhabitants, w
others round about, were called in Bede's time, before England was divi
into counties, *Wiccii.* (1) Wirecester must be a corruption of Wigora,
Wigracester, its name under the Conqueror and his sons, and Wigrace:
a contraction of Wic-wara-cester, the city of the men of Wiccia. (2) 7
name of *Wigornia* occurs in Florence of Worcester, who died above s:
years before Joseph of Exeter wrote. (3)

But I rather subscribe to Mr. Camden, who gives the name a Saxon c
ginal, and derives it from the Wiches, or briny wells, that with little lab
yield salt, the staple of this province from the earliest ages. He had rea:
to think, that such wells were anciently found in several parts of Wicc:
and afterwards closed up to prevent too great consumption of wood, wh:
was the only fuel for the furnace in those times. The old Chartulary me
tions a salt pit in the boundaries of Scepwæscetune (4) (Shipston up
Stour) ; a salt well adjacent to Iccumb (5) on the west ; a road called Sa
street, (6) near Euinlode ; a salt brook, salt pit, or saltere wællan *(salito*
puteus) (7) in the limits of Wulfrington, a village to the east of Worcest
But the springs that were most famous, and have survived the memory
all their rivals, were those near the river Salwarp ; which gave both na:
and subsistence to a town that grew up on their margin, now distinguish
by the name of Droitwich (8)

There was at first but one bishop for the Mercian kingdom, with no settl
place of residence A cathedral was built at Litchfield for Ceadda, or :
Chad, the fourth of the Mercian bishops, who died in 672 Saxulf, one
his successors, is commonly deemed founder of the first Saxon church

(1) Bede's Lccl Hist c 22. Camden, Gough's edit. vol. II p 351 , in Worcestershire.

(2) Ibid p 365

(3) Gal., ibid Camden had supposed, in p 352, Joseph of Exeter to have been the first writer w
had given that name to Worcester He has also said that the Saxons afterwards, probably called
Weogare-ccaster, Wegeorna-cester, and Wire-ccaster, from the forest of Wire This suggestion
however, over ruled, from the too great distance of that forest, and from its being as much in Shropsl
as Worcestershire

(4) Heming, p 339   (5) P. 412   (6) P 214.   (7) P 359, 360.

(8) This name is of no great antiquity In Domesday book, where this town is frequently mention
it is called Wich , in the Saxon charters Wic, and sometimes Salt Wic. Brine springs had this appe
tion from the sacredness ascribed to them for Wic in Saxon is holy , and in a secondary sense, a sa
tuary or asylum In Tacitus, Annal. l xiii. c 57. a remarkable instance of German superstition w
regard to such springs

Worcester, dedicated to St. Peter: in which, so soon as erected, a bishop was placed by King Ethelred, to preside in ecclesiastical affairs over the whole Wiccian province. This king, who succeeded his brother Wulfere, in the very beginning of his reign, made an useful regulation, by dividing his kingdom, the most extensive that the heptarchy could boast of, into five dioceses. Osric, the Wiccian viceroy, prevailed with him, that one of the new bishops might be assigned to his metropolis. (1) Accordingly Bosel was consecrated A D 679, with the title of Episcopus Huicciorum. The other Mercian sees constituted about this time, were Hereford, Sidnacester, and Leicester The see of Litchfield subsisted, but with a diocese much contracted.

After Osric's time there is a silence about the viceroys of Worcester, till the reign of King Offa. Uhtred, *propriæ gentis Regulus*, is a Wiccian prince frequently mentioned in the charters of that time, as also his brother Aldred, who signs himself Wigra Cestres Under Cining, *i. e.* Deputy King of Worcester. (2) This Aldred was also A. D 778, stiled " Regulus et Dux propriæ gentis Huicciorum." Ruler and Duke of his own nation of the Huiccii, or Worcestershire men.—" Subregulus Wigorniæ Civitatis." Lieutenant of the City of Worcester.—" Regulus Wicciorum licentiâ Regis Offani Merciorum." Governor of the Worcestershire men by licence of Offa, King of the Mercians (3)

At the death of Offa, in the year 796, the kingdom of Mercia was arrived to its summit of glory, and greatest extent. It was the last kingdom the Saxons established, and was named suitably to the circumstance of its erection. Mercia, signifying end, or bound, or else famous, great, because it was the largest kingdom of the heptarchy (4) It was divided from that of Northumberland by the rivers Mersey and Humber; extended eastward to the fens of Cambridgeshire; southward to the Thames and to the Avon, that runs by the city of Bath; and was bounded on the west by Offa's famous dyke, which he carried on from sea to sea, along the frontiers of Wales Not less than seventeen of our present counties, included within this compass, were subject to the Mercian dominion· viz Cheshire, Derbyshire, Nottinghamshire, Lincolnshire, Huntingdonshire, Northamptonshire,

---

(1) Florence of Worcester   (2) It must be owned that some of the grants, which bear the names of these princes, are but of suspicious authority   (3) Abingd MS p. 3.   (4) See Dr. Hickes's Preface to his Anglo Saxon Grammar, dedicated to Sir John Pakington. Dr. Nash, Pref. p iv.

D

Rutlandshire, Leicestershire, Warwickshire, Staffordshire, Shropshire, Herefordshire, Worcestershire, Gloucestershire, Oxfordshire, Buckinghamshire, Bedfordshire, and part of Hertfordshire. King Wulfere had his residence at Wedon, in Northamptonshire: but Tamworth, in Staffordshire, was the most celebrated of the royal seats of Mercia.

The great Alfred, whose paternal throne was that of Wessex, was the first king in England who had all the provinces of the heptarchy under his immediate dominion. Yet he thought it expedient to govern the Mercians by a prince of their ancient nobility, Duke Ethelred, to whom he had given his daughter Ethelfleda, a very heroine, in marriage. Several towns in Mercia (Chester, Shrewsbury, Stafford, Warwick, and Bridgnorth,) are indebted to this noble pair; at least to Ethelfleda, who, surviving the duke seven years, died A D 919. Worcester also has obligations to them: for, by a charter of theirs, (1) signed in King Alfred's reign, (i e. before A. D 900) upon Bishop Wærfred's desire, that the city of Weogernaceastre might be improved and fortified with bulwarks for the security of its inhabitants, they granted to the church or minster there one half of the royal dues or tolls, arising either from the market or the street, reserving only the wainshilling and the seam-penny (2) entire to the king. But out of all his landrents, and the mulcts for fighting, theft, fraud, &c and the other forfeitures that might accrue to the crown, they assigned a moiety to the use of St. Peter's church and see.

In consequence of this grant, the castle, we may suppose, of Worcester, (the ancient seat of the Wiccian viceroys) was repaired; and some fortresses erected round it, of which only one has reached our time. This is the tower commonly called Edgar's, because the statues of that king and of Elfleda and Elfrida his queens are placed on its eastern front (3) But it was erected in the time of his son King Ethelred II. if we may depend on

(1) Heming Chartul p 3   (2) This was a duty on wares carried out; one penny each horse load, and twelve times as much a loaded wain

(3) On the opposite side there is a remarkable bust, prominent from the building, and not inelegantly finished It represents a monk leaning forwards, in a position almost horizontal, supporting himself by his left hand, and holding in his right, which is drawn in towards his breast, something oval; whether a chrismatory, or other vasculum, or any kind of fruit, I leave to the curious in the minutiæ of antiquity to determine There is also in this west front, in a niche over the gateway, a very well executed bust of King George II erected at the expence of the dean and chapter of Worcester. Underneath, in gold letters, is written, " Georgius Secundus "

West Front   Erected 1793   G. Byfield Archilect

HOUSE of INDUSTRY.

an inscription extant upon it not many years ago; which was judged by the ablest antiquaries to express, in Gothic letters, the year from the nativity MV, i. e A. D. 1005. Instead of which, the repairers of this building, when its surface was last scaled, have set up the date A. D 975, in our modern numerals; supposing that these were the characters intended by the ancient sculptor. whereas the Arabic method of numeration, now in use, was not introduced in England till long after the tenth century. (1)

(1) See the Philosophical Transactions, No. 439 p 136. Memoirs of the Royal Society, Vol. X p. 148 plate vi fig 6 p 281 where we have a delineation of the date on this tower in the antique characters, such as it originally appeared, a copy of which is subjoined at the bottom of the annexed plate, representing the east front of this building.

In farther considering this subject, I shall treat first of the fabric, and secondly of the ancient date found upon this tower, both of which have so much engaged the attention of the antiquarian world, and among others, that of my late learned friend, the Rev Mr Garbet

That this tower might have been erected at the time of the supposed date, said by some of the learned commentators to have been originally inscribed upon it, viz. ℳⅭ. i. e. 1005, the 26th year of the reign of King Edgar's second son Ethelred, surnamed the Unready, is not so difficult to imagine, from one circumstance, namely, the nearness of that time to the death of his father, King Edgar, as that it is highly improbable from another, viz. that the stile of architecture in which it is built, was totally unknown to the Saxons

After the demise of King John, an occasion arose, which appears to warrant the propriety, I may add the necessity, of raising this edifice, and which also authorizes the stile of its building, which began about that time to obtain in England. This was the grant to the monastery of that moiety of the castle which occupied the space south of the present cathedral, now known by the name of the College Green. On the demolition of that part of the ancient fortress, a general inclosure of the newly granted possessions of the church seems to have taken place It had been the custom in those ages to encompass the precincts of the church with strong and high walls [Somner's Antiq Cant Part III. p. 89] In Henry the Third's time the bishop's palace at Worcester is said to be *infra clausum*, within the close The wall which now forms the south boundary of the college precincts, dividing them from the present castle or county gaol, was raised at this period, in its direction from the river eastwards, this wall ended at the knoll, where the ancient portal or entrance into the castle originally stood, to which Edgar-street served as a grand avenue, and on the site of which Edgar's Tower now stands. Under the direction of the monastery another (the present) portal was substituted, in a stile of magnificence that bespoke the sense they entertained of the royal favour, but not with a view of having vested in the church the government of a military fortress, the rule against which had already been laid down * Its more direct purpose

* The castle of Old Sarum was vested in the king, in which the old cathedral stood In the council held at Winchester in 1140, the then Archbishop of Roan in Normandy, who was present, maintained this position, that by the canons of the church, bishops could have no right to hold castles, and that if they were tolerated to do so by the royal sufferance or indulgence, they ought at least upon apprehensions of danger to deliver up the keys Here then the important question at that time arose, whether bishops might be governors of such strong holds, or not? This question was determined by a great churchman against bishops in general, and against the then Bishop of Sarum in particular. [Daniel in K Stephen, p 61 Camden in Wilts Godwin, in Roger, third Bishop of Sarum W Malmsb. Hist Nov, l. ii See also the Account of Old Sarum, p 35]

Wiga-erne signifies in Saxon the warrior's lodge, the hero's place of

was certainly to perpetuate, in the character of Edgar, their first and greatest benefactor, the obligations their church had to him in particular, as well as to some preceding and succeeding kings The tower has accordingly received his name, and, as appears in several ancient writings, that name has in consequence devolved also on the street at the head of which it stands, and which it retains to this day The statues, representing Edgar seated between his two queens, in a range of parallel niches in the east front of the building, are not of that class of figures which usually form the decorations of our ancient castles, or other civil edifices not connected with a church , on the contrary, sacred imagery is mingled with the sculptured representations of a Saxon king and his queens , and our Saviour crowning his blessed Mother formed a central group, which was placed over the head of Edgar, indicative of that reward he had merited of heaven, in his care of the church. Under his feet the date 975 was inscribed this date other commentators have better deciphered than explained its purpose , for it is the date of his death These are circumstances appropriate and illustrative beyond the imputation of fiction, and apply strictly to the objects before us they also strengthen the opinion I have always entertained, that this building was raised under the immediate direction of the monastery, and on that account, even supposing it to have been erected prior to the time of King John, it was suffered to remain untouched, whilst the castle itself was doomed to destruction The precise time at which this tower was erected, is not of importance to its designation. It is saying enough, that " the pure Gothic stile which prevails throughout the whole " structure is alone a sufficient proof that it was not erected in the Saxon times " •

The remarks of Mr Abingdon on this tower can only be placed among the minutiæ of the observations this subject has engaged He says, " King John, a great benefactor to the church of Worcester, did by " all likelihood build the stately gatehouse of his court, which after served the priory, and now the col- " lege In the front whereof, under the statues of our blessed Saviour crowning his blessed Mother, is a " king armed, with his legs crossed, which may represent King John, who, An Dom 1215, in St Paul's " church, London, took on him the sign of the cross for the holy voyage, or King Richard the Ist, " whose lion's heart so conquered the infidels " †   Dr Lyttelton does not appear to have much assisted these conjectures by a comparison of some figures found at Exeter and at Wells, which are said to have a resemblance in their stile and execution with those at Worcester, as I may venture to affirm, that although in sepulchral cumbent figures the *crossing of the legs* in many of them is to be taken as one mark of their having been devoted to the crusade , *a sitting figure, with his right leg laid across his left knee,* is not to be considered in the light suggested, and that a knight of the holy voyage is no where to be found so represented That action however, as far as regards the figure in question, whatever may have given rise to the choice, was extremely well executed by the sculptor

In the same dissertation in which the learned author has considered the suggestions of Mr Abingdon, (notwithstanding the support he has given to those which regard the time of the erecting of this tower) by adverting to the two female figures between whom the king is seated, and finding that neither King John, nor Richard the First had either more than one wife, ‡ we are brought back again to the precise point from whence Dr Thomas and other writers had set out, and King Edgar and his two queens are left in the quiet possession of their honours, as we now find them, and which they may probably hereafter enjoy without further controversy

In the rich volume of the Memoirs of the Royal Society, plate vi fig 6 p 281, we have a delineation in the old English black letter, in which character the date was originally inscribed on King Edgar's tower at Worcester, and of which the following is a copy, viz ꝺ D·ꝯꝓꝺ ‖ This, taken at the first

* Bishop Lyttelton' MS note on this passage in the Survey, p 18 19 penes me   † Abingdon's MS p 24   In the archives of the dean and chapter   ‡ Archæologia, vol I art XXXIV. p. 140
‖ This date is also engraved in the Gentleman's Magazine for March, 1748, p 122.

retirement. Perhaps this may account for the name which the Saxons gave to the Ceastre or Roman fort they found here: which they called Wigerna, Weogerna, (1) Wigorna, and in process of time more contractedly Wegrin, Wigra-cester, and Wigornceaster: (2) this, afterwards, was corrupted into Wircestre, a mode of writing that prevailed about the

glance, appears to denote A D MV ι e 1005, according to some   Whilst others supposing the date to be in Arabic numerals, by dividing the 𝕸 thus, ¶ 9, ⫇ 7, with the 𝕭 5, it then appears that 975 was the date inscribed   Here, however, it must be noted, that the two first figures only are of the Arabian character, the last being the black letter 𝕮 *   If this mixture or combination of character be allowed in these numerals, we have then a direct application of the number to the date of the year in which Edgar died, an event, as has already been observed, proper to be inscribed beneath his statue   And this I conceive to be a sufficient reply also to Bishop Lyttelton's MS note on this passage in the Survey, p 19 viz. " As to the *pretended* dates of MV or 975, no argument can be drawn from them, as neither of them can " possibly be ascertained " †

Dr Nash has informed us, that Mr Wilkinson, architect to the cathedral, when he chipped this tower in the year 1730, he found the walls in several parts covered with fine work, like lace-work, and in many parts gilt and painted like some parts of Westminster Abbey.   And so far from thinking the building prior to the reign of King John, he judges it to have been erected some years subsequent to that period ‡ From an account of this structure given by Mr Cope, and printed in the Memoirs of the Royal Society, it appears that the date was only *painted, in black upon a gold ground*   This account, he says, was communicated to him by Mr Joseph Dougharty of Worcester, who lived in the house over its gateway, and who also informed him that it went by the name of the oldest house in five counties. ‖

I imagine it probable that this date had been so affixed, to correspond with the other *gilt and painted* parts of the building   That Dr Thomas saw it, and that it was legible in his time, there can be no doubt, notwithstanding Dr Ward has questioned it, as he was cotemporary with Mr Joseph Dougharty, and that this date was legible to more advantage in Mr. Abingdon's time is still less to be questioned, although Dean Lyttelton has doubted the fact §   On the repair of the tower as mentioned by Dr Nash, and already quoted, the date as we now see it, was put up in modern numerals, A D 975, cut in stone

When Dr Stukeley took his drawing of the east front of this tower in 1721, ¶ there was then in being a single figure in a small niche above that which contained the group of Christ and the Virgin Mary, the top of this small niche rose parallel to the points of the present windows, this figure is now gone, and the group beneath it so defaced, as renders Mr Abingdon's account of it, which Dr Thomas has followed, valuable, in having ascertained its design   Dr Stukeley's plate has, however, reversed the view of the tower in the impression

(1) Weogerna-ceastre very often occurs   The dipthong eo in Anglo-Saxon was pronounced like ee in modern English   thus the ancient words deop, weod, treo, hweol, beo, &c are now written deep, weed, tree, wheel, bee, &c   (2) Hence some of the monastic writers call it in Latin " Monasterium in Wigorna castello " [Heming 169] " Episcopalis sedes Wigorniensis castri " [Mon Angl tom I. p 138   Tanner's Notitia Monastica, p 613 ed 1744]

* According to Dr Wallis, our present numerals were not known in England before the year 1130 [Phil Trans No 439 p 136]   † Bishop Lyttelton's MS note in p 18, 19 of the Survey
‡ Vol II p clv Worcester, Appendix   ‖ Grosse's Antiquities, vol IV in Worcestershire
§ Archæologia, vol I p 142, Dr Lyttelton'. Dissertation.   ¶ See his Itin Curios plate 23.

Norman Conquest, and gave way in a succeeding age to the present form of spelling,—Worcester; which the invention of printing has effectually established.

———————————

SECT. III.

OF THE COLLEGE, FROM ITS FOUNDATION TO THE TIME OF KING EDGAR.

THE church, which the Britons had in this place, had doubtless been rebuilt several years before Bosel was appointed to preside as bishop here. It was not a cathedral however, till A D 680, when Ethelred King of Mercia placed in it the chair of that bishop of the Wiccians, with the concurrence of Archbishop Theodore, who had consecrated him (1) This church was dedicated to St. Peter, but in the next century was more generally called St Mary's. (2)

Till about this time, cathedrals and the churches of monasteries were almost the only places of religious worship among the Anglo-Saxons. But now, churches and oratories were beginning to be erected in country towns. At these, no stationary priests were as yet fixed . all the clergy of the

(1) Heming places it in 670, [see p 529] but 680 is more consistent with the time of the council of Hatfield, where the division of this diocese was decreed. ['Tanner's Not. Mon p 613 ed 1744]

(2) Heming, p 322, &c Tanner, ibid

The church of St Peter at Worcester it is most probable was built of stone, as it was still in being in the time of St Wulstan, who sometimes kept his midnight vigils in it [Angl Sac II p 247] When, or by whom it was demolished, we have no account It is even uncertain where it stood

Stone buildings, even of churches, were in the seventh century very rare , it is said that about 680, Bennet, Abbat of Weremouth, master to venerable Bede, first brought artificers of stone houses and glass windows into this island among the Saxons, who had before constructed all their edifices of wood William of Malmsbury has, however, carried this custom much farther back into antiquity he states that the blessed Confessor Ninias, about the middle of the fifth century, built a church of polished stone in the confines of England and Scotland, which at that time was beheld as a miracle by the Britons, and that thence it had its name, *Candida Casa*, which Bede himself has noticed [Beda, Hist lib iii cap 4 circit. at 625 Hunting p 328]

Cathedrals were generally the first built churches here, and were either founded by piously disposed princes, or by their respective bishops, assisted by the contributions of devout persons, for the honour of God, and the service of religion They retained also great pre eminence above other churches, the right of baptism and sepulture belonged anciently exclusively to cathedrals, which therefore were termed the mother church [Stavel, p 128 ch]

diocese lived with the bishop in one great family . he preached himself in his cathedral, and sent them out to preach in whatever parts of his diocese he pleased · they were his Sunday missionaries, and returned to the service of the cathedral during the other days of the week   All ecclesiastical dues throughout the diocese were remitted to the episcopal or mother church, and thrown into a common treasure; some part of which was assigned for the repair of the buildings, and the rest for the maintenance of the bishop and his college, and the enabling them to furnish entertainment to the traveller, and relief to the poor

In the next century, the state of the clergy was greatly altered   Preachers were no longer itinerant.   They were fixed in particular districts , and the ecclesiastical dues arising from those districts had, by the bishop's allowance, been appropriated to them. (1)   Still it was necessary, that about ten or twelve priests should in every cathedral be kept, for the performance of the choral services every day, and the supply of all the canonical hours.   These each diocesan was now well enabled to maintain, from the profits of those lands, which were frequently, by the devotion of Saxon princes, granted in perpetuity for the augmentation of their sees   These clerks lived with the bishop in a conventual way, near his cathedral.   They were a fraternity of religious, though not tied down to the abstinence of the monastic life   The bishop was to them in the place of an abbat, to govern and instruct them · and in his absence, one chosen from their own body, under the name of *Prӕpositus*, or provost, was his substitute

We have extant many charters, or copies of charters, made in the eighth and ninth centuries to the bishop and his family (as it is called) at Wigornaceastre, by royal or princely patrons   The viceroys of the Huiccii were considerable benefactors to them   Athelbald, Offa, Kenulf, Ceolwulf, Beornulf, Wiglaf, Berhtwulf, and Burhred, successive kings of Mercia, outdid the

(1) As Christianity prevailed, the lay nobles and gentry erected churches and oratories by degrees in every part of the kingdom, for the use of themselves and their tenants who were too distant from the cathedral to assist in their devotions   These they endowed for the maintenance of incumbents who were to reside and officiate in them   The rights of tithes, sepulture, and baptism were granted to them by the bishop, without which privileges they could only have been considered as chapels , but being confirmed in those rights, they also became rural parochial mother churches

Collegiate and conventual churches were built mostly by the founders of those religious houses, or the cities to which we have found them annexed or belonging, such as abbies, or priories, and such as at present belong to colleges [Staveley p 108 ch 7]

munificence of eastern Magi; (1) for they offered at St. Peter's altar entire villages, or manors, with their various lucrative appendages, their native bondmen, woods, fisheries, cattle, &c. Some of these territories were part of royal demesne, (2) and, as such, were conveyed with great immunities; (3) and for the rest an exemption from secular services was not difficultly obtained.

In these ages, moreover, the bishops had the superintendance of all the monasteries in their respective dioceses; and, when abuses were found in any of these religious societies, they could eject or transplant them, and appropriate their revenues to other monasteries, or to the colleges of their own cathedrals; or even could gratify rich laymen with a grant of the lands of the suppressed abby. Such steps indeed were not taken without the consent of a provincial synod, wherein the king and his principal thanes, as well as the prelates and many abbats, were present (4) But in these assemblies the influence

(1) See Dugdale's Monasticon, from p 121, to p 136, and from thence to p 140, a recapitulation of their lands and endowments

(2) Croppethorn on the Avon had been a royal hamlet ; perhaps a hunting seat of the Mercian kings. Offa has been reckoned the donor of this, and its fifty manses or farms, to the episcopal see But the grant of it under Offa's name, A D 780, is manifestly supposititious For we find from Hemingus, (p 70) that Croppethorn continued threescore years to be a place of residence for the kings of Mercia

(3) The manner in which the supremacy of the ancient kings over the church is recognized, and the general form of all those cartularies by which the Saxon princes endowed the abbies and other religious establishments they erected in England, appear in the " Fundatio Monasterii Sancti Albani," which is given at large by Weever, in his Funeral Monuments, p 97 ch 14

(4) The charters of our Saxon kings are generally witnessed by lords spiritual and temporal, and, as Sir Henry Spelman observes, the custom seems to imply a necessity of their consent to the disposal of the possessions of the crown , • the chief men also abiding at or near any place were chosen to be witnesses to deeds, to give strength and confirmation to the passing thereof It is, however, curious to remark, that during the period from the seventh to the eleventh century, that by many charters granted by persons of the highest rank , and which are preserved, it appears that they could not subscribe their name Several of these remain, where kings and persons of great eminence affix *signum crucis manu propria pro ignoratione literarum* From this is derived the phrase of signing, instead of subscribing a paper † They used no seals but the cross, and as whatsoever bore that sign was looked upon by them as sanctified, so they religiously and uniformly applied it as an amulet or preservative of their charters against injuries and evil minded persons Where our Saxon ancestors sold or gave land absolutely, they usually did it verbally, but where they gave it in a special manner, as with a limitation of time, heirs, or how it should be employed, they did it by writing The lands disposed of in the first manner were denominated *Folkland*, those sold in the last were called *Bokeland* This division is found in the laws of Edward the Elder, cap 2 1

• See his Works, part II p 233 Peck's Ann of Stamford, lib ix p 47 ex Burton's Leicest

† Robertson's Hist Charles V vol I p 21, 22, ex Du Cange, voc Crux, vol III p 1191 and note E in 2nd   ‖ Spelm part II p 233

of the bishops was very great: convents in favoured situations were augmented, while others were doomed to impropriation or suppression. Thus in Gloucestershire, the monasteries of Clive, Wythington, and Westbury; in Warwickshire, the monastery of Stratford upon Avon; in Worcestershire, that of Sture in Usmern, hodiè Kidderminster: the abbies of Kemesey, Bredon, Blockley, Deylesford, Hanbury, and Fladbury, were dissolved, or rather swallowed up in the see and college of Worcester.

Bishop Wilfrith obtained a synodal decree, that the monastery of Wudi-andun (Wythington in Gloucestershire) should, after the death of the abbess, who then possessed it, be annexed to his see of Wegrin-cestre. (1) His successor, Bishop Milred, in whose time this monastery lapsed, made a fresh grant of it, A. D. 774, to Lady Æthelburga, abbess of a religious house at Worcester, on condition, that both this, and also her own monastery at Worcester, should, upon her death, devolve to the church and chair of St. Peter in that city (2) And the bishop thought this no unreasonable provision, as it was the intention of her father Ælfred, (3) the founder most probably of her monastic establishment at Worcester, that the whole of that, with all appertenances, should be hers for life only, and pass in reversion to this cathedral church.

There is great reason to suppose, that the religious house at Weogerna-cestre, of which Æthelburga was governess, received, after her death, by the appointment of Bishop Tilhere or Heathored, Benedictine monks in lieu of nuns. Recluses of both sexes, as was the practice in very many Saxon monasteries, had been assembled here, under the government of an old maid: after her time, however, no other abbess occurs; and monks only seem to have possessed the convent of St Mary

The first mention of St Mary's minster is in a charter of King Æthel-bald, dated A D 743 (4) It was then probably a new foundation, under the noble abbess already mentioned The grants of Uthtred, the Wiccian viceroy, and several of King Offa s charters to this monastery, are manifestly spurious but there is less reason to doubt of several grants to it, made by the devotion of Mercian princes of the next century The convent of St.

(1) Heming Chart p 464, 465   (2) Ibid p 467
(3) This perhaps was that Ælfred, who was one of the principal nobles of Mercia in K Æthelbald's time, and signs some of his charters [Heming Chart p 69 219 35]
(4) Ibid p 56

E

Mary, however, was in no capacity of being a rival to its neighbour, the college of St Peter, before the days of Bishop Oswald and King Edgar.

That was the reign of monkery . the colleges of canons, or secular clerks, had then lost their credit. The popes had found it their interest to exact celibacy from the clergy, They incited the monks to raise an outcry against those, who, instead of devoting their whole time to spiritual employments, gave a part of it to the company of their wives, the dalliance of their children, and the cares of a family. Priests, that were members of cathedral colleges, had not as yet been restrained from marrying. Many of them had wives ; and what was almost held as criminal in that age, they had hawks, and dogs for game, and lived in such splendour and luxury, as was more mortifying than any rigours of Benedict's rule, to the poor Benedictines. A general opinion prevailed, that if the vast revenues of collegiate endowments were transferred from these secular clerks, into the hands of the monks, they would make a more religious use of them. The utter abuse of wealth in a monastery (of which succeeding ages had sufficient experience) was a sight not yet seen

King Edgar found that he could not take a more popular measure than to worm out the secular clerks from their most opulent foundations, and to place monks in their room Dunstan, his great favourite, whom he had promoted to the primacy of Canterbury, strongly incited him to this reform: Ethelwold, Bishop of Winchester, and Oswald of Worcester, were his principal instruments in the execution of it (1) Ethelwold went with rapidity into the work, and dislodged the seculars from the old and new minsters of Winchester in the very first year of his consecration (2) Oswald was more cautious his first step was, his frequent attendance at the church of St. Mary, and performing of divine offices there . this artifice brought the crowd from the cathedral, for his reputation was high, and the people would flock any where to receive the blessing of so holy a prelate (3) He found a fit tool in Cynsige, or Wynsige, one of the clerks of his college ; this man he made Circward, i e. keeper or treasurer (4) of St Peter's

---

(1) These three prelates are said to have ruled England under King Edgar [Fuller's Church Hist p 131] (2) A D 963 (3) Edmer, de Vit Oswald Angl Sacr Pars II p 202. [Malms de Gest Pontif I iii fol 153] (4) Circweard Sacracrinarius, Alfric's Glossary The precious vessels shrines, and records of the church were under his care

church, in the room of Æthelstan, and he added to this the vicarage of St. Helen's, (1) (a very profitable preferment at that time, when no less than eleven parochial chapels were dependent upon it). To Wulfgar, another collegiate priest, he gave the church of St. Peter by the south wall; (2) and for his life, and two lives after his, the manor of Batenhale (3) This grant was made A D 969. he found means to gain over so many of his canons, that no obstruction was made to the surrender, which, in that year, Wynsige as Circward, made of the keys of St. Peter's cathedral, and of all its emoluments, territories, &c to the use of the monks (of St. Mary's) for ever. (4) Nay, out of the eighteen seculars, of whom the college consisted before, we find but two (Ælfred and Ælfstan) wanting in the subscriptions to Bishop Oswald's charters in the year 977. Ælfred had been a collegian in the time of Bishop Koenwald, and probably was dead in the interval between 969 and 977. Wynsige, and four of the other clerks of the college, actually submitted to the monachal discipline, and became regulars professed (5) The rest were permitted to keep their stalls, and obliged to acquiesce in being subordinate officers to a society of monks. (6)

The grants of the lands of the see of Worcester by Bishop Oswald to his friends and followers, for life, or for three lives, imposed a sort of feudal tenure upon them, by which they were subjected to a variety of charges and services, as well civil as military, and these instruments were ratified by the king himself. The following are among the articles of obligation to which they were made liable, as contained in a charter intitled " Indiculum Libertatis de Oswaldes-Lawes-Hundred," as cited by Sir Henry Spelman, chap 26 of his works, part II. p 41. " Feuds and Tenures," viz.

" His tenants shall perform all the duties of horsemen.

" They shall pay all dues, and perform all rights belonging to the church.

(1) Heming p 428   (2) The present church of that name, situate in Sidbury
(3) Heming p 137, 138   (4) A D 969 Chartul Wig p 530   (5) Heming p 197.
(6) The number of seculars in this college at different periods of time, is easily collected from the subscriptions to the charters of lease granted by the bishop and his venerable family One provost, seven presbyters, and a deacon, were consenting to a grant of Bishop Alhun in 849 A provost and fourteen clerks composed Bishop Werfrith's family in 872, and 899 Thirteen sign with Bishop Koenwald in 954. Bishop Oswald had at first eighteen when two of these were dead or expelled, the addition of St Mary's society (who seem to have been but ten) augmented his number to twenty six This was his complement from 969 to 982, when, from the sudden reduction of his number, I suspect five or six of his clerks might be expelled

" They shall swear to be in all humble subjection, and at the command of the bishop, as long as they shall hold lands of him.

" That as often as occasion shall require, they shall present themselves ready to furnish him with horses, and ride themselves.

" They shall perform all the work about the steeple of the church, and for the building of castles and bridges.

" They shall fence the bishop's parks, and furnish him with hunting weapons when he goeth a hunting

" That in other cases, when the bishop shall require them, whether for his own or the king's service, they shall in humble subjection be obedient to the chief captain or leader of the bishoprick, for the fee granted, or benefit done unto them, and the quantity of land which every one of them possesseth

" That after the expiration of the three lives, the lands shall return again to the bishoprick.

" That if there be any default in performing the premises, by reason that some shall vary or break the agreement, the delinquent shall make satisfaction according to the justice of the bishop, or shall forfeit the land which he had of his gift "

The grants of Bishop Oswald, as extracted and chronologically arranged by Dr Thomas (1) from Hemings' Chartulary, begin A D 962, and end in 991, during which period 190 hides of land were disposed of by him in seventy grants, of which thirty were made prior to the year 972, when he was promoted to the archbishoprick of York, and as he held Worcester in commendam, he added forty more to the number   During the latter period two grants occur in favour of two characters of some note in the church history of Worcester, viz. In 985 Archbishop Oswald gave to *Godinge*, a priest, three hides at *Bredicot*, and one yard-land at *Genenofre*, and seven acres of meadow at *Tiberton*, upon condition that he should be the amanuensis of the see, and write all things that should be necessary to be inserted in their registers   This service Godinge appears to have performed with ability, having written many books for them (2)   The other is a grant to his faithful man *Ælstan*, of one manse at *Icbington*, com Warwick, in 991. He was

(1) See his Account of the Bishops of Worcester, from p 41, to p 48, inclusive

(2) Ibid p 46   Hem Chart p 139, 265, 266

the father of St. Wulstan, Bishop of Worcester, and died a monk of this church. (1)

Upon the death of his kinsman Oskitell, the see of York becoming void, Oswald was thought a fit person to preside in his place, but he was not permitted to leave the see of Worcester, lest the new institution of the monks there should be endangered by being deprived of their patron. (2)

Oswald is farther said to have ejected the married clergy out of seven monasteries in the diocese of Worcester, and to have had their removal confirmed by the pope; a caution he found necessary, because in some places they had broke in upon the settlement of the foundation; of which the church of Worcester itself is an instance, having, as appears by the acts of the council of Worcester held under Wulstan, been originally furnished with secular canons (3)

From this detail, it appears that the zeal of this saint of the monks had by no means the start of his prudence There was no law to support him in a forcible expulsion, even of married canons, from his cathedral. He was wise in proceeding gently, till a national synod should enable him to act with greater vigour. Dunstan had laboured to obtain a synodal decree that might crush the married clergy He had success at the council of Winchester in 975; where, as the monks pretend, heaven itself declared in their favour, by an audible voice from a crucifix which hung aloft in the room. The seculars were not to be convinced by such miracles that their marriage was a crime They made great efforts at the council of Calne, in 978, to be restored to their colleges; but in vain.

There is a charter extant, under the name of King Edgar, dated at Glouceastre, Dec 28, A D 964, which represents this reform in the minster or cathedral of Wearecestre, as then already accomplished; and speaks in strong terms of the expulsion of the clerks who had possessed it before; who chose, if this writing can be believed, to be degraded rather than to serve God canonically, and preferred their wives to their benefices But this charter is of no authority, as Dr Hopkins, who wrote the additions to Camden's account of Worcester, was sensible Its spuriousness is clear from a great number of indubitable records of transactions between Oswald and the

(1) Dr Thomas' Account of the Bishops of Worcester, p 48 Hem Chart p 126
(2) W Malmsb p 153 (3) Aug Sacr. Pars I p 546, et Pars II p 202. Collier's
Eccl Hist vol I b. iii p. 191

beneficiaries of his church. The members of the church were constantly called in to ratify these transactions by their consent and subscription. No change in their body appears till after the year 969; and then almost all the old members are continued, with the addition of several new ones to them   Wulfric, as provost, and five other priests, take precedency of Wynsige till after that year · (1) and yet, according to this charter, Wynsige had the priorship or government of this convent five years before. Ancient historians have said, that Edgar founded forty-seven houses for monks or nuns during his reign , and intended, if he had lived, to have increased the number to fifty   but this charter, most improbably, makes him the founder of seven-and-forty, even in the six first years of his reign   The piece of apocryphal history, that Edgar had subdued the greatest part of Ireland, which Mr. Camden reports solely upon authority of this instrument, decisively tends to confirm my opinion (2)

The acts of Bishop Wulstan's synod may be depended on, which place the surrender of the cathedral and its endowments to the monks, in the year 969, and Indict XII   From that time the church of St. Mary's became the cathedral of Worcester, (3) though, being erected for the use of a private society, it must have been quite unsuitable for that purpose

In this church of St Peter an episcopal throne had been established by Sexulphus, the last of the Mercian bishops, who placed in it secular canons so early as A. D 680, eighty-three years after the see of Canterbury had been founded by St Augustin

In 983 Oswald, the great patron of the monks, completed the building of a new and more stately cathedral in the churchyard of the now neglected St Peter's, (4) which he dedicated to the blessed Virgin Mary, and furnished with no less than twenty-eight altars (5)   The displacing of the

---

(1) Heming p 163 214

(2) In my opinion of this charter I am not singular   Bishop Burnet long since objected to its authority , merely from the superstitious mention it makes of the number fifty, the number of the years of pardon   Now the invention of jubilees, says the bishop, being much later than Edgar's time, gives occasion to believe this also was forgery [See his Abridgment of his Hist of the Reform, vol 1 p 147]

(3) In a grant of Oswald' , dated anno 965, the episcopal chair is said to belong to the monastic convent of the Virgin Mary But the names of the subscribers shew, that the date is erroneous Athelstan was not then primus , nor Oswald yet archbishop   The date should undoubtedly be 985, at which time the monastery consisted of those very members who appear at the bottom of that charter

(4) Heming p 1-

(5) From a memorial in the first or east window of the south aile of the choir, in which king Edgar

secular canons, or married presbyters, from St Peter's cathedral, a measure which had been for some time in a gradual progression under the management of Bishop Oswald, was, on the opening of his new church, finally completed, and the cathedral of St Mary, which from that time became the cathedral of Worcester, was filled with monks, to the utter exclusion of the secular clergy. (1)

During the building of this new cathedral, and before, this bishop was wont to preach to his crowded audiences in the open area by St. Peter's church, taking his stand near the cross (2) that was erected over the stone monument of Duke Wiferd and his lady Alta, (3) who had been considerable benefactors to that church. This monument, which is said to have been a work of admirable art, was taken down by Archdeacon Alric, in the time of King Edward the Confessor, in order to enlarge the choir of St. Peter's. Duke Wiferd's monument appears to have been at the end of the High-street, for, a mile being measured from it northwards, another stone pile with like carvings, was erected at the mile's end, which was called the White Stane, (4) and gave name to a district or tithing, without the city, called Whitstanes to this day

and St Oswald were set out as supporting the cathedral church, and from these words of the charter, " Monasterium amplificavit," it is conjectured by Mr Abingdon that Edgar and St Oswald joined in the foundation of the monastery. [See Abingdon's MS. p 6 And in the Appendix to Sect IV No. V. p xiii]

Ednoth, a monk of Worcester, was sent by Bishop Oswald to direct the building of the abbey of Ramsey, in Huntingdonshire, finished A D 974, founded by Ailwin, Alderman of all England, as he is called (Hist Ramesiensis, cap 20 p 399 inter XV Scriptores, edit per Gale) This Ednoth most probably afterwards directed the building of the cathedral of St Mary at Worcester, founded by St Oswald, and for which service he was in process of time made Bishop of Dorchester [Dr Thomas's Account of the Bishops of Worcester, p 50]

(1) W Malmsb de Gestis Pont l iii p 154 Angl Sac. tom II. p 202.

(2) In the elder ages, in some places before they had a church built, our Christian ancestors were obliged to perform divine service under a cross, in some open and convenient place, instead of a church, such was originally the custom at St Paul's cross, in London, and the practice was continued there on special occasions till the Reformation. It is on this account singular, that Stow in his Survey, fol 357, professes " that the original, or antiquity of Paul's cross was to him unknown " [Staveley's Hist. of Churches in England, chap 7 p 102 See also Dr Thomas's Account of the Bishops of Worcester, p 21, and Pennant's London, 2d ed p 370   (3) Heming p 342.   (4) Id. p 343.

SECT. IV.

OF ST. MARY'S CATHEDRAL AND MONASTERY; WITH THE HISTORY OF
THE FABRIC, TO THE TIME OF THE REFORMATION.

THE new cathedral, raised and dedicated by Archbishop Oswald, would not
have perpetuated his name, if he had done nothing else that was memorable.
It could not escape in the conflagration of the city, which was abandoned to
the cruelty of Hardicnute's soldiers, in the year 1041 (1) But the ravages
of fire on a stone edifice might be soon repaired. The improvements in architecture, which the Normans introduced, brought Oswald's structure into
contempt. What is now called the Gothic architecture was then approaching to its perfection ; the art of vaulting roofs with stone, in angular compartments, and the fashion of adorning blank walls with batoons, horizontal
and columnar, and arches interposed, luxuriant in their mouldings, (2) were
now becoming the familiar practice of the architects of churches ; the
pointed arch, the tracery work, the ornamented columns, composed of small
toruses, were so skilfully diversified in their application, and displayed on a
scale of such magnificence that astonished and capitvated the beholder Bishop Wulstan had a magnificent spirit ; he was determined to leave posterity
proofs of it He accordingly in 1084 laid the foundation of a new church,
and in the year 1089 he finished both that and the monastery, which was
now called " Monasterium S. Mariae in Cryptis." (3)

(1) W Malmsb p 83 Flor Wig sub anno
(2) The Saxon architecture, which continued with little alteration near one hundred years after the
Norman conquest, was a debased, corrupted, Roman stile The Gothic stile did not come in till Rich.
I or King John's reign, and it is far from certain that it was brought from Palestine [Bishop Lyttelton's MS note on the text]

Dr Wilson also strongly controverts the opinion of Sir Christopher Wren on this ground, who had
derived its origin from the Holy Land ,* and Mr Ledwich disallows it in toto " Time (says he) has
revealed its errors , no such Saracenic works exist in Spain or Sicily, or in any other place to which the
Arabian power extended And that there are enough of the productions of ancient art, to evince that the
pointed arch was known and used many centuries before the Gothic power was established, or the
romantic expedition to the Holy Land commenced "†
(3) Heming p 521, Tanner's Notitia Monast p 614
If I rightly understand a note of Dr Hopkins, the bishop carried on his building westward, as far as

* Ornaments of Churches considered, p 92
† Observations on Ancient Churches, Archæol vol VIII p 190, 192

S.W. VIEW OF WORCESTER CATHEDRAL, 1789

The building of churches was much forwarded by the indulgences granted by the popes, in the middle and dark times of the hierarchy. Dugdale, in his History of St Paul's, London, has given us a copious catalogue of the number and nature of those indulgences, which were granted for building and repairing of that cathedral. The like provident powers were granted to Joffrid, Abbat of Crowland, to enable him to rebuild his abbey in 1112, (1) and to Bishop Poore, when he built Salisbury cathedral, in 1220 (2)

It does not appear, however, that, on the occasion of the building of this cathedral by St Wulstan, any of the means we have mentioned had been resorted to, or that he received any assistance in carrying it into execution. The example set by him, in offering upon the altar of his new church, when he opened it, the manor of Alveston, (3) which he had recovered of the Conqueror, at a great expence, and another gift of lands of considerable value, the deed of which Wulstan himself, about four months before he died, offered up to God on the altar of St Mary, on the day of her nativity, A. D. 1093, (4) did not stimulate to similar acts either royal or private benevolence.

the first, or great cross ile of the present church, which ile seems to have been the ante-temple, or narthex, in the ancient structure. So that we owe to him the noblest part of the present cathedral a better monument of him, than any shrine which the superstition of his successors could raise. [Willis's Mitred Abbies, vol II. p. 262]

(1) See Camden, in Lincolnshire Staveley's Hist of Churches, ch vi.

(2) Price's Description of Salis Cath. p 5. " The great south ysle of Gloucester churche was made by oblations done at the tombe of Kynge Edward the second." [Leland's Itin vol VIII. p 64]

(3) The manor of Alveston in Warwickshire, which formerly belonged to the episcopal see, had, for some time, been in the hands of powerful laymen this bishop obtained, for a sum of money, the restitution of it from William the Conqueror, and on Whitsunday, A D 1089, in the first year after the commencing of divine services in the new minster, he made upon its altar an offering of that manor, to the perpetual use of the monks of his church • " Anno ingressionis nostræ in novum monasterium, quod construxi in honore Dei genitricis, primo." Such are the words of the charter And yet the laborious Dr Thomas, in whom such slips are not frequent, tells us, on the authority of this instrument, that Whitsunday of the year 1089, was the time when the monks were removed into their new monastery and church, and that the grant of Alveston was presented on the altar the same day. See his Survey, p 3. and his Account of the Bishops, p 87 The word Monasterium, was indifferently used in that age, either for the buildings in which a society of monks was lodged, or for the minster, i e the conventual church and seems to be used in this grant for the latter. From this charter we learn, that on his accession to the government of the convent, he found in it scarce more than twelve monks, but had now augmented their number to fifty ‡ The rest of this charter, which is given at length in Dr Thomas's edition of Dugdale, vol II p 6 is noticeable for the devout trust it has for the piety of its purpose.

(4) Hem Chart p 421

• Hemin p 411   ‡ Paulo plus quam duodecim.

The only instance at all similar to that custom, which occurs in the church history of Worcester, was during the prelacy of John Barnet, bishop of this see, who, A. D 1362, following the example of other dioceses, ordered, to the praise of Almighty God, the blessed Virgin, St Oswald, St Wulstan, and All Saints, that in all parochial churches throughout his diocese, the priest every Sunday, after sprinkling of the holy water, should enjoin the people to kneel, and pray for the brethren and sisters, the benefactors of his cathedral church, and of the fabric thereof, saying a Pater Noster, an Ave Maria, and some other collects; and to all that should do this, or should give any thing to the fabric, or confraire of the said church, he granted forty days indulgences (1)

The ceremonies anciently used in the founding of a church, were, as in modern times since the Reformation, many and various ; but their dedication to saints was entirely dependent on the will of the founder, who selected which he pleased, or, as was most likely, that which he himself had chosen as his patron saint.   The minor are often joined in those dedications with the higher order of sanctified persons, as in this instance . " To Mary, the holy mother of God, the blessed Apostle Peter, and to the Saints Oswald and Wulstan." But to the saints or martyrs, as to the objects of their adoration, the practice is disclaimed ; to God only was the offering made, and by this solemn and public act, that right which the founders might have in the places of devotion thus erected by them, was renounced and assigned to God as the owner, and for ever given up for the purposes of his holy worship. (2)   The days of the anniversaries of those saints, to whom churches were thus dedicated, were kept as festivals, and were also honoured with great privileges, confirmed by the sanction of ancient laws (3) Wakes are the common name by which they are known ; their devotional observance has been wholly superseded by sports and pastimes, till the clamour of the puritans against them, as remnants of popery, in 1627 and 1631, induced orders to be issued for their suppression. They are still, however, to be found in the midland and northern parts of the kingdom. (4)

It is related of Bishop Wulstan, that upon seeing the workmen employed in

---

(1) Dr Thomas in Ap No CVII p 120, 121; and Acc of the Bishops of Worcester, p. 182, 183.
(2) Durandus, Rationale Divinorum, lib 1 cap 6 fol 13   (3) Int Leg Edw Confes. cap. 3.
(4) Dr Thomas's ed. Dugd p 682, 683, vol. II. in which the ancient ceremonial of consecrating churches is also given, see p 647

pulling down the old church, he wept   One of his attendants expostulating
with him, and reminding him, that he ought rather to rejoice, as he was
preparing in the room of it an edifice of greater splendour, and more proportioned to the enlarged number of his monks ; he replied, " I think far
" otherwise ; we, poor wretches, destroy the works of our forefathers, only
" to get praise to ourselves ; that happy age of holy men, knew not how
" to build stately churches ; but under any roof they offered up themselves
" living temples unto God ; and, by their examples, excited those under their
" care to do the same ; but we, on the contrary, neglecting the care of souls,
" labour to heap up stones " (1)   On the finishing of his new church, he
caused the relicks of St Oswald to be inclosed in a new shrine, prepared for
that purpose, and solemnly deposited them therein, on the twelfth of October
the same year, at the expence of seventy-two marks of silver, or about forty-
eight pounds of the present money.

Of the fabric of St Mary's cathedral little has hitherto been said.   The
silence of writers on a subject so replete with curious matter, is only to be
accounted for by the want of authentic materials to make a satisfactory
narrative of the progressive stages of its building, till it had finally become,
through a succession of ages, and through various hands, that venerable and
extensive structure we behold it at this day.   By whom, in what manner,
and at what periods, since the time of St. Wulstan, this edifice has been
carried on to its present general appearance, is in this place my design to
examine.

In order to assist in the discussion of this subject, the principal events
relative to the fabric of the present cathedral will be stated in chronological
succession, after recapitulating,

First.   That the ancient cathedral of St. Peter was probably raised as early
as the time of the foundation of the see itself, viz A D. 680 , a period
marked by the numerous instances of religious houses, which the munificence
of the princes, the piety of the nobles, and the devotion of the prelacy of that
age, erected and endowed   Of the last order we find, that Egwine, the third
Bishop of Worcester, A. D 702, began building the famous abbey of Evesham, and that he, after resigning this bishopric, in 710, became its first abbat.
We may, therefore, place the building of St. Peter's cathedral at Worcester,

between the years 680 and 690.   This church, as we have already said, was still in being in the days of St. Wulstan.

Secondly. That St. Mary's minster, or convent, at Worcester, was founded in the beginning of the eighth century ; this convent, after the death of the abbess, Æthelburga, who governed it A D. 743, became a monastery, to which the endowments of St Peter's cathedral were surrendered in 969, and from that time the church of St. Mary became the cathedral of Worcester

Thirdly. That, the church of St. Mary having been erected for the use of a private society, and not being suitable for the purposes of a cathedral, St. Oswald began a new one, which he built in the churchyard of St. Peter's, completed, and dedicated it to the blessed Virgin Mary, in 983.

Fourthly. That St Oswald's cathedral was destroyed by Hardicnute, A. D. 1041, and

Fifthly That St Wulstan began building the present cathedral A D. 1084, and finished it A D. 1089.

There are few examples to be found among our ancient churches, in which such a variety of stile of building is combined as in the cathedral of Worcester ; and it has proved from thence an object of no small difficulty to divide and arrange those parts of which it is composed, and which vary so much in the time of their erection, and also in the mode of their construction.

The form of the eastern part of the cathedral, as built by St Wulstan, is that of the cross, and its principal entrance was at the west end, from a vestibule or porch, which now forms the great cross ile of the nave, on a plan similar to that of the chapel of New College, Oxford.

On the internal face of the west wall of the north and south transepts of that ile, there is no trace of any aperture that could serve as a principal entrance, nor indeed is there in any other part of this first church ; here then most unquestionably the western boundary of St. Wulstan's fabric was terminated, and its grand approach provided

From this ante-temple, or narthex, of the original cathedral, the entrance to its nave (the present choir) was under the rood loft, where now the organ is placed. Two descents into the crypt were then open ; the one under the present ascent to the north ile of the choir, the stone steps into which are still visible within it , and the other, now in use, and remaining under the ancient ascent, through the great Saxon arch into the vestries on the south.

This Saxon arch, at the west end of the vestry, formed a collateral entrance into the cathedral, from the present great cross ile ; a like arch was provided on the north side, to correspond with it in appearance, leading to the ancient lodgings of the sacrist. The confined extent of that appendage to the church, which never could have gone eastwards beyond the first window of the north ile of the choir, together with its situation, shew it to have been erected for a peculiar and select service. As the office of the sacrist was the care of the church and its furniture, it is probable this might have formed the treasury of its sacred vestments, and vessels for the service of the altars. A small balcony of stone, with glazed windows, and a flight of stone steps, descending from it within the wall, underneath which was a door of communication with the church, now closed up, formed a part of the plan on which it was constructed, and are still visible in the wall, between the entrance of the north ile of the choir, and near to the first window (1) It might also have served as a vestry for the bishop, separate and detached from those of the subordinate clergy, a provision not uncommon in episcopal churches. (2)

That this church had a principal tower at the time of its first erection, is to be gathered from Mr Abingdon, who says,—" in 1175 the *new tower* fell down ."(3) and also from the account in the Worcester annals, of the destruction of its *two lesser towers*, by a storm (4) The situation of the first was most probably over the centre of the upper cross ile, supported by the four massive pillars, which now encompass the area of the communion table, or high altar. And the sites of the two lesser ones seem evidently to have been at the two extreme north and south ends of the great cross ile of the present nave ; a supposition well warranted by the stile of building of those transepts, being so totally unlike any other part of the whole fabric ; a circumstance resulting from the necessity of an immediate repair, for the church had no other accessible entrance than in that part of it which was become ruinated by the fall of those towers. Without reference, therefore, to precedent in stile of architecture, we find this part of the church supplied

---

(1) See the plan of the cathedral, reference O.

(2) This building, which at the Reformation was appropriated to the use of the first prebendary, was taken down, and the Saxon arch closed up in the beginning of the present century

(3) Abingdon's Antiq. of Worcester Cathedral, p 5. Willis's Mitred Abbies, vol I p 302.

(4) Anno 1222, about the feast of St. Andrew. Annal. Wig. Dr. Thomas's Survey, p 5.

with a specimen of building belonging to no age or sort then in use, and wholly dissimilar to what had either preceded, or since followed it, throughout the whole fabric, and which may thence safely be pronounced the mere fancy of the architect.

THE CRYPT.

We can have little hesitation in adopting Bishop Lyttelton's opinions respecting the antiquity of the crypt. (1) Crypts, or undercrofts, are certain evidences of the high antiquity of those cathedrals in which they are found; as that of St. Faith, under old St Paul's, London, Canterbury cathedral, and St Peter's, in Oxford, &c. (2) It is observable also, that they are found in the most select and dignified situations in our ancient churches, uniformly bespeaking their uses to have been of the most sacred kind. The primitive Christians were necessitated to assemble themselves, not in the fittest and most convenient, but in the safest places, such as the state and temper of those times would permit, to avoid the persecutions which awaited them whenever they were discovered in the act of worshipping God after their own manner. For their greater safety they sometimes congregated *sub dio*, in the open fields; at others, *subter terram*, under the earth, in caves and vaults, the remains of many of which are still to be traced in the famous catacombs in Rome. In these they used to assemble at their devotions, bury the bodies of their martyrs and confessors, and frequently held their councils. In memorial of these ancient subterraneous places of worship, many of our cathedrals have those crypts or vaults under their choirs; which by the Germans, in whose principal churches they are very frequent, are called kruft, and by us croft, undercroft, or vault. (3) In many churches on the continent they are called martyrdoms, and confessionaries. Some also have conjectured that crypts were the remains of either Saxon or British churches, and that they have been embosomed within the present structures, from a veneration of their having been the places sanctified and consecrated to God, by the piety and devotion of their forefathers, in the first ages of Christianity. It appears that many of these crypta have had their distinct and peculiar dedications, as at Canterbury and London; that they were furnished with chapels and altars anciently

(1) See his letter to Smarte Lethiculhier, Esq in the preface   (2) Weever's Fun Mon p 324.
(3) Staveley's Hist of Churches in England. chap 3 p 26, 27

set apart and dedicated to particular saints; and also that they were appropriated to obituary services, and that the most distinguished and eminent characters among their saints, martyrs, confessors, princes, (1) bishops, and founders, have had interment in them, as in the most sanctified part of their respective churches   We have, however, no trace of the dedication of the crypt in the cathedral of Worcester to any of the saints of the Romish calendar, nor even of a single altar, by which we might find that it had ever received such a distinction.   And there appears but one item of any part of it having been used for obituary purposes; and that occurs on the south side, nearly opposite the entrance of the vault from the great cross ile of the nave   This part, which seems to have been separated from the crypt at large, as a kind of chapel for this purpose, is immediately under the east or second vestry, and of nearly the same dimensions.   On the north wall of this inclosure, in a sort of recess, are still visible three coats of arms, of the family of Clare, Earl of Gloucester, some of whom may probably have been buried there (2)

A general uniformity may be perceived in the position of most churches, being built length-wise, east and west, with the tower or steeple at the west, and the chancel at the east end, representing the sanctum sanctorum, where the symbols of divinity were placed, and from thence communicated.

The ancient catechumeni, at their baptization, when they renounced the devil, they turned their faces to the west ; but when they pronounced the creed, they turned to the east. (3)   In these formulæ it is easy to trace the eastern adoration adopted into the Christian system.

The sculptured decorations, with which this ancient part of the cathedral was originally embellished, consist of a series of ornamented arches pointed at their tops, which runs under the foot of the lower tier of windows, beginning in the bishop's chapel, or north transept of the cross ile, and con-

(1) Edward the Black Prince had a chapel founded to his memory in Canterbury crypt   [Somner's Antiq of Cant by Battely, p 97]

(2) See the plan of the crypt (fig A) which is introduced in the plate of that of the cathedral, parallel to the situation it occupies beneath the choir   Under a drawing of the ichnography of this vault, in the library of the Society of Antiquaries, (not very correctly made) the following note is subjoined   " Th s " is the form of the ancient basilicas at Rome, particularly Constantine's, which was the model on which " the earliest Christian churches were built "   It is certain that Rome is famous for its catacombs, or subterraneous repositories for the interment of their illustrious dead

(3) See the Diatribe of Jo Gregory, notes. cap 18.   Staveley's Hist. of Churches, chap 10.

tinuing entirely round the Lady's chapel, ends in the corresponding transept on the south side, now called the Dean's chapel. On the intermediate planes or spandrels between those arches, which are supported by pillars attached to the walls, is a curious and regular arrangement of ancient sculpture, representing a great variety of subjects, many of them grotesque, others of the history of the foundation of the church, and others of scripture history. Of the latter classes a few of them may be described. Of those, however, in the Bishop's chapel, no certain account can be adduced of their design; a great proportion of the grotesque, and a still greater of obliteration and decay, renders inquiry respecting them fruitless. The same may also be said of that part of this work which formerly extended along the extreme east end of the Lady's chapel, where in many parts it may be traced, but where also it has been mutilated and destroyed, to make way for the monuments now seen there. At the east end of the north side-ile, over the second pillar, and beneath the second window, a bishop is represented mitred, kneeling, and offering a church on an altar within the compartment; above, and behind him, a dove is seen descending, expressive of the spirit by which his piety is actuated, as is also the favour of heaven towards his devotion, by an angel with extended arms, ready to receive it at his hands This subject was probably meant either for St Oswald, as founder of the first cathedral church of St. Mary, which event the respect of Wulstan thus chose to commemorate; or it was designed for himself, to the same purpose, with regard to the present church. Over the three next pillars in order, are the annunciation, the visitation, and the nativity.

The first intelligible subject which occurs in the south side-ile, after passing several grotesques, is on the last spandrel to the west, under the second window. An angel is there represented as appearing to a devotee, and enjoining him to some act of piety The succeeding subject explains what that act should be. He is there instructed, that to build a place for the worship of God would be the most acceptable service; and in consequence, the next represents him delivering his plan to an architect, to carry it into execution. The two last subjects alluded to are over the first and second pillars beneath the third window Following the course of this work into the Dean's chapel, on the south wall, we find Christ sitting in judgment, represented in one of those compositions in another, the resurrection of the dead; and in another, on the west side, the wicked delivered over to eternal punishment, entering the mouth of hell, which is figured as a monster, whose capacious jaws are opened to receive them as his prey (1)

Among the various ancient masks dispersed through this part of the church, many of their characters are well conceived, and as well executed. Over the great Saxon arch at the west end of the vestry, in the roof, is a half length figure, represented reclining its head on the right hand; which from the character of the face, and the pensive posture it assumes, appears to have been meant for Christ, as an Ecce Homo In a parallel situation, over the arch of the south side-ile of the choir, are the mutilated remains of a seated figure, which, from the staff it yet holds, seems to have been designed for some pastoral character, either of a bishop or an abbat.

Respecting those sculptured figures, we find at the west end of this portion of the church, all of them directing their looks eastward, they may be considered as very strong evidences that the extreme western boundary of St. Wulstan's sanctum sanctorum was formed at this line or division of the present cathedral; for it is to be observed, that all the other heads or masks, applied as ornamental brackets, are made to look across the ile, at the opposite or corresponding head or mask; among which are found those of kings and bishops, with too great a sameness of character about them to become objects of much attention.

(1) The ancient sculptures of this kind found in our churches, the example under consideration, and a similar one in Westminster abbey, which was carried round its cross iles, may be considered as certain evidences of the early age in which they were erected The mixture of the historic with the hieroglyphic and the grotesque sculptures, appears to have been a refinement upon those examples of the two latter sorts in the crypts at Oxford and Canterbury, of which species these evidently are, at least so far as relates to the allegory they contain • If the crypt at Canterbury be anterior to the Christian era, and that it is the remains of an Iseum, or Roman chapel sacred to Isis, as suggested,† we become at once reconciled to the ingenious explications proposed, and are improved by their erudition But seeing the same objects presented in churches of later date, without any of the same reasons for their appearance, we are led to consider some of those in no other view than as the vagaries and idle fancies of the sculptors, or at best but as mere imitations of what they had probably either seen or heard of at Canterbury, Oxford, or elsewhere For the motives that are said to have induced those representations in the former instances, can hardly be supposed to influence the mere decoration of other churches built four hundred years afterwards, and much less so if the crypt at Canterbury had really been a heathen temple, and erected still so much earlier than the ancient cathedral

• See Archæologia, vol I. p 151 on St Grimbald's Crypt at Oxford, by Mr Theobald, and vol. VIII p 176 on that at Canterbury, by Mr Ledwich, who also observes, that grotesques were mostly confined to crypts, and thence got their appellation [Ibid p 80, note (a)]   † Ibid. p 179. The undercroft at Canterbury was founded antecedent to the year 742 [Angl Sac vol I. p 75]

To these internal embellishments is only to be added the foliage in the capitals of the pillars, most luxuriantly wrought, and the cheveron-work, or zig-zag moulding, the most general manner of ornamenting the arches of that age, found traversing those of the choir only. These and the *corbel-table* ornament, extending entirely round the external part of this building, immediately under the parapet, form the entire suite of decorative appendage known to the venerable founder.

LEADEN STEEPLE

Immediately opposite the north transept of the cross ile of the Lady's chapel, a clochium was erected, in which the bells, anciently but five, were placed. These bells had been newly cast, and were consecrated, some of them to the Saviour and his Mother; Hauteclere and his compeer, to St. John the Evangelist (1) The base of this cloche was eight sided; the height of the stone work was sixty feet, equal to the battlement of the cathedral; the diameter of the base was sixty-one feet; the thickness of the walls ten feet (2) On this base stood a spire, wholly covered with lead, fifty

---

(1) " The scripture apon the iiij bells in the leddon stepull "

The furst bell—" Campanas dia serves has Virgo Maria "

The 2ᵈ bell—" Cristus vincit Cristus regnant Cristus imperat Cristus nos ab omni malo "

The iijᵈ bell—" Johannes Lyndesey, hoc opere impleto, Christi virtute faveto "

The iiijᵗʰ bell—" Ave Maria gratia plena Dominus tecum."

The clock bell—" Thomâ Mildenam Priore "

        " En Ego Campana, nunquam denuncio vana ,
          Laudo Deum verum, plebem voco, congrego clerum."

Funera plango,	-	{ Men's deaths I tell { By doleful knell
Fulgura frango,	-	{ Lightning and thunder { I break asunder
Oblata } Sabati } pango,	-	{ On Sabbath, all { To church I call
Excito lentos,	-	{ The sleepy head { I raise from bed
Dissipo ventos,	-	{ The winds so fierce { I do disperse
Paco cruentos " •	-	{ Men's cruel rage { I do assuage †

(2) St Wulstan, whilst he was prior of this church, inter 1051 and 1062, built a tower for the bells; most probably this base, on which the spire was afterwards raised   Ang Sac. p 474 Willis's Abb v I. p 306.

* From the archives of the dean and chapter of Worcester   † Fuller, in his *History of Abbeys*, sect 2 b vi p 301, has given this rhiming translation of the Latin inscriptions, which he says have sometime been found on sets of six bells, but which it appears have been collected into one for the clock bell at Worcester

yards high; from which circumstance it obtained the name it was afterwards known by, viz the Leaden Spire. The whole height of the base and
spire was seventy yards. The weathercock was on a level with the former
spire of St. Andrew's church, which was seventy-seven yards high. The
timber work of the leaden spire was all of Irish oak, not sawed, but wrought
with the axe (1) The ceremony of the consecration of the bells was performed in 1220, by William de Blois, then Bishop of Worcester (2) Tradition has said, that this spire, with two others at York, were built by King
John; but this report has no certain foundation. In Strype's Annals of the
Reformation, I. p 402, it is said to have been built by King Henry III. (3)

The new cathedral suffered more than once by fire, in the ages subsequent
of its erection ; but at each reparation received addition of ornament and
splendour.—June 14, A. D. 1113, when the city and castle were burnt, the
church and monastery were involved in the same calamity One monk, two
servants of the convent, and fifteen citizens perished in the flames (4)
The walls of the church had little damage; as we may collect from the
silence of William of Malmsbury, who particularly mentions the destruction of its roof, which was undoubtedly of wood.

On Wednesday night in Easter week, April 17, A. D. 1202, the church
was again abandoned to all the injuries of a conflagration; which had
its rise in a different quarter, (5) and reduced to ashes first a great part
of the city After this misfortune, it was long before the cathedral was
repaired. It was not consecrated anew till June 7, 1218. when in the
presence of King Henry III. and a great assembly of nobility, bishops,
abbats, and knights, Bishop Sylvester dedicated it to Mary, the holy Mother
of God, the blessed Apostle Peter, and the Saints Oswald and Wulstan :
in particular, the great altar was dedicated to St Mary and St Oswald ;
and the middle one to St. Peter and St Wulstan. (6)

The church was now restored but William de Blois, the next bishop,

(1) Ex Chartis W Hopkins, D D   (2) Ab Hist Worc Cath p 3
In the year 1647, the leaden steeple adjoining to St Michael's church was pulled down, and the materials sold for £617 4s 2d the principal part of which was given to repair several churches damaged
during the civil war Dodderhill had £80. Castle Morton £80 and the rest in proportion [Dr Nash,
Introduction, vol I p 38]
(3) Jan 16, 1539. The four bells in the leaden steeple were taken down, broke, and carried away.
[Bishop Blandford's MS]
(4) Flor Wig   (5) Igne conflagravit alieno [Annal. Wig]   (6) Ibid.

appears to have formed a nobler plan, that of enlarging and extending it.
Accordingly, in 1224, he laid the foundation stone of a new work, designed
for the front, (1) or nave of the church; an improvement he had undoubtedly seen the propriety of adopting, to complete Wulstan's plan, and to
which the recent accident that had befallen its original front most probably
stimulated him.

We are now come to that portion of the cathedral which may properly
assume the distinction of what is generally termed the modern Gothic stile
of architecture. The skill evinced in attaching this magnificent appendage
to the ancient church is abundant and striking, and forms one of the many
instances in the Gothic taste, on which we can contemplate with satisfaction, without a dread of meeting with the barbarisms of the less refined
structures of the earlier ages, and in which both the delicacy and the impressive grandeur that form its true characteristics are most judiciously
united and preserved

The ruinated parts of the great cross ile were at its north and south ends
only ; the west side or front of it was supported by flying buttresses, one
of which, attached to its south-west side without, is still clearly to be traced,
arising from between the two first windows from which the south wall of
the nave commences. Of its companion buttress on the north side no appearance remains. But we are attracted by the ingenuity of the architect
in his management of the double buttresses within, corresponding in
respect of form and height with the one just mentioned   The shaft of the
inner buttress on the south side has been transformed into the first or easternmost pillar of the nave, and the lower part of its curve, arising from the
capital, forms the western limb of the first arch, from the apex of which it
is continued, and intersects two arches of the first series of arcades above,
and joins the south-west column which supports the tower, parallel to the
spring of the transverse principal arch of the nave to the east   The shaft of
the second, or outer buttress, forming the second pillar, its curve in a parallel
direction with the first, traverses both the lower and upper arcades, and
joins the supporting column of the tower in a proportionately higher part.
The corresponding buttresses on the opposite side of the great ile are pre-

(1) Inceptum est novum opus frontis [Annal Wigorn] In old writers, the western end of a church
is usually called its front, with respect to which the north and south sides were considered as wings, alæ
whence the modern term, ailes, or iles

cisely of the same construction and dimensions, with this only difference in the outer one, the lower part of its curve, apparently discontinued over the second arch, is seen only to arise from the foot of the upper arcade over the first pillar, from whence it reaches the supporting north-west column of the tower In this manner were those lofty and projecting buttresses, (originally on the outside of this west front of the ancient church), incorporated with, and made a part of, those noble ranges of columns and arches which form the magnificent nave of the present cathedral

An object occurs at the west end of this additional building, which has given rise to much conjecture, and it has remained to the present time undecided, why the two lowermost arches of the present nave should be, as they most unquestionably are, of so much older construction than any other part of it, or indeed, as may easily be believed, even older than any other part of the whole church, and yet constituting a portion of the most modern of the additions which have been made to it. It is among my duties to attempt a solution of this problem.

That we are not warranted, by any account or record whatsoever, to say that those arches formed any part of St Oswald's structure, is fully allowed: yet the stumbling-block which Dr Thomas incautiously put in our way, in his endeavouring to ascertain the locality of that structure, by stating that the present cathedral was begun by St. Wulstan " a little to the south of the old one," being so entirely and completely removed, we are thence emboldened in our conjectures to conclude, that those arches really did form a part of St Oswald's building, from the following reasons ·

First, it is not probable that those arches could have been a part of the ancient church of St. Peter, which had barely survived till the days of Wulstan ; for although in the time of St. Oswald it had been the episcopal church, it cannot well be imagined to have been of the dimensions proportionate to those arches, with their superstructure, which are very little short of the height of the present nave; an elevation much exceeding all examples of the age in which St Peter's church was erected

Secondly, the church of St. Mary's monastery, which, prior to the building of St. Oswald's, had been the cathedral of Worcester, appears much more likely to have been the *Old Church,* which, with its monastery, Wulstan ordered to be pulled down, when he removed his monks into his new monastery, as stated by Malmsbury, than that of St. Oswald's church,

the remains of the latter, although in ruins, could not so properly be termed
old in the days of Wulstan, as either those of St Peter's or St Mary's
churches: and we have some authorities to say, that Wulstan's work was
but a repair of St Oswald's church It behoves us also, that we should
dispose of the two old churches of St Peter and St. Mary, which certainly
were situated near the present cathedral, as appears by St. Oswald's church
having been built in the churchyard of St. Peter's, before we entirely destroy
the more modern work of St Oswald's structure That both of them sunk
when Wulstan's arose, and that many of their remains now form parts of
those ancient substructures, on which some of the present prebendal houses
are raised, and on which some of the offices of Wulstan's monastery were
constructed, need not be questioned. But it is not probable, that either of
them would survive any relics of St. Oswald's cathedral, which had been
erected but one century before it was destroyed, and in a stile, as may be
supposed, much more nearly approaching that of St. Wulstan's, than either
of those very ancient churches could be thought to have been.

Lastly, it is not easy to conceive the use to which an insolated building
of this kind could be applied, consisting of two arches only, surmounted
by two others, and accompanied with the same number in the collateral
iles to the north and south, with their vaultings and roofs complete, and
furnished with two tiers of windows strictly appropriated to the form and
fashion of the church architecture of the Saxon era, unless we admit it to
have been part of such an edifice, which most evidently was the fact. From
its form and dimensions (the first of which so well agreeing with its present
use, and the last, particularly in its altitude) it is sufficiently demonstrable
that its erection must have been little anterior to the Conquest; and although it be older than the eleventh century, and therefore not belonging to
Wulstan's building, yet with still less certainty can it be placed in either the
seventh or eighth centuries As, therefore, it cannot be a part either of St.
Peter's, nor of the ancient church of St Mary's monastery, it necessarily
follows that this portion of the present nave is an authentic vestige of St,
Oswald's cathedral, and which survived the vindictive outrage of the Danes
in 1041.

We are hence not only irresistibly led to this conclusion, but also persuaded
that Bishop Blois first connected those remains to the present church, by his
introduction of the intermediate arches of the nave, between them and the

great cross ile. And in this persuasion we are still more strongly supported in observing externally the difference of the stone work of which those arches are formed, and comparing it with that of Bishop Blois's work : the last is wholly of the red Ombersley stone, whilst the first is of the same stone of which the east end of the church is built, none of which it appears was ever used in any of t e additional buildings belonging to the cathedral subsequent to Bishop Blois's time. (1)

In many of our cathedrals, it appears that the nave was an addition made to the original structure in succeeding ages. The cathedral of Canterbury, which had been destroyed by fire, A. D. 1174, according to Gervase, a monk of that church, and an eye witness to its destruction, was rebuilt in ten years; (2) but it was not till two hundred years afterwards that the nave was added to it: the church of Worcester had that addition made to it one hundred and sixty years before that of Canterbury, and nearly the middle of the second century after its erection, by St. Wulstan.

It is not easy to ascertain how many examples of this kind in other churches Bishop Blois had to follow, nor whether he proceeded upon any plan which Wulstan had laid down, or left to his successors, on which his church should afterwards be completed. A variety of circumstances, however, concur to establish the latter proposition as a fact, and as such marks this part of the cathedral as an object of singular curiosity to the attentive examiner.

First, the attention that Wulstan's architect appears to have bestowed upon those ancient arches of St Oswald's church, in placing his structure in the precise line of their direction, and that so justly, that but for those in the side iles being a little lower in the elevation of their roofs than the rest with which they are now connected, the whole series might be said to have been raised at the same time.

(1) It must, however, be admitted that the two lowermost arches of the north ile, in the internal appearance of their vaulting so much alike to the rest of its preceding arches, and so unlike to the two in the south ile, that they would seem rather to have been of Bishop Blois's raising, or at least that Bishop Cobham, when he vaulted the upper part of that ile, had effected the uniformity of appearance their roofs now have to the others, but I conceive the fact to be, that this reform was effected by Bishop Wakefield, to render his work the more complete; he was, however, prevented from availing himself of the same advantage in the arches of the south ile by the buildings adjoining to the dormitory, which had been erected over them, preceding the finishing of his work in this part of the cathedral

(2) Duncombe's Hist of Cant Cath p 148

Secondly, the proportions and subdivisions of the principal portions of the church between the extreme points of distance of the east end of the Lady's chapel, and the west end of the cathedral, including the ancient arches, appearing from accurate measurement so correctly to correspond with certain other divisions of it, to which they are compared, confirms the belief that the whole fabric, although the work of different ages, is the result of one regular and systematic plan, laid down and founded on the measures of the area of those ancient arches, which were in existence one hundred and one years prior to any other part of the present cathedral, although not united to it till two hundred and ninety-six years after St. Wulstan had finished his building (1)

Thirdly, it appears that the plan of the double cross on which the cathedral, as we now see it, is constructed, was adjusted, and its several proportions affixed and combined with each other by the ingenuity of Wulstan's

(1) For a full illustration of the preceding remarks, see the Diagram of the Cathedral in the Plate of its plan, fig B, in which the *relative proportions* of its foundation, beginning at the west end, are found to occur as follow, viz.

I. The area of the Saxon arches from east to west, being 45 feet is equal to one-fourth of the length of the nave, viz 180 feet.

II The length of the nave being 180 feet is equal to the distance from the west end of the choir to the great east window, viz 180 feet

III The breadth of the great cross ile, in its north and south transepts, being 32 feet : is equal to one fourth of its length from north to south, viz 128 feet

IV The same is equal to the breadth of the great window, viz. 32 feet

V The distance from the west side of the great cross ile, to the pillars on the west side of the upper cross ile, being 120 feet is equal to the length of the upper cross ile, viz 120 feet.

VI The length of the choir, from its west entrance to the steps at the ascent to the altar, being 90 feet is equal to one half of the length of the nave, its whole length being 180 feet.

VII The length of the Lady's chapel, from the east end of its side iles to the west side of its cross ile, being 74 feet is equal to the breadth of the Lady's chapel, viz 74 feet

VIII The breadth of the two side iles of the Lady's chapel, and of the choir, each 18 feet 6 inches, being in the whole 37 feet is equal to the breadth of their respective middle iles, viz 37 feet each

IX The depth of the recess of the great east window, from the collateral ends of the side iles of the Lady's chapel, being 16 feet is equal to half the breadth of the window, its whole breadth being 32 feet.

X The distance from the great east window to the pillars on the east side of the upper cross ile at the back of the altar, being 60 feet is equal to one half of the length of the upper cross ile, its whole length being 120 feet

XI The height of the stone work of the tower, from the floor of the great cross ile (over which it arises in the precise centre of the cathedral) to the points of its pinnacles, being 196 feet is equal to the whole length of the nave (180 feet) added to the half of the breadth of the transepts of the great cross ile (16 feet), total 196 feet

architect, who, notwithstanding he raised only the east and choir part of the fabric, and perfected only its upper or lesser cross, at the same time projected its lower or great cross, which he applied as a vestibule to his church, in effecting of which he most judiciously and correctly designed the whole of its relative dimensions in that curious order of regular arrangement, that each cross now occupies its respective extent of space on its own scale of proportion, and, although raised at different periods, and formed to stand independent of each other, they are yet found so united and combined, as to compose that most dignified of distinctions in ancient church architecture, the double cross, perfect and complete in all its parts. (1)

(1) The following *relative proportions* occur in the arrangement of the double cross, on which the plan of this cathedral was laid.

The upper or lesser cross, erected by St Wulstan, it appears, is governed in its proportions by the measure of 60 feet, thus varied and applied

The head, formed of the distance between the great east window and the pillars at the back of the altar (*a*), contains 60 feet

The body, formed of the distance between the west side of the upper cross ile (*b*), and the west side of the great cross ile (*c*), contains 120, or twice 60 feet

The arms, formed of the length of the upper cross ile, contain also 120, or twice 60 feet

The lower or greater cross, completed by Bishop Blois, is regulated in its proportions by the foregoing measure of sixty feet, being augmented in its amount to ninety feet, that scale is thus applied to its construction

The head, formed of the length of the present choir, from its west entrance (*c*) to the pillars at the ascent to the altar (*b*), contains 90 feet

The body, formed of the length of the nave (*d, e*), contains 180, or twice 90 feet.

The arms, formed of the length of the great cross ile, contain 90 feet, and the following fractions of the same measure, viz one-third, or 30 feet, and one-sixteenth, or 8 feet, total 128 feet. [See the Diagram of the Cathedral, in the Plate of its plan, fig. B]

" It was the fashion (says Mr Essex) to apply the name of Gothic to every irregular or disproportioned building, and strange as it must appear, the noblest of our old cathedrals, and other ingenious works, have been no better esteemed than the productions of a rude people, who were ignorant of all the principles of designing, and the art of executing But under whatever denomination the conductors of those noble fabrics may be placed, whether we call them Goths or freemasons, we must acknowledge that the stile of building which they used, was brought to a more perfect system by them, than the Greek or Roman has been by modern architects, and that the principles on which it was founded were unknown to the greatest professors of architecture since the Reformation, is evident from the attempt of Ingo Jones, Sir Christopher Wren, and others of inferior abilities, to the present time, who have endeavoured to imitate it without success But we are not to conclude that the conductors of those stately fabrics had no principles to direct them, because these great men did not discover them, for if any one who is properly qualified, will divest himself of his prejudices in favour of the mode of building which fashion has made agreeable, and impartially examine the merits of those Gothic buildings which are perfect, he must acknowledge, that the ancient freemasons were equal to our modern architects in taste for

H

These points surely attach too strongly to judicious arrangement and contrivance, and have too much of ingenuity in their application, to be supposed the offspring of mere chance On the contrary, I conceive that they present a most decisive and convincing evidence of a regular and connected plan on which the whole fabric was intended to be completed, and the ancient remains of St. Oswald's cathedral united to it to make all its proportions perfectly accord, as we now find they do, with the utmost exactness

designing, (agreeable to the mode of their times) and superior to them in abilities to execute ; that they perfectly understood the nature and use of proportions, and knew how to vary them when they wanted to produce a striking effect   The Gothic, like the Grecian architecture, has its different orders or modes. and every order its peculiar members, by which it may be distinguished from the rest , and the whole is regulated by just proportions founded upon geometrical principles, as capable of demonstration as those of the Greek or Roman •

   " The structures of our Saxon churches were gloomy, heavy, and confined , their roofs and lights, which were lattised, were small and mean , their walls without buttresses, and their columns thick and massy, consequently the whole was dark and damp , their entrances were by descents inwards, and the arches drawn over the top gradually declining with the steps   The Norman plans for building our ancient churches were laid out at first, not the work of a few years, but left to succeeding ages to finish. They were usually begun at the east end, or the choir part, and when covered in, were consecrated   They were large, sumptuous, and magnificent, of great length and breadth, and carried up to a proportionate height, with two, and sometimes three ranges of pillars, one over another, connected together by various arches, forming thereby a lower and upper portico   Their roofs and windows were high, large, stately, and lightsome, and their entrances formed by ascents , the whole possessing an air of solemn grandeur, which never failed to inspire reverence and awe into every beholder +

   " Arches and pillars were in use in the early Saxon structures, but the Normans are said to have introduced the mode of stone buildings raised upon arches The church of Worcester is admitted as one of the most early instances of the practice   its vault or crypt having given occasion to its being called the church of " St Mary in Cryptis," in many of its ancient records

   " The stile of what we term the modern Gothic architecture, but which more correctly speaking, should be called the Saracenic refined by the Christians, first appeared in Britain towards the latter end of the reign of Henry the Second, and gained complete footing in the succeeding reign   It was then that the circular gave place to the pointed arch , the massive column yielded to the slender pillar, and many ancient and solid buildings erected in former ages were taken down, to be re-edified in the new taste, or had additions made to them of this mode of architecture ‡

   " The fashionable pillars in our churches during the same reign, were of Purbeck marble,§ very slender and round, encompassed with shafts a little detached, so as to make them appear of a proportionable

   • Archæologia, vol IV. Art XIII p 149   Observations on Lincoln Cath by Mr Essex, ibid Art. VII p 108, 109

   † Staveley's History of Churches   Bentham's Ely

   ‡ No part, however, of St Wulstan's cathedral appears to have received any of these reforms, unless it be the two arches at the west ends of the north and south ales of the choir   These were probably round Saxon arches, similar to the adjoining ones on the north behind Bishop Hough's monument, and on the south in the vestry

   § A stone, said to be a concretion of shells, from a quarry in the isle of Purbeck, now worked out

and precision   The projecting of this plan appears also to have provided for the certainty of covering the whole of the ground originally occupied by that church, the interesting ruins of which, from their stile of building and situation, the pious founder was persuaded would so far bespeak the favour of posterity, that his successors at some future period would unite them to his own work, and thereby perfect his original design (1)

thickness , these shafts had each of them a capital richly adorned with foliage, which clustering together formed one elegant capital for the whole pillar   The long, narrow, sharp pointed windows, of the lancet form, and usually decorated with marble shafts, are also said to be of the same age *

" The smallness of the windows, and the consequent darkness of our Saxon churches, are supposed to have been owing to their not having been skilled so well as the Normans in the art of making glass   the improvement in the appearance of the Norman churches was certainly much benefited by the advantage they had of better furnaces, to make their glass not only larger, but clearer †

" The windows in the time of Edward II were greatly enlarged, and divided into several lights by stone mullions running into various ramifications above, and dividing the head into numerous compartments of different forms, as leaves, flowers, and other fanciful shapes , and more particularly the great eastern and western windows (which became fashionable about this time) took up nearly the whole breadth of the nave, and were carried up almost as high as the vaulting "‡

(1) The suggestion contained in Browne Willis's prefatory epistle to Dr Tanner, in the second volume of his History of Abbies, respecting the dimensions of our cathedrals and other large conventual churches, advances but little towards adducing any useful insight into the principles of their construction, neither are the comparative dimensions found but in very few particulars to agree with the rule he recommends to be applied to certain parts of their plans, by which other portions of their elevations are supposed by him to have been governed But although those means have failed, future researches after those principles may probably be assisted from the result of the *relative proportions* found to exist in so many of the principal sections of the plan of this cathedral   Beyond this boundary, however, I pretend not to advance   the application of the principles on which the foundation of this church is formed to the proportions of its superstructure, and their immediate or remote dependencies on each other, together with their various bearings and combinations of strength, by which the whole structure has been cemented so firmly, as to have stood thus inflexibly the test of time through so many ages, is left to the professors of architecture to develope and compare

* Of this fashion is the addition made by Bishop Giffard, of the small shaft or columellæ representing grey marble, which are of artificial stone, fastened by rings of gilt copper to the originally unadorned columns of the choir, the Lady's chapel, and the whole series of windows in this ancient part of the cathedral   [Leland's Itin vol VIII p 177]

These, however, have not shared the fate of those of which they are but imitations, for they still remain firm and entire, whilst the columellæ raised in other churches being formed of long pieces of marble, cut horizontally from the quarry, and having been placed in perpendicular situations, have split asunder and broke to pieces, which was the supposed cause that this sort of architectural embellishment was laid aside in the next century

† Strutt's Manners and Customs of the Anglo Saxons, vol I p 34 35
‡ Bentham's Ely p 40 Norman Architecture

In the constructing of the nave by Bishop Blois, we perceive that he had
planned the principal entrance of the church to be continued at the west
end, for on the north no access whatsoever was provided to it ; and the two
entrances on the south side were exclusively for the use of the monastery.
The ancient arch or west entrance into St Oswald's cathedral was still in
being, and of that advantage it was Bishop Blois's plan to avail himself, and
to make the whole of that ancient part of the church serve as a vestibule to
the new nave   In this state, together with the defects and incongruities
arising from a dissimilarity of the whole internal appearance, and a want of
uniform connection of the old with the new work remaining, Bishop Blois
left the west end of the cathedral (1)

It was doubtless soon perceived that light was wanting, more sufficiently to illumine the extent of the nave. The Saxon windows (probably
two or three small ones) which had originally served the purposes of this
part of the ancient church, were insufficient to dispel the gloom that must
have pervaded the extended length of the church westward, and through
which the beauty of the whole nave was destroyed This defect, however,
could not be wholly overcome but by raising the vaultings of the iles internally, and more especially that of the middle ile, and uniting it with the
new vaulting of the nave, which was elevated so much above the level of
the Saxon arches   This is that part of the reform made by Bishop Wakefield, to which Leland adverts, " Superior pars basilicæ forsan id temporis
aucta, &c " as cited by Bishop Lyttelton, and replied to by Mr Garbet, in
their remarks on this operation, as already stated in their letters, given in
the Preface

In the year 1380, under the auspices of Bishop Wakefield, these ornamental and useful reforms were undertaken and accomplished   the ancient
arches were completely attached to the new work of Bishop Blois, and the
great west window was opened (2) It is to be remarked of the erecting of
this window, that it is always stated as a distinct operation from all the

---

(1) He left it not, however, without some provision for carrying on the work he had so spiritedly begun William de Beauchamp III hereditary constable of Worcester castle, paid £75 as his relief for
lands held by his family under this see to the Bishop William de Blois, who dying soon after, bequeathed
it, with £ 200 more to the finishing the fabric of the church   [Ann Wig]

(2) As in Rochester cathedral , the great west window of which was enlarged to its present dimensions
by destroying part of the walls on either side of it   The other windows of its nave were enlarged in the
same manner [Hist of Rochester, p 59, 60]

others in the accounts of the improvements of the church by Bishop Wake-field, and in such a way as clearly indicates that it was formed in a part already built This noble and useful improvement had nothing of Saxon in its design, although constituting a portion of a Saxon arrangement ; on the contrary, it was one of those magnificent windows which the Normans brought in to our churches, and without reference to its Saxonic situation, was more judiciously composed to correspond with that in the east end of the church, and totally different in its construction to either the end or the side windows of the two collateral arches, which are the original windows built by St Oswald, and evidently of a more ancient stile than any other throughout the whole cathedral.

The opening of this magnificent window, it is probable, suggested the expediency of closing the entrance beneath it, which, together with its being so far removed from its ancient situation prior to the building of the nave, and the approach to it withal so circuitous and inconvenient for the congregation, from the narrow and confined pass between the cathedral and the charnel house, the present north entrance or porch was erected and opened opposite the centre arch of the nave, in 1386 ; a situation that at once provided an access suitable to the magnitude and dignity of the structure to which it led , commodious in its approach to the city and the episcopal palace, and a ready and direct communication with its cemetery, and the chapel of the charnel house, to which it was contiguous. The ancient west entrance to the cathedral was in consequence finally closed up (1)

The operations at the west end of the cathedral having been so completely effected by the munificence of Bishop Wakefield, that prelate might (as has been heretofore often stated) with seeming propriety be said to have added those two arches to it, by having thus rendered them fully conformable to the rest of the nave, in the manner already related, both in their appearance and in their uses , but by no means can he be considered as the founder or builder of those arches, as I trust has already been satisfactorily proved. The cathedral has, however, been equally benefited by his liberal attention to its improvement in this part of its structure, for the more this reform is

(1) The situation and dimensions of that entrance are still visibly denoted, externally, by the appearance of a spacious, but low arch, filled up with stone work , and internally by a handsome black Gothic arrangement, executed in wood, expressive of the original purpose of that part of the church, and set up in 1756

contemplated, the greater cause we find to applaud it, as a most judicious and provident measure, in adding or connecting so substantial a work to its extreme west end ; by which the strength of the whole edifice has been greatly augmented, and its durability and security most essentially assisted.

As a great number of bodies interred on the outside of St. Wulstan's building, must be dug up in the prosecution of Bishop Blois's plan of adding the nave to it, he provided a subterraneous vault for their reception, over which he raised a chapel, called Capella Carnariæ, or the chapel of

THE CHARNEL HOUSE ; (1)

and which, in another respect, proved a great convenience to the monastery. In the earlier ages, the cathedral and its cemetery were the common places of interment, not only for the city, but also for the principal families of the adjacent country   they were now become crowded with their dead.   But on the opening of this crypt, the bones that were occasionally displaced on the preparing of new graves, were also deposited in this general sepulchre ; a practice not objected to, under the persuasion of participating in the spiritual advantages to be derived from the devotional purposes of its chapel, in which, on its foundation, three chaplains were maintained to perform daily services for the souls of those whose remains were deposited there.

Walter de Cantelupe, successor to Bishop Blois, confirmed the work begun, dedicated the chapel on its completion to God, St. Mary, and St. Thomas the martyr, in whose name and honour it was built; and A. D. 1265, gave it a new institution.   He appointed four chaplains for its service, to be continually resident in it ; one of which was to be perpetual master, chosen by the bishop, and was to provide for the expences of the chapel.   The sacrist had the care of its repairs   The duties of these chaplains commenced in the morning, on the sounding of the first bell in the city.   They celebrated one mass for the day in the chapel, before their teaching in the schools began, and afterwards three others were daily celebrated for the dead (2)

On the third of the ides of April, 1287, Bishop Godfrey Giffard made an augmentation to the chapel of the charnel house, ordering six priests to officiate there instead of four , and for their maintenance, appropriating to

(1) Strype, Annal Reform vol. I p. 402.
(2) See Dr Thomas,' Account of the Bishops, p. 134, and in Appendix, No XLIII p 26

them the church of St Helen in Worcester, and on the fifth of December following, the church of Newenton, in Cotswold

Upon this new endowment, Hugo de Walingeford, the master, promised the bishop to release unto him and his successors, their right and title to the yearly rent of ten pounds, out of his manor of Hembury, in Saltmarsh, and to give up the writings belonging to the same, which we may suppose he did, for in 1298 the bishop restored to them that ten pounds a year also (1)

In the reign of Richard II. it being found that the rents appropriated for the support of the establishment were insufficient, and that the building was going to ruin, the king's licence was obtained to put the charnel house and the chantry under the care and superintendance of the sacrist of the cathedral, who was to repair the building, and to provide a chaplain to perform the offices of the chapel, and daily to celebrate mass for the souls of the deceased bishops and their successors.

In the 37th of Henry VI the charnel house received new grants and a new foundation. By the statutes then formed, the sacrist of the cathedral (to whose office it was still annexed) was to maintain in the charnel house one chaplain, to celebrate mass in the chapel; he was to be a bachelor of divinity, and to have the custody of the library and books therein; he was also to read publicly in the chapel, once or twice a week, a moral lecture on the New Testament, or, according to the discretion of the bishop, deliver a sermon in the cathedral, or at the cross in the same churchyard, on every Friday for ever   This deed is dated the last day of September, 37th Henry the VIth, witnessed by Bishop Carpenter, William Vause, archdeacon, and others, and confirmed by the chapter. (2)

(1) Dr Thomas's Account of the bishops of Worcester, p 141. See also his Appendix, No LXI. p 45 ex Reg Giff.

(2) Abingdon's MS. p. 33, 37. " Upon the dissolution of the priory of Worcester, the chapel of the charnel house, with other chapels, churches, and appertenances of the priory, were vested in the crown   Amongst other things, this chapel, with all within the circuit of the sanctuary, 24 Jan 1542, King Henry VIII endows the dean and chapter of Worcester, by letters patent, which were confirmed 1 Edw. VI cap 14; and 1 and 2 Phil and Mary, cap. 8.

" Anno 1578, Nov 25, 20 Eliz by virtue of their foundation and charters of endowment, the dean and chapter granted the chapel of the charnel house unto John (Whitgift) Bishop of Worcester, together with the house and priest's chamber,* at the west end thereof, for twenty-one years, if he should so long continue Bishop of Worcester, at the rent of 6s 8d Upon Bishop Whitgift's promotion to the archbishopric

* Erected temp Henry VI

About the time of Bishop Giffard we are to date, I presume, another considerable change in the internal arrangement of this church. In primitive cathedrals, the principal altar was near the eastern end, with only the bishop's throne behind it When the doctrine of transubstantiation was afterwards introduced, a natural consequence of it was, that the host was an object o adoration, and as such should be exhibited in a part of the church the most

of Canterbury, it was granted, Feb 9th, 1586, to Roger Folliott, of the city of Worcester, gent. for 40 years, at the same rent , with a covenant that the dean and chapter should have and take all the lead belonging to the said charnel house This lease determining in Feb 9th, 1626, Bishop Thornborough afterwards used it as a hay barn.

" By an order of the chapter, held Oct 29th, 1636, the chapel was prepared and fitted up as a school for the scholars of the college and city, and on the 18th March following, on a hearing of differences between Bishop Thornborough and the dean and chapter, and the mayor, aldermen, and citizens of Worcester, before Archbishop Laud, his grace decreed that the school should be kept in the chapel This decree was observed till 1641, when the differences were renewed, and a complaint made from the city of the damps and unwholesome smells of the charnel house, that were prejudicial to the health of the scholars These were collectively brought before the parliament in May, 1641, and the school was afterwards removed to the refectory, and the chapel from that time suffered to go to ruin In the Survey of the manor of Guestenhall, fol. 91, the chapel of the charnel house is declared to be in so ruinous a state, from its roof being uncovered, its walls in danger of falling, its inside so incumbered with weeds and rubbish, and its floor overgrown with alder trees, as to threaten destruction to the roof of the vault beneath ; and a part of it also made use of as a workhouse for masons, stone-cutters, and labourers, by whom it was so defiled as to become a common nuisance June 28th, 1676, a lease was granted of the two chambers and garden ground to James, Lord Bishop of Worcester, for 21 years ; who, in consideration of faithful service done to his lordship, and to the episcopal see of Worcester, by John Price, B L. surrendered the lease into the hands of the dean and chapter, to the use of the said John Price, 23 Nov 1677 The dean and chapter on the 25th Nov 1677, accordingly granted the ruinous charnel house, except the vault, with the tenement at the end of it, and the garden ground adjoining, to the said John Price, with a power to take down the walls of the charnel house to the stools of the windows, and to employ the materials in inclosing the garden ground, with a free use of the floor of the chapel for a passage to the tenement, for 40 years, at the yearly rent of 6s 8d

" By virtue of that lease, those conditions were fulfilled by the said John Price, and a new house was erected by him upon the ground whereon the old tenement stood , and he became tenant to the dean and chapter for it, at the yearly rent of 6s 8d under a new lease granted to him, dated 25th Nov 1679 Those premises therefore still belong to the cathedral church of Worcester, as before the dissolution "*

The only vestiges of the chapel that remain, are part of the north and south walls, which now inclose the court before the abovementioned house but the crypt, which is underneath it, and bounded by the same walls, and extending the whole space of the court, remains entire, its length is 58 feet, its breadth 22, and its height about 14 It contains a vast quantity of bones, which, although now in some disorder, seem to have been curiously assorted, and piled up in two rows along its sides, leaving a passage between them from its west entrance (which was closed at the time the chapel was demolished) to its east end. The only entrance at present into it is by one of its windows on the south side, but it is generally stopped up. [See the plan of the vault, in the Plate of that of the cathedral]

* Ex MS. J. Price, B. L.

elevated and conspicuous.   Hence it became necessary, that, in the largest and most frequented churches, the high altar should be placed in the centre of a cross ile ; so that, at the elevation of the host, the crowds in the transepts on each side, the women especially (1) (who were excluded from the choirs of the monks) might have an opportunity to see and adore (2) This conveniency was attained, in some places, by the addition of a new cross ile at the east end of the choir, and of a new chapel beyond it ; as at Gloucester, Ely, St Paul's in London, Litchfield, Croyland abbey, &c. (3) and in other places, by removing the choir so far westwards, that its chancel and altar might lie open to a cross ile of the church   This last method appears to have been taken at Westminster abbey ; and, as some circumstances induce me to think, in Worcester cathedral also.

In the due consideration of this object it is absolutely necessary that we should wholly detach our ideas from the present arrangement of the Lady's chapel, the choir, and the great cross ile, as we now find them ; these originally formed the whole of the cathedral, as built by St. Wulstan.   But

(1) We are told, that anciently women were prohibited from entering into the monastical church of St. Cuthbert, at Durham, beyond the blue cross, in the pavement at its lower end ; the prohibition is attributed to the miracle wrought by St Cuthbert, upon a lewd woman that would have slandered him, by charging him with incontinency. [Rites and Monuments of Durham, Camd. Brit. in Durham   Staveley, p 281, 282] The story as related in the legend, is copied at length by Grose, in his Antiquities, vol. I. But it seems this inexorably chaste saint had not forgot his resentment against the sex from the time of his death, A D 687, to the time of Edw III a period of 650 years.

Philippa, queen of Edw. III having followed the king to Durham, was conducted to him through the gate of the abbey to the prior's lodgings, where, having supped and gone to bed, she was soon disturbed by one of the monks, who rudely intimated to the king, that St. Cuthbert by no means loved the company of her sex   The queen, upon this, got out of bed, and having hastily dressed herself, went to the castle for the remaining part of the night, asking pardon for the crime she had inadvertently been guilty of against the patron saint of their church. [Angl. Sac vol I. p 760 Brand's Hist. of Newcastle, vol II. p 408, 409] The prohibition of the women extended to all the churches of the Picts, dedicated to St. Cuthbert, by an ordinance of the king of that province, whose daughter it was that had traduced his character   [Antiquities of Durham Abbey, 12mo p 38, 39, 40]

(2) Nor was this sufficient. The synod of Reading, held in 1179, required a tabernacle to be placed over the altar, under which the host, deposited in a handsome pyx, might be suspended. Thus the eucharistic wafer, cased in a box, became an object of daily adoration to all who frequented the service of the church.

(3) In all these places, the new fabric, for lengthening the church eastwards, was raised in the reign of Henry III. Edward I or Edward II and, in all of them, except Ely, was dedicated to the particular service of the Virgin Mary, who, in these ages, began to be called Regina Cœli In the charter of the foundation of Bordasley, in Worcestershire, by the Empress Maude, for Cistercian monks, dedicated to the most blessed Virgin Mary, she is stiled Regina Cœlorum. [Monast. Angl. vol. I. p 803. Epitom. p. 96.]

I

those parts were then known by other names, and had other uses assigned
to them   There was at that time no such division in this church as the
Lady's chapel.   That portion of the church, at the time we are now treating
of, was the ancient choir, extending from the great east window to the
western pillars of the upper cross ile, where now are the steps, to the present
altar.   From that division to the west end of the present choir, was the nave
of the ancient church, to which the ascent was from its vestibule, the present great cross ile.   Such was the cathedral of Worcester, when it was for
the last time nearly consumed by an accidental fire in 1202.   The subsequent repairs it received, were carried on very slowly ; they were not completed A. D 1216, when King John was interred in this cathedral, in its
original choir, between the Saints Oswald and Wulstan, and before its high
altar, at that time placed under the great east window.   It was not till two
years afterwards, that the church, being restored, received consecration
anew, viz on the seventh day of June, 1218.

From hence I conceive we may gather, that, in the interval between
the interment of King John, and the reconsecration of the church, the
change we are here speaking of took place, when the eastern part of the
middle ile, beyond the screen of the present altar, was converted into a
stately chapel to the Virgin Mary, who, in almost all the large conventual
churches, had a peculiar chapel in the middle ile, either at the east or western
end. (1)   The appointment of a daily mass to be sung at her altar, and of

(1) In the year 1292, 5 id June, Nicholas, the sacrist, adorned the church with tables of images,
placed on each side of that of the Virgin Mary. [Willis's Mitred Abbies, vol I. p 303]

The image of the Virgin here mentioned was probably set up in her chapel.

Mr. Bentham has produced sufficient authority to prove, that what we generally term the chapel of a
particular saint in a church, is no other than the porticus ; which term has constantly been applied to
the porch or entrance into the church.   The highest authorities are cited, to support the conjecture, that
a more considerable part of the church is certainly intended by porticus, than what is commonly understood by the church porch . and it is clearly inferred, from all the instances he has produced, (and they
are many and strong) " that the writers meant by it, either what is now called the side ile of the church,
" or sometimes it may be a particular division of it, consisting of one arch with its recess ," which are
often termed chapels, and dedicated to some saint   Of this sort we may presume was Jesus chapel in this
cathedral   The ancient Kentish kings, and the first archbishops of Canterbury, from St Augustine to
Brithwald inclusive, Earl Leofric and his Countess Godiva, and many others, are therefore more reasonably conjectured to lie within those churches, where their interment was expressed to have been in the
north or south porticus, a word synonymous with atrium or vestibulum, denoting a building withoutside
the church, at the entrance into it, which is generally translated by the English word, porch [Bentham's
Ely, p. 19, 20]

We may conjecture form hence, that the custom of burying in churches was permitted and practised

particular priests for her service, began to take place in the thirteenth century.

In dedicating an altar to the Virgin, we may well suppose that altar to have had the most dignified situation in the portion of the church now set apart for her worship; it took place, therefore, of the high altar of the ancient choir, under the great east window of her chapel, where it remained till the dissolution of the monastery. The distinction here made of the *great altar* being dedicated to St. Mary, is to be understood as compared to the adjacent altars placed at the east ends of the collateral side iles of that part, now collectively called the Lady's chapel, which at that time were devoted to other saints, and had each their peculiar services.

The middle altar, dedicated to St. Peter and St. Wulstan, points out its own situation in relation to the surrounding ones; this unquestionably was the choral, or high altar of the cathedral.

In this transfer of the sacred offices of the church it was considered that the royal remains of King John partook of the reverence paid to the Holy Virgin, and that they had received additional sanctification, in being left undisturbed before her altar, and between the sepulchres of the Saints Oswald and Wulstan.

On the separation of the ancient choir from the original nave of the church, an inclosure was formed of the area of the four sectional pillars of the upper cross ile, the stone work of which was faced with a series of small arcades, extending entirely round its north and south sides, and its east end; an embellishment which it appears to have had both within and without; for in 1792, on removing the two inner pilasters of the centre of the present altar screen, to admit the picture which now occupies that part, those arcades were discovered, and parts of an inscription were observable in the spaces between those small pillars; but too much divided to be connected, or satisfactorily explained This range of the arcades is most probably entire. On the outside, at the north end of the altar, the mutilated remains of those small pillars are visible; their derangement in this part was occasioned by the erecting of Bishop Bullingham's tomb, (1) and on

---

at a more early period than what some authors have stated, and whose accounts would lead us to imagine, that it had obtained, by degrees, from the cemetery to the outer walls of the church, from thence into the porch, or entrance, and, lastly, into the church itself

(1) At that time the wall above it, within the arch, was raised, to secure a dangerous failure in the

the south side by the building of Prince Arthur's chapel   The form and dimensions of those small pillars within and without are precisely the same, and, when entire, must have formed a very beautiful termination of the choir, from its uniformity, and the simplicity of the Gothic mode of decoration.

We are here attentively to notice, that before this inclosure was effected, the east end of the crypt, which prior to that time had formed the western extremity of the ancient choir, was a visible object to that part of the church, its circular end presenting itself to view between the two pillars west of the upper cross ile.

I have taken some pains to establish this fact, not only with a view to ascertain the sepulture of King John, but also to reconcile a note which the learned Dr Hopkins has made, relative to this subject, but in terms so general, as to need an explanation. It is the doctor's remark, that " anciently " the choir extended westward to the second pillar below the belfry." (1) To get at the true import of this assertion, (for it can be nothing more, without proof) we must again recur to the ancient principal tower of this church, which stood on the section of the middle and upper cross iles, immediately over the area of the present altar, in which, doubtless, bells were fixed for the immediate purposes of the church service, besides those in the leaden steeple; more particularly the sanctes bell.   Here, then, was the belfry to which Dr. Hopkins's remark refers; and if we say farther, that " the choir extended westward, to the second pillar *beneath* (instead of " *below*) the belfry," the information contained in the note is then correct; but it cannot apply to any other arrangement of the church in any of the reforms it has undergone subsequent to that period.

On examining the extreme eastern part of the undercroft, it is observable,

structure, visible at the east end of the north ile of the choir. Similar means of strengthening part of the fabric about the Dean's chapel were applied at the same time

It is highly probable that these parts of the upper cross ile were thus damaged by the fall of the ancient tower, which originally stood between them

These modern addenda, with the stone screen under the organ loft, are the principal architectural blemishes in the whole church, as far as regards its general appearance as a Gothic edifice   They were the produce of that age, when the miserable attempts at the Grecian architecture arose, and when the Gothic, which had just attained its perfection, was falling into disuse

(1) See Browne Willis's Hist of Mitred Abbies, vol. II. p. 262. Abingdon's Hist of Worcester Cathedral, p xxii and Dr Thomas's Survey p 4.

that in parts of one or two of its arches, where some of the loose stones with which they have been stopped up are displaced, and where the outer face of the stone work of the circular end can be in part explored, it is found to have a regular wrought surface, and that the external angles of the sides of those arches, of which there are five, are finished with projecting mouldings, or, what is most probable, small columellæ, in form corresponding with those in the inner part of the circle. The whole cavity and extent of the area, as then inclosed, from the present altar screen east, to the circular end of the undercroft west, (1) which is precisely under the space between the foot of King John's tomb and the first step of the ascent to the altar, was entirely filled up with earth to the height we now see it, and which, from the level of the vault, is about thirteen feet. Since that era many interments have taken place about the high altar, of which we shall hereafter have farther occasion to mention (2)

It will be much less difficult to believe that the body of King John is still in possession of its original sepulture in this chapel, than that St. Oswald was ever buried beside his grave. The death of that saint is stated to have happened A. D. 992; and that he was buried in his own church is most probable. Ten years after his death, many miracles having been wrought at his tomb, Adulph, his successor, A. D. 1002, honourably translated St. Oswald's bones from his grave into a shrine he had prepared for that purpose. The body was found reduced to powder; but his episcopal garment, in which he was wrapped, was as fresh as when newly made, and continued so, says Malmsbury, to his time, which was in the twelfth century. (3)

In 1089, the relics of St. Oswald were inclosed in a new shrine, at the expence of seventy-two marks of silver, by Bishop Wulstan, at the time of his opening his new cathedral, and 48 years after the destruction of St. Oswald's cathedral. This, as well as the former shrine, we may gather, was of the portable kind, which upon various disastrous occasions had been brought forth in procession, to avert threatening calamities, and, as we may imagine, with various success. The last service but one, to which the remains of this saint were called, proved unfavourable to their reputed influence. In 1139, when the forces of the Empress Maude

(1) The plan of the crypt is inserted in the Plate of the ichnography of the cathedral, and is placed parallel to the situation it occupies in its foundation   (2) See Appendix, No VIII p xxvi
(3) Malmsb de Gestis Pont lib iii. p 154. Dr Thomas, in Bishops of Worcester, p 56

attacked the city of Worcester, the relics of St. Oswald were carried in procession from one gate to the other, with the choir singing before it in form. But the assailants, regardless of the ceremony, forced their way into the city, set fire to it in several places, and plundered it without mercy.(1)

In Mr. Abingdon's time, there was extant in the ledger of rectories and impropriations of the diocese of Worcester, a letter, written in English by holy King Henry VI. to this priory, to obtain of God rain, at a time of extreme drought, by a procession joined with the relics of St. Oswald. (2)

It is most likely the procession took place; but what was its success we are not informed of, as neither the letter, the year of the king's reign, or any trace of the circumstance, is now to be found. It serves, however, to shew, that the relics of St. Oswald continued in a state of requisition so late as near the middle of the fifteenth century.

That the grave of St Wulstan was here, may be admitted as a certainty. In 1201, one hundred and six years after his death, his remains had the reputation of working miracles, and fifteen or sixteen persons in a day were said to have been cured of their diseases This we may suppose was the effect of the outrage committed upon their repose by Bishop John de Constantiis, during his short prelacy, from November, 1196, to September, 1198 : for in 1204, Bishop Malger replaced the bones of the blessed Wulstan in the same grave from whence they had been irreverently removed by his predecessor. (3) They had, however, been long enough above ground, to prove that such a treasure was not literally to be buried. Their fame soon found its way to the Vatican ; and Hubert, Archbishop of Canterbury, Eustace, Bishop of Ely, and the abbats of St. Edmund and Wlburn, in 1202, received the commands of Pope Innocent III. to visit Worcester, and to inquire into the truth of those miracles ; where receiving full satisfaction of the fact, they returned with joy, and sent letters of attestation to the pope by Walter de Bradwas, and Randolph de Evesham, monks of Worcester ; whereupon Wulstan was canonized at Rome with great solemnity, (4) on the ninth of the calends of May, 1203.

(1) Flor Wigorn. (2) Abingdon's MS p. 47
(3) Annal Wig. Dr Thomas, in Account of the Bishops, p. 121, 122.
(4) An Wig See also 4 C. fol. 2 art 3 " Bulla Innocentii Papæ pro Canonizatione Wulstani Wi- " gorniensis Episcopi . data anno sexto."—The last page. On parchment. Casley's Catal. of MSS. of the King's Library, p 52. Mus. Brit

We may conclude that the bones of Wulstan were not enshrined after they had been taken from the grave by Bishop de Constantiis, and that his successor, induced by the sanctity which they had newly acquired, entombed them again, from motives of veneration and devotion. King John, A. D. 1207, three years after St. Wulstan's second interment, paid his devotions at his tomb. But he was not suffered to rest long with his kindred dust; for we are told by the Worcester Annals, that Bishop Sylvester, on the day of the dedication of the cathedral, in 1216 as before related, put the corpse of St. Wulstan into a sumptuous new shrine, the old one having been melted down two years before, to enable them to pay the contribution of three hundred marks, which was at that time imposed upon the convent, for their having submitted to the dauphin, and receiving William, the son of William Mareschall, to maintain his interest among them. (1) The death of Bishop Sylvester, which happened on the 16th day of the following month, (July) was said by some to have been a judgment upon him, for having with his own hands sawed in two some of the bones of St. Wulstan, and divided them in several places Of this indecent transaction it seems he gloried.(2) This is farther confirmed by Florence of Worcester, who says, that at this time the relics of Wulstan were divided, and that one of his ribs was given to the monks of St. Alban's, who received it with procession, and inclosed it with gold. (3)

In the pontificacy of William de Blois, it was decreed in 1224, that the profits arising from the tomb of St. Wulstan, at which many miracles continued at that time to be performed, should be divided between the bishop and the convent. (4)

Edward the First was much devoted to this saint, and often resorted to his tomb; to which, in 1300, he sent an offering of eight candles, to burn before it.

After this period, we may presume that the shrines of these canonized saints became stationary in the side iles of the Lady's chapel, whilst their tombs were also permanent before the altar of the blessed Virgin in its middle ile.

That St. Oswald's remains shared the same fate as St. Wulstan's, in being

(1) An Wig. sub anno 1216.   (2) Annal. Waverl. p. 184.   (3) Lambarde, ex Flo.
P 409, 410.   (4) Ang. Sac.

divided, although we cannot trace the date of the circumstance, we are led
to believe, from his shrine being also a portable one: the fixed shrines, such
as the Confessor's, in Westminster abbey, St Cuthbert's, at Durham, and
a few others, are supposed to contain the bodies entire of the persons whose
names they bear. In the Harleian Collection of MSS. (1) in the British
Museum, we find in part of an inventory of the plate, vestments, utensils,
&c belonging to the priory of Worcester, under the head " The Tumbary's
Office," the following " Item. Seynt Oswalde and Seynt Ulstans hede,
" with selvͬ and gylte—and certen relyquis of Seynt Oswalde and Seynt
" Ulsta—, coveryde with selvͬ."

One other view of their bones was afforded " to the up-turn'd wondering
" eyes of mortals," before they left " the glimpses of the moon." In 1538,
The *shrines* of St Wulstan and St Oswald were taken down, and their
bones (with the bones of Bishop de Constantiis) were laid in lead, and
buried at the north end of the high altar; all which time there was such
lightning and thunder, that every one thought the church would have
fallen. And in 1541, the *tombs* of St. Oswald and St. Wulstan were taken
down and removed (2)

From the preceding account of the posthumous labours of those saints,
to their final disappearance, we are no longer to suppose them deposited
under those stones which bear the effigies of two ancient bishops, so uniformly sculptured in the same kind of stone, and so exactly placed at equal
distances from the sepulchral covering still remaining over the grave of
King John. But in suggesting, that on the removal of their tombs, these
figures, which had been placed upon them, were laid down on the floor,
where those tombs anciently stood, still denoting where the real grave of

(1) No 604 Plut 2—v F art 48 p 102   See also the Appendix to this Section, No III. p vii.
(2) Bishop Blandford's MS ——Quære   May not the collection of mosaic bricks laid in the form of
an oblong square, in the north ile of the Lady's chapel, cover this deposit? The situation accords strictly
enough to the place described " at the north end of the high altar " The disorder in which those bricks
were till lately found, prove, that either they were the spoils of the ancient sepulchres of those saints,
brought into use upon the present occasion , or that an interment, subsequent to the time of their being
first laid down, where we now find them, had taken place. The present order of the arrangement of those
bricks has been effected by the industry of a very meritorious servant of the church, by whose careful
attention in replacing them, the original design of this ancient sepulchral covering has been restored

It represents a cross, about which flowers are disposed, some of the bricks are ornamented with birds,
and others at the angles with mitres, denoting the spot as the sepulture of some prelate——of whom no
account has reached us.—It is also to be remarked as the only tessellated pavement in the whole church.

St Wulstan and the reputed one of St Oswald had formerly been, will, I trust, be thought easily reconcileable to positive fact (1)

On the festivals of the translation of these saints it was customary to pay devotions at their shrines, but on the anniversaries of their deposition (or decease) at their graves: that of Oswald's deposition, January the 19th, continued to be observed by the Roman catholics in the last age, who were wont to visit, on that day, a gravestone with an effigy upon it, in the pavement of St. Mary's chapel (2) In matters of *la petite religion* the tradition of the Romanists is faithful enough, and may safely be allowed its authority.

Bishop Giffard, in his last will, (dated 1301, Sept. 13) very clearly distinguishes between the great or high altar, and the altar of the glorious Virgin's chapel, (3) in the cathedral church of Worcester, and bequeaths precious vestments to the use of each So that the separation of her chapel in this cathedral must have been made before that time. He expresses also his desire, that he might be buried in the tomb he had prepared for himself on the north side of the great altar. This tomb, says the register of Canterbury, was *supra beati Oswaldi feretrum*, (4) whence I collect, that the shrine

(1) Mr Gough, in his valuable and learned work, has decidedly settled the point respecting the fashion of tombs in different ages In his class of those of the eleventh century, the first in the order of his arrangement, he thus treats of those of " St Oswald and St Wulstan, at Worcester, (miscalled, by " Dr Thomas, Bishops de Constantiis and Giffard, who lived one and two centuries later) are very much " in the stile of those of Roger and the other bishop at Sarum, the same attitude and the same foliage " under their heads as under the latter It is remarkable, that both the Worcester statues hold a mere " baculus, or staff, instead of a crosier, (though both Thomas and Green call them crosiers) and have a " rose on their breasts " [Sepulchral Monuments, p 13 Century XI]

It is, however, to be noted in favour of the engravings of those figures in Dr Thomas, that they represent the staff correctly in each, although it is certain both his account and mine have mistermed them crosiers

(2) Angl Sacr I p 497.

(3) It is extraordinary that Dr Thomas, who, in his Appendix, No 69 p 77. gives us a copy of this will should not perceive a distinction so strongly marked He tells us, that the bishop made himself a magnificent tomb, near the great altar of the Virgin Mary's chapel. [Dr. Thomas's Account, p 152] We often read of the great altar of a church, and of the altars in its several chapels but who ever heard of the great altar of the chapel of a church? It is certain, that the great altar, meant by Bishop Giffard, was the choral, or high altar, near which he had already buried his sister Maude, close by the place that he had destined for the lofty position of his own tomb " juxta locum ubi episcopus frater ejus deposuit " subt mius sepeliri " [Annal Wig] It is clear to me, that the bishop was desirous of having his own sepulchre at the top of the northern ascent to the altar, where the monument of Mrs. Goldisburgh is now seen (4) Angl Sac I p 497

h

of that saint stood on the north side of the choir : this is indeed confirmed by the register of the priory, *sede vacante,* in the following account

The raising of this sumptuous tomb gave great offence to Winchelsea, at that time Archbishop of Canterbury, as it had occasioned the removal of that of John de Constantiis, who had been considered as a saint, and whose claims on that distinction were now much strengthened in the public opinion, upon its being found that his body, after being interred for near one hundred years, remained uncorrupted   The shrine of St. Oswald was also incommoded by the new tomb, which had the appearance of a tabernacle over it.   These circumstances, added to the encroachment it made upon the choir, so as to obstruct the priests in serving at the high altar, induced the archbishop to issue orders to the prior to remove it   The prior, by letter, excused himself from doing it in the time of the bishop's last sickness, lest the grief occasioned by it might hasten his death.   But on the decease of Giffard, which happened 26 Jan A. D. 1301-2, the orders of the archbishop were fulfilled, and the tomb was taken down (1)

In the last will of Bishop Giffard, (which Dr Thomas has inserted in his Appendix, No. 69 p 77) he earnestly entreats the prior and convent, that his body may be deposited on the dexter or north side of the altar   But this was not likely to be granted   He had too much chagrined them by tedious and expensive law suits, which he carried on against them   Yet as he had been a noble benefactor in ornamenting the church, they could not refuse his remains a place near the altar, in a situation, from which no annoyance could arise ; and he was accordingly interred at the bottom of the south ascent to the high altar, over which his tomb was placed

The erecting of Prince Arthur's chapel in 1504, occasioned a second derangement of Giffard's tomb, *pro tempore.*   It was then divested of its sculptured appendages, and, in the simple form we now find it, was accommodated to its present situation, still remaining over his grave, beneath the chapel of Prince Arthur (2)   The adjacent tomb of the Countess of Surrey was submitted to the same operation at the same time. (3)

---

(1) Abingdon's MS p 38   (2) Browne Willis, in his MS. Addenda to his Cathedrals, vol I p 627.
(3) In Symonds's Church Notes, vol II [No 965, in the Harl Coll. MSS. art. 16. Brit Mus] He says, " Under Prince Arthur's chapel, in blue marble, lies the statue of a bishop upon an altar tomb, for " St. Wulstan, who gave all the marble pillars to this church, in all 250 "   Here we see a compound of truth and error, jumbled together by oral tradition.

The tomb of John de Constantiis was, doubtless, replaced in its former situation ; and the tomb of Bishop Cantelupe occupies the adjoining sepulchral arch eastwards. (1)

Two facts, hitherto obscured and much disputed, are established beyond a doubt in this extract from the register of the priory ; namely, the place of the sepulture of Bishop de Constantiis, and the situation of the shrine of St. Oswald. We have henceforth only to recollect that the graves and shrines of St Oswald and St. Wulstan were distinct objects ; that the first were emptied of their remains, to supply the last ; and that each retained a degree of sanctity and imposing reverence deeply rooted in the faith of those who resorted to them Their graves, as already described, were on each side of that of King John ; their shrines were brought forward to the view of the congregation; that of St. Oswald on a line with Cantelupe's tomb, and that of St Wulstan parallel with the tomb of Giffard, at the north and south ends of the high altar. On the destruction of the shrines of those saints, the hallowed honours of their names were transferred to the adjoining tombs ; and thus the Bishops Cantelupe and Giffard, if they never received papal beatification, have been sanctified in their graves, by a vulgar error, which has reached through two centuries to the present times.

The miracles wrought by King John were not of such a nature, that monkish devotion would either raise up its eyes or its hands, in support of his claim on the order of its saints. He had, however, done something in favour of the church, and that of Worcester had a share of his attention. To the political world he gave much greater cause of remembrance. History and experience have handed down to us the importance of the benefits derived to the constitution of England ; and past and succeeding ages have already felt, and will hereafter continue to feel, that more was ceded towards the emancipation of a brave people from the iron hand of power, by that extraordinary compound of majesty and meanness, than could have been wrested from kings more just, more wise, and more magnanimous.

A simple stone coffin, with his figure upon it, of the fashion of the thirteenth century, (2) raised a little above the surface of the earth, was all the

(1) See the Plan of the Cathedral, No 18, 16   See also Gough's Sepulchral Monuments, p. 30, ex. Green's Survey, p 72.   (2) Sandford pronounces the figures of the king, and the bishops Oswald and Wulstan, between whom he is represented, all of one stone, to be as old as the time of Henry III. [See his Genealogical Hist p 85]

K 2

memorial left, for posterity to contemplate the personal character of a monarch to whom it has casually been so much indebted. This stone was
removed at the Reformation, for the evident purpose of perpetuating in the
public mind the new policy of that important era. The influence of papal
authority having been compelled to yield to regal supremacy, the image of
that same king, whom two centuries before had seen basely surrendering
his dignity and his crown to that overwhelming tyranny, was now brought
forward, and most appositely made the visible sign of that important part
of the Reformation having taken full effect in the church of Worcester but
his corporeal remains, as if unworthy to assert a right so legitimate and just,
were left to their repose in obscurity and neglect, and in so marked a manner, as at this time it remains a question with many, where they really are:
—a question we shall endeavour to resolve

The evidences necessary to establish this point have been in part already
produced.   But that which I conceive to be the most conclusive is yet to
be noticed.

There still remains (1790) in the Lady's chapel, in the precise situation
pointed out in every account left us of the place of the interment of King John,
a sepulchral stone, of a dark colour, so truly corresponding in form with
that on his tomb in the choir, as at once to assure us that it was the original
plinth or base, on which that stone, now bearing the effigy of the king,
was laid (1)

The perplexities which attended this monarch through life seem to have
taken up their habitation with him in his grave   It does not appear, however, that they broke out till after the removal of his effigy from the place
of his sepulture, when it was laid upon the new altar tomb, which was raised
for its reception before the high altar in the present choir   Of this transaction, Leland, who lived nearer the time in which it took place, than any

(1) The following are the measures of the stone on which the effigy of King John is represented on his
tomb, compared with the sepulchral stone over his grave

	Stone in the Choir					Stone in the Lady's Chapel.	
	Ft	In				Ft	In
Length	6	4	-	-	-	6	9
Breadth at the head	2	5	-	-	-	2	6
Breadth at the feet	1	2	-	-	-	1	3

Whereby it appears that the plinth now over the grave presented a regular projection beyond the lines
of the superincumbent stone now in the choir, of two inches and a half on each side, and half an inch
at each end

other writer who has at all adverted to it, furnishes the following item from
his own observation . " In Presbyterio   Johannes Rex, cujus sepulchram
" *Alchirch* Sacrista nuper renovavit." And further, " Sacellum in quo Ar-
" turius Princeps sepultus est ad austrum " (1)   From hence we learn
two things . First, that the renovation of King John's tomb could not
allude to the ancient tomb in the Lady's chapel, but must refer only to the
present one in the choir, on the south of which he points out the station of
Prince Arthur's chapel   The renovation, therefore, implies the rebuilding
or reconstructing anew in the choir a tomb for King John, and placing his
image, which was removed from the old tomb, upon it   Secondly, the time
when this change took place, namely, when *Alchirch*, or *Alchurch* (the same
person) was sacrist, that is, a little before the dissolution of the monastery.
For although no regular list of the sacrists of this church on the monkish
establishment be found, yet sufficient evidence, proving Alchurch in that
office at that time, occurs in the inventory of the church plate in his possession, and under his care, as sacrist, when the treasures of the monastery
were surrendered in 1540 (2)   It appears not, however, that this reform
was effected at his own charge, although we find him in the same account
a benefactor of plate to the treasury ; and afterwards as sub-prior, having
presented a blue arras cloth, ornamented with his own device or rebus,
used as a covering for the stone seat of the church dignitaries assisting at
divine service, which remained a hundred years after his time fresh and in
good condition, although in constant weekly use ; for such was its state, at
the time of the civil wars (3)   But the question, whether the body of the
king was translated from his grave to his tomb at that time, is not at all
assisted by the notice Leland has taken, as above   Many, however, have
been of opinion, that it was inclosed in the tomb above ground   Mr Willis
was well apprized, that no grave could be dug beneath this tomb. (4)   But
Dr Thomas has denied this, on a presumption that the great vault, which
he sets down but sixty feet long, does not extend so far under the eastern
part of the choir, but that graves might be made there, and under the parallel arches of the side iles   It is with some pain that I point out the errors of this antiquary of Worcester. I am conscious of my obligations to

(1) Leland's Itin vol VIII p 129.
(2) See Appendix to this Section, No II. p iv
(3) Dr Thomas's Survey, p 9
(4) See his Cathedrals, vol I p. 626.

his industry : his name is venerable with me : but truth is sacred. He certainly had not examined this vault, when he asserts that it extends but half the length of the choir. Its western end is under the first arch of the choir; and it extends eastwards beyond the king's tomb, quite to the foundation of the western pillars of the upper cross ile, or the foot of the ascent to the altar. Its length is sixty-seven feet, and the ground between the pavement of the choir and the level or floor, cast immediately over the arches of the vault, is not more than one foot deep ; much too shallow to admit of any grave being dug therein

In a manuscript note inserted at the bottom of p 35, in Dr. Thomas's Survey of this cathedral, by Mr Joseph Dougharty, to whom the author had presented it, (and which is now in the possession of Sir Charles Trubshaw Withers, Knight, who very politely suffered me to copy it) it is stated, " July 24th, 1754, on examination, the sepulchre of King John was within " the tomb. It is of Purbeck marble, the same with the relievo, and is " painted of a vermillion red ground, ornamented with lions in *or*. The " sarcophagus is covered with wood, over which are some flat sand stones : " the rest filled with rubbish   When it was first deposited, the figure lay " on the stone coffin, and both were environed with gilt pallisadoes, which " I suppose were destroyed in 1651 ; after which the present embellishments " of the sides were added   His body remains within "

In the first edition of the present work, p. 40, the late Rev. Mr. Garbet has noted in his copy, in the possession of Dr. Nash, that " there is within " the tomb a sepulchral case, or stone coffin, adorned with nine lions, with " a plank over it : but no bones were found in it "

On these informations I have only to remark, that both agree with respect to a sepulchral case being within the tomb, and also as to its decorations. But it appears, that although the first concludes by saying " His " (King John's) " body remains within" (that sepulchre) yet that it had not been examined · whereas, the latter states, " but no bones were found in " it ," which could only have been known from actual inspection.

We must also question the opinion of Mr. Dougharty, on the first deposition of the stone coffin, that the figure lay upon it, &c.

Symonds, in his Church Notes, vol II p 81, has not given the least item of this tomb being inclosed by pallisadoes, nor that the figure, or stone coffin, were so disposed ; but he has particularly described the armorial embellishments of the tomb, which, Mr Dougharty has stated, were added after the destruction of the inclosure in 1651. Symonds wrote his notes on this church in 1645; in which he has farther said respecting this tomb, that " the body" (the effigy of the king) " in the beginning of Queen " Elizabeth's time, was gilt "

Dr Stukeley says, King John is not buried where his monument now stands, but under a little stone before the altar of the easternmost wall of the church   On each side of him, upon the ground, lie the two Bishops Oswald and Wulstan   The image of the king he supposes likewise lay upon the ground. (1)   Dr. Nash, as Mr. Gough has quoted him, thinks the body was left in the ancient choir, when on its being ruined, the tomb was brought forward. (2)

The conjecture of Dr. Stukeley appears to be well founded, and is much strengthened by the foregoing accounts of the sepulchral case contained within the present tomb in the choir   That stone coffin could not have been suffered to remain over the grave of the king in the Lady's chapel when the figure that formed its covering was taken off; and had the stone, which now remains over his grave on the floor, been continued on the ancient tomb, the absurdity of duplicate tombs in the same church, for the same king, was too glaring to be adopted ; neither was it of a form or fashion at all correspondent with the era of its translation, to become an ornament suitable to the situation the present tomb now occupies, however well it suited its ancient site, whilst the figure remained upon it.   The royal insignia which embellished its outside, and at that time visible, formed the same object in its original state as those now seen on the present tomb ; and the whole, as a vestige of royal antiquity, has very properly been inclosed in the present cenotaph to preserve it

Having explored, as far as the best authorities can warrant, the tomb, where the body of King John is not, it is necessary, in order to trace out where it is, again to resort to his grave.

I have already said in page 40 of the Survey, that the body of King John is supposed to be still preserved in a deep sepulchral vault in St Mary s chapel, that has been discovered between the gravestones that bear the effigies of two bishops, which have been generally shewn for the tombs of John de Constantiis, and Godfrey de Giffard   The vault is of stone, very ancient;

(1) Stukeley's Itinerarium Curiosum, p. 65   (2) Sepulchral Monuments, p. 37. Cent. XIII.

and contains a strong chest, in which, upon the opening, was found a leaden coffin; (1) yet without any characters or symbols that might certainly determine the deposite, so carefully preserved, to be the royal body.   And farther, that if this be not the body of the king, we must be content with an absolute ignorance of the place where it lies This opinion is still retained in its full extent, with respect to the remains of King John being deposited in the vault discovered. This grave has been repeatedly opened, and each time has to a certainty proved those remains to be still within it · but the coffin is of stone, and the chest must either have been destroyed, or covered in the subsequent ruin of this vault, if the first report be to be depended upon, of the coffin being contained within a chest (2)

As I trust it is made evident that the bodies of the Saints Oswald and Wulstan are neither of them in the graves in which they were at first interred, and that neither the remains of the Bishops John de Constantius nor Godfrey de Giffard, are deposited in the reputed sepulchres of those saints, as asserted by Dr. Thomas We have here another obituary investigation to encounter before we can leave this spot, so pregnant with incertitude and doubt.

The learned gentleman who has honoured the author by the communication of some curious particulars relative to the last opening of the grave of King John, and in whose presence the whole operation was performed, in having opportunely suggesed the temporary removal of those two stones, on each of which the sculptured figure of a bishop is represented, and laid on the respective graves of the Saints Oswald and Wulstan, on each side of that of the king, fortunately for the subject, has brought the whole to a direct issue The proposition he made being forthwith carried into effect, the following was the result of a careful inspection —In each of the graves a stone coffin was found, similar to that of King John, at the same depth from the surface of the earth, and each containing a skeleton, laid in its right position of burial The remains of their vestures (3) sufficiently ascertained both of them to have been of the prelatic order of ecclesiastic dignity.

(1) Drak_ Ebor p 37 Weever's Fun Mon p 37 The use of leaden coffins was known to the Romans

(2) The demolition of the ancient vault was occasioned by making room for a new one adjoining to it, of no very distant date

(3) A small piece of that in the grave to the north, on which a figure, inscribed IEREMI, is embroidered, about four inches long, is in the author's possession It is of a fine texture, of a brownish colour, the effect of time, and parts of the embroidery are of gold thread

On this circumstance I have first to observe, that the grave of St. Wulstan, after a period of about 112 years after his deposition, and about eight years before the death of King John, had been emptied of his remains, which were then inclosed in a shrine : and, secondly, that St Oswald's translation from his grave to his shrine had taken place more than two centuries before that period. But although it be probable he never was buried where his reputed tomb was placed, some relic of him might be there deposited, to which devotions were offered by the people ; an object sufficiently sanctified and attractive, to render that spot equally sacred to spiritual purposes, as the real grave of St. Wulstan could possibly be ; and, as such, equally desirable as a place of sepulture to any succeeding bishop, who might either select or command it.

If the cowl of a monk was deemed by King John to be a helmet of salvation for him in a future state, we may conclude that the untenanted graves of two of the most celebrated saints of the monkish calendar would be sought, as places of refuge, by those who had the power to secure them to themselves, for the repose of their mortal parts, unless they would either abandon or betray the avowed principles of their practical faith. The royal sepulchre had derived new and important consequence to the part of the church in which it was placed ; and from that part also having been recently devoted to the peculiar service of the blessed Virgin, it was then literally and devoutly considered as the sanctum sanctorum of the cathedral.

I conceive it is not presuming too much, to suppose that Bishop Sylvester would, without much hesitation, assume to himself one of those vacant graves. This prelate had arisen from the rank of a private monk of this church, to its episcopal throne. He had been personally known to, in having been consecrated by the Pope, Innocent III ; he had buried the late King John within his church, between the tombs of its sainted founders ; and he had newly consecrated that church, in the presence of the young King Henry III. who had ceded to its use a moiety of his castle · doubtless, therefore, Bishop Sylvester, who considered himself as the patron of the church, wanted no other stimulus than his own pleasure, to determine which of the two hallowed sepulchres he would direct should receive his remains at his death We shall therefore state the probability, that the grave of St. Oswald was selected ; as his irreverent treatment of the bones of Wulstan had ren-

L

dered it in a great degree improper for him to lay a decent claim to the grave of that saint.

The real services his successor, William de Blois, had rendered to this cathedral, in erecting its magnificent nave, and building the charnel house, in aid of its overflowing cemetery, entitled his remains to the first obituary distinctions the church had yet in reserve to dispose of; and, at his decease, the sainted sepulchre of Wulstan most probably received them

Now, it appears, in support of the foregoing conjectures, that of the twenty-eight bishops of Worcester, being the whole of the number who have been interred in the present church, from St Wulstan to Bishop Madox, both inclusive, the grave of each has been ascertained, upon the earliest and firmest historical evidence that can be adduced, with the exception of three only, namely, the Bishops Sylvester, William de Blois, and Wulstan de Braunsford. Of the inhumation of the two first of those bishops, enough has been advanced, to shew the probability that it is they who are in possession of the graves of St. Oswald and St. Wulstan ; and which is now reduced to a moral certainty, from the knowledge derived of the sites of those of every other prelate buried in the cathedral.

With respect to William de Braunsford, it is Willis's opinion that he was buried here, as he had been a considerable benefactor to the church . (1) of this fact, however, we have no other testimony, than that a tomb, formerly under the second window eastwards of the north ile of the choir, was supposed to be his . a bishop, mitred, and vested for the altar, being represented cumbent upon it   But Mr Abingdon, having expressed a strong doubt whether it was a bishop or a prior, from observing in the second pane of the window over the tomb the figure of a prior with two mitres, one on his head, and the other in his left hand, and in his right a staff of authority, and the inscription, " Johannes Evesham, Prior, privilegium de " mitra . . " has been induced to suppose the tomb belonged to him. And Willis, in his account of the priors of this monastery, says, that he was buried in the north ile, and was one of the first of that dignity, who had interment in the cathedral (2)

(1) Willis's Cathedrals, vol. I. p 641   (2) See Hist. Mitred Abbies, vol. I. p. 309. Dr.
Thomas's Survey, p 43.

THE BISHOP'S PALACE,

Is a very ancient and interesting remain of antiquity. It is situated on the northern verge of the college precincts, near the Severn , the date of its erection is not precisely known. We find it to have been existing before 1224, when Bishop Blois built the chapel of the charnel house, between the cathedral church and his palace, " which in my opinion," says Mr. Abingdon, " declareth the ancient hall to have been, in former ages, nearer than this " modern to the cathedral. The palace itself is, I think, equal in continu- " ance with the bishopric " (1)

In 1270, Bishop Giffard obtained the royal licence of King Henry to fortify it with an inclosure of embattled walls , (2) and probably added much to the structure, but the cellarage has the appearance of being a work of early Norman antiquity. Its arched vaults, its noble and spacious kitchen, and the chapel originally over it; the essays of various improvements and useful modern additions, clinging round and supporting the venerable remains of the ancient mansion, to which the Bishops Sandys, Hough, and Johnson have liberally contributed, and to which the present prelate has given the finish, evince that neither the munificent intention of its founders has escaped the observance of their successors, nor its ancient hospitality lost any thing of its value or its dignity in the present times.

In all conventual cathedrals the bishop's house was not within the close of the monastery, but on the outside of its gates, yet adjacent to it ; his house, and a convenient space for offices round it, was a royalty of his own, as the ground within the convent close, was the free and unalienable fief of the prior and chapter.

An episcopal residence in London for the bishops of Worcester, appears to have been very early provided

In 857, King Bertwulf gave to Alhune, Bishop of Worcester, a piece of ground without the west gate of London, called Ceolmundinge-haga, paying 12d a year for the same, where afterwards the bishops of that see had a

(1) Abingdon's MS p. 33 and 37. It may be questioned whether the Saxon bishops had any other house of residence in the diocese than this The Norman prelates were fond of their manor-houses in the country, whence those at Kemsey, Northwyke, Bredon, Blockley, Wydindon (Gloucestershire), and Hartlebury, became in different ages episcopal seats.

(2) Dr. Thomas's Bishops of Worcester, p 137

palace, for the conveniency of attending the king's courts and affairs in parliament, as other noblemen and prelates had ; and for this he gave the king 60 shillings in silver (1) In the time of Maugerus, Bishop of Worcester, to whom it was again confirmed, temp King John, by Fulco, abbat, and the convent of Lesnes : the mansion was then deemed a manor. (2)

Wulstan de Braunsford, Bishop of Worcester, 22 August, 1344, granted the keeping of his house in the Strand, London, to William de Netherton, during his life, who was to receive for his labour 40 shillings and one robe yearly.

Tideman, Bishop of Worcester, granted to Henry Cambrigge, citizen and fishmonger, for his service to the bishop and his predecessors, the keeping of his house, situate without the gate of the New Temple, London, together with the easements of all the houses lying between the great gate of the said mansion and the Savoy, and annexed to the same mansion ; also a certain void piece of ground, whereon to build a house, to hold for his life, paying yearly a pound of pepper, repairing all the houses without the gate, and finding the bishop and his successors in herbs, during their residence in the said mansion ; dated at Hyllingdon, 21 Rich II. (3)

Bishop Carpenter, 29 Hen VI granted the keeping of this house, together with the gardens, &c to Thomas Andrews; the bishop giving him a livery suitable to his valets, 26 shillings and 8 pence yearly, and a dish of meat, with bread and ale daily, during the bishop's residence there. (4)

St Mary le Strand was a very ancient church and parish, a rectory in the gift of the bishops of Worcester, who had near it their inn, or town residence. This church with the house, gardens, &c. together with Chester inn, belonging to the see of Litchfield and Coventry, and another belonging to the Bishops of Landaff, were all levelled to the ground by the Protector Somerset, to make room for the late magnificent palace which bore his name, and on the site of which Somerset Place now stands (5) These victims to sacrilege were

(1) Dr Thomas, in Account of Bishops, p. 29. ex Hem Chart. p 44
(2) Lib Alb Episc Wigorn. f 139   (3) Ibid f. 104, 105
(4) Dr Nash, in Intr vol. I. p 35
(5) Pennant's London, p 149 Fuller, b iii. p. 62, 63 and Weever's Funeral Monuments, p 215.
It would seem that both Dr Nash and Mr. Pennant had not been aware that the following transaction had taken place Bishop Heath, temp Edw VI exchanged Hillingdon in Middlesex, and his palace and church in the Strand, London, for the manors of Grimlege and Hallow, and the advowson, with the advowson of St Martin's Vintry, and Newington, Com Surrey, which remain to the see to this day. Cited

thus devoted without the least atonement or compensation made to the pro-prietors for the loss, other than to the Bishop of Worcester, who had in re-spect to his former house, a house in the White Fryers, which he enjoyeth. (1)

THE DEANRY.

In 1225, William de Bedeford, the twenty-third prior of this monastery, built a new house, with offices adjacent, for the residence of the priors This ancient edifice is still in being ; it hath, however, been much enlarged and modernized by one or other of its successive possessors   At the dissolution it was appropriated for the residence of the deans of this church, and as such it has ever since been called the Deanry. (2)

THE GUESTEN, OR AUDIT HALL.

There remains one public office of the old monastery that may give us some idea of its original hospitality. This is the Audit House, anciently called the Guesten Hall ; built in 1320 by Wulstan de Braunsford, then Prior, afterwards Bishop of Worcester, for the entertainment of strangers exclusively ; the rules of the order not allowing them to sit with the monks at the tables of the refectory (3) In this hall the convent held their monthly court, called Guesten hall court, for the determining of differences between their tenants · (4) and it was a custom, preserved even to the days of King Charles I. that the tenants of this church might not sue each other in actions for less than forty shillings, in any court but this   The building is still sacred to hospitality : and the noble entertainments furnished here at the annual audits, do honour to one of the most eminent capitular bodies, established by one of the greatest of our kings.

THE CLOISTER.

The present cloister was built anno 1372   The east cloister is 125 feet long, the south, west, and north cloisters 120 feet each, and the whole series 16 feet wide. The body or nave of the cathedral is contiguous to them on

from Strype's Eccl. Mem. vol II. p 25   See Dr. Thomas's Acc of the Bishops of Worcester, p 207, 208 In the Pepysian library, Magd College, Cambridge, are Hollar's drawings of Suffolk, York, Durham, Salisbury, Worcester, and Somerset Houses   [Gough's Topogr ed. 1. p 314.]

(1) Sir Henry Spelman's Works, part II. p 212, 213. fol ed 1723

(2) Ann Wig   (3) Its length is 68 feet, its breadth and height of well regulated proportions, and was originally lighted by a single series of handsome Gothic windows.   (4) Dr. Thomas.

the north side, and communicates with them by two doors from its south ile, the one opening into the east cloister, and the other into the west It is a remark which generally applies to the cloisters of most of our conventual fabrics, that their situation is, as at Worcester, to the south of the church.

According to the Worcester annals, we find that King John upon his coming to Worcester, A D. 1207, after having paid his devotions at the tomb of St Wulstan, and giving to the prior and convent certain great privileges in their manors of Lindridge, Wulvardely, Stoke, and Clive ; he gave them also one hundred marks to repair their cloister and offices, which, together with the monastery had been destroyed by fire five years before Of the situation of those ancient cloisters we have no account. It is most probable they were constructed of wood, as well as the other offices of the church, which were either greatly damaged, or wholly destroyed by that conflagration. (1)

THE CHAPTER-HOUSE, AND LIBRARY.

On the east side of the cloister is the chapter-house, in form a decagon, fifty-eight feet in diameter, and forty-five in height Its roof is supported by a fine round umbilical pillar, arising in the centre, exactly corresponding with that at Ely. It was erected at the same time with the cloisters ; and now most aptly serves a double use, being not only the council room,

---

(1) The vaulted roof of the present cloister is adorned with a profusion of sculptures, particularly the north and south cloisters in the former, on the keystone of the centre arch, is a well wrought figure of the Virgin Mary, with our Saviour in her lap , the heads of both are gone Round them are placed the hieroglyphics of the four Evangelists, between these four angels are represented kneeling The remaining sculptures of this cloister consist of a series of angels, represented on the centres of the other arches, bearing shields, on which coats of arms were most probably painted In the latter a regal genealogy of Judah and Israel, or a compendium of the history of the Old Testament, is arranged in the following manner, beginning at the west end on the keystone of the first arch is a figure with a branch issuing out of his bowels (the customary manner in which the old genealogists denoted the founders of families), which may well be supposed Jesse, from whose root the kings of Judah sprung This sculpture is followed by the figure of David with his harp, on the next keystone, and that by a succession of other kings to the keystone of the centre arch of this cloister, on which is a group of figures representing, most probably, the ceremony of their great prophet Samuel anointing their greatest king, David, in the presence of his brethren At the east end, on the first keystone, is a figure similarly represented as that of Jesse, and probably meant for Nebat, father of Jeroboam, king of Israel , a succession of regal figures is continued from this to the same centre, each holding a scroll in his hand, on which it may be supposed their names were inscribed in the order of their succession, but now defaced .

several heads of kings, bishops, and monks, are also dispersed about this cloister as architectural ornaments And on the first keystone at the north end of the east cloister, is a group of three female figures standing, but without any mark of distinction by which to ascertain for whom they were designed.

INTERNAL VIEW OF THE C

CHAPTER-HOUSE, WORCESTER.

J. Landseer. Sculp.

but also the library of the church, in which is preserved a valuable collection of printed books, and many old manuscripts, chiefly of canon law, of which 169 are in folio, and 82 in quarto   The collection of books has been greatly augmented of late ages by the care of the deans, and the benefactions of private persons ; and their judicious arrangement amply evinces that great attention has been paid to put them before the inquiring eye to the utmost advantage   This room wants but little of the grandeur of a perfect rotund

In Heming's Chartulary, p. 261, 262, we find the first mention of a library belonging to the church of Worcester   *Godiva*, the wife of Leofric, Duke of Mercia, upon the death of her husband in 1057, among other presents which she made to the church of Worcester, to obtain their consent that she should hold certain possessions during her life, which Leofric had promised to restore to the monks at his decease, gave them a *library* (1) But it was not till the prelacy of Bishop Carpenter that a regular establishment of a library appears to have taken place for the use of the convent.   In 1461, June 24th, that prelate erected a library in the charnel house, adjoining to his cathedral, and Jan 24th following, endowed it to the value of ten pounds per annum for a library keeper   This event, in the register of that bishop, is dated as above ; see vol. I. p 175 ; but in Abingdon's Account of the Charnel house, he has placed the same occurrence, A. D. 1459, 37 Hen. VI   From this place, A D. 1641, the library was removed to the chapter-house, and the king's school from the chapel to the refectory, where they have ever since remained

The ancient library is supposed to have been in one of those rooms over the south ile of the body of the church, extending over the whole of the ile, and where also the ancient parvis, (2) or school was kept.   The ascent to those rooms is by a circular stone staircase, contained within the extreme

(1) Literature, science, taste, were words hardly in use during those ages of feudal tyranny. **Persons** of the highest rank, and in the most eminent stations, could not read or write   Many of the clergy did not understand the breviary, which they were obliged daily to recite , some of them could scarcely read it, Private persons seldom possessed any books whatever , even monasteries of considerable note had only one missal   When any person made a present of a book to a church or a monastery, in which were then the only libraries, it was deemed a donative of such value that he offered it on the altar, pro remedio animæ suæ, in order to obtain forgiveness of his sins   [Robertson's Hist Cha V vol I p 21, 22 , and note K, p 282]

(2) See Staveley's Hist of English Churches, p. 159, 160 — And Jacob's Hist. of Faversham, p. 43.

south-west angle of the cathedral, and from which all communication with the rest of the church is entirely cut off, the entrance to the ascent being from without (1)   In this place is now deposited a vast collection of the church writings, wills, &c. to which use it has of late been very judiciously applied, for their preservation from fire or other accidents.

THE REFECTORY.

In the south cloister is the entrance of the ancient refectory, or monks hall, now known by the name of the College hall ; a spacious and lofty room, one hundred and twenty feet long (the exact length of the west cloister, to which it is contiguous), and thirty-eight in breadth. Here the king's school is kept ; and here also are performed the oratorios, and other select musical compositions of the most eminent masters, at the grand triennial meeting of the three choirs of Worcester, Hereford, and Gloucester, for the benefit of the widows and orphans of the clergy of their respective counties. (2) This room was also built at the same time with the cloister.

THE KITCHEN

At the back of the seventh prebendal house, which anciently belonged to the coquinarius, or kitchener of the monastery, on a line with the west end of the refectory, the remains of a spacious octagonal apartment has lately been explored with attention, and ultimately with success, as far as regards the ascertaining of the use to which so singular and so secluded a structure had originally been designed. Its diameter is 34 feet, and its height from the present bottom of it (which appears to be much raised above its original flooring (3) by its own ruins, or by those of adjacent buildings) to the heads of the windows, 11 feet. Its open and blank windows, of which there were seven, of a well proportioned and uniform Gothic shape and size, occupy in series the planes or sides of the building, the wall of which is in the highest parts 12 feet, and in others not more than 4 feet above their points. From the following remarks I conceive we may with certainty conclude this to have been the ancient conventual kitchen.

---

(1) See reference Z in the Plan   (2) Of this establishment, see more in Sect XX.
(3) The floor of the kitchen now in use in this prebendal house, is 8 feet below the level of the surface of the earth within this building.

In Ducarel's History of Normandy, p. 49, a view of William the Conqueror's kitchen is given ; it is an eight-sided building, has four chimnies in it, and a skylight in the middle of its arched roof   But as that kitchen was not an appendage to a monastical building, we shall accept the aid of its similarity to this at Worcester no farther than just to note, that among the Normans such things were, and that from them we have received and adopted them at a very early period.   But we come at once to a decision on this matter, by minutely comparing the arrangement of the conventual offices of Durham cathedral and Worcester, which, with regard to their cloisters, refectories, kitchens, chapter-houses, and dormitories, are the exact counterparts of each other ; (1) and what is remarkable, the kitchen at Durham is also octangular, in which were seven fire places or chimnies, and a skylight in its vaulted roof   The arched roof of the kitchen at Worcester has either fallen in, or been taken down, for it is now entirely open at top ; and no trace of chimnies or fire-places remaining, either on its sides, or in the angles of the building ; it is probable, therefore, that they were placed in its centre, as we see in the rotunda of Ranelagh, and that they had one common ventige in the roof   for it is to be remarked, that the necessity of a skylight in this kitchen was entirely superseded by the ample light afforded from its surrounding windows   Its former connection with the refectory may still be traced, by several divisions of covered passages directing their course towards its west end, where, under a large arch, long since closed up, their common intercourse was carried on (2) The date of its erection is not known

As we are now on a research that regards a very important point of accommodation to the wellbeing of the ancient fraternity, it may be proper to notice that the CELLARAGE beneath the refectory appears to have been equal to the services to which it was devoted by its founders.   The OVEN of the monastery was situated at the extreme south-west corner of its precincts, near the Severn, on the site of which Mrs Hopton's house now stands.

---

(1) See the Ichnographies of Durham cathedral in Willis's Cathedrals, vol I p 223, and in Grose's Antiquities, vol I quarto

(2) To the vigilance of Mr Ed Jeal, one of the sextons of this cathedral, who first noticed this building to the author, he owes the satisfaction of having personally examined it, and of being enabled to state many of the foregoing particulars respecting it

M

THE LAVATORY.

Near the south end of the west cloister, are still to be seen the remains of the old lavatory, or cistern for washing; but its tin, or leaden lining is gone. The lavatory in convents was usually placed near the entrance of the refectory hall: it was a small reservoir of water, in which the monks were required to wash their hands when going to, or returning from, their meals. Water to drink was supplied from another cistern, I suppose within the door of the refectory: and pipes were branched to the kitchen, and to the infirmary

This lavatory was supplied with water from a spring on Hinewick (Henwick) hill, a place distant from the cloister about 1600 yards, on the other side of the river; whence a leaden pipe was laid along Hilton-lane, and drawn over the Severn underneath the pavement of the old bridge; it was thence conducted along the river side, and conveyed fountain water to the cloister.

King Henry IV by deed, bearing date the eighth of May, in the eighth year of his reign, enjoined the bailiffs and all officers to be aiding and assisting to the prior and convent in the work of this aqueduct; and directed that they should have free liberty at all times to mend these pipes whenever they required it (1) In pursuance of this there was a composition made, and interchangeably sealed, between the prior and convent on the one part, and the bailiffs and aldermen of the city on the other part The condition on the part of the prior and convent was thus expressed · " That, for the more worship of the bailiffs and aldermen, their maces might be borne before them (2) within the precincts of the cemetery, or the sanctuary, although out of the liberty of the city, and likewise in the parish of St. John's in Bedwardine." (3) The condition on the part of the citizens was: " That the prior and convent should have free liberty to lead their conduit pipe over

(1) Lib Pens Wig f 47   Lib Albus f 439
(2) A former King Henry had granted a charter to the convent which expressly restrains the bailiffs, or their servants from bearing a mace within the church, cemetery, or priory of Worcester, unless in the presence of the king himself, or some of his children [Hearne' Chartul Wig p 550]
(3) In pursuance of this composition, the mayor and officers of the corporation walk once a year in their formalities, and with their maces into the suburb of St John' on the Friday before Palm Sunday, which is the fair day of St John, and the day before the great fair of Worcester

the bridge, and through such streets and lanes as were most convenient." This pipe, in the civil wars, was every where torn up (1)

Towards the latter end of the prelacy of Bishop Polton, A D. 1432, Richard Osney (2) and William Boghton being at that time bailiffs of Worcester, a covenant was made and executed between them and the commonalty on the one part, and John Fordham, then prior, and the convent of Worcester on the other part, for the conveyance of water from the city conduit to the monastery   The line of the pipes to be laid for that purpose is thus described :—" in the king's highway, and up the street leading before the cottages of the prior and convent, in the suburbs of Worcester, near the castle ditch, which John Feckenham, shoemaker, held, and which is and are opposite to the town ditch of Worcester, under the castle ; then, extending from thence within the city, to the priory gate, and land of the priory and convent, according as it is limited and divided " The prior and convent agree to pay to the bailiffs and their successors, for this grant, a red rose (3) at the feast of the nativity of St John the Baptist.   Dated at the Guildhall, Worcester, the Monday next after the feast of St Michael, the eleventh year of Henry VI. (4)

THE TOWER

The furnishing of the cathedral with a tower was the next labour undertaken in carrying on the improvements of the monastery   Near a century before the present tower was erected, Nicholas, Archdeacon of Ely, and Chancellor of England, who was bishop of this see not quite two years, gave among other benefactions to this church, sixty marks for re-edifying the tower. This donation was paid by his executors to the sacrist of the monastery, A. D 1281 (5)

(1) There was a more ancient lavatory, mentioned by Hemingus, adorned with the carved stones from the famous cross at Whitstanes, which was taken down in the reign of William the Conqueror [Heming Chart p 113]

(2) Richard Osney was the high or first bailiff of Worcester in the 9th year of Henry VI his coadjutor for that year was Thomas Swiney   The list of bailiffs of Worcester is deducible no higher than that year with certainty   He lies buried in St Alban's church, and was a considerable benefactor to the cathedral   See Dr Nash, vol II p cxi who writes his name *Oldney* —Quære if not at present *Oldnal?*

(3) The royal badge or ensign   (4) Abingdon's MS p 55, 56.

(5) An Waverl p 224   Dr Thomas's Account of the Bishops of Worcester, p 135   See also Wil lis's Hist of Abbies, vol.I p 303

The rectory of Wiverslawe (Wolverley) was given to the priory by Roger, Bishop of Worcester, who

M 2

The tower was finished in the year 1374; it is 162 feet high, arising from the centre of the great cross ile, and dividing the choir from the nave of the church. The external embellishments of this structure are excelled by none in the kingdom for their richness The series of tabernacle-work which surrounds its upper stage, comprehending the windows of the bell-room, and the figures (1) placed about them, is an arrangement of the modern Gothic decoration, that has left little of improvement discoverable in the same stile of embellishment, even in the latest instances of its use in Europe, in a period of near two centuries, and when that species of architecture had arrived at its *ne plus ultra* of perfection

The top of the tower is terminated by four handsome pinnacles of open work, and surrounded with a corresponding battlement The chapter Worcester about the close of the last century erected those pinnacles, and new cased some of the outward walls of the cathedral, at the expence of several thousand pounds. (2) At that time also, we may suppose the figures round the tower were cleaned and made visible, as they now appear to great advantage

It is evident that the constructing of towers for the use of churches was not well understood by the Saxon builders, from the frequency of their destruction, as at Worcester and other places. The tower and turrets built by the Normans to their churches, erected in the first century after their

died 1179, and upon the petition of Prior John de Evesham, and the convent, it was impropriated by the pope, the reason of which impropriation was, the re-building the fair tower of the cathedral church and monastery [Dr Nash, vol II p 472.—See also Dr Thomas's Survey, p 6]

(1) The figures on the east façade of the tower have evidently an allusion to its founders, from the instruments which are held in some of their hands The centre one is a king, probably Edward III towards the latter end of whose reign the tower was completed The two bishops we may reasonably conclude to be Nicholas de Ely, a benefactor to the work, and William Lynn, at that time Bishop of Worcester, doubtless also a benefactor

On the south side is a king in armour, robed and crowned it is not improbable it was meant for King Henry III who had granted the outer ward of the castle to the use of the church, for the purpose of enlarging its precincts to the south, and in whose presence the church had been newly consecrated in 1218 On his right is a bishop with a church in his hands, and on his left another with a ...

Those on the west front are figures of two bishops and a king disposed in the ... de ... the preceding ones, only that the king is uncovered, and represented with a beard

On the north side, which faces the city, the Virgin Mary with the infant Saviour in ... the centre niche, in that to the east is St Oswald and St Wulstan in the one to the ... of these figure are in every respectable ... of sculpture for the age that produced them

(2) Wild's Cathedrals, vol I p 628

coming, were covered as platforms with battlements, or plain parapet walls. Spires and pinnacles are not of very ancient date, and were additions since the modern stile of pointed arches prevailed. One of the earliest spires we have any account of is that of old St Paul's, London, finished A D 1222; it was of timber covered with lead, as was that at Worcester (1)

Bells, no doubt (says Mr Bentham), at first suggested the necessity of towers, and were built not only for necessary use, (2) but often symmetry and ornament, in different parts of the fabric, and particularly where the plan of a cross was adopted, the usefulness of such a building appeared in the intersection of the cross, adding strength to the whole by its incumbent weight on that part (3) This is the short history of the origin of towers and steeples; which always have been, and still are, considered as the pride and ornament of our churches (4) To these remarks may be added, that to the variety those structures have in their local forms and situations, the relative beauty and dignified appearance they give to the cities and towns of which they form a part, is no less an object of delight to the beholder, than their immediate use And few of the principal cities and towns in England can better exemplify the force of this observation, than the city of Worcester itself, viewed from any point of the compass whatsoever.

ROOFS AND VAULTING

The vaulting of the several parts of the cathedral, the roofing of which was originally principally constructed of wood, (excepting the side iles of the choir and St Mary's chapel, which had their roofs vaulted, or arched with stone) was now undertaken and completed in the following order Bishop Cobham vaulted with stone the roof of the north ile of the nave,

(1) Bentham's Ely, p 40
(2) The campanile, or that particular tower allotted for the use of bells, was sometimes a distinct separate building of itself (as anciently at Worcester, in the leaden spire, and at Evesham, in latter times in Abbat Litchfield's tower, continued indeed to this day), but was more commonly adjoined to the church, so as to make part of the fabric, and usually placed at the west end [Vide Monast Angl vol 1 p 995]
(3) See this explained by Sir Christ Wren, in his letter to Bishop Sprat, in Widmore's Hist of Westminster Abbey, p 53 In his Parentalia, p 301, he further observes, " that addition of weight is required to establish solidity and firmness in buildings where their thickness cannot be added to, and this is the reason why in all Gothic fabrics of this form (Westminster Abbey) the architects were wont to build towers or steeples in the middle, not only for ornament, but to confirm the middle pillars against the thrust of the several rows of arches which force against them every way "
(4) Bentham's Ely, p 30

which at his own expence he completed A. D. 1327, the year in which he died, and was interred in it, opposite the window west of Jesus' chapel. (1) This is the first mention made of vaulting this church with stone. That bishop is also said to have vaulted some other parts of it with the same material. The ancient covering the church received prior to this era was formed of wood; an opinion strongly supported by W. Malmsbury, in his remark on the first calamity it sustained from fire, A. D. 1113, that " not " the whole church, but only the roof was burnt." (2)

In 1375, the chapel of the blessed Mary Magdalen was vaulted

In 1376, the choir, the great cross ile, and the altar of St. Thomas were vaulted

In 1377, the vaultings over the nave of the church, the library, and the treasury, were completed.

The fashion of these vaultings partakes both of those of the time of Henry III. and of Edward II. The ribs are of freestone, arising from their imposts and spreading themselves over the inner face of the arches, and with transoms dividing the roofs into angular compartments, ornamented at their intersections by orbs, foliage, heads, and other embossed devices. (3) Under the belfry the springers are more enriched with tracery, than in any part of the roofs, which has a very rich and beautiful effect   This sort of tracery in vaultings is among the graces peculiar to the Gothic mode of building, and is never found in the Saxon or Norman structures   The arches of these roofs are of tuftstone, the tophus of the ancients, a concretion, in quality rough, light, and hollow. (4)

(1) Abing MS   Lel Itin vol VIII p 127   See also Appendix, No. VIII p xxxi
(2) Lib de Gestis Pont   (3) Bentham's Elv, p 39
(4) Sir Henry Englefield, Bart in his " Observations on Reading Abbey," says of the semicircular arch of the hall, that " it was vaulted in the intervals of the stone ribs with a curious substance, evidently " a tophus, formed by some petrifying spring, and inclosing the impressions of twigs, &c   One leaf was " very fair   The substance is very soft, and extremely light, bearing only the proportion of 66 to 161 of " Portland stone " [Archæologia, vol VI p 61 Art 5]

It is in this place necessary again to advert to the sculptural decorations of the church which yet remain unnoticed   I mean those heads and groups of figures which appear on the keystones of the roofs, more especially those in the Lady's chapel, and in the middle ile of the nave   To begin with the former, the one to the east has the holy Virgin with the infant Saviour in her lap   The next has a bishop, whom we may conclude to be St Wulstan, the founder of the church, the third, St Oswald, and the fourth, a crowned figure of King Edgar, the most munificent of the patrons of the ancient monastery   These are all whole length figures, and form the finishing point of the four arches included in the Lady's chapel   The keystones of the arches of the choir having only composition of foliage upon them, we pass to the

THE DORMITORY (1)

Near the lavatory, about the middle of the west cloister, is a door very handsomely arched, which was formerly the entrance into the dormitory, or great room, where the beds of the monks were placed. That building was begun A D. 1375, and in August of the year 1377 it was furnished with beds It was 120 feet long, and 60 feet wide; and its vaulted stone roof was supported by five large pillars, ranged along its centre. (2)   It was at first an open hall, presenting at once to the keeper's (3) view the whole range of beds on each side, and all his sleeping family reposed therein Afterwards the monks had their cells divided.   Their rule obliged them to sleep always in their clothes, without taking off even their girdles.   The ruin of this building forms now a garden inclosure, wherein may yet be seen,

latter, which has many excellent masks in it, particularly that in the centre of the last arch but one in Bishop Wakefield's work, it is a head encompassed with foliage, giving it much the appearance of the antique Medusa Angels, bishops, and kings chiefly occupy the rest, some singly, others in groups, and each respectably

On the South side, at the junction of the Saxon arches with the nave, are two figures on a line with the plane of the lower arcades, but attached to the Saxon pillar The upper one is a grotesque, something resembling the harpy, as we find them represented, the lower one is a man standing in a sort of rostrum, as if preaching, but the head is gone

It is at this part where we have another instance of demarkation in the building of this church   that the boundary of its nave, as designed by Bishop Blois, terminated at this place, these figures were meant to denote, in the same manner as those already spoken of at the west end of the choir had done, by directing their looks eastward   These figures are coeval with the nave, as are also those heads at the springs of the outer mouldings of the principal arches on the north side.   The arches on the south side are wholly destitute of ornament

The series of figures which are uniformly placed on the divisions of the arcades on each side of the middle ile of the Lady's chapel, the upper cross ile, the choir, and on the north side of the nave, were among the most respectable of the sculptures which adorned this cathedral   Many of them were single figures, others were groups of two figures, some seated, and others standing, and from their elevated situation appear to be the size of life   But them having received so general and severe a visitation from the ruthless reformers of another age, and their mutilations being so completely destructive, not a single trace of information has survived, to shew us under what order of the monkish tribes they should be classed It may, however, be concluded, from the injuries they have sustained, that they held no subordinate rank in their legends The heads of the whole assemblage are gone, enough, however, still remains of many of their figures, to confirm an opinion of their more than common merit, is the productions of art so ancient as near the middle of the fourteenth century

(1) There was a more ancient dormitory in this monastery, part of which fell down A D 1302 [Willis Abbies, vol I p 303]   (2) Willis, from Dr Hopkins Abbies, vol II p 263

(3) The doctor, doctor, or dormitory was under the care of the sub-prior called also master of the frater house, and keeper of the frerctory, or vice-prior [Antiq of Durham Abbey, 12mo]

along the sides of its patched up walls, traces of windows and doors, after the Gothic model.

The spital, for lodging poorer travellers and pilgrims, was a room 50 feet in length, and 20 in breadth. (1) I know not where this building stood, if it were a detached one for that purpose; it is, however, probable, those lodgings were in a chamber, over the present west entrance into the north cloister, between the cathedral and the dormitory.

In the month of October, A. D. 1375, the new work about the stalls was begun. What this new work was, is uncertain, unless it were the preparation for erecting the stalls, which was done in the year 1379 (2)

A D 1376, the altar of St. Thomas was set up.

A. D. 1378, the treasury, library, and the water gate were erected   We have already pointed out the situation of the ancient library ; the treasury was contiguous to it, over the south ile of the nave of the cathedral. It is supposed there must have been a gate to the river before this period

In 1379, the area of the choir, and the chapels of St. Thomas and Magdalen were paved.

THE INFIRMARY

Of the convent was built the same year   The site of this structure was immediately westward, beyond the dormitory, from which it was separated only by a narrow passage, now called the Dark Alley, and on the verge of the Severn   It was there the monks, when sick, had suitable attendance, medicine, and diet   It was not unusual even for priors, under desperate disease, to be removed thither, in order to partake of its benefits   Two lofty walls of this building yet remain, and constitute, one of them the southern side of the eighth prebendal house, and the other the north side of the ninth prebendal house   The space now uncovered between these walls was anciently a public room, as appears from the stateliness of the windows, whose arches, still preserved in the north wall, were elaborately wrought   Either the hall or the chapel of the infirmary must have been on this lower floor , and in the story above were the lodgings of the patients

I have already stated the particulars of the addition of the two Saxon arches to the nave, and making the great west window in 1380 ; and also

(1) Willis's Abbic., vol II p 263 from Dr Hopkin
(2) Exar hive of the Dean and Chapter

of erecting the north porch to the cathedral in 1386 ; some additions and improvements that were made about the altars of Sanctæ Crucis, and Sancti Edmundi Archiepiscopi, complete the catalogue of the very munificent works carried into execution under the auspices of Bishop Wakefield, between the years 1375 and 1386; during which period, John Lyndsey was sacrist, and William Poer was cellarer of this church. It is conjectured that the prior and convent were surveyors of those works under the bishop (1)

To the preceding accounts of the progress of the building of the cathedral and the offices of the monastery, it will be proper in this place to notice those articles for devotional purposes, with which our cathedrals and conventual churches were usually supplied (2)

THE ALTAR

Forms the principal object in all churches In cathedrals, and even in rural churches, there were often more than one ; and where that was the case, one of them was distinguished as the high altar, and always so called The church of Worcester, as founded by St Oswald, was furnished by him with no less than twenty-eight altars (3)

Those altars with which the present cathedral was furnished, either by

---

(1) See Dr Thomas's Survey of this Cathedral, p 6. ex Chartis W Hopkins, D D, Preb. hujus ecclesia Abingdon's Antiquities of Worcester Cath p 22, 23 Willis's Abbies, vol. I. p. 304 vol II p 262, and his Cathedrals, vol II p 628

(2) For a detail of the lesser class of church furniture, see Appendix, No IV p ix

(3) Abingdon's Hist of this Cathedral, p 2, 3

The reason for so many altars being erected in the same church, is said by a learned author (Thorndike, Epil p 254) to have been this " There was a custom, which seems to come from undefiled " Christianity, to bury the remains of the bodies of eminent saints, especially martyrs, under those stones " upon which the eucharist was celebrated " Hence, at Canterbury, the head of St Swithin was inclosed in one altar, the head of St Fruseus in another, the head of St Austreberta in a third, an altar was built as a repository of the body of St Wilfrid, and one was erected at the tomb of St Dunstan. The superstition incited by them, and their numbers increased so fast in different churches, as to exceed all bounds. But this evil cured itself, for the respect due to them from their votaries was at length abated by the imposition of false relics, insomuch, that when it was found that the same saint or martyr had more heads than one, and that it was become a dispute whether the right one was at Canterbury, or some other place, it was with some embarrassment that a priest of principle could repeat the litanies, the supplications, and the prayers ordered by the church for the true saint, to a doubtful one, and thereby abuse the faith of his auditors •

• Battely's Cantuaria Sacra, Part II p 25

St. Wulstan, its founder, or subsequent to his time, which have come to our knowledge, from their situations being known, are the high, or choral altar; the altar of the blessed Virgin, in the Lady'schapel, beneath the great east window; the altar of Sanctæ Crucis, or the Holy Cross, in the great cross ile, where now the monument of Bishop Hough is placed; the altar of St Simon and St Jude, in the same ile, and where Bishop Madox's monument is erected; the altar of St. Edmund, whose chapel was in this south transept of the great cross ile, and the altar of St John the Baptist, at the second pillar from the north-west support of the tower, in the nave. In addition to those, we find the following altars frequently mentioned, but their precise situations, or rather their true designations, cannot be satisfactorily ascertained, viz the altars of St Mary Magdalen, St. Nicholas, St George, and St. Thomas It is to be remarked, that although the high altars were not always placed against the walls, yet most of the lesser or requiem altars were; and that as the high altars have an eastern position in churches, so the lesser ones have generally that station in the various chapels, oratories, and other parts of the churches where they are erected. This distinction is evident throughout the cathedral of Worcester, in places where altars have anciently stood, whose names are now unknown In the Lady's chapel the ascent to her altar still remains In the north ile of that chapel, and parallel in situation, the ascent to an altar, formerly there, was taken away when Lady Middleton's monument was placed under its east window, prior to that of Mrs Rae, since erected. In the south ile, under its east window, where now the consistory court is held, the ascent to an altar remains In the Bishop's and Dean's chapels the ascents to their respective altars remain The altars of the Holy Cross, of St Simon and St Jude, and of St. Edmund, in the great cross ile, had the same ascents to them The altars of St John the Baptist, in the nave, and of Jesus' chapel, which last was taken down by Dean Barlow, A D 1550, had each the like ascent to them Every trace of the five last named altars was swept away by the late reforms made in those parts of the church, and for the reception of the monuments already mentioned The altar in Prince Arthur's chapel had also an elevation at its foot

The present times have much to lament the effects of those differences which formerly subsisted on the notable choice of two words—altar, or table, and also about where the article meant by either was to be placed

for use Hence the incongruous appearance they make in our old churches'
and more especially in our cathedrals; and hence the unnatural and barbarous conjunction of modern Grecian architectural forms and embellishments, that continually offend our sight, about an altar placed in an ancient
Gothic structure

The original altars, or tables, were all taken away, or destroyed, at the
time of the Reformation, as objects of superstition The destruction was
continued through the puritanical period of the Usurpation, and its ruinous
effects were so complete and general throughout the kingdom, that there
is not at this time, in England or Wales, one to be found of greater antiquity than the Restoration This fact was lately discovered, upon an inquiry
of some judicious Antiquaries, with a view to the erection of an altar in the
church of St Catherine, near the Tower, that should correspond with that
ancient fabric. (1)

Bishop Blandford gives us the following particulars respecting the ancient
high altar of this cathedral, at the time it was receiving the prescribed
regulations of the grand reform.

1547 The great brass candlestick, and the beam of timber before the
high altar, were taken down.

1548 On the 20th of October was taken away the cup, with the body of
Christ, from the high altar of St Mary's church, (i e. the cathedral,) and
from other churches and chapels, (in Worcester).

1550. King Edward VI. commanded that all altars, crucifixes, and rood
sellers should be pulled down, and to have long tables of wood, and there-
upon mass said in English.

1551, August 12th. The high altar was demolished.

1556. The Lady's chapel was furnished with an altar (2)

THE HOLY ROOD

The rood was an image of Christ upon the cross, generally made of wood,
and placed on a loft (3) erected for that purpose, just over the passage out

(1) Antiq Rep vol IV No VI. p 134 From Sir J Hawkins   (2) Bishop Blandford's MS
This took place when the choir was restored, after it had been destroyed in 1551, at which time also
the high altar was replaced, and the upper windows of the eastern part of the church were new glazed
   (3) The place bearing the rood-loft was called a reredosse   Rode, or rood, is a Saxon word, signifying
a cross

of the church into the chancel, in the lesser or rural churches, where we now usually find the king's arms; and in cathedrals, and the larger churches, in that part which separates the choir from the body or nave, and where, as at Westminster, Canterbury, and at this and other cathedrals, the organ is now placed. The rood was not considered as complete, without the images of the Virgin and St. John standing on either side of the cross, in allusion to chap. xix. v. 26, St John, " Jesus saw his mother, and the disciple stand-" ing by, whom he loved " The mystery covered by this device is said to be the church militant, denoted by the body or nave of the church; and the church triumphant, signified by the chancel, or choir; and that those who will pass from the sanctum to the sanctorum, a distinction by which the same places in churches are also known, must go under the cross, and suffer affliction, ere they can arrive at that felicity This conceit exactly corresponds with the ancient heathen probation through the temple of Honour, in their progress to the fane of Virtue These holy roods were of great esteem, and many miracles are pretended to have been done at and by them; one of the most famous was at Boxley, in Kent, of which Lambarde, in his perambulation of that county, has given a description. The festival of the exaltation of the cross, Sept. 14, and holy-rood day, is the same (1)

CROSSES,

Were anciently as numerous in this, as in any other nation. Public crosses form a feature of church influence, that was contrived to embrace every possible means of arresting the attention of such, whose disinclination to, or whose situation in life admitted not of, the convenience either to attend the public duties it imposed, or to the forms of practical devotion They assisted in spreading and establishing the powers of the church so universally, as to leave none ignorant of the obedience meant to be enforced and exacted of all, whether on their journeyings in their own, or in other countries, or whether in the transaction of any worldly affairs within their own, or in other cities, towns, or districts Among the most celebrated in England, of modern construction, was the cross at Coventry, begun A D 1541, and finished 1544, an example of the perfection to which the Gothic stile of ornamental building had arrived It was founded by Sir William

(1) Staveley, p 199, 200

Hollies, Knight, some time lord mayor of London. (1) The most eminent among the ancient crosses were those which the affection of Edward the First raised to the memory of his beloved Queen Eleonora ; of which, that near Northampton, another at Geddington, and a third near Waltham, are existing instances of superior excellence, and objects of admiration, to the present times   Of the several crosses erected in and about the city of Worcester, the high cross (2) before the ancient guildhall may be supposed to have been the most elegant, as well as the most eminent. It is, however, in vain to conjecture what its particular construction might have been   The grass-cross, situated where now the market is held, and still known by the name of the Cross, appears to have been next in consideration and consequence (3)   The cross at Losemore, the cross at Red-hill, that without Sidbury gate, and the one on the Tewkesbury road, as mentioned in the ancient perambulation of the city bounds, and in the visit of Queen Elizabeth to this city, may be considered as road crosses, stationed at the several entrances of the town, of which, probably, there were also others near some of the city gates, and at the bridge , but of those we have no certain accounts   The ancient cross at the monument of Duke Wiferd and his Lady Alta, within the sanctuary of the cathedral, and that at Whitstanes, in the north suburbs of the city, were entirely devotional structures, and served the more immediate purposes of the church establishments near which they were situated, and of which they were appendages. They served also as places for receiving spiritual instruction from preachers appointed to give sermons in public, in imitation of the primitive practice, as hath already been observed, and as stations, at which religious ceremonies and processions began or ended, in the public pageants of the church   To the latter purpose, also, were those crosses appropriated, which were erected before the stadthouses, tolseys, townhouses, or guildhalls, of cities or corporate towns ; and may therefore not improperly be called civil crosses, from the general uses to which they were applied by the magistracy

The ancient grants of our Saxon ancestors, from their brevity, even on matters of the utmost importance, shew us sufficiently that in those ages

(1) Antiquities of Coventry Illustrated   Collected from Dugdale's Warwickshire

(2) That cross was defaced A D 1529 [Bishop Blandford's MS]

(3) The grass cross taken down, and market-house set up, A D 1578 [Ibid.]

civil contracts were not so frequently committed to legal forms for ratification, as since is become the practice

In those ages too, when the qualifications of reading and writing were so confined, as to be considered as very rare accomplishments, even in characters of the highest eminence among the rulers of nations, and consequently still more rare among the common people, compacts were therefore simply made and entered into by men who intended no fraud, with the single but solemn appeal to that visible emblem of the Christian faith, the cross; an appeal considered by them as a confirmation sufficient to hold good every sort of obligation, that the laws of the realm had not already specially provided a written process by which to render them binding

This summary way of legalizing civil transactions, by saluting, touching, or swearing by the cross, (forms readily to be comprehended, and quickly dispatched) was among the provident expedients founded by the only power which alone had influence sufficient to establish its validity, the church (1) Hence arose the crosses we find, or hear of by name, in those open places in cities and towns, where anciently all ordinary public business was transacted, and where now their marts, fairs, statutes, or markets, are still held, throughout these kingdoms   But at that important period, when the mask was withdrawn, that had so long shrouded the Supreme Being from men's eyes, which had been taught to view him through the most gross and vitiated mediums ; at that time, when crosses and images, blindly adored, were crumbled to dust, or reduced to ashes, before the face of the newly enlightened multitude, those oaths and asseverations, that had heretofore been conscientiously and decently addressed to either, were now heard on all and every frivolous occasion. It was now, that the tide of that senseless vice of common swearing broke in upon the orderly and decorous manners of society ; and " by the rood," " by the mass," and by every saint on monkish record, which but a while before would not have been uttered but with fear and trembling, became modes and phrases of general application, and mingled insensibly in the most common topics of conversation (2)

(1) This custom, apparently, had its origin in patriarchal practice   The covenant on Mount Gilead, between Laban and Jacob (Gen ch xxxi v 44) was witnessed by a heap of stones gathered together, and a pillar set up by Jacob, which he called *Galeed*, and seem to have been the prototype of those civil crosse

(2 Sir John Perrot, supposed natural son of Henry VIII is said by Dean Swift in his preface to his

The evil soon rooted itself too deeply to be wholly destroyed; for, instead of ceasing with its cause, the effect has evidently descended upon the present age, with accumulated atrocity, through the foul mouths of a too numerous crowd of common swearers and impious blasphemers.

IMAGES

Among the ancient church furniture, images have made a considerable part, from a very early period of church history. To Egwin, the third Bishop of Worcester, and first Abbat of Evesham, is attributed the first pretence for introducing images into the churches of Britain and their worship gained great fame to the church of Worcester, not only in England, but abroad; (1) for, according to Bale, Egwin was enjoined by the Virgin Mary, when she appeared to him, to make her an image, which she would have worshipped at Worcester (2)

In a council held at London, about the year 708, under Brithwald, Archbishop of Canterbury, and authorized by Pope Constantine, it was decreed, that images should be placed in churches, and honoured with the celebration of masses and adoration (3) These are, however, supposed to have been only the images of the blessed Virgin, and of Christ, to whom those marks of devotional distinction were to be paid; for it does not appear that the images of saints, martyrs, or other subordinate characters, were set up, or presented as objects of adoration, till near the end of that century, after the second Nicene council, held in or about the year 792 But upon the general admittance of images into the church, which then began to prevail, the second commandment was made to give way, and was accordingly left out of the decalogue: this omission may be observed in the preface to the laws of King Alfred, and in the old copies of the Saxon laws. The worship of images, therefore, obtained in the English churches from that time, until they were suppressed by an *ejectione firme* of the Reformation, a period of upwards of seven hundred years (4)

Polite Conversation, to have been the first that swore by G**'s w****s He was the son of Sir Thomas Perrot, Gentleman of the Bedchamber to Henry VIII and Mary, daughter to James Berkley, Esq [Granger's Biogr Hist vol 1 p 141 4to]

(1) Lambarde, p 408   (2) Bale's Cent 709
(3) This account is given by the Magdeburgensian Centuriators, out of Nauclerus and Bale —Cent ?6? cap 91. 94. 99   (4) Staveley, ch 14 p 238
In the metropolitical visitation of Robert Winchelsea, Archbishop of Canterbury, (temp Ed I) he

The abuses and pious frauds, discovered even in the best endowed and most celebrated convents, contributed to reconcile very many of their votaries to their suppression : and, as if one of the most atrocious deceptions practised in the worship of images should be reserved for public exposure and contempt, in the very place where the artifice was first broached, on the visitation of the church of Worcester, a very large image of our Lady, held in great reverence, was found, when stript of the veils that covered it, to be the statue of a bishop, ten feet high. (1)

On the 10th of January, 1547, all the images on the high altar, and throughout the church, and all the other churches (of Worcester) were destroyed And on the 17th of May, 1560, the cross and images of our Lady were burnt in the churchyard (2)

CHAPELS.

The example of almost every cathedral and principal church in Christendom proves the custom of chapels, dedicated to other saints than the patron saint of the general fabric, being erected, and set apart for their peculiar service; many of which have been constructed within them, and others have been attached to them from without   These internal subdivisions of, or external addenda to, the original churches, have often been made by families and persons of eminence, for the select purposes of their devotion whilst living, and for places of their sepulture at their decease. This custom has prevailed, from the earliest ages of the church in Britain, down to the Reformation, in the instances of kings, princes, prelates, nobles, and private individuals. The most remarkable and splendid of this kind is that which Henry VII added to the church of St. Peter, at Westminster, emphatically called by Leland, Orbis Miraculum That king is said to have built a ship and a chapel at an equal charge . and it is remarked, that whilst not so much as a plank of his ship remains, his chapel stands to this day, a lasting monument of his munificence and devotion This chapel, however, as Mr. Walpole has justly observed. is properly but the mausoleum of that monarch,

made an order, or decree, which was confirmed by his successor, that the image of the saint, to whom the church was dedicated, should be set up in the chancel of every parish throughout all the archdeaconries of his province [Ibid ch 8 p 125 126 [

(1) Burnet's Hist of Ref vol 1   Collier's Eccl Hist vol II ; 147   Staveley's Romish Horse leach p 79   (2) Bishop Blandford's MS

he having built it solely for the burial place of himself and the royal family; and accordingly ordering by his will that no other persons should be interred there (1)

In the church of Worcester we are enabled to trace the following chapels Our Lady's chapel, at the east end of the cathedral . of the foundation and dedication of which we have already treated. The inclosure of this chapel is described by Bishop Blandford to have been of white stone, and iron, within and without It was demolished by Dean Barlow, A. D. 1550.

In the collateral iles of that chapel, the altars anciently placed under each of their east windows, sufficiently denote that a chapel was included in each but to what saint or martyr they were respectively devoted, we remain uninformed.

A similar account to the preceding is all we can render of the two chapels in the north and south transepts of the upper cross ile, where altars were also placed. But we have farther observations to make on each. The chapel in the south transept appears to have received a name derived from the uses to which it has been formerly assigned, as the place of sepulture of the deans of this church No less than four out of the first five of those dignitaries in succession, from the suppression of the ancient monastery, were interred there ; and, as if laying claim to the church, in bar of the exploded interest of papal pretension, and in favour of the reform, it has from thence been denominated the "Dean's chapel."

The chapel in the north transept has latterly been distinguished by no particular denomination Its patron saint and its altar, which probably bore the name of that saint, are now no longer known Modern events have frequently given occasion for substituting new names to places and things, formerly known by others. It has, doubtless, already been so with the Dean's chapel ; and the same fate, it is probable, may attend this, which the author humbly suggests may hereafter appositely enough be recognized by the name of the "Bishop's chapel," in contradistinction to the former, and in reference to the interment of Bishop Parry, whose monument is placed therein, its forming the right arm of the upper cross, and its being on that side of the cathedral on which the episcopal residence is situated It would,

(1) Dart's Antiquities of Westm. Abbey, vol 1 p 32 Walpole's Ancc of Painting, vol 1 p 49 in notes,

however, have been infinitely more gratifying to him to have been enabled to restore both those chapels to their original ancient patronage, than to have suggested the alternative proposed. Meantime, present possession may have its claim allowed, without material injury to past or future pretensions

The vestry to the east we may conclude was also anciently a distinct chapel, the ascent to which remains at its present entrance

The chapel of St. Edmund, wherein was a pair of organs, was situated in the south transept of the great cross ile, near the altar of St Simon and St. Jude; and the chapel of St George, made of timber, grated with iron, and furnished with a great pair of organs, the site of which is, however, not pointed out, were both pulled down by Dean Barlow, A D 1550 Chapels of the kind of the two last mentioned were mere inclosures at the end of an ile, or in the recess of some arch, as already intimated It is probable that of St George corresponded in situation with the chapel of St. Edmund, and was placed in the north transept of the same ile.

Jesus' chapel is still in being, and is coeval in its erection with the north side of the nave, to which it is attached. (1)

The chapel of the charnel house, in which a service adapted to its uses was appointed, had also its altar; that chapel, and we may conclude its altar also, were dedicated to St. Thomas the martyr. (2)

PRINCE ARTHUR'S CHAPEL,

Or mausoleum, (for I conceive it may properly enough be called by either name) is the most distinguished and elegant example of that class of structure, in the Gothic stile, raised within this, or, I presume, any other church in Britain. It was erected A. D. 1504 Its form is an oblong square, situated intermediately in the space of the south sectional pillars of the upper cross ile, at that end of the high altar where its entrance is provided An altar was placed in its inside, at the east end, beneath the figure of a dead Christ

(1) Over this chapel, and also over the north porch, it appears that lodgings had anciently been provided for those who were appointed to watch the church a fire place is found in each, and over Jesus' chapel a small oven is made in the wall of the north ile of the nave

(2) On the obituary chapel, in the crypt of the cathedral, supposed to have been a place of sepulture of the family of Clare, Earl of Gloucester, we have nothing to add to what has already been stated respecting it Chapels are frequent in crypts, and are usually dedicated to the patron saints of their respective founders But of the dedication of this no account appears It is indeed but conjecturally, that it can be classed as a chapel

SOUTH FRONT OF PRINCE ARTHUR'S

CHAPEL, IN WORCESTER CATHEDRAL

at the foot of the tomb Here prayers were offered by the devout, for the repose of the soul of the deceased prince To the service of this altar, it is not improbable, that the affection of Henry VII had provided a priest to administer religious duties, and a suitable endowment for his support No proof, however, empowers us to offer this as a fact

Unique in its design and execution, a decided deviation from the cumbrous mausoleums that had preceded its erection, the chapel of Prince Arthur appears an effort of considerable power, to get rid of that superincumbent decoration, with which too many of the monumental structures of that age are burthened , inducing no other sentiment in the mind stronger than that of a compassionate concern for the fate of a tomb, over which such a tremendous load of useless ornament hangs suspended, as by a thread, and threatening destruction to all beneath. (1)

The general design of this chapel is the history of the union of the two contending parties, that, under the distinct banners of a white and a red rose, had recently deluged an innocent and an unoffending nation with a waste of kindred blood, that would have appalled a savage to contemplate —The closing of this direful scene the skilful hand of an unknown sculptor has treated with all the faithfulness and becoming decency, that the hand of pity itself would have bestowed, in veiling over a story never to be repeated, but with indignant execration, on the inhuman sacrifice made of the simple many to the sanguinary purposes of a tyrannical and ungrateful few. On

(1) The monument of Humphry, Duke of Gloucester, at St Alban's, seems to have led in this heavy rule of tomb architecture   [Sandford, p 318]   Those of Cardinal Beaufort and Bishop Wainflete, in Winchester cathedral, are of the same fashion   The chapel of Bishop Fox, in the same church, may also be classed with the others, as another instance of heavy grandeur   [See Vetusta Monumenta, vol II Plates XLV XLVI L]   Bishop West's chapel, in Ely cathedral, is one of the nearest approaches to the refined taste for which this at Worcester is so distinguished   [Bentham's Ely, p 41]

On this class of Gothic structures, and on tomb architecture, we are led to expect superior attention to the niceties of high finishing, than in more enlarged subjects   And here we may also remark, that excepting pinnacles, there is scarce any sort of Gothic ornament, which does not branch from the trefoil, quatrefoil, and cinquefoil, being but various modifications of it, of which species also are all the ramifications of the modern Gothic windows * The various modes that have obtained at different periods in this rule of architecture, may be thus exemplified, *absolute Gothic*, unmixed with the Saxon, about 1220, (Salisbury cathedral) , *ornamental Gothic*, 1440, (St George's chapel, Windsor) , and *florid Gothic*, 1500, (interior of King's college chapel, Cambridge, and Henry the Seventh's chapel, Westminster) †

* Mr Walpole's Letter on the Subject of an History of Gothic Architecture
† Oracle, Oct 21, 1790

the face of this sepulchre it is evident, that neither York nor Lancaster can boast a pre-eminence in the regard of the king: for it is a monument he has evidently devoted as a peace-offering to all who had borne a part in, or suffered from, the destructive effects of those perilous and distracted times, than raised as a trophy of supreme power exulting over an adversary sub- dued   The meek and pious Henry VI (1) he has placed in contact with the impatient and impetuous Edward IV. Foes in the senate and in the field, at peace in their sepulchres, he has compelled them here to meet, and, as it were, in penance deplore the enormity of their ancient enmities, so ruinous to the welfare of civil society.   Between these opposites, the universal Me- diator " for peace and good will towards men," he has represented as having expiated all mortal offence, and reconciled man to his Maker   These con- tending kings are also brought forth, to witness the weakness of those bands, that, after their deaths, had been tied between their descendants, to bind up the wounds of public and private misfortune, burst asunder by the death of a prince, the first fruit of that union, and fondly thought to have been born to cement every jarring interest into one,—the public good. But alas! that hope, nipped in its bud, lies blasted and prostrate before them, and all its blushing honours compressed within the narrow limits of an unadorned tomb, and, as Speed in his Chronicle says, without any remembrance of him by picture. (2)

The figures of these kings have but lately become visible: the following is an extract from an account of their discovery in 1788, read before the So- ciety of Antiquaries, London, March 19th, 1789, communicated by the author to the Rev Mr. Brand, secretary (3)

" SIR,

" In my visit to Worcester, in November last, for the purpose of com- pleting my collections for a new edition of the History and Antiquities of that City and its Suburbs, a review of the cathedral made a part of my em-

(1) Henry the Seventh proposed to Pope Alexander VI and to his successor, Julius II, to canonize this pious and unfortunate monarch , but through the extreme avarice of those pontifts, it was never effected. Fuller has preserved some account of this transaction, and has rendered it in a very entertaining manner

(2) P 763   Images and statues were often termed pictures

(3) With that paper the two drawings were also laid before the Society, made by Mr James Ross, of Worcester, from which the engravings were executed for this work   See the annexed Plates of the " Internal View of the East End of Prince Arthur's Chapel in the cathedral of Worcester, as it appeared in November, 1788," and the same object, " in its present state " The notes and illustrations are now first added

ployment. On entering the chapel of Prince Arthur, the most complete example of what is usually called the Gothic stile of architecture that church has to boast, I was struck with the appearance of that part of its east end, which had ever been considered as a *ruin*, the consequence of the severe visitation of that city by the Oliverians, after the battle of Worcester, in 1651. That blank of rude plastering, formed of the coarsest kind of mortar, and occupying nearly one third of the whole façade, had not hitherto met with the attention it merited It was not long before I convinced myself, that instead of its being the remains of an outrage committed on the embellishments of the chapel, it was, on the contrary, the friendly covering of something meant thereby to be preserved from injury · and this became the more apparent, by observing the projection of the whole mass of plastering to be nearly as forward as the projections of the canopies over the several niches The divisions of the niches were easily traceable from those canopies, and are enriched with the same series of small imagery of bishops and confessors, as the corresponding divisions at the west end of the chapel.

" The remarks I had made were communicated to the honourable and reverend Dean St John, to whom I had not then the honour of being personally known , but from whom, in consequence, I received a very polite invitation to accompany him to the chapel, where, in a few moments, he himself became so much assured of the conclusions I had formed on the subject being founded, that he could not forbear beginning the operation of removing the mortar, by the application of a penknife; and making a slight opening in the centre niche, struck upon the fibula (1) on the breast of the dead Christ, which unites the drapery on that part, and was found covered with gilding, a distinction on the ancient sculptures which occurs but in very few instances in this cathedral, excepting in armorial bearings

" Evidence enough was now in view, that the chief ornaments of the chapel, as originally designed by the artists who constructed it, were there deposited, and would be found on clearing away the heavy mass of mortar with which they were enveloped But before this operation should take place, I requested the indulgence of having a drawing made of that end of the chapel, as it then appeared · adducing as a reason, that how unpromising

(1) The fibula in the dress of the ancients was fixed to the mantle or chlamys It is also the fastening of the chlamys either on the shoulder or on the breast The tunic under the chlamys is fastened by belt [Introd to Gough's Sepulchral Monuments]

soever the appearance the object then made, it might tend to encourage the attentive examiner into the constituent parts of an edifice so important as that of an ancient cathedral, to bestow more than a cursory view on those features of it, where something more than blank walls might be expected to appear, either from their situation, or some other local circumstances.

" As soon as the drawing was made, (which I may venture to remark is as accurate and intelligent as it is possible to be on so small a scale) the Dean and Chapter ordered the niches to be laid open ; which was accordingly done with the utmost attention and care, and the figures, as they are represented in the drawing, were discovered.

" First A religious character, on whose right shoulder a cross (1) is represented

(1) It is necessary here to remark, that I had not seen the figures when this account of them was drawn up, and which is formed on the communications I received from Worcester The signum here mentioned is not a cross, but more resembling the Roman capital T , and being placed high on the right breast, upon the chlamys, is not found to correspond with any of the insignia by which several others of the orders of the religeux are recognized, many of whom had crosses on their vestures, but were always on the left side, or on their breast The Trinitarians had them on both

It remains, therefore, difficult to decide, whether this figure be meant to represent the glorious Confessor, St Nicholas, as he is usually called , the saint who may be said to have presided at the birth of Henry VI (December 6th) to whom and to the Virgin Mary he has dedicated King's college, Cambridge, as appears from the charter of its foundation ; or whether it be his patron saint, Thomas of Canterbury, denoted by that mis-shaped letter, and the ornament that appears resting on the bend of his right arm, somewhat resembling the fleureted top of a portable cross, often borne about by the ancient bishops, or, lastly, whether it be St Antony, to whom the following particulars relate, are questions that may take place among the millions already propounded, and which still remain without solution

The monks of St Antony, who follow the rule of St Austin, are habited in a cassock, a patience, * a plaited cloak, and a black hood They have the letter T, of a blue colour, on the left side of their clothes St Antony is represented with a fire at his side, to signify his power in the cure of the sacred fire called by his name He is also represented with a hog, denoting his curing those animals of all the disorders to which they are subject [Lmillianne's Hist of Monastic Orders, chap. 14. p 128]

In the " Histoire du Clergé Seculier et Regulier," vol I p 192, under the article " Les Chanoines " de Saint Antoine de Viennois, Onzième Siecle," it is said,—" their habits were black, marked with a " T in blue (un Tau bleau) on the outer robe and inner vest, on the left side or breast, in enamel, after " the manner of the knights "

James, King of Jerusalem and Sicily, recommended to his heirs and successors always to have a particular devotion for St Antony, and always to wear hung round the neck a T in gold, and a little bell, the symbol of that saint, for whom he had great veneration, as appears by his will, made in the year 1403 [Ibid p 196]

Quere Did not the fashion of the ——— " Cross she wore
                    " Which Jew might kiss, and infidels adore,"
descend from this ancient injunction down to the present times, without Pope's knowing the fact ?

* The patience is only another name to signify the two sides of the scapulary [Ibid p 224, 225]

PERSPECTIVE VIEW OF THE INSIDE OF PRINCE ARTHUR'S CHAPEL IN THE
CATHEDRAL OF WORCESTER as it stood in 1610.

Plate

" Secondly. A king, crowned, in his regal vestments, and at his feet an animal, which is too much defaced to have its species ascertained.

" Thirdly. In the centre niche, a mutilated figure of the dead Christ, the head and hands gone, and the lower extremities much injured   On the body are represented red spots, expressive of the blood which had issued from his wounds   The drapery in which this figure is placed is upheld by two angels, represented near the top of the niche, and is partly gilt.

" Fourthly. Another king, crowned, and in his royal robes

" Fifthly. A figure in armour, much mutilated ; the arms and the right leg gone   At the feet of this figure are the remains of an animal, sufficient to shew that it was meant as a dragon ; and to establish an inference, that St George was meant to be the character represented.

" It requires no great depth of research, I conceive, to prove that the statues of the two kings were intended to represent Henry VI and Edward IV   If the religious character which precedes the pious Henry, and was designed allegorically as much to depict the image of his mind, as the figure of a king does that of his person and elevated station ; or if St. George, the Mars of England, be not enough to characterize the intrepidity of the Fourth Edward, who delighted in the feats of arms, let the external decorations of this chapel be put in the balance, and it will soon be found, that from the arms of each party, together with their several devices, and the symbols of union with which its south side is embellished, this mausoleum was erected as much to commemorate the important event of the coalition of the houses of York and Lancaster, of which those kings had been respectively the principals, as it was to form a repository for the remains of Prince Arthur, the first issue of their immediate representatives.

" Of the internal ornaments of this chapel, Abingdon, the Worcestershire Antiquary, who wrote in the time of Queen Elizabeth, has given the following description, in his " Account of the Cathedral of Worcester," p 14. " The east end, where once an altar stood, was sometime graced with rare " imagery work.   Here are now painted *France* and *England* quartered " within the garter, supported with a dragon and a greyhound, all covered " with an imperial crown, and under, *vival regina*," &c. (1)

(1) To that description should have been added—" garnished about with red crosses, inclosing the " white, and next the same arms, also quartered, with a label of three, argent, supported by two stags, " proper, tyred and unguled, or   and over all a prince's crown, the rest adorned with ostrich feathers,

" Dr. Thomas, in his Survey of the same cathedral, p. 36, has literally copied Abingdon's account, but he has somewhat more illustrated the subject by giving a plate of the north front of the chapel (1) These were the authorities followed by me in the " Survey of Worcester," p 76 Sandford in his " Genealogical History," p 476, 477, has given a plate of the prince's tomb, (2) and an external view of the south side of the chapel, (3) but no account of its inside.

" From what Abingdon has stated as above, it appears that the statues had been hid from public view before he took his account of the chapel, and that he had never seen them, but had received information that " rare imagery work had formerly graced that part of it " The mutilation of the figures appears to have been anterior to their being covered up, as near three parts of a bushel of their fragments have been found mixed with the mortar, and placed in the different cavities about them (4)

" The altar which Abingdon has noticed to have been in this chapel, was placed underneath the centre niche, at the feet of the dead Christ, and opposite the foot of the prince's tomb ; it was destroyed at the time the

" the badges of Wales, within princely crowns " Two displays of royal arms were therefore painted on the same canvas or panel, the first belonging to Queen Elizabeth, and the other to Prince Arthur, her uncle

(1) A very imperfect performance   (2) A decent representation

(3) So incorrect as to become a reproach to the name of Hollar, whose work it is

(4) Among which, painted in black upon the stone, was the following part of an inscription, viz Zpari
According to Bishop Blandford's MS A D 1547, Jan 10th, all images on the high altar, and throughout the church were destroyed This operation appears, therefore, to have preceded the act passed 1549, 3 Ed VI enjoining, " that any images of stone, timber, alabaster, or earth, graven, carved, or painted, which heretofore have stood in churches, be removed " A proviso, however, is added in this act, " that it did not extend to such images as were of a civil use, or of a monumental kind." This is evidently the period when the figure of the dead Saviour was defaced, as an object of worship, and most probably the altar beneath it was destroyed at the same time It is probable, therefore, that those figures were left, and remained nearly in the state we now see them, till about the year 1560, or 1561
Those who had been commissioned by Henry VIII and Edward VI to clean the churches of objects to which devotion had actually been paid, entered upon their business with too great a zeal for the reform, to give that discriminating attention to the objects, which their curiosity, value, or use entitled them to, and the consequences were that much property, learning, and valuable antiquities, were sacrificed to the blind fury of ignorant zealots, which the present times have to lament and execrate Queen Elizabeth in the beginning of her reign found it so disgracefully unjust and barbarous, as to induce her to issue, " a proclamation against breaking or defacing of monument of antiquitie, set up in churches or other public place for memory and not for superstition " To each of which the more to manifest her zeal, and to strengthen it, she appended her own name, and caused them to be dispersed throughout all her dominions [- - proc Annal p 16, Spelman Hist of Sacrilege, p 270 Weever Fun Monum

figures were covered up, and when the painted arms he has described were placed before that plastering which has just now been removed Of those arms it must be noted, that no trace is left of the time they were taken down, nor of what has since become of them. (1) I can readily admit that some of those parts of the figures, which originally projected beyond the line of the canopies above, or that of the base below, on which they are placed, were broken off to reduce the whole to an even surface, for the purpose of re-

(1) It is, I conceive, most likely that they gave way in their turn to democratic prejudice against regal power, and that the parliamentary reformers tore this insignia of royalty down, at the time of the siege of Worcester in 1646, and left that part of the chapel in the state in which it remained in November, 1738

The following extract from a collection of letters, published by J Carte, 1739, (2 vol octavo) will serve to shew what was then done in the church of Worcester by that party Vol I p 15,—" *Arthur Trevor to the Marquis of Ormond*

" From Oxford I came to Worcester, which I found under the government of Sir W Russel, the high sheriff for the county, and therein a good garrison for his majesty, and well fortified by the parliament, who, when they were there, were fain to employ their soldiers in throwing up ditches at 12d *per diem,* who would else be pulling down the cathedral for nothing

" The organs, being two fair pair, all the bishops beards, noses, fingers, and arms and all, if they had white sleeves, were broken King John, and the other kings that he interred there, have not passed better in this quarrel than with cracked crowns

" In all the corners of the church are the droppings of these unclean birds visible, preserved almost without putrefaction, to witness the impiety of that party A grave man, one for his life and learning I may call a father of that church, shewing me these *purgamenta,* with tears in his eyes told me, that with those eyes he saw divers of them ease themselves in the font, and upon the communion table, calling to them that cheerfully looked on, to name the child, and sign it with the sign of the cross This I am bold to acquaint your honour withal, to let you see they have raised a spirit that they cannot tell how to lay again, for in all this hurley-burley their general or officers durst manage no other instrument of correction in their hands than their hats "

To the same purport is another extract from, " A Short View of the late Troubles in England, &c " printed at Oxford,* 1681, wherein, under the date of " Sept 24th, 1642, page 557," it states that " When their whole army from London, under the command of the Earl of Essex, came to Worcester, the first thing they did was the profanation of the cathedral, destroying the organ, breaking in pieces divers beautiful windows, wherein the foundation of that church was lively historified with painted glass, and barbarously defacing divers fair monuments of the dead And, as if this were not enough, they brought their horses into the body of the church, keeping fires and courts of guard therein, making the quire and side isles, with the font, the common places wherein they did their easements of nature Also, to make their wickedness the more complete, they rifled the library, with the records and evidences of the church, tore in pieces the Bibles and service books pertaining to the quire, putting the surplices and other vestments upon their dragooners, who rode about the streets with them "

So wantonly wicked and shamelessly indecent were they in this their savage visitation of the church of Worcester, that whenever their subsequent enormities committed at other places want force in their description of them, they are usually pronounced ' to have been as truly horrible as those they perpetrated at Worcester "

* Said to be written by Sir William Dugdale Vide Grey's Hudibra

P

" Dr. Thomas, in his Survey of the same cathedral, p. 36, has literally copied Abingdon's account, but he has somewhat more illustrated the subject by giving a plate of the north front of the chapel. (1) These were the authorities followed by me in the " Survey of Worcester," p. 76 Sandford in his " Genealogical History," p. 476, 477, has given a plate of the prince's tomb, (2) and an external view of the south side of the chapel, (3) but no account of its inside.

" From what Abingdon has stated as above, it appears that the statues had been hid from public view before he took his account of the chapel, and that he had never seen them, but had received information that " rare imagery work had formerly graced that part of it." The mutilation of the figures appears to have been anterior to their being covered up, as near three parts of a bushel of their fragments have been found mixed with the mortar, and placed in the different cavities about them. (4)

" The altar which Abingdon has noticed to have been in this chapel, was placed underneath the centre niche, at the feet of the dead Christ, and opposite the foot of the prince's tomb ; it was destroyed at the time the

---

" the badges of Wales, within princely crowns " Two displays of royal arms were therefore painted on the same canvas or panel , the first belonging to Queen Elizabeth, and the other to Prince Arthur, her uncle

(1) A very imperfect performance   (2) A decent representation

(3) So incorrect as to become a reproach to the name of Hollar, whose work it is

(4) Among which, painted in black upon the stone, was the following part of an inscription, viz **Span̄**
According to Bishop Blandford's MS A. D 1547, Jan 10th, all images on the high altar, and throughout the church were destroyed This operation appears, therefore, to have preceded the act passed 1549, 3 Ed VI enjoining, " that any images of stone, timber, alabaster, or earth, graven, carved, or painted, which heretofore have stood in churches, be removed " A proviso, however, is added in this act, " that it did not extend to such images as were of a civil use, or of a monumental kind " This is evidently the period when the figure of the dead Saviour was defaced, as an object of worship, and most probably the altar beneath it was destroyed at the same time It is probable, therefore, that those figures were left, and remained nearly in the state we now see them, till about the year 1560, or 1561

Those who had been commissioned by Henry VIII and Edward VI to clear the churches of objects to which devotion had actually been paid, entered upon their business with too great a zeal for the reform, to give that discriminating attention to the objects, which their curiosity, value, or use entitled them to , and the consequences were, that much property, learning, and valuable antiquities, were sacrificed to the blind fury of ignorant zealots, which the present times have to lament and execrate Queen Elizabeth, in the beginning of her reign, found it so disgracefully unjust and barbarous, as to induce her to issue, " A proclamation against breaking or defacing of monuments of antiquitie, set up in churches or other public place for memory and not for superstition " To each of which, the more to manifest her zeal, and restrain the sacrilege, she signed her own name, and caused them to be dispersed throughout all her dominion [Strype's Annals, p 185 Spelman's Hist of Sacrilege, p 290 Weever's Fun. Monum p 50, 51 52 53, chap 10]

figures were covered up, and when the painted arms he has described were placed before that plastering which has just now been removed. Of those arms it must be noted, that no trace is left of the time they were taken down, nor of what has since become of them. (1) I can readily admit that some of those parts of the figures, which originally projected beyond the line of the canopies above, or that of the base below, on which they are placed, were broken off to reduce the whole to an even surface, for the purpose of re-

(1) It is, I conceive, most likely that they gave way in their turn to democratic prejudice against regal power, and that the parliamentary reformers tore this insignia of royalty down, at the time of the siege of Worcester in 1646, and left that part of the chapel in the state in which it remained in November, 1788

The following extract from a collection of letters, published by J Carte, 1739, (2 vol. octavo) will serve to shew what was then done in the church of Worcester by that party Vol I p. 15 ,—" *Arthur Trevor to the Marquis of Ormond*

" From Oxford I came to Worcester, which I found under the government of Sir W Russel, the high sheriff for the county, and therein a good garrison for his majesty, and well fortified by the parliament , who, when they were there, were fain to employ their soldiers in throwing up ditches at 12*d per diem*, who would else be pulling down the cathedral for nothing.

" The organs, being two fair pair, all the bishops beards, noses, fingers, and arms and all, if they had white sleeves, were broken King John, and the other kings that lie interred there, have not passed better in this quarrel than with cracked crowns.

" In all the corners of the church are the droppings of these unclean birds visible, preserved almost without putrefaction, to witness the impiety of that party A grave man, one for his life and learning I may call a father of that church, shewing me these *purgamenta*, with tears in his eyes told me, that with those eyes he saw divers of them ease themselves in the font, and upon the communion table, calling to them that cheerfully looked on, to name the child, and sign it with the sign of the cross This I am bold to acquaint your honour withal, to let you see they have raised a spirit that they cannot tell how to lay again , for in all this hurley-burley their general or officers durst manage no other instrument of correction in their hands than their hats "

To the same purport is another extract from, " A Short View of the late Troubles in England, &c " printed at Oxford,* 1681, wherein, under the date of " Sept 24th, 1642, page 557," it states that " When their whole army from London, under the command of the Earl of Essex, came to Worcester, the first thing they did was the profanation of the cathedral, destroying the organ, breaking in pieces divers beautiful windows, wherein the foundation of that church was lively historified with painted glass, and barbarously defacing divers fair monuments of the dead. And, as if this were not enough, they brought their horses into the body of the church, keeping fires and courts of guard therein , making the quire and side iles, with the font, the common places wherein they did their easements of nature Also, to make their wickedness the more complete, they rifled the library, with the records and evidences of the church, tore in pieces the Bibles and service books pertaining to the quire, putting the surplices and other vestments upon their dragooners, who rode about the streets with them "

So wantonly wicked and shamelessly indecent were they in this their savage visitation of the church of Worcester, that whenever their subsequent enormities committed at other places want force in their description of them, they are usually pronounced " to have been as truly horrible as those they perpetrated at Worcester "

* Said to be written by Sir William Dugdale Vide Grey's Hudibras

ceiving the queen's arms as an object of civil worship, superseding what
was then become obnoxious to religious veneration

" So long since, therefore, as that period of Queen Elizabeth's reign, in
which she assumed the decided independent government of the church,
have these statues been secluded from observation, and this elegant structure bereft of its choicest ornament   I am, Sir, &c.

     March 12th, 1789   V. GREEN "

The design of this chapel was evidently defective while those figures
were detached from it, and remained unseen   They were intended to form
the groundwork of its purpose, to which every other part of the structure
has a reference. And as indispensable to its history, they are thence seen
to occupy the first station in its arrangement.

It is neither incurious, nor unworthy of remark, that these objects which
had their origin in the purity of paternal affection, mingled with the ardency
of pious devotion that characterized the age in which they were produced,
in less than fifty years afterwards became utterly obnoxious, from that very
devotion that had called them into existence, which, from its having not
only become suspected, but convicted, of fostering principles inimical to civil
authority, for that offence was rooted up and abolished   To that exploded
influence, regal power, consolidating spiritual and temporal interests, succeeded, and in both functions became absolute. The next century saw the
complete overthrow of that system, and the iron age of democratic usurpation and fanatic hypocrisy prevail   Scarcely half another century elapsed,
in the early part of which period a restoration of royal authority was effected,
and in the latter part a Revolution took place, that elicited a constitution
capable to stand the test of time, guarantee the blessings of union and peace
to future ages, and has thence " made these odds all even." Such have been
the great national vicissitudes the two last centuries have witnessed, and to
which the narrow spot we have thus long been busied about, has borne
more than a common share of interesting testimony (1)

Considered as one of the earliest efforts existing of that class of refined
Gothic art that has ventured to address itself to the sublimity of sentiment,
and not less successfully directed to the judgment than to the passions, we
cannot but admire the skill with which its leading points are managed   As

(1) For the measures of this chapel, see Appendix, No XXXII p cxxix

a lesson prepared with profound reasoning, capable of inducing wholesome reflection in minds at all susceptible of thought, this " sermon in stone," which even he who runs may read to the most useful purpose ; this spectacle of solemn magnificence, teeming with instruction, produced in that eventful age for pure Gothic architecture, in which its modest and simple beauties bloomed and expired, cannot be contemplated without pleasure, nor studied without advantage.

From the dates of the foregoing events we may gather that either the figures in this chapel, which had been defaced in 1547, remained exposed in their mutilated state till the first of Queen Elizabeth's proclamations appeared, enjoining all destruction of that sort to be made good, and that then the expedient was resorted to of setting up her arms to cover the outrage altogether, by a political act of ecclesiastical grace, after they had openly borne their injuries for fourteen years ; or that the same expedient was postponed till after the appearance of the second proclamation, which extends their ruinated exposure to the term of twenty-six years, and brings the restoration of that part of the chapel, by the introduction of the painting of the queen's arms, to within two years of her majesty's visit to Worcester, A D. 1574, and so opportunely as just to save the church from her probable displeasure.

SHRINES.

In this church there is now no trace to be found of either the fixed or the portable shrine The usual situation of the former sort was between the high altar and the extreme east end of our cathedrals, as at Canterbury, Durham, Westminster, &c   The fixed shrines are supposed to differ in little else from the grand sepulchral monuments, than as the former contained the relics of canonized persons, and the latter those who were not so The portable shrines were used in processions, and were called Feretra ; the immoveable ones had also that name, though not with equal propriety The cost and magnificent splendour bestowed on the fixed shrines in many instances, made it necessary to appoint a *custos feretri* to prevent their being spoiled of their jewels and other valuable enrichments by those who might visit them for other than religious purposes. The one at St. Alban's, and the Confessor's at Westminster, were so watched, each by a monk , and at Canterbury, an inclosure of Becket's treasures preserved them from the hands of the sacrilegious, and kept the wondering spectator at an awful distance, to admire and to adore   The shrine of the three kings at Cologne, rich beyond computation in its jewels and precious stones, can only be entered by one or two persons at once, who are always attended by a canon of the church.   The history of all those churches wherein the tombs or shrines of sanctified persons were deposited, prove that the manufacture of miracles was among the most productive sources of their revenue.   In the ancient church of St. Peter at Worcester, it appears there was more than one shrine ; for the spoils of the Conqueror from *off the long shrine*, were 8 pounds of gold or silver ; another shrine at least is therefore implied in that account.   It is probable one of them was that of St. Oswald, whose relics on the opening of the present cathedral, were put into a *new shrine* , but to whom the other might belong is not known.   The tombs and shrines of our Worcester saints were in existence at the same time . and at each the devout were accustomed to offer up their prayers ; for their reputed holiness was second to none in the calendar of those ages.   Their shrines seem to have been of the portable kind, as distinguished by Dr. Stukeley. (1)

RELICS

Of saints, martyrs, and holy men, according to the eminence of the characters to whom they belonged, acquired a proportionable reverence for those churches in which they were deposited.   Of these there have been only two in the church of Worcester, to whom miracles, or any supernatural influences, were ever attempted to be attributed, those were the Saints Oswald and Wulstan.   In the Monasticon Anglicanum, and therein as a specimen for the whole, let the abbey of Glastenbury suffice for all their extravagancies united.   In the instance of St. Wulstan, already stated, we find one of their practices of dividing the bones of the objects of their veneration, and thereby of enhancing the reputation of some less fortunate churches, by retailing to them a rib, an arm, a toe, or any other portion of the body ; and the certain consequence of such benefactions was an augmentation of their revenues, from the piety of those who resorted to them as objects of adoration.

We find also that to enrich the stores of relics in the greater churches, they were frequently not only presented, but most probably bartered and

(1) Phil Transac No 490, p 580 Archæologia, vol I p 23, Art V Observations upon Shrines, by John Loveday, Esq.

exchanged. It appears from the paper already quoted, that the church of Worcester had supplies from other quarters, among which were, " a arme of Seynt Edmunde the Bysshoope ; a arme of Seynt Romane the Bysshope coveryde yn certen placis with selver ; una vitta cirra caput Ste. Margarete, with selver with other garnyssynge with selver abowte the hede, xi thousande v̄gyns, in parte of a skul ; of Herffords tombe garnyssyde in gold and gylte." In the same paper we have already found, in " the farce their miserable relics played," that the Worcester saints had not been suffered to remain idle after their deaths, and that while some parcels of their bones lay in their tombs, and others in their shrines, their heads became furniture for the treasury ; and in this third remove from the grave, were again made subservient to the avarice of religious imposition on the multitude, and shared a third time in their devotions within the pale of the same church.

In the council of Trent a provision was made, that no relics should be admitted but such as were first approved by the bishop. And that of the Lateran, which decreed that none should be worshipped but such as were stamped with the pope's authority, was approved and confirmed, in a synod held at Exeter, by Bishop Wyvil, A. D. 1287, with farther provision to prevent counterfeits. Another held at Winchester, A. D. 1308, decreed similar preventives ; but all could not effect a cure. The measure of their imposture was not yet full, and it remained for the Reformation at once to discover the meanness of the fraud, and to abolish it altogether (1)

FONTS.

When the first use of fonts began, they were set up in private houses That sacrament, in the times of persecution, was obliged to be administered in solitary places, amongst other ceremonies used by the primitive Christians, till in more peaceful times, they drew nearer, and placed their fonts at a little distance from the church or oratory. They were afterwards placed in the porch ; and lastly in the church itself. Their situation is usually near the entrance, because baptism is the sacrament of initiation, or admittance into the church Anciently there was but one font in a city, and that was placed in or near the principal of its churches. Its name is retained from the primitive custom of baptizing in rivers and fountains Their first introduction was into cathedral churches, where the bishop re-

(1) Staveley, chap. 13. p. 200.

sided, and where the right of baptism and sepulture belonged (1) Among the ceremonies of the ancient church there was one called " Font hallowing," and which was performed on Easter even, and Whitsunday eve. That ceremony ceased in this cathedral on Easter even, A D 1549. (2)

The ancient font of this church was placed on the west side of the second pillar, below the great cross ile, near the upper south entrance of the nave, and opposite to the altar of St John the Baptist, which stood at the foot of the corresponding pillar on the north side of the nave, near Jesus' chapel ; according to Leland, it was of black marble, with an inscription upon it, which he copied, viz. Inscriptio baptisterii in nigro marmore.—" Hic fons est vitæ, mundandi quicunque venite   Suscipit ista reos, et parit unda deos." (3)

It is not unusual to find the more ancient fonts much embellished with sculptures of saints, and scriptural history; and being a part of church furniture, not unfrequently votive, they are sometimes distinguished with armorial ensigns, denoting their benefactors

PAINTED GLASS

Is supposed to have been general in its use in our churches in Henry the Third's time ; although even plain glass windows were very rarely found in any other building, excepting the houses of people of the highest distinction, before the time of Henry VIII (4)

The church of New Sarum was one of the first that received this captivating ornament in its windows, of which they had both painted and stained glass (5)

The ancient windows of this cathedral had never any very remarkable decoration of this kind to boast, beyond crowned or enthroned kings, praying prelates, or priors, kneeling knights, or pious ladies, and these very " thinly scattered to make up a show," compared with many others of our cathedral churches, of inferior note (6)   The number of coats of arms was so considerable at the time Mr Abingdon took his account of them, that he judged it proper to notice none that had been put up within one hundred years preceding his taking his survey of this cathedral. (7)

(1) Staveley, chap 13 p 216   (2) Bishop Blandford's MS   (3) Lel Itin. vol VIII. p. 129.
(4) Aubrey's MS Ashm Mus Oxon Antiq Rep No II vol. III p 46
(5) Pile's Observ on that Cath p 65.   (6) For a list of the figures formerly put up in them, see the Append to this sect p xii No VII   (7) See p 1, 2 His list is notwithstanding very numerous.

The names and arms of other benefactors to the monastery were also painted on the windows of the cloisters, the chapter house, and the refectory, of which Symonds has drawn many, and noticed near two hundred others (1)

These combined objects formed the whole of this species of embellishment the church of Worcester possessed.

The vigilant discrimination of Dr. Thomas has given names to many of them, which had not been known to Mr. Abingdon, and many illustrations of which they stood in much need, to be at all useful, (2) and to the same end Dr. Nash has also been eminently instructive in his collection of the arms of the Worcestershire families (3) These heraldic memorials of personages and families formerly connected with this church, either as members of, or benefactors to it, are so amply enumerated by those learned Antiquaries, to whose accounts reference may be had, as to preclude the necessity in this place, to repeat what is already more than a twice told tale

PICTURES,

Had never found a reception in our churches to any considerable extent. The art of painting in England had not arrived to an eminence sufficient to add incitement to devotion, or strength to the interest of papal delusion, to be called into the service of the church, or to reap the fruit of its powerful patronage, (4) whilst on the Continent it had been so successfully cultivated, as to have become one of the most attractive expedients the subtlety of the conclave could have devised, whereby to augment the splendour of the ecclesiastical establishment, and confirm its duration. At that period, when the power of the church in England had become obnoxious to the will of the king, and when, in consequence, its altars were stripped of their embellishments, the Raphaels, the Michael Angelos, and the great masters of the other Italian schools, were rendering their churches and their palaces, the result of their superior talents, and themselves immortal by their works

(1) See his MS. church notes, vol. II. Harl Coll No 965 Art XVI Brit Mus He says " in the convocation or treasury windows, a circular building (the chapter house) now used for the magazine of the garrison, were fifteen coats," drawn by him.

(2) See his Survey of this Cathedral, p 11   (3) In Appendix, vol II. p 83.

(4) On this subject, see farther in " a Review of the Polite Arts in France, at the time of their establishment under Louis XIV compared with their present State in England," in a letter to the late Sir Joshua Reynolds, President of the Royal Academy, by the Author Quarto Cadell, 1782.

But excluded here from the only prospect they could have hoped, by which to have become known and respectable, chilled and repressed in their outset (for Holbein had appeared among us), the arts sought and happily found refuge in climes more congenial and propitious to their growth ; and it has remained till the present age, to see them called forth, and become a new source of honourable estimation, in a country unaccustomed to act secondarily in whatsoever relates to intellectual and elegant refinement.

The church of Worcester has had no example of ancient art that has survived the wreck of the Reformation, or that has even obtained the honour of a place in the inventories of its spoliations

ORGANS,

As we now have them, supplied with bellows, and played by keys, are among the very early articles of furniture introduced into our churches; they are said to be an Eastern invention, and as early as the fourth century At what period they were first brought here has not been ascertained.

Sir Henry Spelman conceives there were organs in England in the time of King Edgar, about the year 958. (1) This is confirmed by William of Malmsbury, who says the famous Dunstan gave to the church of Malmsbury an organ with brass pipes. (2) And Alwyn, alderman of all England, who flourished about the same time, laid out the sum of thirty Saxon pounds, in building an organ in the church at Ramsey abbey, which had pipes of brass or copper, and was blown into by bellows, played upon with keys, and furnished with proper stops (3)

The Anglo-Saxons were so much attached to psalmody, that the services of their cathedrals and monasteries seemed a continued strain of chanting and sacred harmony, kept up by a succession of priests day and night (4) The introduction of the organ was a happy and great improvement to that taste , the vocal chorus became more full and grand in its musical effect, and more solemn and sublime in its devotional sentiment   Most of the penances imposed were redeemable by singing a number of psalms, or repeating the Lord's prayer so many times   The pater noster, and the 119th psalm, sung six times over, would redeem the penance of a day's fasting. (5)

(1) Spelm Gloss in verb organum.   (2) Malms de Pontif.
(3) Hist Ramsiens apud Gale, c 54.   (4) Muratori Dissert. T. 4
(5) Johnson's Canons, A D 963. Strutt's Chron vol. II ch 9 p. 256, 257

In the injunctions of Queen Elizabeth respecting the Reformation, singing in churches was among the first of the clauses   She recommended it to be kept up, to preserve the science and advantages of music ; that therefore all maintenances settled for the service of the choirs should be continued   That the affectation of skill should not be carried so far as to make the use of the church service less significant , and that the common prayer should be sung in so plain and distinct a manner that the pronunciation might be altogether as well understood as if it had been read.   However, for the satisfaction of those that were particularly pleased with music, a religious anthem was allowed at the beginning or end of the service.   Pursuant to this order, in most parish churches the psalms were sung in plain song, being changed from antiphones into metrical psalmody, which was at that time called Geneva psalms. (1) In the queen's chapel, in cathedrals, and in colleges, the hymns were sung in a more refined manner ; and to render the performance more solemn and impressive, organs and other instrumental music were made use of (2)

In the cathedral of Worcester, we find mention made of several organs having been erected for the use of its choir and chapels.   The chapel of St Edmund, wherein was a pair of organs, and the chapel of St George, in which was a great pair of organs, were pulled down by Dean Barlow, A D 1550   The great organ (supposed to have been in the choir) was taken down on the 30th of August, 1551.   In 1556, a pair of organs was set up on the north side of the choir (3)   These, it may be supposed, remained till the civil wars in the next century, when it appears that the two fair pair of organs, which were found in the cathedral, were broken. (4) Mr. Townshend in his Journal of the Siege of Worcester, A. D. 1646, thus mentions the same fact —" 23d July   This day many gentlemen went to six o'clock prayers to the college, to take their last farewell of the church of England service, the organs having been taken down the 20th " (5)

The organ of this cathedral, which with its gallery terminates the west end of the choir, consists of nine stops, and is esteemed a fine instrument.

(1) Archæologia, vol II p 22 Art. IV.   (2) Collier's Eccl. Hist of Brit. vol II, B vi. p. 433.
In the great Synod held at Westminster in Jan. 1562-3 Dr Wilson, afterwards Dean of Worcester, was one of those who voted for the removal of organs out of churches, which was thrown out of the lower house of convocation by one vote only, viz. 59 against 58   [Dr. Nash, vol II. p 318.]
(3) Bishop Blandford's MS   (4) Carte's Letters, vol I. p 15.
(5) Dr Nash, in Appendix, vol. II. p 105

Q

It is of a dimension proportioned to the church, and forms a magnificent object, viewed either from the nave or the choir   In the account of its erection, in the archives of the Dean and Chapter, as produced by Thomas Dallam, organ maker, in 1613, it is termed " the new double organs " The expence attending its building was defrayed by a voluntary contribution. On the west front of its gallery, on the cornice, is the following inscription . " These honourable and worshipful gentlemen, whose arms are here placed, were contributors towards this gallery, anno Domini, 1614 " (1)

On a plane in the centre of this front, is a painting of the Virgin Mary, with our Saviour in her arms , underneath which the arms of the see are represented, displayed by two naked boys withdrawing a large drapery from before them

The east front of the gallery towards the choir, has a good imitation of a marble parapet, or screen, inclosing the floor of the gallery over the stalls of the choir.   On this side the lesser or chair organ is seen, as communicating with the great one , it consists of five stops.   In its painted decorations, the arms of the see are represented as on the west front, over which, answerable to the situation of the virgin and child, as already described, an angel is seen sounding a trumpet, and holding an olive branch in his left hand   The carvings on the top are the king's arms, without the supporters, from which, on each side, a bold festoon, richly composed of flowers, fruits, &c is suspended   At the bottom of the larger pipes, on each

(1) In the centre are three coats, viz the arms of the see of Worcester, impaling those of Bishop Parry, beneath which are those of the Dean and Chapter, and Talbot, Earl of Shrewsbury   Then beginning on the north side of these are, Thomas Lord Windsor, Sir John Pakington and his lady, Sir Henry Bromley, Sir Edward Blount, Sir Thomas Russel, Sir Arnold Lygon, Sir William Walsh and his lady, Sir Edward Pitt, Sir Thomas Biggs, Sir Francis Egiocke, Sir John Buck, Sir William Sandys, Sir John Rous, of Rouslench, one unknown, Humphrey Pakington, of Chidsley, Henry Lygon, Thomas Russel, John Hanford, Edward Newport, of Hindley Williams, Leonard J ffreys, of Earl's Cromb, —— Dingley, of Carlton, William Savage, of Elmley, John Washborne, Cornwall Baronn, Esqrs. Sir Edmund Wylde, one unknown; Sir John Acton, of Wolverton   On the south side Lord Compton, —— Lucy, Sir John Scudamore, one unknown, —— Verney, one unknown, Sir Clement Throkmorton, Sir William Somervil, Thomas Spencer, of Cliverdon, Esq two unknown. —— Talbot two others unknown, Thomas Coventry, Esq —— Peto, quartering Loges, and Langley, the same, one unknown, William Gower Francis Harewell, —— Warmstry —— Copley, of Bredon, Esqs one unknown, Thomas Cocks, Esq of Crowle, one unknown, William Richardson, Esq and Dr Haln, chancellor   in the whole fiftys even coats   These , however, form but few more than half the contributors to the setting up of this organ   for the rest, together with the sum subscribed, and other particulars respecting this arsel , see the Appendix to this section No VI p xv, xvi, xvii

side, are carved heads of cherubins   The pipes of the chair organ have their tops inserted behind the expanded plumes of a large cherub's wings, which spread over the whole line ; a pretty design, but indifferently executed.

This organ appears to have survived the outrages committed upon the others found in the cathedral at the time of the great rebellion, without much damage : no account of its being either removed or repaired occurring till the early part of Dean Waugh's time, when the following chapter order was made, to complete the liberal repair it received under his direction, viz. " 6 March, 1752, whereas it appears, upon experience, that two hundred " pounds, formerly agreed on, will not be sufficient to add the stops that " are wanting in the great organ, and to make it full, perfect, and complete " in all its parts, ordered, that one hundred pounds more be allowed : in " all three hundred pounds, effectually to repair and finish the same "

The trumpet stop introduced at this time is esteemed the finest of the kind in England   the stopped diapason is also peculiarly excellent.   The great characteristic of this noble instrument is its sweetness and fullness of tone, to which this part of the cathedral, well adapted for sound, does the amplest justice, and " to the full voiced choir below " (1)

BELLS

When the tower of the cathedral was completed, the bells, anciently but five, were removed out of the cloche, or leaden steeple, and placed therein ; they were supposed to be equal to those of York, of which the largest weighed 6600 lb.   There are now eight, but cast at different times ; on which are the following inscriptions

1 God save our king. 1640 —3 In honore Sci Wolstan. Epi +.—5 Richardo Eedes Decano 1602 J G B M —6 Hoc opus inspicito, Jesu virtute faveto —7. Miserere Deus meus · habeo nomen Gaufreus. (Arms France and England.)—8 I sweatly toaling, men doe call, To taste on meate that feads the soule.   1648

Bells have always been considered a very convenient and necessary part of church furniture   Paulinas, Bishop of Nola, a city of Campania, about the year 400, has the reputation of their invention   But when or by whomsoever bells were first invented, it is certain that no country hath more of

(1) Milton, Il Penseroso

Q 2

them, proportionably to the number of churches, than England, which from thence has often been called " the ringing island." The use of the great ringing bells appears to have been very ancient among us   Ingulphus describes the first and best regular ring or peal of bells in England, cast and hung up in the church of Croyland abbey by the famous Abbat Turketulus, who died about the year 870 (1)   St Dunstan, who died A. D. 988, presented to Malmsbury abbey some large bells, and organs, at that time wonderful and strange in England (2)

Early, therefore, after this period, we may date the building of those bell towers, or clocheriums, found erected near our cathedrals, for the reception of bells, which were now become a part of the appendages to all the great churches, more especially the episcopal ones of the island   Hence those of York, Canterbury, St Paul's London, and Worcester.

Hence it may be supposed, that those churches which now have, or formerly had, those belfries erected near them, are of the most ancient now existing ; the tower or towers that are found attached to, or erected upon them, being chiefly structures of a much later date than the churches to which they belong   Of this the cathedral of Worcester is an example.

Another church bell yet remains to be noticed. The small bell, (called formerly the sanctes bell) which we still find in many of our churches, was only used and rung out when the priest came to that part of the service, " Sancte, sancte, sancte Domine Deus Sabaoth !" purposely that they who could not come to church might understand what a solemn office the congregation were at that instant engaged in, and so even in their absence become at least sensible of their duty to God. For this reason the sanctes bell was generally hung where it might be heard farthest. (3)

CLOCKS AND DIALS

Were set up in churches in the middle of the seventh century (4)   There remain, however, no certain traces to whom this invention really belongs The Greeks had their dials from the Jews; and to the diagram described upon the steps of the palace of Ahaz, a gnomon was added at Sparta, by

(1) Collier's Eccles Hist b iii p 198 Ingulph fol 53   (2) Malms de Pontif lib v Edit Angl Sac vol II p 33   (3) Pe k's Annals of Stamford lib viii p 51 52 Art 37
(4) Stow says that clocks and dials were commanded to be set up in churches by Savianus, the sixty-third pope [Stow's Chron p 56]

Anaximenes   The Romans distinguished the day merely by its two natural periods, sunrise, and sunset.   Noon was ascertained and proclaimed by the crier of the consuls, when the sun was perceived betwixt two particular points of the forum   The first dial among them was placed on a pillar by the rostrum ; and although inaccurate, from the lines not answering with precision to the hours, it continued their standard for the division of time, till Scipio Nasica invented a horologe, which could be serviceable under a cloudy, as well as a sunny sky ; (1) the first of which was introduced into Britain by Cæsar (2)   The one has received the appellation of horarium, or hour-glass, and the other the name of diale, a dial, or day-piece, among us (3)

The honourable Daines Barrington, in his " Observations on the earliest " Introduction of Clocks," says, " Dante seems to be the first author who " hath introduced the mention of an orologio, which struck the hour," and has quoted the passage, (Dante Paradiso, C x)

In England, precisely about the same time, the famous clock-house near Westminster hall was furnished with a clock, to be heard by the courts of law, out of a fine imposed on the chief justice of the King's Bench, A D 1288   At Canterbury was another, A D. 1292.

There appears no evidence of the exact time when this useful and important invention was introduced into this church, or rather into its service ; as it was first placed in the leaden steeple; and on the demolition of that structure, and the removal of the bells, it was fixed in the tower of the cathedral, in which it now remains.   Chimes were also added to its movements, but they are at present disused.

At the interment of King John, a present much more valuable than that of his body was made to this church.   The close of the monastery had hitherto been much too narrow for the offices belonging to it.   Ever since the reign of the Norman conqueror, whose sheriff, Urso d'Abitot, had carried the graff or mote of the castle nearer the church than had been attempted before, and had even, if we may believe William of Malmsbury,(4) taken away part of the burial ground of the monks, there had been strong complaints   A favourable opportunity of redress was offered in 1216, when

---

(1) Pliny, lib vii c 60   (2) Cæsar, p 89   (3) Whitaker's Manchester, vol II ch 10 p 127, 128   (4) Hemingus, who often complains of Urso's injustice, and mentions several encroach ments that he made on St. Mary's land, says nothing of this

the Earl of Pembroke and the pope's legate brought the king's corpse to be interred here This great general, soon after made regent of the kingdom, undertook the enlarging of the church precincts, by granting, in the young king's name, the northern moiety, or outer ward, of Worcester castle, to the use of St Mary's convent for ever. (1) The Italian legate, as if his master had a property in the demesnes of the English crown, concurred with the regent in the grant Fifteen years after, the king himself confirmed it. The water gate, towards the river, (2) and Edgar's gate, which was the eastern avenue, are the only edifices belonging to this ward of the castle that were preserved But on the site of it several modern buildings have been erected, to the east and south of the area, now called the College Green Nay, Dr Thomas adds, (on what authority I know not,) that even part of the present cloister stands on the ground that before belonged to the Norman fortress (3) Soon after this donation, the prior and convent raised an embattled wall, to separate their new acquisition from the other moiety of the castle, which was reserved to the use of the king and his sheriffs Part of this wall, extending from Edgar's tower, more than half way towards the river, is now remaining (4) But, notwithstanding the grant of Henry III the site of the demolished ward of the castle was still claimed by the sheriffs, who were Earls of Worcester, till in 1276 they relinquished all farther pretensions to it, in due form of law, in consideration of one hundred pounds paid by the monks (5)

(1) Dugdale's Baronage, I p 227
must have been a gate there before

(2) The present water gate was built in 1378; but there
(3) Dr Thomas's Survey, p 7

Nor is it in the least improbable for admitting the mote of the ancient castle to have approached no nearer to the cathedral than on a line from Edgar's tower, between the college green and the refectory, in its direct course to the Severn, there was then no great cause for Archbishop Aldred's denouncing the sheriff for his intrusion on the church, as there was then nearly as great a distance between the mote and the cathedral, as the cemetery on its north side occupied between the church and the bounds of its precincts towards the city It is here also to be remarked, that in no less a period than 155 years after Urso d'Abitot's time, that any building we now see south of the cathedral and belonging to it, was erected, the first of which was the priory, and more than 300 years before the refectory, cloisters, and chapter house were built To have been, therefore, that sort of annoyance to the church, as to have induced the venom of episcopal anathema, the course of the drift of the fortress most likely, entrenched on holy ground so far as to cut off nearly half of the whole of the cloisters, as we now see them in a direct line from east to west

(4) Without this wall there was left a freeboard, or open passage to the river, at least sixteen feet wide which has been since taken away, to prevent the escape of prisoners, and the county gaol (called the castle) is now contiguous to the wall See Dr Thomas's Survey, p 8

(5) Gough's Camden, vol II p 366 in Worcester
This agreement took place in the time of William de Beauchamp, IV

Having carried down the history of this monastery to the time of its greatest opulence and splendour, it may not be unseasonable to speak, in this place, of its constitution and government.

A cathedral in the possession of monks appeared to foreigners an extraordinary sight. (1) There were in England seven cathedrals besides this of Worcester, so appropriated Canterbury, Durham, Ely, Norwich, Rochester, Bath, and Winchester Every cathedral-convent was governed by a prior, the bishop himself being in the place of abbat. but in process of time these priors obtained of the pope the honour of the mitre, and were placed in every respect on a level with the greatest abbats, except the honour of sitting with the barons in parliament. In the reign of Henry III. they had summons to parliament with the mitred abbats; but this privilege was not continued to them, because they held their baronies, not *in capite* of the crown, but under their respective bishops Only one summons of the prior of Worcester appears this was to the parliament of 1265, 49 Hen. III (2)

In the earlier ages of this convent, the prior had the title of dean, which soon after the conquest was dropped; and in the times next preceding the Reformation, the more magnificent title of lord prior. He presided as judge in the courts-leet within the manors of the convent : to which anciently belonged *jus furcarum*, or the right of punishing felons by death on the gallows (3)

The PRIOR when the monastery became void of the prior by death, preferment, or removal, the convent chose seven of the most sufficient monks, whom they presented to the Bishop of Worcester, that he out of these

(1) Annal Waverl p 157   (2) Steven's Mon Append p 16

(3) Hearne's Chartul Wig p 541, 551 There was in this church a prison for convicted clerks, such as are now in gaol deliveries saved from death by reading. The porter of the palace was their keeper his office was considered of that importance, that the chapter once refused to confirm a grant made of it by the bishop, unless the porter gave security for the safe custody of the prisoners, for in the vacancy of the see, the prior and monks being the chapter, stood accountable for the prison Every clerk convicted was delivered out of this prison by the verdict of twelve clerks, by proclamation, which was called his purgation * We can, however, neither trace its dungeon, nor the execution of any clerical criminal in consequence of the powers vested in the monastery to punish their delinquency Of an imprisoned monk we have one example the nature of his offence is given by himself, † but his fate is unknown.

* Abingdon's MS p. 37.   † See Appendix, No I p 1.

might elect one to be their prior, whom he had power to place, but not to
displace   During the vacancy of the priory the bishop might present to
the parsonages and churches of the monks, and dispose of their escheats,
wards, and marriages in their manors, but without prejudice to the priory
The convent, when the priory was vacant, did instantly certify the bishop
thereof, and if the bishop was negligent in ordaining a successor, he was to
lose the advantages which by the vacancy might otherwise accrue to him.
The prior had in the precincts of the sanctuary a fair house, and all things
answerable thereunto, and maintained continual hospitality; yet had nothing
proper to himself   The officers of the monastery disposed of all, giving the
prior money for the expences of his chamber only, as appeareth in the registry of the priory (1)

   Boniface, Archbishop of Canterbury, confirmed the following powers to
the priors of this monastery, A D. 1268

   " On the death of the Bishop of Worcester, the prior shall signify the
same to the Archbishop of Canterbury, who shall appoint the prior to execute all things appertaining to the bishopric, during the vacancy "   The
first instance which occurs of the exercise of this delegated authority, was
on the death of Godfrey de Giffard, Bishop of Worcester, by John de la
Wyke, the then prior, as commissary or official of the Archbishop of Canterbury   It appears from the various transactions of this monastery that
the powers of the priory, as the chapter of the bishop, were very extensive
and important (2)

   The Obedientiaries, or the principal officers of the church and monastery
under the prior, were these: the sub-prior, sacrist, cellarer, chamberlain, hospitalarius, almoner, pittancer, coquinarius, infirmarius, præcentor, master of
the chapel, and tumbarius.

   The sub, or Vice-prior was principal assistant to the lord-prior when he
was present, and acted in his stead when absent.   He was also master and
keeper of the frectory (3)

   The Cellarer's was a place of great trust, he had charge of all the grana-
ries, storehouses, and cellars of the monastery; and delivered out meal to
the bakehouse, salted provisions (4) to the kitchen, cheese and liquors to

(1) Abingdon' MS p 42   (2) Ibid p 45, 46, ex Registry of Worcester Priory, sede vacante
(3) see Durham Abbey   (4) The monastic rule required a total abstinence from flesh, ex
cept in case of great decay, when a physician might direct the use of it   But as wealth increased, the

the refectory, hay to the stables, and fuel to the hearths.   This officer must of necessity have many servants under him.

The Camerarius, or chamberlain, was overseer of the dormitory, and had the care of providing for it beds, towels, &c. and shoes and habits for the monks.   He was also to provide for the accommodation of strangers while they lodged in the monastery

The Hospitalarius, or hostler, presided in the guest-hall, entertained and attended on strangers, and was obliged to see that they wanted no suitable accommodation.

The Almoner had the distribution of the loaves and other alms to the poor.

The Pittancer was entrusted with the *pietantiæ*, which were extraordinary allowances of more generous aliment on certain holidays ; as, the seven great festivals, and the anniversaries of founders and principal benefactors. In academical language, he was the furnisher of the gaudies : the stores of the cellarer being spared on those days, as liable to no demands but for stated and regular commons. (1)   The live cattle kept by the convent were under the pittancer's care.

The Coquinarius, or kitchener : Mr. Tanner, in his preface to Bishop Tanner's Notitia, confesses ignorance of the nature of this office ; but it is very clear from the records of Evesham abbey, (2) that he was the market-man, who bought fresh provisions, fish, &c. for the convent.   The hiring of cooks, and the whole government of the kitchen might belong to this officer

The Infirmarius superintended the infirmary, had the care of the sick monks when carried thither, provided them physic and all necessaries while living, and washed and dressed their bodies for burial when dead. (3)

The four other officers had the care of the church and its service allotted to them.   On the sacrist it was incumbent to provide incense, and wax-candles, (4)   and the furniture of the high altar, vestments, &c. to super-

rigour of the rule was relaxed   and prelates were empowered to dispense with the eating of flesh   [See Ann W·g A D 1300   See also an instance of this indulgence granted by a parochial priest of the parish of St Martin, in this city, in the Appendix, No XXXV p cxxxiii]

(1) Steven's Mon Append p 131, 132.   (2) Ibid. p 131   (3) Tanner's Pref

(4) The company of wax chandlers was in a flourishing state during the time of the Romish church ; gratitude to saints called frequently for lights   Candlemas wasted its thousands, and those all blessed by the priests, and adjured in solemn terms   "I adjure thee, O waxen creature, that thou repel the devil and his sprights " [Rev Mr. Brand's edit of Bourne's Antiquitates Vulgares, p 222 Pens. Lond. 2 ed p 414]

R

intend the fabric of the church, and receive oblations and legacies for its repair ; to keep the consecrated vessels, administer baptism, and bury the dead. The sacrist was chosen by the bishop, as appears in the prior's registry, *sede vacante :* and to him were committed by the bishop the keys and custody of the cathedral. (1)

Of the Tumbary I can only collect what the name imports, that he had the care of the tombs   Probably, he received and accounted for the offerings made at the sepulchres of St. Oswald and St Wulstan. (2)   The bishop had the right of appointing these two officers, the sacrist and the tumbary.

To the Præcentor, or chanter, belonged the direction of the choral service, the providing of missals and anthem-books, and the repair of the organs he was also the librarian and registrar of the convent ; penned warrants and letters for the chapter ; and had custody of their seal, and the oversight of the Scriptorium, which was the room wherein the novices, or younger monks, were employed in copying books (3)   The novices studied in the cloisters, and when properly qualified were sent to the universities

The salary of this officer prior to the year 1314, was only 40s. per annum. In that year Bishop Maydenstone appropriated the church of Tyberton for the augmentation of his income (4)

Of the Magister Capellæ I can speak but conjecturally : I suppose he presided over the priests of St Mary's chapel, as well as over the service of the chapel of the infirmary, to which his lodgings were contiguous.

To these several offices, possessed by the monks, belonged manors and lands, which they could neither alienate or dispose of to their own use (for they were capable of none), but to the benefit of the convent at large   The monks, therefore, who possessed those offices, held the courts of their several lordships, accompanied with a steward, and an esquire of the priory, stiled Armiger, appointed, I think, to defend the unarmed religious.   They had horses, and every one a garçon on foot to attend them   Every one of

(1) Abingdon's MS p 42   (2) Dr Thomas's Account, p 65 Append p 161

(3) The Scriptorium at Worcester was part of the cloister, the windows of which were glazed, for protecting the desks of the writers from the weather   There is a very fine MS Bible in folio, written in the cloister of Worcester monastery, now in the library of Benet college, Cambridge, it stands at present at No 48 in that valuable collection   A note at the beginning of it is published at length in Nasmith's Catalogue, page 31, intimating that the writer lived in the reign of Henry II his name *Senatus*.   The MS is on vellum, and written with uncommon clearness and beauty of penmanship

(4) Dr Thomas, p 161

those esquires had his diet, and a robe furred, of six ells of good cloth, the whole value 20s. (1) livery of hay and provender for his horse, and a chamber. In regard whereof he was sworn, if it pleased the prior, to perform his diligent and faithful service in the office of an esquire. Divers had in this priory *largitions*, which I may call *largesses*, and corodies; and of those, some had them in regard of monies given to the monastery, for a provision of maintenance in diet and lodging for themselves, and, if their estate required it, for their servants and horses during life. Those were such as the king, out of his royal prerogative, did sometimes challenge, to give to his followers, without any consideration paid. Sir John Beauchamp of Holt, Knight, had one of them, which he, rising after to great honour and authority, requited with true charity to the religious of this monastery. (2)

THE SANCTUARY.

The church of Worcester was among those that enjoyed the privilege of sanctuary in its fullest plenitude Its institution is of very ancient origin, and its confirmation, where once permitted, has been uniformly conceded by successive kings, both before and since the Conquest. The refugees were admitted in various manners in different places. They were to confess the crime or cause of their seeking sanctuary; which, with their names, were registered (3) At Durham the refugee knocked at the door of the Galilee of the cathedral, and was let in even at any hour of the night: the tolling of the Galilee bell announced that some one had taken sanctuary. He was then dressed in a black gown, with the yellow cross of St. Cuthbert on the left shoulder; and being totally disarmed, was lodged within the church. (4)

The ancient grant of sanctuary in the church of Worcester was confirmed by charter, by Henry IV. A D. 1400, in the second year of his reign; by which it was ordained, that " no bailiffs, serjeants, minister, or other person " of the city of Worcester, shall hereafter carry or bear any mace or maces, " but only in the presence of the king or his children, within the church- " yard, priory, and sanctuary of Worcester, nor intermeddle within the

(1) See the Register of the Priory.   (2) Abingdon's MS. p. 44   (3) Stowe's Survey, I p 607 Lord Bacon's Hist Hen. VII p 104, as cited by the Rev Mr Pegge, in his Hist of the Asylum, or Sanctuary, in Archæologia, vol. VIII. Art. I.   (4) Sanderson's Antiq of Durham Abbey, P 43 Stowe, ibidem Pegge, in Archæologia, vol VIII

" aforesaid liberties." This grant was also confirmed by King Henry VI. in the thirty-seventh year of his reign, to John, (Carpenter) Bishop of Worcester, and Thomas, (Musard) Prior, with this farther privilege: " that " no sheriff, escheator, coroner, constable, &c. shall arrest any man for any " cause whatsoever, (treason against the king's person only excepted) within " the churchyard and precincts of the monastery." (1)

The limits of the sanctuary begin from the great door of the north entrance of the cathedral, near to the carnarie, otherwise called the charnel house, by a great stone wall of the palace unto the great gate thereof, and from thence to the house of John Smith, called John Smith's house, dividing the churchyard, or sanctuary, from the king's highway, called the Leech street of the said churchyard of Worcester, and including all the buildings from the great gate aforesaid, even in and unto Smith's house, being itself situate on the King's street; and from the same house to the angle called Stodesmorisknoll, by dividing that street called Sudbury from the sanctuary, and inclosing all the houses near the king's said highway, from the house of the said John Smith, even to the angle aforesaid, excepting three houses in the parish of St Peter of our city; and from Stodesmorisknoll to the great gate of the priory, dividing the king's highway, called Stodesmorisknoll, from the churchyard, and including all the buildings from the said angle even to the gate of the priory, and from the priory gate by the Ymbrie, otherwise a channel near the walls of the gardens of the prior, unto the great stone wall seated near Severn; and by the said wall, including all buildings, gardens, &c within the said channel, towards the cathedral church, and extendeth itself by the said stone wall situate on the Severn, unto another stone wall reaching from Severn to the chapel of the charnel house, including it, and from the charnel house to the door of the church, dividing the palace from the churchyard.

Dated at the Bishop of Worcester's house, without the New Temple-bar, London, 20 May, A. D. 1640 (2) In the prelacy of Carpenter.

Sanctuaries and their privileges were suppressed by statute 1 James I. c. 25 sect 34.

The renouncing of worldly possessions was a first principle in the institute, and a prime engagement in the vow of monks. But when they had

_____

(1) Abingdon's MS. p. 46, 47   (2) Ibid p. 46, extracted from the Ledger of Rectories and Impropriations

SALISBURY CATHEDRAL

Nave

thrust themselves into the richest establishments of the secular clergy, they knew how to distinguish between dominion and stewardship, fruition and agency, the possessing of baronies for themselves, and the possessing them for God and the church. This distinction would not always pass upon the world; especially, as they lived too much like barons.

When the pope's supremacy in England was once annulled, Henry VIII. met with little opposition to his grand design of suppressing the monasteries. All the greater ones were wrought upon to make him a voluntary surrender of all their possessions and privileges The priory of Worcester was dissolved Jan. 18, A D 1540, (31 Hen VIII.) by the surrender of Holbech the prior, and his monks, to whom pensions were allotted for life; but those pensions to be withdrawn whenever they should accept of preferment The income of this monastery was then valued at £ 1386. 12s 10$\frac{3}{4}$d. per annum; but was reported to be only £ 1290. 10s. 6$\frac{3}{4}$d. clear rent (1) no very profuse provision, even as money then went, for the maintenance of fifty monks and their prior, and the keeping a constant table for strangers (2) But there were reasons for setting down the valuation of each religious house extremely low It is certain, that among all the great monasteries there were but fourteen which had a more ample endowment than this of Worcester.

The suppressing of forty of the smaller monasteries in England by Cardinal Wolsey, under the licence of Pope Clement VII. in 1525, intending on their spoils to erect two colleges, one where he was born, in Ipswich, the other where he was bred, in Oxford, was thought ominous with regard to what followed, by their being wholly suppressed by the king " In a " word," says my author, " this dissolution of forty small houses by the " cardinal, made all the forest of religious foundations in England to shake, " justly fearing the king would finish to fell the oaks, seeing the cardinal " began to cut the underwood " (3)

It is allowed that Henry VIII was friendly to learning. nor was it til

(1) Bishop Tanner —The temporal and spiritual possessions of the monastery or priory of the cathedral church of Worcester, as returned by the commissioners, amounted to the clear annual sum of £ 1299 12s 8$\frac{1}{2}$d [Bacon's Liber Regis, p 963]

(2) How very expensive this article of hospitality was, from the continual resort of strangers to Worcester, or passage of travellers through it, may be understood from the complaint of the monastery in the time of king Edward II [See Dr Thomas's Account, p 160] A clear revenue of £ 1290 at that time of the dissolution, was equivalent to an income of about £ 4500 in the present age

(3) Fuller's Church Hist Sect III b vi

the two succeeding reigns, that the barbarous inroads on the provinces of science and literature were made to any ruinous degree It was enough for Henry to have rooted up the power the church was ever inclined to exercise, under papal direction, against his regal will for the notorious frauds committed on the property found in the suppressed monasteries, not only in the embezzlement of the contents of their treasuries, the ornaments of their altars, shrines, &c. (1) but often in their lands and inheritances, which were neither restored to them on their refoundation, nor accounted for to government, fully evinced, that had he formed ideas of merely filling his coffers with their riches, the amount of their aggregate value fell infinitely short of gratifying his avarice, if that were the motive for acting as he did . on the contrary, the deficit excited not the chagrin of disappointment in him, from its being so much below the estimated value of the property. His grand desideratum was achieved · he had laid the hierarchy and its powers at his feet, humbled in its pride, and shorn of the splendour of its beams.

Bale, a notorious and professed reformer, laments the injuries sustained by literature during this violent conflict, and more especially deplores the ruins of the labours of Leland, who by the command of Henry VIII had bestowed six years research into the libraries of the English monasteries, and collected an immense treasure of national history and antiquities, with an intent to publish it under the royal sanction (2)

By an order of council, A D. 1550, the king's library at Westminster was purged of its missals, legends, &c. and the garniture of the books, being either of gold or silver, was taken away. Baliol, Exeter, Queen's, and Lincoln colleges, Oxford, together with the public library, which last had been chiefly formed of the books given to it by Angerville, Bishop of Durham, Cobham, Bishop of Worcester, and Humphry, the good Duke of Gloucester, were all stripped of the labours of the schoolmen, and their books devoted to the flames. This barbarous inquisition upon science and learning was deridingly called by some of the young members of the university, " Sco-" tus's funeral " (3)

The destructive force of this storm of religious reformation did not wholly subside till the time of Elizabeth, who found it expedient to grant farther powers to the commissioners for their regal visitation, by which images, pictures, crucifixes, and other external appendages of church worship were swept away. It is, however, remarked, that the queen herself could not be persuaded to part with the crucifix and lighted tapers in her own closet. (1)

When the royal fiat had pronounced that the tyranny of pontifical power should cease in England, we trace the operation of that mandate in this church through a regular progression of its effects, to the final closing of that important scene   The consequent removal and destruction of chapels, altars, shrines, tombs, relics, images, crosses, missals, &c. which took place in this cathedral, and in other churches and parts of this city, have in part already been noticed under their respective heads and dates   Bishop Blandford's Manuscript furnishes the following detail in addition, which appears to complete the eventful history of the overthrow of the ancient church discipline on the monkish system at Worcester, carried down to the time of the full adoption of the ritual of the reformed church of England, as by law established

" In January, A D 1539, the monks of this church put on secular habits, and the priory surrendered.

" A D. 1547 On candlemas day, no candles were hallowed, or borne. On Ash Wednesday no ashes hallowed

" A D 1548 March 25th, being Palm Sunday, no palms hallowed, nor cross borne on Easter eve; no fire hallowed, but the paschal taper, and the font On Easter day the pix, with the sacrament in it, was taken out of the sepulchre, they singing " Christ is risen," without procession. On Good Friday, no creeping to the cross.

" Also on the 20th October was taken away the cup with the body of X^t from the high altar of St. Mary's church, (i. e. the cathedral) and in other churches and chapels

" A D 1549 No sepulchre, or service of sepulchre, on Good Friday. On Easter even no paschal hallowed, nor fire, nor incense, nor font On the 23d April, this year, was mass, matins, even-song, and all other service

---

(1) Collier's Eccles Hist vol II p 434, 435   Cecil's Memoirs   See also Tanner's Notitia Mon. fol pref p 41   Wharton's Spenser, 8vo vol II p 247   Gunton's Peterborough, p 173, in which abbey we are told there were no less than 1700 manuscripts destroyed or dispersed in that ruinous outrage on science

in English. All books of divine service were brought to the bishop, viz. mass-books, graduals, pies port, and legends, and were burned.

" A D. 1551. In all the time of Bishop Hooper were no children confirmed.

" A D. 1559 Midsummer service altered "

At this point the boundary of papal dominion over the church of Worcester appears to have been fixed It was here all its powers were suspended, and its influence totally overthrown It was now the hallowed fires of its delusive religion were extinguished, the sweet scented odours of its incense evaporated, and the glories of its splendid altars faded away · it was now that the solemnity of its processions and pageants closed, the voice of its tide and even-songs died away, and all the functions of its vast and ponderous machinery ceasing their movements together, presented to the world an awful example of the mutability of power, in which even that, whose foundation was thought to have been laid on a rock deemed impregnable, and held sacred from the supposed divinity of its origin, disappeared like a vapour from before men's eyes ; and its customs and ceremonies, whose observance was the familiar duty of our forefathers, in the present times become obsolete, a bye-word, and almost wholly unknown among us. (1)

(1) The monastery of Worcester was of the Benedictine order St Benet, patriarch of the monks in the west, and founder of this order, was the son of a Roman senator, born at Nursia in the dukedom of Spoleto, in Italy, in the year 480, he founded twelve monasteries himself, which were endowed by the benevolences of the Roman nobility, the chief of these was that of Mont Cassin, where he pulled down an old temple of Apollo, and erected a monastery on its ruins, desiring to establish in the west the same manner of living which St Basil had begun in the east • This order is said by many to have been brought into England by St Augustine, A D 596, but others think it was little known before King Edgar's time, when St Dunstan and St Oswald (the latter of whom had been a Benedictine monk at Fleury) not only favoured the monks against the secular clergy, but also so much advanced the Benedictines, that William of Malmsbury saith, " This order took its rise in England from St Oswald." Of this order were all our cathedral priories, except Carlisle, and most of the richest abbies in England The revenues of the Benedictines are said to have been nearly equal to those of all the other religious orders in Britain †

• Emillianne's Hist Monast Orders, ch 8 p 67

† Reyner, vol I p 217.—Tanner's Notitia Monastica —Batteley's Additions to Somner's Canterbury, p 133.—Grose in Pref to his Antiquities, p 35, 36 An abstract of some of the Benedictine rules, which the founder divided into seventy-three chapters or canons, and which, indeed, were mostly followed by later fraternities, is given in the Appendix, No XXXV p cxxxii, as it will serve to shew in what manner the ancient members, possessors of this church, either were, or ought to have been employed in it

SECT. V.

OF THE ESTABLISHMENT MADE BY KING HENRY VIII.

HENRY VIII having driven the monks out of the cathedrals, placed in their stead secular canons; those whom he thus regulated are called the deans and chapters of the new foundation, viz Canterbury, Winchester, Worcester, Ely, Carlisle, Durham, Rochester, Norwich; and besides these, he erected five cathedrals *de novo*, and endowed them out of the estates of dissolved monasteries; viz. Chester, Peterborough, Oxford, Gloucester, (1) and Bristol, (2) which he made episcopal sees.

The greatest part of the ancient manors and revenues of the priory of Worcester, were granted again to the church by King Henry VIII (3) whose foundation charter bears date, Jan. 24, 1541-2, in the 33d year of his reign, for the endowment of a dean, ten prebendaries, ten minor canons,

(1) The charter of erection of the see of Gloucester, which was taken out of that of Worcester, bears date, Sept 3d, 1541 [See Rymer's Fœdera, vol XIV p 724] The charter of its endowment, and the founder's statutes, are given at large in Sir Rob Atkyns's Hist of Gloucestershire

(2) In 1542 the king appointed a Bishop of Bristol, part of whose diocese, namely the deanry of Bristol, likewise belonged to the see of Worcester [Lib Regis p 20]

(3) The diocese of Worcester at present contains almost the whole of the county, except the following parishes, and eight chapelries, which are in the diocese of Hereford Abberley, Brockleton, Bayton, Clifton, and Lower Sapy, Edwin Loch, Eastham, with the two Hanleys, and Orlton, Kyre, Lindridge, with Knighton and Pensax, Mamble, Ribbesford, with Bewdly, Rock, with Hightington, Stanford, Sheldesley, Stocton, Tenbury, these are in the deanry of Burford, and archdeaconry of Salop The diocese of Worcester also contains about a third part of Warwickshire, the parishes of Brome and Clent in Staffordshire, and Halesowen in Shropshire It is divided into nine deanries, in which are contained 116 rectories, besides St Nicholas in Droitwich, now united with St Andrew's, 79 vicarages, 26 curacies, and 41 chapels, viz

In the deanry of	Rectories	Vicarages	Curacies	Chapels.
Worcester	25	8	2	6
Pershose	25	12	7	10
Kidderminster	10	8	3	2
Witton, or Wich	10	6	0	5
Powick	9	6	4	6
Evesham	1	5	7	0
Blockley	4	1	0	0
Kington	18	17	0	6
Warwick	15	16	3	6 *

* See Dr Nash, in Introd vol I p xxxiii

S

ten lay clerks, ten choristers, two schoolmasters, forty king's scholars, and some inferior attendants or servants of the church (1)

To the dean was allotted nearly the whole of the prior's house ; to the first prebendary, the sacrist's, which was on the north side of the church (2) To the second prebendary was allotted the tumbary's house , to the third, the sub-prior's ; to the fourth, the hospitaller's ; to the fifth, the infirmarian's ; to the sixth, the pittancer's, and part of the cellarer's ; to the seventh, the kitchener's ; to the eighth and ninth, the house of magister capellæ, and the site of the infirmary and its chapel , to the tenth, the almoner's, and a part of the prior's house, on the site of which Dr. Byrch, about fifty years since, erected a new one, which is considered the best of the prebendal residences.

The members of this church at present are, the Bishop, Dean, Archdeacon ; ten major canons or prebendaries, of whom three are annually elected to the offices of sub-dean, receiver, and treasurer ; eight minor canons, originally ten, in the number of which are the chanter, and sacrist, a head schoolmaster, and under schoolmaster ; two of the minor canonries, and likewise the offices of diaconus and sub-diaconus, or epistler and gospeller, have long been suppressed ; one organist ; eight lay clerks, or singing men; ten choristers, who are usually scholars on the royal foundation ; forty king's scholars, ten of whom are nominated to the school by the dean, and three by each prebendary ; two virgers (formerly four) ; two sub-sacrists, or sextons , two butlers ; one caterer, or manciple , one cook ; two porters ; ten beadsmen, or eleemosynarii, i e almsmen (3) The Bishop of Worcester is, by the founder's statutes, visitor of this collegiate body

When the constitution of this conventual church was thus changed, and a dean and prebendaries placed in it, a body of statutes was drawn up for its government, the substance of which, *mutatis mutandis*, may be found at full in the Antiquities of the Cathedral of Rochester, octavo, 1717 : that the

---

(1) Bacon's Liber Regis p 962, 963   (2) That house was taken down in the present century , the site of it is now inclosed within the wall on the north side of the cathedral, between the ends of the two cross iles, and a garden is formed upon it   The first prebendal house is to the east of the college green, where the organist's house formerly stood, and was erected about the year 1713

(3) Almsmen, in the great monasteries, were such paupers as were ordered to attend daily at the gate, to receive the charity loaves, and the offals of the refectory   Beode, in the Saxon, signified table , from which their name of beadsmen seems to be derived (implying, men that were fed from the table) , or, as others suppose, from the string of beads they usually bore in their hands, at the door of the choir, during divine service   The beadsmen of the present establishment, instead of alms, have a settled pension.

statutes for this church were not so attentively revised and corrected as was requisite, and that they stood in need of being rendered, in some instances, more decided, and in others less ambiguous, will be gathered from the measures subsequently taken to render them practically useful to the new establishment. On these accounts it will be sufficient to the present purpose simply to give the procemium statutorum, with the heads of the chapters, which are as follow, viz. *(1)*

(1) Statuta ecclesiæ cathedralis Wigorniensis edita per serenissimum ac potentissimum Princip. Henricum Octavum, Angliæ, Franciæ, et Hiberniæ Regem, fidei defensor, et in terra Anglicanæ et Hiberniæ ecclesiæ supremum caput, ejusdem ecclesiæ Wigorniensis fundatorem •

Henricus Octavus, Dei gratiâ Angliæ, Franciæ, et Hiberniæ Rex, fidei defensor, ac in terra ecclesiæ Anglicanæ et Hiberniæ supremum caput, universis sanctæ matris ecclesiæ filiis, ad quorum notitiam præsens scriptum pervenerit, salutem.

Cum nobis, et regni proceribus nostri universoq, senatui (quem parliamentum vocamus) visum sit (Deo ut confidimus nos huc movente) monasteria quæ passim in regno nostro extabant, tum propter graves ac multiplices illorum enormitates, tum ob alias justas rationabilesq, causas supprimere, abolere, et in meliores usus convertere—nos, et divinæ voluntati conformius, et maxime in rem Christianum esse ducentes, ut ubi ignorantia et superstitio regnabant, ibi sincerus Dei cultus vigeat, et sanctum Christi Evangelium assiduè et purè annuncietur, et præterea ut ad Christianæ fidei et pietatis incrementum, juventus regni nostri in bonis literis instituatur et pauperes perpetuò sustententur, in ipsorum monasteriorum loco ecclesias ereximus et constituimus, quarum alias cathedrales, alias collegiatas, vocari volumus, pro quarum ecclesiarum gubernatione et regimine leges et statuta quæ sequuntur præscribenda curavimus, quibus tam decani, et utriusq, ordinis canonici, quam cæteri omnes ministri, pueri et pauperes qui in ipsis ecclesiis commoraturi sunt, pareant et obsequantur, ijsq, ut a nobis conditis et perfectis, regantur et gubernentur, id quod si fecerint, ingens sane pietatis incrementum in hoc regno nostro proventurum esse confidimus, et nos expectatione, ac voto nostro, qui ad Dei optimi maximi gloriam, ac fidei Christianæ augmentum eas ecclesias ereximus, varijs ministrorum ordinibus exornavimus, haud quaquam fraudabimur.

Tabula Capitum

Cap		Cap	
1	De numero integro eorum qui in ecclesia cathedrali Wigorniensi sustentantur	5.	De visitatione terrarum.
2	De qualitalibus, electione, et admissione decani.	6.	Dimissio terrarum et tenementorum ad firmam.
3	De juramento decani.	7	De traditione bonorum decano.
4	De officio decani	8	De residentiâ decani.
		9	De obedientiâ decano præstanda.

* In Misc XX 401, 409, Benet college library, Cambridge, the title of the Worcester statutes, is " Statuta ecclesiæ cathedralis Wigorniæ, facta 36 anno regni sereniss. R Henrici 8, et tradita per N. " Wigorn, Georgium Cicestrensis, et Ricardum Cox, Archid Eliensem." The following note is subjoined.——" Manus M^d Pedder, Decani —Architypus horum statutorum ut fertur Cardinali Pole tra- " debatur, per Seth Holland decanum, tempore R Mariæ, nec postea restitutus "

The " Procemium Statutorum" at page 409, runs thus —" Henricus Octavus, Dei grâ Ang Fran et " Hibern Rex, fidei defensor, ac in terra supremum ecclesiæ Anglican et Hibern. caput, universis " sanctæ matris eccles. filius, &c "

S 2

SECT. VI.

A SURVEY OF THE CATHEDRAL SUBSEQUENT TO THE REFORMATION.

It is unnecessary here to retrace the accounts of the particular portions and offices of this cathedral, as they were anciently arranged, they having already been fully stated and described in the fourth Section, and regularly

Cap.

10 De qualitatibus, electione et admissione canonicorum

11 De juramento canonicorum

12 De residentia canonicorum

13 De concionibus in ecclesiâ nostrâ habendis

14. De mensa canonicorum *

15. De stipendio decani, et canonicorum

16. De electione officiariorum, et electionis tempore.

17 De officio vice decani

18 De officio receptoris

19 De officio Thesaurarij

20 De qualitate, electione, et admissione minorum
canonicorum et clericorum

21 De juramento ministrorum

22 De residentia ministrorum

23 De præcentore, et ejus officio.

24 De sacristâ, et subsacristis, et virgiferis

25. De choristis et ipsorum numero et magistro

Cap

26 De pueris grammaticis et eorum informato-
ribus

27 De pauperibus et eorum officio

28 De inferioribus ecclesiæ ministris

29 De communi mensâ omnium ministrorum *

30 De vestibus ministrorum quæ liberaturas vo-
cant

31 De stipendiis ministrorum in ecclesiâ nostrâ †

32 De celebratione divinorum

33 De communi ærario, de custodiâ sigilli et
munimentorum

34 De ratione seu computo quotannis reddendo

35 De corrigendis excessibus

36 De eleemosynis et studentibus in academijs

37 De capitulis celebrandis ‡

38 De visitatione ecclesia

39 De precibus in ecclesia dicendis

40 De scholâ et classibus ac ordine in ea obser-
vandi.

* The commons table of this church was dissolved by petition of those who partook of it, about the year 1560, or 1561, see a MS in answer to certain articles exhibited by the queen's high commissioners for causes ecclesiastical, in which Roger Folyott, chapter-clerk in 1587, on behalf of the prebendaries of the church of Worcester, against whom charges were exhibited, declares that the crosses, chalices, censers, candlesticks, paxes, and other ornaments of the church, all of silver and gilt, also copes vestments, hangings and curtains for altars of divers sorts, of which plate, part thereof made a silver pot and cups for the communion table, and other plate, as salts, and cups of silver and gilt for Mr Dean, and common hospitality, and the copes and vestments, and other ornaments of the church, some made coverings for the communion table, some cushions for the choir and church   [Return of the Report of the commissioners, from a MS in the evidence room, Worcester Cath]

† This chapter, as matter of some curiosity, is given at large   ‡ The chapters or statutes in the MS at Benet college, are regularly numbered to the 37th, which, with four others not numbered, are entitled— De capitulis celebrandis ——De visitatione ecclesiæ ——Preces in schola mane dicenda ——
" Preces in schola vespere dicenda——Preces pauperum " Then follows the—" Confirmatio statuto-
" rum " [For the endowment of the church of Worcester, see Appendix to this section, No VII p.
xvi, and the alienation of lands from the chapter, p xxii.

classed under the respective epochas of their construction. What, therefore, yet remains to be noticed under this head, is the principal alterations and improvements that have taken place subsequent to the grand Reform, and which will necessarily comprize the history of this church under the Protestant establishment, from that period down to the present time.

De Stipendiis Ministrorum in Ecclesiâ nostrâ —Cap 31

Statuimus et volumus ut ex bonis communibus nostræ ecclesiæ, præter communias, et liberatus superius assignatas solvantur stipendia omnibus ministris ecclesiæ nostræ per manus Thesaurarii singulis anni terminis per æquales portiones ad hunc qui sequitur modum, videlicet

	£	s.	d		£	s.	d
Singulis minoribus canonicis pro portione suâ	5	2	0	Obsonatori	1	18	0
				Coquo	1	18	0
Superiori informatori grammaticæ	15	2	0	Cuilibet ex choristis	0	15	0
Magistro choristarum	11	13	0	Singulis pueris grammaticis	0	1	8
Inferiori informatori grammaticæ	6	5	10	Singulis decem pauperum	4	10	0
Diacono	4	5	10	Sub-coquo	1	10	0
Subdiacono	4	5	10	Vice-decano	2	13	4
Singulis clericis	2	19	2	Preceptori	5	0	0
Cuilibet ex virgiferis	3	0	0	Thesaurario	2	14	4
Cuilibet ex subsacristis	2	18	0	Præcentori	2	0	0
Cuilibet ex pincernis	1	18	0	Sacristæ	2	0	0
Uni janitorum qui et barbæ tonsor erit	2	18	0	Senescallo, seu clerico terrarum	3	6	8
Alteri ex janitoribus	1	18	0	Auditori *	4	0	0

De horum Statutorum firmit ite et robore

Volumus et per præsentes concedimus Decano et Capitulo dictæ ecclesiæ cathedralis Christi, et beatæ Mariæ Virginis Wigorniensis, et successoribus suis quod decanus ecclesiæ cathedralis illius pro tempore existens, omnes et singulos ejusdem ecclesiæ cathedralis inferiores officiarios et ministros et alias præ-

---

* In the British museum, vol 856, MS "Letters and Warrants of King Charles the Second" Art 112, is the following letter

"To the Deane of Worcester, about the Vicars choral.

"Trusty and well beloved, wee greete you well Our princely care that moved us to make provision for vicars rural, carrieth us on also to advance piety by providing for vicars choiall, that dayly attend God's service in cathedralls Now that these having decent maintevnance may bee both obliged to singular exemplary regularity of conversacon, and incouraged constantly and reverendly to praise Almighty God for his goodnesse to all, especially for o' miraculous restauration, and to pray for the psperity of o' pson, governm', and kingdoms, it is o' will and pleasure, that you increase the sallary of every quier man to £ 16 or £ 20 per annum, by improveing for theire use the rents or Warton, Thornton, or any other rectyries or lands you shall thinke meete And by psueing that worthy psident begun by the now Lord Arch Bishop of Canterbury,† and continued by Dr Potter, yo' former deanes, viz to improve one bushell of wheate, and two of barley upon every coppy hould estate where the old rent s tenn shillings per annum, and so pporsonabley, bee the rent more or lesse, except coppy houlds of inheritance, and in markett townes which have noe land annexed, and out of this improvem' farther

† Dr William Juxon he succeeded to this deanry 1627, and died Archbishop of Canterbury, 1663

The cathedral makes a most venerable appearance ; and though raised to what it is by architects in different ages, has yet sufficient uniformity to please the less searching eye Its general plan is that of the double cross, the most eminent of the architectural distinctions in the construction of our ancient cathedrals ; an advantage which the discernment of Bishop Blois judiciously secured to this church when he added the present nave to the original structure, as built by St. Wulstan Both the delicacy and magnificence of which the Gothic stile of building is susceptible, are here united ‧ The whole from east to west is divided into three iles by two rows of well proportioned columns, sustaining on each side a series of eighteen grand and capacious arches, viz. three in the Lady's chapel, five in the choir,

dictæ ecclesiæ cathedralis Christi et beatæ Mariæ Virginis Wigorniensis quasquncq; personas prout casus seu causa exiget, faciet, constituet, admittet, et acceptabit de tempore in tempus in perpetuum , ac omnes et eorum quemlibet sic admissos, vel admissum, ob causam legitimam non solum corrigere, sed etiam deponere, et ab eadem ecclesiâ cathedrali amovere, et expellere possit, et valeat

Nos Nicholaus Wigorniensis, Georgius Cicestrensis, et Ricardus Cox, archidiaconus Eliensis, metuendissimi Domini nostri Regis Henrici Octavi, Dei gratiâ Angliæ, Franciæ, et Hiberniæ Regis, fidei defensoris, et in terra ecclesiæ Anglicanæ et Hiberniæ supremi capitis, mandato et nomine vobis decano, canonicis cæterisq, ministris omnibus dictæ ecclesiæ Wigorniensis statuta hæc diligenter, et bonâ fidè observanda tradimus, anno ejusdem domini nostri regis tricesimo sexto, et mensis Julii die ultimo

Ubi authoritas statutorum authoritate invictissimi principis piæ memoriæ Henrici Octavi editorum in quæstionem venit, nos Ricardus Morison, Ricardus Tracie, Armigeri, Henricus Siddall, et Robertus Ferrar, sacræ theologiæ et legum respective baccalaurei, illustrissimi in Christo principis et domini nostri Domini Edvardi Sexti, Dei gratiâ Angliæ, Franceæ, et Hiberniæ Regis, fidei defensoris, ac in terris ecclesiæ Anglicanæ et Hiberniæ supremi capitis, commissarii generales ad visitationem suam regiam per dioces Wigorniensem exercendam, pro robore, et valore eorundum pronuntiamus et decernimus, eademq, statuta ab omnibus et singulis istius cathedralis ecclesiæ ministe̅ inviolabiliter̅ observari subpænis in eisdem contentis, permittimus tamen decano, et cuivis alii canonico privilegia, commoditates et emolumenta quæcunq, sufficienti authoritate regia illis, aut illorum cuilibet prius concessa

Concordat cum Decreto   CONSTANTINE, Register.

to augm[t] the quier men's p̅vision according to the division by these former deanes assigned, and for the good of succession wee further requier you strictly to keepe yo[r]selves to the litterall observance of such statutes made by o[r] royall predecessors as enjoyne you to demise leases for the just terme of 21 yeares only, in number and not in value , and that noe coppy hould estate be filled with more than two lives in one coppy of reversion , and for the good repaire and maintainance of the fabric of o[r] cathedrall church, wee order that you imploy the benefitt of all donacions meant for that end only for that use continually, and alsoe that you keepe up the impropriacions demised by the late comitties at the improved rents, and imploy them upon repaire of the cathedrall onely, unlesse you can make it appeare that the p̅sent exigent of the church will bee better satisfied by taking fines of some of them that lastly itt is o[r] pleasure that these o[r] injunctions be registered in the Statute Booke, and observed as statutes And soe wee bid you farewell   Given, &c

" To o[r] trusty and well beloved the Deane and Chapter of Worcester."

and ten in the great cross ile and nave. The middle ile, to a spectator that advances from its west end, exhibits a grand perspective; (1) which must have been more striking before the view of the choir was cut off by the organ at the entrance of it. The vaulted roof of this ile has a light and sprightly appearance, to which perhaps its loftiness contributes, as well as the elegance of the smaller arcades which surmount the greater arches on each side   The curious eye is gratified by the justness and symmetry of the work in this ancient pile; whilst a most pleasing sense of awe is impressed on the minds of more cursory beholders (2)

The ancient stalls in the choir were made in 1397; these remained till 1551, when, with all the choir and the bishop's seat, they were taken down. Five years afterwards, viz. in 1556, the choir was removed from the clock-house, to which it had been transferred, the present stalls were set up in the order in which they stand at this time, a goodly loft to read the gospel, and the whole order of the choir restored. at the same time the upper part of it, from the end of the stalls to the foot of the altar, was inclosed with stone, grated with iron, and two doors on each side. (3)   The stalls extend from beneath the rood loft, where the organ is now placed, to the second pillar on each side of the choir. Those on the south side are terminated by the bishop's throne, and on the north side by the archdeacon's stall. They are in number fifty-two, being twenty-six on each side; of which the bishop's throne takes up two, and on the opposite side the archdeacon has two; which, before the see of Gloucester was taken out of this, were occupied jointly by the Archdeacon of Worcester, and the Archdeacon of Gloucester.

The bishop's throne is a plain, respectable, and characteristic object.   On its top is the type of ecclesiastical jurisdiction, the mitre on a cushion; below which are the emblems of peace, denoted by the olive branch.   The whole, with the stalls, are made of fine Irish oak, with an abundance of carvings interspersed about the seats, pillars, and cornices.   On the north side, and on the cornice of the last stall, in a shield, are displayed armorially the five wounds of Christ, the same device is cut in stone in Bishop Alcock's chapel in Ely cathedral.   In the next stall are the arms of the see of Worcester; corresponding with these on the south side, on another shield,

(1) See the annexed plate,   (2) For the measures of the cathedral, see Appendix, No. XXXVI.
p cxxxv.   (3) Bishop Blandford's MS.

is represented a cross, on each arm of which is hung a scourge ; this, with the foregoing device, are emblematical of the sufferings and crucifixion of Christ. Over the next stall is a coat of arms, probably those of Philip Hawford, at that time dean of Worcester   Above the stalls are two spacious galleries on each side, furnished with seats for ladies Adjoining to the archdeacon's stall, on the north side, are the seats of the civil magistrates of the city, who on particular occasions use this church   This part of our ancient cathedrals was called the Greece, or gradus chori, *i e* the part next beyond the stalls towards the altar, in the centre of which the tomb of King John is placed (1)

The pulpit, which was originally set up near the west end of the nave, against the second pillar from the window on its north side, was removed from thence at the time the reforms were made in this church by Dean Martin and his

(1) Will of Henry VI Acct of King's coll chap Cambridge, p 7 In the notice already taken of the ancient sculptures in the Lady's chapel (sect. IV p 41) the principle and the motives on which those heterogeneous representations were introduced there, have been briefly questioned

The investigation of these matters naturally leads us to inquire into the no less singular, though much more modern, decorations of the seats and stalls of our choirs, about many of which an abundance of carvings of a variety of subjects is found

The seats of the stalls of Henry the Seventh's chapel, Westminster, abound with a great variety of carvings of many subjects, the authorities for which are unknown, and represented for purposes as little to be understood When those stalls were set up, the monkish system was in the zenith of its glory, why is it then that some of those subjects are representations of the excesses and lascivious manners of that order of the religious, and so placed as to become the objects of the derision and contempt of a congregation assembled for so opposite a purpose to that of laughing at their spiritual instructors? But it would be in vain to follow this vulgar, coarse, and indecent train of satire to any other purpose than, after a fruitless search for motives which could eligibly have authorized their introduction into so many of our ancient churches, and about the same period too, to conclude with Dr Stukeley, as far as these examples have gone, and in charity to the conservators of the religion of the times, that most of the subjects are only the licentious inventions of the workmen

It would require more than the erudition of Reeks, who produced that ingenious illustration of the hieroglyphics in the interior of the quadrangle of the cloister of Magdalen college, Oxford, in his " Oedipus Magdalenensis," or that of the late Dr King in his Essay on Allegory, as applied to the fine arts, to connect and form a system that could possibly serve any useful or valuable purpose, in the places in which we find them, and to adduce even the true reason for such an eccentric feature in our churches, might perhaps prove of little moment to their concerns, but in tracing its course through the progress of the arts, it is found that those subjects are the works of Florentine artists, at the head of whom was Torrigiano, the scholar of Michael Angelo, whom Benvenuto Cellini has celebrated for his savage exploit of breaking the nose of his master by a blow which he gave him, an exploit of which he boasted, that although he had not killed (which he intended), he had set his mark upon the first artist in the world. To

successor Dr Waugh, and fixed to the third pillar from the altar, on the north side of the choir. It is of an octagon figure, most elegantly carved in the Gothic mode In the front pannels are the four evangelic hieroglyphics; beneath which, on the dies of the base, are the quarters of the imperial arms of England, with the coat of the see of Worcester These appropriate decorations illustrate the purposes of the structure in the most comprehensive manner; the old and the new law are exemplified and combined to indicate the system of the Christian religion; the imperial insignia denote the source of the temporal government of the church, and the whole referring to the divine power for guidance and protection, is beautifully indicated by the eye of Providence placed over the series of emblems in each compartiment. The new Jerusalem, as described in the Revelations, and represented on the plane of the inside of the pulpit, may be considered as the climax of the whole composition, in as much as it is the object to which all our views should be directed.

The top is a well designed canopy, the festooned drapery of which, with its embroidery, is formed and suspended at the several angles by a hand emerging from beneath, and is surmounted by a folding riband running round it. The ascent to the pulpit is by a flight of stone steps arising from the north ile, the supports of which are enriched with sculptured embellishments corresponding with its other ornamented parts; the whole of this very elegant structure is executed in stone, and forms the most chaste example of that species of church furniture any where to be found.

The altar screen is an object no otherwise noticeable as a part of the garniture of the cathedral than that, like others hastily set up to cover the outrage committed on the ancient altar, and to be as much dissimilar to them, or

this Torrigiano (who fled hither to avoid punishment for the outrage) and his followers it appears that we owe those marks of irreverent impertinences that still disfigure some of the otherwise most venerable churches in the kingdom Henry the Seventh's chapel at Westminster, and St. George's chapel at Windsor, are, in that line of embellishment, the work of his prolific genius Partial reform has, indeed, in a late instance or two, begun to correct the atrocities of this evil, not with the violence of a destroyer, nor the rage of fanaticism, but with a moderation and temper, aided by judicious discrimination, from which the inoffensive has nothing to dread, and the guilty alone receives the stroke of distributive justice.

It is a satisfaction to find, upon a close examination of the carvings in the choir of this cathedral, that if some of the subjects are not altogether strictly applicable to their situations, they are none of them offensive or disgusting, many of them are instructive, others entertaining, and mostly very curious. •

• See Appendix, No XXXVIII. p cxxxvii, cxxxviii.

T

to any other part of the church, as possible, as well in form as in use, it stands distinct in its appearance from every thing that surrounds it, a Greek among Goths. But that appearance will no longer be considered as singular, since we have seen from what cause it has arisen, and that every other of our ancient churches is marked by the same defect   The screen is formed of plain oak, divided into large pannels by a series of Corinthian pilasters (1)

The seats between the east end of the stalls and the altar appear to have been placed there so early as 1623, as may be gathered from a chamber order of the city, dated Nov. 14th, 21 James I. when " It was agreed that every one of the company of xxiij^{ue}, and every one of the xlviii^{ue}, shall pay unto the chamberlaines that were for the last yeare for and towards making of the newe seats in the cathedrall church, the sum of v^s a peece, and that Mr Townclarke shall likewise pay the sum of v^s, and which was paid accordingly." (2)

In the time of Dean Talbot the iron gates at the west end of the choir beneath the organ loft were put up ; his arms, as Bishop of Oxford and Dean of Worcester are painted on their outside, and the date 1701 is inscribed on their inside

The electioneering dispute between Sir John Pakington and Bishop Lloyd and his son, in 1702, produced in its consequences much benefit to the fabric of the cathedral. Before that period it had been much neglected, and fallen to decay in many of its parts ; and the ravages of the grand rebellion were still reproachfully visible about it ; but those storms which had shaken the ecclesiastical foundations of the whole kingdom to the centre, and threatened a general dissolution of the hierarchy, left in its ministers little inclination to care for the structures of their churches, when their revenues were wrested from their hands, and individual ruin was looking them in the face   The funds of this church having been, in consequence of those disastrous and unsettled times, so much deranged, and the fabric itself having

(1) The altar of this cathedral had stood wholly unadorned and plain till 1792, when the late honourable and reverend the Dean St Andrew St John, and the reverend the Chapter of Worcester did the author the honour to accept a copy of " the Descent from the Cross," of the dimensions of nine feet high, by seven feet wide, painted by Mr Thomas Phillips The original picture, one of the sublimest productions of the pencil, painted by Sir Peter Paul Rubens, formed an altar-piece in the cathedral at Antwerp, but has lately been carried to Paris   in its removal it is said to have been much damaged.

(2) See Chamber Orders from 1602 to 1650

sustained more than a common share of this brutal violence, it may well be imagined it stood much in need of reparation. It is of little moment in this place to be assured whether the motive that suggested the necessity of its repair originated in the pique the baronet might have had against the bishop and the chapter, or from a real regard to the safety and preservation of the structure ; or lastly, whether it arose from a resolution of the chapter itself to effect it · this general derangement was represented to government, and its repair was soon afterwards entered upon. Substantial repair was what was now necessary ; and this appears to have included the providing the stone-work that fills the space between the two pillars at the north side of the altar, over the tomb of Bishop Bullingham , the inclosing of the Bishop's and Dean's chapels, with the modern arches above the latter, for the better security of the superstructure of that part of the church , the taking down the sacrist's lodgings, near the west end of the north ile of the choir, and closing the Saxon arch before which Bishop Hough's monument now stands: to these may also be added the paving of the choir, the glazing of many of the windows, the white-washing the greater part of the church, and the erecting of the first prebendal house, at the east end of the college green

Under this date also, I conjecture, we may place the raising of that handsome set of spires so ornamental to the external appearance of the cathedral, and which distinguishes it from every other in Europe : these arise in series, two from the angles of the middle ile at the east end, and four from those at the west end, denoting the extremities of the principal and collateral iles ; and two at each angle of the north and south ends of the two transverse or cross iles. These spires are of a subordinate but well adjusted proportion of altitude to the tower, and of a uniform dimension of height and diameter respecting each other, excepting those at the extreme angles of the west end, which are not so high, having a relative proportion to the elevation of the side iles of the nave, to which they are attached In support of the opinion that these spires were raised at this time, it is observable that in the print of the cathedral as given in the Monasticon, and in another or two which I have seen, anterior to the present century, the angles of those parts now occupied by them were terminated by short pinnacles rising on the parapet of the church The expenditure upon these operations, which were begun in 1712, and were three years in completing, amounted to upwards of £ 7000.

T 2

The most considerable reform and repair this church has received since that time was commenced about the year 1748, and completed in 1756 in the course of that period the north end of the great cross ile of the nave was rebuilt, with its window and spires, (1) by the ingenious Mr. Wilkinson, who had just then raised that beautiful ornament to the city, and monument of his own abilities, the spire of St Andrew's church   The stone pulpit was removed from the nave and placed in the choir, which, with its side iles, was then newly paved.   The present floor of the choir has been laid over the old one, which lies about eight inches beneath   it is a party-coloured pavement, blue and white.   In the floors of the side iles, gravestones, that had been removed from the nave and the great cross ile, have been laid by their walls (2)

The steps ascending to these iles, and to the choir at the west end from the great cross ile, and those leading from their east end into the Lady's chapel, together with the iron gates that inclose them, were formed and set up at the same time ; also the passage round the west end of the cathedral, leading on the left into the cloisters, and on the right into what is called the Dark alley, in a direction towards the Water-gate, was laid open, by which improvement the indecent annoyance of passengers conveying every kind of burthen through the principal north entrance, across the nave of the cathedral to the cloisters, even during the time of divine service, was properly and effectually removed, and a ready communication with the residences south of the church was provided, to the great convenience and accommodation of the inhabitants (3)

The old floor of the great cross ile, and of the nave and its side iles, were taken up, together with all the sepulchral stones, and several monuments and tombs, and in its stead was laid the present white stone floor, which has rendered that part of the church eminently beautiful ; and since which time no graves are suffered to be made in it (4)

The consistory court formerly occupying the west end of the south ile of

---

(1) See Appendix to Sect VII No VIII p xxii   (2) See a further account of them, No VIII p xxvi, xxvii, in Appendix   (3) In 1751, June 21st, a fire broke out in one of the rooms near the vestry, called Oliver Cromwell's Chambers, which burnt part of two large beams, and melted a great quantity of lead , but by timely assistance it was put out before it had reached the library, which is contiguous to that part of the building   [See Worcester Journal, No 2188]

(4) For an account of the gravestones, monuments, and tombs taken away and displaced on occasion of this reform , see Appendix, No 1 III. p xxxi—xxxiii

the nave was removed, and their sittings are now held in the east end of the same ile in the Lady's chapel.

There was anciently in the churchyard, a lofty stone cross. At this place the sermons were wont to be delivered in the open air   On the south side of it, near the church walls, there were seats for the accommodation of the principal citizens   On its demolition in the civil wars, it was, with the sacrist's lodgings, converted into the first prebendal house   After which the place for sermons was within doors, at the bottom of the cathedral, and was continued there till the new floor of the nave was laid. A stone bench, set under the great west window, and covered with fine blue arras cloth, was appropriated to the chief citizens   The bishop's chair was placed under the second lowermost pillar on the south side ; the pulpit stood beneath the opposite corresponding pillar   Near the bishop's chair were the seats of the dean and prebendaries, on a stone bench, covered also with blue arras cloth; on which was wrought a design of Robert Alchurch, sub-prior of, and a considerable benefactor to, this church. Near these, under the third arch on the south side, was an organ, long since removed from the church.

The font was erected soon after this time, in the centre of Jesus' chapel, which had been newly laid open to the nave   Its form is that of a term, elevated on a double plinth, making an ascent to it of two steps. Its situation is nearly parallel with the ancient baptistry   The whole is of marble, and from its elegant simplicity, is very ornamental to the station in which it is placed. (1)

The cloisters received an entire new series of window frames of stone about 1762 ; the old ones, which were ruinated in the civil wars, had formerly been enriched with arms and inscriptions painted on their glass, of which some notice has already been taken. No glazing has hitherto been put up in the new window frames

The whole of these very essential and evident improvements were effected during the decanal administrations of Dr. Edmund Martin, and his successor, Dr John Waugh

To the care and attention of the succeeding deans this church owes much of its present truly respectable and venerable appearance, in having restored those of its spires that had formerly been damaged, and partly broken down.

---

(1) The time of the first use of this font appears, by the register of the cathedral, to have been " July 11th, 1770."

The library has been completely fitted up, and the whole of its contents classed and arranged in the most perfect order, to every article of which a copious index or catalogue refers   The magnificent windows at the east and west ends of the cathedral have been rebuilt, with the spire of its south-west end ; and the entire roof the church east of the tower has been newly covered.   Internally the Lady's chapel has been prepared to receive here-after a reform in its flooring similar to that in the nave ; an improvement much wished, and probably meant to have been a part of those completed by Dean Waugh   The Bishop's chapel has also been laid open, and its orderly appearance greatly restored.   Little indeed is now wanting in this part of the cathedral to make the sober grandeur and magnificence of the whole edifice uniform and complete ; in the contemplation of which the eye of the spectator will encounter nothing of irreverent negligence to offend his feelings, or disturb the reflections that must naturally result from the impressive, solemn, and awful scene that surrounds him . where

> " The high embowed roof
> " With antique pillars massv proof ," (1)
> " Where through the long drawn ile and fretted vault,
> " The pealing anthem swells the note of praise " (2)

The east window has a few panes of painted glass introduced in it, on which some of the churches of the city are represented.   The arms of the see are also a part of its decorations , but the blemish in its blazoning stands in need of a reform   In the upper space of the new west window, the arms of the bishopric are also placed, and properly displayed ; underneath is a preparation for the reception of another coat, which might well be supplied with the arms of the deanry.   In the points of the two principal divisions of the window, shields are prepared for other armorial decorations   Beneath the great transom on each side of the centre of the lower division, the arms of England are set up ; there are also parts of other coats collected from other windows of the church introduced, but so disposed, that it cannot be ascertained to whom they belonged. (3)

At some future period these windows may probably receive embellish-ments from art more decidedly appropriate to their stations, and to the his-

---

(1) Milton, Il Penseroso   (2) Gray's Elegy   (3) These windows were built by Mr Thomas Johnson, architect of this city   See their elevations, with those of the ancient windows, in the Plan of the Cathedral, referred to by the letters i, k, l, m.

tory of the church, than those they at present possess. The spur of the occasion of its erection did not allow the time necessary to the arrangement of a plan of decoration suggested for the west window, the design of which was to commemorate the honour the church received by the presence of their Majesties at the triennial meeting of the three choirs of Worcester, Hereford, and Gloucester, for the relief of the widows and orphans of the clergy of those dioceses, held at Worcester in 1788, on which occasion the royal visitors were seated in a magnificent gallery erected immediately under that window.

PRECINCTS OF THE CATHEDRAL.

The cathedral and its precincts make no part of the city, though contiguous to it. Exemption from the least interposition of the civil powers was what all the great monasteries sooner or later obtained ; but this of Worcester had a long struggle with the hereditary sheriffs of the county, before its absolute immunity from their officers could be established The Reformation has introduced great changes , it has abolished the right of sanctuary in cathedrals , subsequent laws have weakened the barrier between royal and ecclesiastical jurisdiction; the precincts of the church are now part of the outer county, but still remain independent of the city, or county interior, being a separate district, under the jurisdiction of the dean and chapter. The limit of these precincts, beginning at the Severn, is bounded on the south by a wall, extending from thence between the castle and the deanry ; a line from that wall, including part of the eminence or ridge leading from the Castle hill to the end of Frog-lane, reaches Edgar's-tower-gate ; from thence to the Knowle's-end, including all the houses on the north side of Edgar-street, on the Sanctuary side, it passes through part of a house, excluding its fore-front, with those of two other houses belonging to the city, being there divided by stones called Monke stones, of a blue colour, and from thence along Sidbury to its upper end, it enters the Leech-street, including all the houses on its south side, to the gate of the bishop's palace , along which line every house on the Sanctuary side have free board and liberty as far as it is marked with blue stones. From the palace gate the line is continued by a wall belonging to the cathedral, to the charnel-house, including which, it extends westward from thence by the end of the bishop's garden to the Severn, which river, from thence to the point where the limit began, forms its western boundary.

SECT. VII.

A SURVEY OF THE MONUMENTS IN THE CATHEDRAL.

CUTHBERT, the eleventh archbishop of Canterbury, during his stay at Rome, observing the custom of burying in and near churches, obtained a dispensation from the pope for making cemeteries or churchyards within towns and cities throughout England, and particularly for himself, that he might be buried in his own church, within the city of Canterbury   He died A. D. 758.

Many of his immediate successors followed his example, and in a few years the most eminent lay personages were also buried in churches, of which the most preferred for that purpose were cathedrals, and churches belonging to abbies and monasteries, in which prayers for the dead were more frequently offered up than in parochial or lesser churches. Lanfranc, Archbishop of Canterbury, upon the rebuilding of that church in 1075, brought up the use of vaults, and of burying near the high altar.   Since those periods the practice has become general throughout Europe.

Monuments and epitaphs are not very commonly met with prior to the Conquest.   Indeed many must have been swept away and demolished in the more ancient churches, to make room for improvements; instances of which practice continually occur.   The veneration all ages have shewn towards these memorials of the dead, has been sanctioned by very severe laws made against those who have dared to violate or destroy them

The connection between sepulchres and places of worship is of the remotest antiquity   Tombs near and in temples, are not unfrequent among the Greeks   Mr Gough (1) has quoted a variety of instances, and draws this inference from them . " what are these but so many prototypes of the disposition of monuments in Christian churches?" The custom has indeed become now so rooted and confirmed, that it occurs as naturally to our recollection on entering a church, that we are also entering the general mausoleum, or tomb of the vicinage, as that we are approaching a place of worship, nor does there appear but one founded objection against their union, namely, the danger to the living, from the crowded interments many of them have admitted in cities, more especially in the metropolis. But that

(1) Introd Sepul Mon. p 3, 4

the remedy being so easily attainable, and the complaint still suffered to exist, is the most extraordinary part of the consideration.

About the middle of the fourteenth century, the interment of the dead within this cathedral and its cemetery had become not only difficult to perform, but also dangerous, to permit its further continuance. And notwithstanding the convenience of the charnel-house, which had been erected for the purpose of receiving the bones of such as the making of graves for the newly deceased had occasioned to be displaced, and that it had been opened but a century before, such were the annoyances suffered, and the danger to which the health of the monks and of the citizens were exposed from the custom, that Wulstan de Braunsford, then Bishop of Worcester, issued his ordinance, dated at Hartlebury, 18th April, 1349, (1) directing the sacrist, at his discretion, to bury such bodies as might be brought to the cathedral or its cemetery for interment in the burial ground of St Oswald's hospital (2) By this prudent measure, not only were the monastery and the city relieved from a very alarming evil, but also the parishes of St. Alban, St. Helen, St. Swithin, St. Martin, St. Nicholas, and All Saints, whose churchyards were very confined, and not equal to the reception of the parochial deceased, were permitted to partake of the same advantage of sepulture; but without detriment to their respective incumbents, in the article of burial fees, agreeable to an ancient ordinance, established to that purpose in a synod held at Winchester, A. D 1102, by Anselm, Archbishop of Canterbury. (3) Hence St. Oswald's burial ground has accumulated that prodigious assemblage of tumulation which, at this time, cannot be viewed with indifference by the most cursory beholder.

From the cause that no interments have taken place either in the great cross ile or the nave, since the present floors of those parts have been laid down, the consequence has been that the number is increased in the Lady's chapel. It is evident, that whatsoever objections some may raise to the depositing of the dead in churches, the practice has been too long authorized and established to be suddenly annulled To be laid near the remains of relatives or friends is a wish so natural and so powerful, that church doors are

---

(1) Bishop Wulstan died himself in the following August, and was buried in the cathedral

(2) Ex Reg Wolst v 1 f 145, b "De sepeliendo in cemeterio hospitalis Sancti Oswaldi." See Dr Nash, vol 1 p 226, 227 in Appendix Art "Claines,"

(3) Fuller's Ch Hist p 16, 18

U

not sufficiently strong wholly to repress it. The attempt might be a service of
difficulty, if not of positive danger. Under these impressions, I conceive that
not only interments might be continued in the whole of the Lady's chapel
and its transepts, after the laying of a new floor, but also that they might
be resumed in the present forbidden ground of the nave, and the great cross
ile, when put under the regulation of a register, opened on the plan judiciously suggested by Mr Bigland, in which, as he recommends, should be
drawn on a large scale the ichnography of the church, with proper references to each person's grave or family vault, an obituary record of their
names, age, dates, as usually inscribed on monuments, tombs, &c should be
kept, in which those entries should be made, and for which a moderate fee
should be paid to the sacrist. Indecent and premature disturbance of the
dead would thereby be wholly avoided, the order and economy of the church
be preserved from the patchwork appearance of flat gravestones of all sizes,
shapes, and colours ; and the living would be rescued from the apprehension
of being excluded the use of the church, by the injudicious and improvident
manner of disposing of tombs and stone coffins, on what should be the open
parts of its flooring ; of the impropriety of which practice a most striking
instance occurs in the Dean's chapel, through which it is rendered difficult
to pass, from the very irregular manner in which its floor is occupied by the
tombs and stone coffins it contains.

The present section reports only the monuments, tombs, tablets, flat gravestones, or other sepulchral memorials, to which references are made in the annexed Plan of the cathedral and such of their inscriptions as have not already appeared in the publications of Mr Abingdon, Dr Thomas, and Dr.
Nash, are given at large The accounts of the rest of the flat gravestones now
in being, within the cathedral and the cloisters, and of those monuments, tombs,
and gravestones, that have been removed subsequent to the year 1736, to which
period Dr Thomas has brought them down in his Survey of this church, are
inserted in the Appendix to this Section, No VIII from p xxiv to p. xxxiii.

MONUMENTS IN OUR LADY'S CHAPLI MIDDLE ILE.

1 On the subject of the interment of King John, and pointing out this as
the spot where his body was deposited, I have already so fully treated in
Sect IV p 67, which admitted of the discussion with equal propriety as it
would have appeared in this, and to a more useful purpose also, as connected

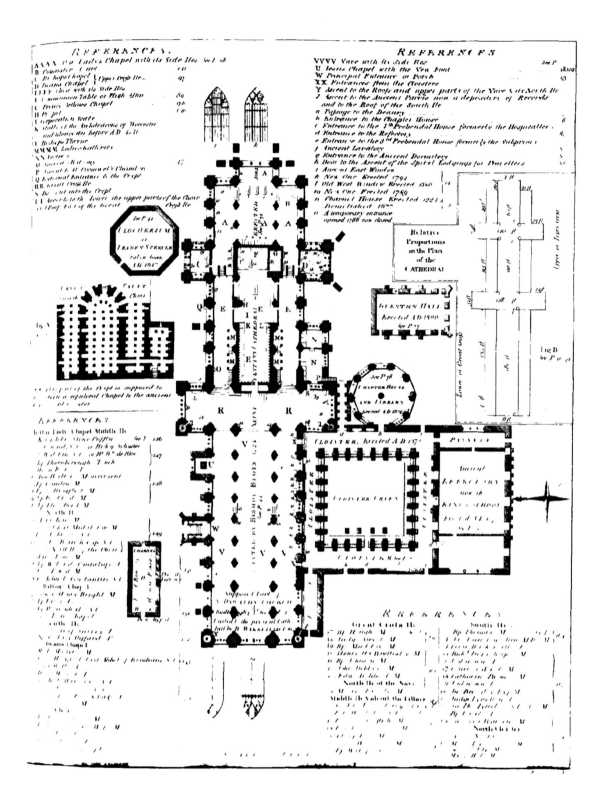

with the investigation of the original arrangement of this part of the church ; the necessity of farther mention of it, than merely as the leading article of the present Section is thereby superseded.

2 3 The same observation applies to the ancient graves of St. Oswald and St Wulstan, placed on each side that of King John, and supposed to be now occupied by the remains of the Bishops Sylvester, and his successor William de Blois They are denoted by the effigies of two bishops, lying at equal distance from the great east window, and are represented as vested for the altar, and mitred ; their right hands lifted up as giving a blessing, and in their left hands a baculus or staff Those are the tombs asserted by Dr. Thomas to belong to the Bishops John de Constantiis, and Godfrey de Giffaid, but which are now more generally and properly considered as the graves of St Oswald and St Wulstan The ground where these saints had lain was always esteemed to possess great sanctity, and was accordingly visited annually by the Roman Catholics with great veneration, on the 19th of January, the anniversary of Bishop Wulstan's death ; (1) a custom which was devoutly continued by them down to the last age But I cannot suppose that any part of the tomb, or of the shrine of either of these saints was left undestroyed at the Reformation ; when all shrines, to which miracles had been imputed, and all monuments that had been objects of superstition, were taken away, broken to pieces, or burnt.

4 Under the first arch, between the pillars on the north side, is a handsome monument erected by Bishop Thornborough, in 1627, fourteen years before his death On the tomb lies his statue in his episcopal robes, his hands elevated as in prayer The arch over him is supported by four pillars, on which are several inscriptions. That above the arch on the north side of the tomb has attracted much notice, but to little purpose —" In Uno 2° 3¹ 4°ʳ 10. Non spirans sper ." may couch a meaning known to its author, but the application of those mystical numbers being lost, we are but little gratified in

(1) Anniversaries and obits were masses yearly celebrated on the day of the death of a particular person or benefactor to the church These masses may be seen in the Romish missals, under the title of ' Missa pro Defunctis " They owed their rise to the notion of praying for souls departed, and continued to be used till the year 1559 " The monthes minde, the yeares minde, the two yeares minde," &c were similar mass to those of the obit and anniversary the word minde in this case implies a memorial or remembrance of the deceased, at the appointed time the ceremony was to be observed The term of monthes minde was changed about the time of the abolition of the practice of observing it, to " monthes monument " See Archæologia, vol I p 11 Art IV , and Morant's Colchester, p 159.

having the solution of an enigma proposed to us, where we might have expected other matter from the character to which the tomb relates. He died at Hartlebury, 3 July, 1641, aged 94

5. Opposite to this, on the south side, under the first arch, is a fine monument of Dean Eedes, on which his figure is represented cumbent, his head resting on a double pillow, and his hands joined in the gesture of prayer; at his feet a lion. The top is supported by four Corinthian pillars. He died 1604 (1)

6. On the north wall, is a small monument of Mrs. Anne Walton; she died 1662, aged 52.

On the west wall of this ile, which forms the back of the high altar of the choir, are the following monuments, viz

7 John Gauden, D D Bishop of Worcester, who died 1662, aged 57. In a concave oval, a half length figure of this prelate of the size of life is introduced, holding in his right hand a book, supposed to be meant for the Icon Basilike. (2)

8 Edward Stillingfleet, D. D. Bishop of Worcester. He died 1699, aged 64.

9. James Fleetwood, D D Bishop of Worcester, died 1683, aged 81.

10. Walter Blandford, D. D. Bishop of Worcester, died 1675, aged 59. (3)

(1) The tombs and monuments erected about the time of Elizabeth and James I. seem to have had their origin from the fashion of the immense bedsteads of those days, on which such abundance of timber and carving are bestowed Of this sort also are the monuments of Bishop Thornborough, Dean Eedes, and Bishop Parry, in the Bishop's chapel

(2) This book was a collection of meditations and prayers of K Charles I composed by him during his troubles The stile of the book is strong, elegant, and perspicuous, and its manly sentiments reflect unfading honour on the royal author His enemies, not content with having deprived him of his life, endeavoured to rob him of the reputation of having written this performance, which they ascribed to Dr Gauden (and his monument seems to countenance that suggestion) but every reader of discernment will find it so much superior in stile, matter, and composition, to any of the doctor's productions, that he will be persuaded, whoever was, Dr. Gauden could not be the writer of the Icon See Smollet's History of Eng vol vii p 371

(3) The four last mentioned monuments are of a mixed stile of construction, ornamental and architectural, in which the departure from the massy heaviness of the last age is very strongly marked, and a fanciful disposition of embellishment begins to appear See engravings of them in succession in Dr. Thomas's Survey, from p 49 to 52 Their inscriptions are in Latin, that of Bishop Stillingfleet came from the masterly hand of Dr Bentley, his chaplain.

The monuments of Mrs Catherine Talbot in the Dean's chapel, of Mrs. Wrottesley in the great cross ile, and of Bishop Thomas, John Bromley Esq and Mrs. Octavia Walsh, in the north ile of the nave, are all of that class of sculpture

NORTH ILE.

11 At the east end of this ile is erected a very beautiful monument to the memory of Mrs. Margaret Rae, who died 1770, aged 29 It is composed of various coloured marble, and enriched with a profile bust of the lady on an oval tablet. The annexed plate will best discharge the duties of description, and put the reader in full possession of the sculptor's design at a single glance The inscription it bears, and which is engraved on the plate, has already appeared in Dr Nash, vol II p. clvi in Appendix. that on the flat stone laid over the vault in which Mrs. Rae is interred, varying in some degree from those on the monument, and having never been published, is inserted in the Appendix to this Section, No VIII. p. xxv.

12 Beneath the east window of the north wall, is the monument of Dorothy Countess of Middleton, who died 1705, aged 71

13 Under the second window on the floor lies a stone coffin of a lady, removed hither from the charnel-house chapel, 13 Jan 1636, where it had been placed on the north side, and was the only tomb that chapel could boast Her figure is lying thereon, of a more than ordinary size; on her head is a coronet, or rather, as it would appear from the plate in Dr. Thomas's Survey, p. 60, the wreath on which the coronet is placed; at her feet a bracket formed of foliage, which runs round the moulding of the tomb. On her chin she has a wimplet, (1) her right hand lying on her breast, is bare, her left has on a glove, in which she also holds the other, and is laid over her body; which form, according to the ritual of marriage, signifies a maiden designed for the nuptial state but who she was is not known.

14. Near this is an ancient tomb of a knight of the holy voyage, armed in mail, with a round helmet and surcoat; his right hand on his sword, which is partly drawn, on his left a long pointed shield, his legs laid across, and at his feet a lion (2) This tomb was removed hither from the north ile of the choir; in a window which was over it were the arms of Beauchamp; from whence it was concluded it might be Sir James Beauchamp.

(1) These wimplets, or rather mufflers, were worn only by persons of the greatest quality. The barbe or wimplet was a kind of chin cloth, of fine linen, worn by mourners No lady under the degree of a baroness was permitted to wear it *on* her chin, knights wives were to wear it *under* their chins, and esquire's wives and gentlemen of note wore them beneath their throats

(2) It is not unfrequent to find the distinction of knights Templars, and knights of the holy voyage confounded and wrongly applied in the obituary accounts of their tombs The former were a religious order, and followed the rule of the canons regular of St Austin, and under a vow of celibacy The latter

15. On a small tablet, surmounted by an urn, and fixed to the second pillar from the east, is the following inscription. " To the memory of Jane Rous, who departed this life the 8th day of September, 1789. Her remains are deposited in a vault near this pillar "

16 Under the easternmost arch of the north wall of the choir, parallel with the altar, is the tomb of a prelate, who is represented on it in his sacred vestments, but much defaced his head lying on a double cushion, supported by angels, and at his feet two lions, (1) the prelate it was designed for, if he were not Walter de Cantelupe, is unknown. It is recorded of that bishop, in the Worcester Annals, that he was buried near the great altar On the subject of his interment I have already treated in Sect IV p. 67 This tomb has not been noticed either by Mr Abingdon nor Dr Thomas

17. Above this tomb on the same wall is fixed a small monument of Mrs. Elizabeth Powel, widow, she died 1697.

18 Under another arch (2) of the same wall is the tomb of John de Constantiis, who died Bishop of Worcester, A D. 1198 He is represented mitred and vested, his hands raised as giving a benediction; his head supported by two angels, and at his feet a lion In Sect IV p. 65, 66, an account is given of the removal of this tomb, to make way for that of Bishop Godfrey Giffard. Dr. Thomas has supposed this to have been the tomb of Bishop Oswald, because it happened to be nearly opposite to that of King John in the choir.

---

included married men, and the custom of representing them cross legged on their tombs, as crusaders, was universal. Antiq. Rep. II p. 226, and note 6 p cxlii. Introd Sep. Mon See also Dr. Nash, vol I. p. 31, in which he remarks, those cross-legged figures on tombs are very difficult to be met with out of England; and that they belong only to married men

(1) Mr Hearne* explains the lions at the feet of sepulchral effigies as emblems of vigilance, industry, and courage, and parallels them with the lion on the tombs of the Bœotians, who died fighting against Philip, and were buried in one common polyandrium † Bishop Cantelupe was however no soldier, he nevertheless distinguished himself so honourably and successfully, as the champion of the ancient English hierarchy against papal innovation, as to have acquired in right of that exertion a distinction I have no where met with besides on the tomb of an ecclesiastic, two lions placed at his feet, another evidence also in support of the conjecture that this is the tomb of Walter de Cantelupe, Bishop of Worcester, whose death happened in 1266

(2) Tombs that are placed under arches formed in the walls of churches, are of the most ancient date Those of Walter de Cantelupe and John de Constantiis are of that class, and correspond with the age in which they lived They are unquestionably the oldest tombs in the cathedral.

---

* Roper's life of More, p 270   † Pausan Bœot p 606, ed Hanov. 1613 Polyandrium was the name given to the common burying grounds of abbies, in which, as it seems from M. Paris, the faithful under *interdict* might be buried See also Anselm's " Palais de l'Honneur," Rule 3.

BISHOP'S CHAPEL.

19. On the east wall of this chapel is placed the monument of Mr. Henry Blight, a native of Worcester, forty years master of the king's school, and then prebendary of this church, celebrated for his intimate acquaintance with literature, and the great number of scholars he trained up He died anno 1626 This monument was removed hither from the west side of the great north pillar of the belfry, to which it was originally fixed, and where the body is deposited

20. Against its north wall is a handsome tomb of Bishop Parry, with a statue of him recumbent and praying Symonds in his MS church notes for Worcester, says, ' this monument was much defaced, and the head of the figure broken off, by the rebels in 1643 "(1) Over the arch, which is supported by pillars, are the figures of Time and Death, with an inscription. He died in 1616

21 On the right of the entrance of this chapel is the stone coffin of Bishop Hemenhale, on which his statue, much defaced, is represented in a cumbent posture; he died A D 1338 His tomb was originally raised in Jesus' chapel; but on its being laid open, was taken down, and the figure laid where we now find it See the Appendix to this Section, No VIII p xxxi.

SOUTH ILE

22 Under a monumental arch, beneath the east end of Prince Arthur's chapel (on the erecting of which the top of the arch was taken down), is the tomb of the Countess of Surrey She is represented lying thereon, having on her head, which rests on a double cushion, a veil, and on her chin a wimplet, or deep muffler, extending over her breast, and holding in her hands a rosary Several escutcheons of arms are dispersed about her ; the whole of the figure has peculiar ease and elegance. About her kirtle or inward drapery, thus blazoned ; or, a fret gules , and others on her mantle, or, chequé, gules, and azure A talbot is couchant at her feet. The arms on her inner garment are Lord Verdon's, and from thence she is reasonably supposed to be of that family ; and by those on her mantle being Warren's, Earl of Surrey, that she was Countess of Surrey by marriage (1) Mr. Willis is

(1) Vol II No 965 Art 16 Harl Coll Brit Mus.

(1) Though the blazoning of arms does not form a part of my plan, yet here I have found it requisite to support truth against a prevailing opinion, that assigns this tomb to the Countess of Salisbury, who dropped her garter whilst dancing before Edward III from whence the order of the garter is by many

more particular, and says, that the Countess of Surrey who lies here, died in the time of King Henry III. which is repugnant to history   The two wives of William Earl Warren and of Surrey, who died both in that reign, were interred in the abbey of Lewes, Sussex , as also were all the countesses their successors, of whom we have any account, down to Joan, the relict of John the last earl of this family, which lady died beyond sea (1)

23 Under another monumental arch adjoining, and also beneath the chapel of Prince Arthur, is the tomb of Bishop Godfrey Giffard, who died in 1301, and who lies interred beneath it   This tomb, which was prepared before his death, and originally placed in the corresponding arch on the north side of the altar, was removed from thence hither, and that of John de Constantiis was restored to its place, as already has been represented in Sect IV p 65, 66   Dr. Thomas and others have erroneously assigned this tomb to St Wulstan, as if determined on fulfilling Merlin's prediction, and let the tomb of King John be where it might, those of St Oswald and St. Wulstan were made to follow it   The figure of the prelate is laid upon the tomb, pontifically habited and mitred ; over his head is a richly ornamented Gothic canopy, in the pediment of which angels are placed to guard his repose ; his shoes are studded on the tops with jewels (the fashion of the times) sculptured upon them   The sides of this, and of the tomb of the Countess of Surrey, are uniformly and richly ornamented with a series of saints, mar-

supposed to have been instituted. The order of the garter was indeed instituted by that king, but from an incident of a very different nature. The king having given his own garter for the signal of a battle that sped fortunately (thought to be that of Cressy), he thence took occasion to institute that noble order, and gave the garter, assumed by him for the symbol of union and society, pre-eminence among the ensigns thereof   [See Ashmole's History of the Order of the Garter , and Sandford's Genealogical History, p 163] Some superficial observer, on seeing the rose circumscribed by the garter on Prince Arthur's chapel a mark only of his dignity, and finding the tomb of this lady beneath it, hastily concluded it was a memorial of the Countess of Salisbury   the fancy gained credit , topographical writers, compilers of gazetteers, tours, &c have caught it up, as might be expected, without examination , a trouble they choose to leave to their readers   This garter, rose, or any other device on that front of Prince Arthur's chapel, has no more connection with the tomb of that lady, than of the bishop, who also lies beneath it

Byshe (on Upton's Asp login, p 64) says the arms on the *inner* garment are *maiden*, and those on the *outer*, *married* bearings " Where the figure of a woman is found, with arms both on her kirtle and mantle, those on the kirtle are always her own family's, and those on her mantle her husband's [Mr. Lethieullier, in Archæologia, vol II p 299 Introd Sepul Mon p cv]

The real fact is that the figure represents ANELA, daughter and sole heiress of Griffin de Albo Mona 'cro or Blanchmin ter Lord of Ichtefeld, Salop, wife of John son of Griffin de Warren, natural son of Williams 6th Earl of Surrey [Watson' Hist of the Warren Family, 1 p 208, where this tomb is re-engraved   (1) Dugdale , Baronage, 1 p 73.

tyrs, and apostles seated in quatrefoils, the spandrells of which are filled with the heads of angels, The stile and fashion of this tomb bespeak it a work of superior excellence of the era in which it was produced, and worthy the taste of its founder and possessor. On removal, it was most probably curtailed in some of its external splendour, more especially about the arch in which it was placed ; but from the evidences it still retains, without looking further into its history, it is strange that this tomb, which belongs to the fourteenth century, should be so pertinaciously assigned to a prelate who died two hundred years before. The tomb of the Countess of Surrey is evidently of the same age

24 On the east wall of this chapel was a monument erected for Dean Pedor, (1) which being taken down, another is there erected to the memory of Franciscæ, the wife of Mr. Richard Moystyne She died A D. 1678.

25 Beneath, on the floor, on the left of the entrance, is the stone coffin of Philip Hawford, alias Ballard, the last abbat of Evesham, who died A. D. 1557 His effigy lies on the coffin, in the robes of an abbat, his head mitred and supported by angels ; at his feet a lion ; his right hand is held up as blessing, in his left is a staff, not with a cross as a metropolitan's, nor a crosier as a bishop's, thereby distinguishing him as an abbat He is represented as having his gloves on, and on the back of each a jewel of a large size is sculptured on the stone, similar to the real ones originally set in those of King John, on his tomb, while it remained in the Lady's chapel. The sides and ends of this tomb have an ornament of quatrefoils encircled.

26 The next is a handsome raised altar tomb of Dean Willis, president of St John's college, Oxford ; he died 1596. On his tomb was an inscription on brass, stolen away before 1641 The arms of the deanry of Worcester and of St John's college, with his own arms, argent, a cheveron gules, between three willow trees, proper, as a rebus of the name, are also on his tomb A MS note by Browne Willis, inserted under the article " Francis Willis," as Dean of Worcester, in vol. I p. 658 of his Cathedrals (in the library of Craven Orde, Esq) says, " this tomb at Worcester was repaired by my greatly importuning it, and promise to give somewhat to it if desired, on coming to Worcester ; but this was never demanded, and so the guinea saved B W "

---

(1) See Appendix to this Section, No VIII p xxxi.

X

27. In the east corner is another altar tomb of Dean Wilson, D D. whose inscription is on a tablet fixed in the south wall over it. He died 1586.

28. Under an arch in the south wall, is an ancient tomb, with a cumbent effigy of Sir Robert Harcourt, a knight of the crusade, in a helmet, surcoat, and coat of mail, exactly corresponding in figure, arms, and attitude, to that of Sir James Beauchamp, before described   A lion is laid at his feet (1)

29. Beneath this, on the floor, is an ancient stone coffin of a lady unknown Her figure is laid upon it ; the coiffure or head-dress is of a peculiar kind, from which is dependent a veil , on her chin a muffler ; over her garments is an outward covering or mantle, held up by her right hand ; her left is placed on her breast, holding her cordon, and at her feet a little dog (2)

30   In the centre of this chapel is an ancient tomb of Sir Griffyth Ryce, as appears by the inscription round its verge   His figure, with his lady's, were of cast brass, inlaid on the top, but now entirely gone (3) At their feet were interred their children Sir Griffyth died, A D. 1522, in the 14th year of King Henry VIII. The date of the decease of lady Catherine his wife, daughter of Sir John Saint John, is defaced

31. On the west wall is fixed a neat monument of Mrs Catherine Talbot, wife of Dr Talbot, Bishop of Oxford, and Dean of Worcester. She died 1702.

MONUMENTS IN THE CHOIR.

32 On the north side of the altar is a very uncouthly compounded monument of Bishop Bullingham , his figure is laid on the tomb, on which the superincumbent wall is most barbarously piled, so that only his head, which is rested on a book, and the upper part of his body, with his arms, appear in one opening of the wall, and his legs in the other   Before that part of the figure which is supposed to be lying under the wall, but which, in fact, cuts it in two, is a tablet with an inscription, over which, to render it uniformly

(1) None of those cross-legged figures are of in earlier date than King Stephen, in whose reign the crusades began , nor later than Edw II or the beginning of Edw III they having ceased about the year 1312

(2) An emblem of faithfulness and vigilance. The figures of dogs are mostly found at the feet of ladies on their tombs   (3) The first instances that occur of flat gravestones, with and without brass ornaments and inscriptions, are in the latter end of the thirteenth century   In the sixteenth century armorial bearings multiplied on tombs and were introduced in great abundance in their canopies, and among other parts of their embellishments   These distinctions appear to have succeeded to the painting of arm on the surcoats, shields, &c. of the armed figures on monuments and tombs [Introd Sepulchral Monument , p c]

absurd, on a shield, the arms of the bishop are placed on the dexter side impaling those of the see, completely contrary to all armorial etiquette. In this state lies the good bishop, with his hands elevated, as if imploring a release from the barbarisms that surround him. An inscription on a stone tablet over his head has been overlooked by Dr. Thomas, viz " All fleshe is grass, and all the goodliness thereof is as the floure of the fielde. The prophecie of Esai, the xl chapter." An inscription in memory of him is also fixed on the other side of the wall, which leads us to suppose that he is interred in the north ile of the Lady's chapel He died 1576.

A more ancient monument, probably that of Godfrey de Giffard, appears to have been removed from this place, the traces of which are still visible within the inclosure of the altar, and without in the Lady's chapel.

33 Near this, within an ornamented arch, flanked by two Corinthian pillars, is the effigy of Abigail, wife of Godfrey Goldisburgh, Bishop of Gloucester She is represented in the dress of the age, kneeling and praying. She died 1613 (1)

34 In a space included between the distances of ten and thirteen feet from the north side wall of the altar, and one foot within its inclosure, the body of William the gallant Duke of Hamilton, slain at the battle of Worcester in 1651, lies interred The position of his grave is marked in the Plan of the cathedral, and referred to under No 35 See also Appendix to this Section, No VIII p xxvi (2)

35 On the south side of the choir, and parallel with the altar, is the chapel of Prince Arthur, elder bother of King Henry VIII. In Section IV. under the article " Chapels," having already given a minute and detailed account of this elegant mausoleum and its decorations, I have only to add in this place, that the tomb in which the body is deposited is of marble throughout, decorated with the arms of England and France, quarterly, painted on the

---

(1) See the engraving of this monument in Dr Thomas's Survey, p 41

(2) The wound which occasioned the death of the Duke of Hamilton was received in one of his legs a little below the knee, by a slug shot, which shattered the bone so fatally as wholly to disable him from keeping the field, and he was forced to retire into the town, where he fell into the enemies hands in the evening of the day of battle He was lodged at the Commandery, where his wound was searched by Mr. Kincaid, the king's surgeon, who pronounced amputation as the only means of saving his life Cromwel ent his own surgeon, Trappam, to wait on the duke, who assured him there was no hazard Two days after the wound had been received by the duke, Sir Robert Cunningham, the king's physician, being found among the prisoners, was brought to him, who reported to him, at his desire, that from the great

several dies of its sides, and ends in quatrefoils; and on the verge of its
covering stone the original inscription has been restored as follows :

" **Heere lyeth buried Prince Arthur, the first begotten sonne of the righte
Renowned King Henry the Seaventhe, which noble Prince departed outof this
transitory life att the castle of Ludlowe in the seaventeenthe yeere of his
father's raygne, and in the yere of oure Lorde God on thousonde five hundred
and two."** (1)

The heart of the prince was buried in the chancel of the church of Ludlow, but the inscription which was put up against the north wall has been
white-washed over, and thence forgotten. The heart was some years since
taken up in a silver box, and was found to be double, or as it is there called,
twinney ; the box was embezzled by the sexton, who was punished for the
breach of trust by a dismissal from his place. (2)

36. In the choir, near to the ascent of the high altar, is the monument or
tomb of King John, the most ancient one that is extant, in England at
least, of all the lineal ancestors of his present Majesty, from the time of
William the Conqueror. (3) That of Henry I. which is the only one
known of an earlier age lies involved in that chaos of ruins, the abbey
of Reading in Berkshire. King John's body was conveyed hither from
Newark, by the Earl of Pembroke His effigy lies on the tomb crowned,
whereon was written *Johannes Rex Angliæ*, which is now entirely defaced
In his right hand is part of a sceptre, in his left a sword lying by him, whose
point is received into the mouth of a couchant lion at his feet. This figure

loss of blood, nothing but an amputation afforded a probability of his recovery Trappam's opinion had
however so encouraged the duke to hope to save so severe an operation, that death alone could extinguish.
At length finding his strength fail, and feeling himself gradually declining, he sent his last thoughts to
his lady and nieces, written with his own hand, and'dated Worcester, Sept. 8th, 1651 , and on the 12th,
about noon, expired, in the 35th year of his age His body was interred before the high altar in the cathedral church of Worcester, notwithstanding he had by his will ordered that it might be buried with his
ancestors at Hamilton, and the earnest request of his servants for leave to carry it to Scotland, it was denied   [Burnet's Memoirs of James * and William, Dukes of Hamilton, folio, 1677 p 427—430]

(1) The old Gothic square letter in which this inscription is written, and in which that on the tomb
of Sir Griffyth Ryce in the Dean's chapel is engraved in brass, was changed into the present Roman letter after the reign of Edward VI. and the phrase " Orate pro anima," with which monumental inscriptions usually begun, were universally omitted. [See Mr Lethieullier, in Archæologia, vol II p 297
Introd Sep Mon. p c A very respectable engraving of Prince Arthur's tomb is given in Sandford's
Gen Hist p 476] His portrait is represented in the north window of Jesus' chapel, in the priory of
Great Malvern, in this county   (2) Gough's Sep Mon. in Introd p lvi lxxiii   (3) Dr. Thomas.

* James Duke of Hamilton, the eldest brother, was beheaded A. D 1648-9, in the 43d year of his age.

is as large as life (1) On each side of him are cumbent images of the bishops St Oswald and St Wulstan, in smaller size, each of one stone of fine grey marble: they are represented as censing him. King John died 19th Oct. 1215, in the 51st year of his age, and 18th of his reign. Being rather corpulent, his bowels were taken out, and buried at Croxton abbey, a house of monks of the order called Premonstratensis, in Staffordshire, the abbat of which was his physician, and who embalmed him; (2) his body, according to his desire, was interred (3) in this church, having on a monk's cowl, which was deemed in those days a good passport through purgatorial regions. (4) As I have in Sect IV p 68, treated of the place of his interment, shall only observe at present that this tomb is a cenotaph (5)

MONUMENTS IN THE GREAT CROSS ILE

37 In the north transept of this ile, and against the east wall, where formerly stood the altar of the holy cross, is a most elegant and magnificent monument erected to the memory of that eminent and distinguished prelate Dr John Hough, Bishop of this diocese He is represented of the size of life, habited in his robes, which are disposed in a bold, free, and graceful manner, and seated in an easy dignified attitude, in a reclined posture, on a sarcophagus, which is formed of black marble, with yellow veins beautifully dis-

---

(1) Mr. Gough is of opinion that effigies on regal monuments may be considered as portraits. The tomb of King John is placed in the class of the thirteenth century, and according to Mr Walpole, was the work of Cavallini, an Italian sculptor patronized by Edward I. The shrine of the Confessor and the crosses of Queen Eleonora are works of his hands [Introd to Sepul Mon p cxiv, cxv]

(2) Hollingshed, p 606 M P his, p 288   (3) His desire is expressed in a clause of his last will. Volo quòd corpus meum sepeliatur in ecclesia S. Mariæ et S. Wulstani de Wigorn. [Dr Thomas's Append No 33, p 19, 20] Agreeing with the prediction of Merlin, " that he should be placed among the saints,—et inter sanctos collocabitur." [Angl Sac P 1 p 483 Annal. Wig sub anno 1216] To supply lights to burn about his tomb, the chapel of Grafton in this county was appropriated. [Willis's Abbies, vol 1 p 303]   (4) It was no uncommon practice for persons to desire to be clothed in the habit of a monk in the hour of their departure out of life, but from the avarice of the church this dress was an article of no small expence to their heirs. [Note in the Hist and Antiq of Rochester, p 119] The Empress Maude, daughter of Henry I was buried in Bec abbey, where her corpse was found wrapt up in an ox's hide [Ducarel, Angl Norm Antiq p 89 Hist of Bec, p 99] The custom of depositing the dead with their feet to the east was practised by the Romanized Britons, and continued by the Saxons   (5) Monumental memorials have frequently been raised for eminent persons who had been dead centuries before they were erected, and often times have been set up in several places for the same individual This practice has served very much to perplex posterity, where the cenotaph has not been discriminated by the sculptor, nor the writer of the inscription, from the tomb in which the person was actually interred

persed over its surface, his right elbow resting on some books, and his hands joined as in the act of devotion The position of his head is inclined towards the left shoulder, and somewhat elevated · the countenance highly expressive of quick sense and religious hope, meek, yet animated ; and if an image of the piety of his mind may be attempted to be drawn from that faithful index, it may be said that in the communion this revered patriarch of our religion seems to hold with his Maker (for he looks beyond this world) he appears to have newly " heard the voice from heaven, saying, blessed are the dead which die in the Lord," and gratefully to feel the comforting inference that " he should rest from his labour "

Beneath, to the right of the prelate, is the figure of Religion standing on the top of the base of the monument, having in her right hand the Bible open, which she supports against her hip ; her left hand is employed in supporting a part of the drapery falling from the bishop, which, it appears would otherwise intercept her view, and also that of the spectator, of the bassorelievo on the face of the sarcophagus The figure of Religion is here viewed profile, standing at due angle with the whole The gentle stooping of her body, as if more minutely inspecting into the above story, is most happily expressed. The centre of gravity is seated in the right foot, supported by the stress of the left hand against the drapery, as before described : the left foot, touching only with the toes, is no sort of support to it This attitude, though intricate, is amazingly easy ; her aspect has the sweetness and complacency which should accompany pure religion ; yet tempered here with the appearance of concern, as though she felt the removal of an advocate whom she had tried and approved

The subject on the bas-relief represents the high commission court held in the hall of Magdalen college, Oxford, on Friday, Oct 21st, 1687, before Cartwright, Bishop of Chester, Wright, chief Justice of the king's bench, and Jenner, one of the barons of the exchequer, as visitors appointed by James II to remove Dr Hough from the presidency of the college, to which he had been duly elected by the fellows, and confirmed by the Bishop of Winchester, appointed by the statutes of the foundation visitor of that college (1) The composition is formed of two groups of figures most expres-

(1) The commissioners were attended by three troops of horse, for the shameless oppression of one of the most considerable seminaries in the university, and in open violation of every principle of justice. The consequence of this mock trial was, that Dr Hough, as president, refusing to deliver up the keys

sively characteristic of their opposite interests in the scene. The first to the left consists of the three tools of tyranny already named, seated on the bench, imperious and overbearing, inflated with all the consequence and importance that could be derived from the impetus of their mission. The second represents Dr Hough at the head of the fellows of his college, attired in their academic habits, making his defence. A lively writer has so well drawn his portrait in this hour of probation, that I shall here beg leave to copy it. "The figure of Hough is so extremely characteristic, and the " countenance so perfectly expresses the sentiments with which his mind " must have been impressed, that without knowing the particulars of the " event which the sculpture records, every one may discern he is a man ar- " raigned, whose consciousness of right makes him bold, but not insolent" (1) This group is judiciously connected with the first, by the introduction of a secretary seated at a table, minuting down the order of the proceedings, as directed by the principal commissioner. the Bishop of Chester. In a word, as an historical composition, this story is treated in the most correct and masterly manner The characters are well discriminated, expressive, and just; the figures are critically understood, and as happily executed. The groups bear out with a well regulated effect, and the perspective is so scientifically adjusted, as that all the objects of the composition approach or recede from the eye, and hold their proportions and places in the most orderly and correct manner possible The principal figures in this subject are about eight inches high.

Opposite the figure of Religion is seated a naked boy weeping, his left hand employed in rubbing his eyes Love, bewailing the separation of a tender pair, is in this figure finely imaged. The right hand of the little

of his lodgings in the college, they broke them open by the hands of a smith , and he with twenty-six fellows were on the 10th of December expelled, and also rendered incapable of any ecclesiastical prefer-ment, and such of them as were not in order s were made incapable of obtaining them, of which sentences all archbishops and bishops, &c were directed to take notice And on the 17th Jan 1688, none of the thirty demies appearing upon the summons from the bishop of Oxford, fourteen of them resident in the uni-versity were expelled,* and the college forthwith received a new president and a new set of fellows, on the popish plan. It was of no avail that Dr Hough had the laws on his side, when bigotry and power over bore and defied them He was firm, however, in the contest , and thereby, when the laws were re-stored, he reaped honours without envy.

(1) Mrs. Morgan's Tour to Milford Haven, Letter lvii p 333

* Proceedings against Magdalen College, 4to, 1688, p 40. A MS. account of this trial is also in the Harl Coll No. 2505. Plut, XXVI. E. Mus. Brit.

genius supports an oval of black marble, on whose plane is a profile head of
the bishop's lady, in demi relievo, with an inscription round it in gold letters Beneath the subject, in basso relievo, is placed the arms of the see of
Worcester, impaling those of his lordship. To use an animated expression,
which the object may well excuse, the larger figures of this sculptured pile
have an air of life, and seem to want nothing but the vital fluid, and the
Almighty's breath; for mind and sentiment were certainly never elicited
from marble with more forcible effect than is found in this admirable production of modern art. We cannot but commend the grateful spirit of the
gentleman who chose so able an artist, to give to posterity a just sense of
his lordship's worth. The memory of a Hough seemed to require the hand
of a Roubillac, to embrace the wide extended honours of his name, to hold
them forth to public veneration, and preserve the full benefit of his illustrious example to the present and future ages; an important duty, of which
that accomplished artist has acquitted himself with infinite honour to his
eminent talents.

The whole is finished with a pyramid of fine grey marble as its ground,
and the monument is happily fixed at a due distance from the north window
of the great cross ile, so that the effect of the claro obscuro is thereby rendered very beautiful Its height is about twenty-four feet. (1)

There are few great men, whose characters may be taken from their epitaphs. Impartial history too often gives the lie to sepulchral marbles But
it is not so with the memory of Bishop Hough The English history has
embalmed it. Satire, that is wont to be unsparing of mitres, has acknowledged his to shine unsullied (2) But the poet and the historian give us
only the idea of his public life Of the private as well as public virtues of
this excellent prelate, the record entered on his monument by the elegant
pen of the late Dr Tottie, Archdeacon of Worcester, and inserted on the
annexed Plate, will form the most correct as well as the most concise account that can in this place be offered to the attention of the reader, as a
faithful picture of the man (3)

38 On the west wall, opposite to Bishop Hough's monument, is erected a
very handsome monument of Sir Thomas Street, Knight It is embellished
with an urn, and his coat of arms A boy is represented displaying the cap

(1) See the annexed Plate   (2) Mr Pope See his Works, vol IV p. 261.
(3) See the order of his funeral, in Appendix, No XXXV p cxxxii

of liberty. At the foot of the urn a book lies open, in which is written, " Articuli Magnæ Chartæ Libertatem ·" to these enrichments are added the insignia of Justice. There is an air of elegant taste that prevails over the whole of this monument, strictly attaching to the character of the person it is meant to commemorate, and does great honour to the hand of Mr. Wilton. A coincidence somewhat remarkable is here to be noticed.—The monuments of two of the most decided characters in opposition to the measures of a prince hostile to the civil and religious rights of his people, to the most tyrannous degree, are here found in contact with each other. (1)

39 On the east wall of the south transept, where the altar of St. Simon and St Jude was anciently placed, is the monument of Bishop Madox, corresponding in situation and dimensions with that of Bishop Hough; the scale on which this work has been executed, with an evident intention that it should form a pendant to that superb monument, evinces the liberality with which it was undertaken, as an honourable testimony of respect to the venerable prelate it commemorates, and a magnificent ornament to the church in which it is placed. (2)

40 Under the great window of this transept is a neat monument of Mrs Henrietta Wrottesley, daughter of Sir Walter Wrottesley. She died 1719

41 Beneath, to the right, on the same wall, is the monument of the late Bishop Johnson A very excellent bust, esteemed a great likeness, and highly expressive of the *animus temperatus æqualibus,* which was always visible in his lordship's countenance, reflects great credit on the talents of Mr Nollekins, as a sculptor The inscription was written by Dr. Lloyd, under master of Westminster school (3)

42 On the great north pillar that supports the tower is fixed a monument of Mr John Dobbins, an eminent practitioner in the law He died 1635

43 Answerable to this, on the great south pillar, is a monument of Edward Archbold, an eminent civilian, Prebendary of Lincoln, who died 1617.

NORTH ILE

44 Below the great north entrance, fixed to the wall under the second window, is a large monument of the family of the Moores, of this city, on

(1) See the account of the place of interment of Sir Thomas Street, in the Appendix to this Section, No VIII p xxviii See also Dr Nash, in Appendix, vol II p clvi (2) See the annexed Plate, and Appendix, No VIII p. xxix, xxx. (3) See the annexed Plate

Y

which are the figures of three men in gowns, and three women by them kneeling, and praying : who, by the inscription, appear to be father and mother, son and wife, brother and sister (1) The son was Thomas Moore, alderman of this city, who died A. D. 1633 He is represented in his alderman's gown, the last figure to the west

Near this is fixed a small stone in the wall, belonging to Mrs. Ann Moore of the same family, who died 1614

MONUMENTS IN THE NAVE AND ITS SIDE ILES.

45. Between the third and fourth pillars from the belfry, on the north side of the nave, is the tomb of Sir John Beauchamp, of Holt, in this county ; on which lies his effigy, in complete polished armour, with that of his lady, Joan, daughter and heiress of William le Fitzwith His figure has on a pointed helmet with (originally) a corded facing, a gorget, on his surcoat gules, a fess or Plated shoes, with large rowels to his spurs. A headless animal at his feet Under his head an helmet, crowned, out of which issues a swan's head and neck, with the two wings. The lady's figure has on a loose mantle, her veil flowing back, a flowered surcoat, with close sleeves, buttoned to the wrist, the apron studded Her head is rested on a swan, and supported by angels, whose heads with that of the swan are broken off The head-dress is reticulated, with a fillet of flowers round it ; the hair plaited behind, the rest flowing about her shoulders The arms, on the panes of the tomb, are those of the Beauchamps, Earls of Warwick, and the Beauchamps, Barons of Powick, but according to Mr. Abingdon's Manuscript, the crest under his head (which is a swan issuing out of a helmet, the head now broken off,) points out the person here represented, to be John the son of Sir John Beauchamp of Holt He received the honour of knighthood in Scotland, having signalized himself in the war with that nation, from the hand of Richard II being then esquire of the body to that monarch, and was the only one of that family so distinguished. He was created Baron Beauchamp, of Kidderminster, by the same king, A D 1388, and was the first peer, according to Mr Selden, who ever received the honour of an English barony by patent. (2) But he did not long enjoy his new honour;

(1) Dr Thomas calls them three men and their wives, and immediately suffers the inscription to contradict him See his Survey of this church, p 102 105 and an engraving of their monument, p 104. (2) 11 Rich II Dugd. Bar I p 251 Selden's Titles of Honour, p 147

MONUMENT OF BISHOP JOHNSON IN WORCESTER CATHEDRAL.

Plate

for the same year appearing in arms in London, with divers other lords, for treasonable purposes, he was attainted in parliament, and after confinement in Dover castle, was beheaded on Tower-hill, in the fifty-eighth year of his age. (1) This nobleman in his younger years having received a largess from the priory of Worcester, gratefully requited them when he became high steward of the king's household, by protecting them from the oppression of the king's officers. Before his death he gave his money and plate to the prior and monks of Worcester, but the king's serjeant at arms demanding it, the whole was conveyed to London. Mr Abingdon, who saw the inventory, says it was very moderate (2) The monks, however, being ancient friends to his family, received his body into their cathedral, in which it was interred, and this tomb erected over his grave. In him expired the ancient name of Beauchamp of Holt.

46. Opposite to those, between the third and fourth pillars from the belfry, answering to that of Sir John Beauchamp, is a fine raised tomb of Robert Wilde, Esq. and his lady, whose figures are cumbent thereon, clothed in gowns nearly alike, their hands uplifted, as in prayer. A lion is placed at their feet. At the head of the tomb, fixed to the pillar, is a handsome ornamented tablet with an inscription, over which is their arms. The pannels on the sides of the tomb have also arms upon them. Two other inscriptions are painted on the adjacent wall Mr Wilde died in 1607

47 Opposite to this, on the pillar at the head of Wilde's tomb, is a small alabaster monument, in memory of Frances, daughter of John Bromley, Esq wife of John Griffith, M A minor canon of this church She died 1682

48 On the south-west side is a small monument of Robert Ludington, Gent factor of the Turkey company, and a great traveller He died 1625

49 On the north-west side of the same pillar is fixed a neat monument to the memory of Philip Fell, B D fellow of Eton college, Oxford He died 1682.

(1) Walsingham, p 365 Knighton, 2705 Sepul Mon p 191   (2) Abing MS

J eland, in his account of some of the interments in this cathedral, says, " In navis ecclesiæ Joannes " Beauchampe, miles, de familia comitum Warwici, ch us Edwardo 3 et Ricardo 2 tandem decollatus " tempore Henrici 4 This Beauchampe was owner of Holt, a pretty pile, a 3 myle by northe owt of Wor- ' cester, on Severne ripa dextra, a mile above Grimley At this Holt Kynge Richard the 2 made at- tointements " [Itin vol VIII p 128]

See the engraving of the tomb in Dr Thomas's Survey, p 93, in which, in addition to the badness of the performance, the view of the figures is wholly reversed The same blunder has been committed by the engraver in the prints of the tombs of the Countess of Surrey, Sir Griffith Rice and his lady, and Robert Wilde, Esq and his lady

50. On the pillar below this, opposite the great north entrance of the church, is a monument fixed to the memory of Mrs. Cicel Warmstry, widow of William Warmstry, Esq. register of this diocese, as was intimated by a sepulchral stone beneath it, now gone. She died 1649 On this monument she is represented in a sculpture near two feet long, wrapt in her widow's veil, cumbent, with her head leaning on her right hand. The muscles of the body are admirably well expressed; the whole intimating the most piteous dejection, and emaciating grief. (1) On the top of the monument two figures are seated, weeping. Above that of the deceased are these words in Greek, taken from Rev xiv. 13. " From henceforth blessed are the dead " which die in the Lord "

51. In the centre of the two lowermost arches in the great middle ile, was a flat stone over the grave of Bishop Wakefield, who added those arches to the church. He died 1394-5. This stone was removed when the present pavement was laid down

52 Under the first window, near the cloister door, is a handsome monument of Dr. William Thomas, Bishop of this diocese, who died 1689 (2)

53. On a white oval tablet, fixed on a grey marble slab, nearly square, as its ground, is the following very classical inscription, by Dr. Parr :

☧

IACOBO IOHNSTONE IVN M D
QUI IN·HAC VRBE PER $\overline{IX}$ ANNOS
ARTEM·MEDICAM EXERCVIT
ET·DVM ÆGRIS IN·CARCERE INCLVSIS
OPEM FEREBAT
FEBRIS·IBI SÆVIENTIS CONTAGIONE CORREPTVS
DECESSIT $\overline{XVII}$ KALEND SEPT
ANNO·CHRISTI $\overline{M}\,\overline{D}\,\overline{CC}\,\overline{LXXXIII}$·
ÆTAT SVÆ $\overline{XXX}$
IACOBVS IOHNSTONE M D
FIL B M F C

(1) Almost all the English cathedrals and conventual churches had one of these skeleton figures, but seldom more In this, however, there were two Besides this of Mrs Warmstry, the monument of Mr. John Howton, removed from the great cross ile, had one leaning its head on its hand Mr Howton died 1608 [See Dr Thomas's Survey, p 91] They are found as early as 1241 [Archæologia, vol II p 300] In the cathedral of Landaff is one of a woman [Arch vol VI p 24] Lincoln cathedral has one, with the figure of Bishop Fleming Under the monument of Archbishop Chichester, in Canterbury cathedral, is one of that prelate in a shroud [Willis's Cath vol VI p 6] In rural and parochial churches they are also found In the church of Westbury, in Gloucestershire, was one on the tomb of

54 Under the second window, beneath an arch in the wall, is an ancient tomb with a cumbent statue of a priest, vested for the altar, with a large tonsure, and at his feet a lion; supposed to have been a prior; and by others said to be the tomb of friar Baskerville (3)

55. Above this, fixed to the wall, is a monument for Mr Richard Inglethorp, who founded an hospital in this city for six poor men.

56. Under the third window, beneath an arch is a raised tomb, on which was a cumbent figure, long since gone To whom it belonged is not known.

57 To the west of that monument is another, for Mrs Octavia Walsh, who died 1706

58 Above which, to the west, is a neat monument of Catharine the daughter of Sir Brian Palmes, of Linely, in Yorkshire She died 1703

59 Near this, under the fourth window, beneath an arch, is another tomb, void of arms and inscriptions Whom it belongs to is unknown

60. Opposite to Wilde's tomb, is erected a handsome monument of John Bromley, Esq son of Sir Thomas Bromley, of Holt castle, knight. He died 1674

61 Under the fifth window, within an arch of the wall, is a plain tomb over the renowned judge Litleton , a justice of the common pleas, in the reign of King Edward IV On the verge of which is this inscription.

Hic jacet corpus Thomæ (4) *Litleton de Frankly, Militis de Balneo, et unus Justiciariorum de Communi Banco, qui obiit 23 Augusti, An. Do 1481.*

On a brass plate on the top was a figure of a judge in his robes, and out of his mouth were issuing these words, *Fili Dei miserere mei.* This plate was torn away in the civil war

62. Next to this, is a handsome monument of Sir Thomas Littleton, Knt. and Bart. and Catherine his lady. He died in February, 1649-50. The

---

John Carpenter, Bishop of Worcester, a native of that place But the most remarkable of this kind that h ive come within my own observation were those of the kings of France in the abbey of St Denis, near Paris, A D 1781 These were placed in the true point of view in which this kind of memento was intended to be most effective in its purpose Above, the monarchs lie in all the splendour of regal magnificence on their tombs Beneath, they remind us only of their mortality, and that " unaccommodated " kings are no more than such a poor, bare, forked animal," as there represented

(2) For the place of his interment, see Appendix to this Section, No VIII p xxvii. The inscription on the flat stone in the cloister being worn out, it is repeated in the continuation of Abingdon's Survey of this Cathedral, p 60. See note (b)   (3) Abing MS

(4) The students of common law are no less beholden to this great man for his Treatise of Tenures, than the civilians are to Justinian for his Institutes.

inscription on the monument refers to a black marble gravestone on the floor, which had also an inscription, now gone.

63. Under the sixth window, within an arch of the wall, is the tomb of Bishop Freake, with several inscriptions about it, and within the arch. On the side of the tomb are his arms impaled with those of the see. He died 1591

64 On a marble tablet, fixed under the seventh (blank) window, is the following inscription. " Mrs. Susannah Warren, daughter of Richard Warren of Redcliffe, Somerset, Esq died March 8th, 1792. To whose ever dear and honoured memory this memorial is erected, as a small, but unfeigned, testimony of the respect and esteem of her truly affectionate niece, D. Mill."

MONUMENTS IN THE NORTH CLOISTER

65 At the east end, near the south entrance of the cathedral, on the stone bench, lies a cumbent statue of a priest, with a large tonsure, vested for the altar; his beard was bushy, a thing not usual in these latter days In his right hand is a staff of authority, and in his left a book. It is said to be in memory of Alexander Neccham, (1) the famous abbat of Cirencester, who died in the year 1217, (2) at the bishop's palace at Kemsey. (3)

66. At the west end, behind a supporter of the church wall, is a monument of Mary, wife of Henry Townshend, Esq She died 1684

67 On a neat mural monument of marble, placed under the north window, having on an urn the arms of the deceased, is the following inscription. " To the memory of the honourable and reverend St. Andrew St John, D D. (second son of John, tenth Lord St John of Blotsoe) Dean of this cathedral, who died 23d March, 1795, aged 64 This monument, the last mark of filial duty and affection, was erected by his son, A. S " (4)

68 On the west wall of this transept, is a handsome marble monument

---

(1) The reader may from hence correct an error in the ichnography of this church, made by Mr Dougharty, for Dr Thomas's Survey, who, in the references, erroneously assigns this tomb to Mrs Barton, whereas she lies beneath a flat stone nearer the corner Compare the plate, reference 65, with Dr. Thomas's description, p 124   (2) Annal Wig

(3) This figure is so much defaced at this time as to render those particulars of it which Mr. Abingdon has described, extremely difficult to be distinguished   [See his Survey of this Cathedral, p 37]

(4) For the place of his interment, see the Appendix to this Section, No. VIII p xxv

of Mrs Hall, (1) formed of a pyramid arising from a base supported by brackets The enrichments are composed of a figure of Religion seated in a reclined posture, leaning against an urn, and holding a book in her right hand, which is rested upon her knee· the following is the inscription on the tablet " Sacred to the memory of Mary, the truly regretted wife of William Hall, Esq of the island of Jamaica, and of Bevere near this city. On the 11th of April, 1794, in the 45th year of her age, she was suddenly taken from this world to a life of eternal happiness Her family most sensibly feel the loss of one of the best of wives, and tenderest of mothers· and the many virtues she possessed make her justly lamented by all her acquaintance." This monument is the production of Mr. William Stephens, a native of this city, in which he is resident.

SECT. VIII.

AN ACCOUNT OF THE BISHOPS OF WORCESTER, FROM THE FOUNDATION OF THE SEE TO THE PRESENT TIME.

Upon the confirmation of the partition of the general diocese of the kingdom of Mercia into five sees, at the synod held at Hedtfield, A D 680, (2) the first bishop nominated to the province of Wiccia, or see of Worcester was

TATFRITH, or Tadfrid, A D 680, who was a monk in Hilda's (3) famous monastery at Streaneshalh, now called Whitby, in Yorkshire, which at that time was the greatest school of learning in all the North. This Tatfrith was taken away by untimely death, before he could be consecrated: and in his place was elected, (4)

(1) She lies buried in the middle ile of the Lady's chapel. See Appendix to this Section, No. VIII. p xxv

(2) Spelm Conc Tom. I p 169 See also Dugd Mon Angl. vol. I. p. 120. Le Neve, fol 294. and Dr Thomas's Account of the Bishops of Worcester, p 3, 4, 5, 6

(3) In a synod held A.D 664, in that monastery, of which she was the foundress and first abbess, she opposed the tonsure of the priests, and the celebration of Easter according to the Roman ritual. [Camden, vol. III. p 18, in N. R. Yorkshire.]   (4) Bede Eccl Hist. l. 4 c. 23.

BOSEL A. D 680, bred in the same school. He was consecrated by Theodore, Archbishop of Canterbury: sat in this see eleven years . when growing
incapable, through extreme infirmities, to continue his functions, he resigned it, A. D. 691, and was by the command of King Ethelred succeeded by

OFTFOR, alias Ostfor, A. D 691, bred also at Hilda's monastery, and
improved by a journey to Rome He was ordained by Wilfride, Archbishop
of York, Theodore Archbishop of Canterbury being at that time dead, and
no other metropolitan appointed in his room (1) He sat in this see not a
full year before he died; and was succeeded by

EGWINE, A. D 692, to whom the monkish historians have given the title
of saint. He was not consecrated till the year after his election In the
year 708, he went to Rome with King Coenred, and Offa, King of the East
Saxons. At this time Egwine obtained from Pope Constantine, *epistolam
privilegii*, or a charter of confirmation of his newly-founded monastery of
Evesham; (2) which, with king Æthelred's leave, he began to build in or
about the year 702; and on his return to England, finished. (3) Soon after,
resigning the bishopric of Worcester, he became the first abbat of Evesham, and died there, 30 December, 717. (4) Brithwald, not the archbishop,
but some other monk of that name, wrote his life.

WILFRED, A D 710, who was coadjutor to St Egwine, after his retiring
to his monastery at Evesham, succeeded him upon his death, and sat in this
see till about the year 743, when he died, and was succeeded by

MILDRED, or Milred, A D 743   He was one of the eleven suffragan
bishops who attended the Archbishop of Canterbury at the council of
Cloveshoe in 747, in which the English clergy asserted their own right, and
disclaimed dependence on any foreign bishop (5) In his time king Ethelbald freed all churches and monasteries of his kingdom (Mercia), from

(1) Abing MS. and Peck's Annals of Stamford, p 37.

(2) Of this once stately abbey scarce any remains are to be seen The tower is preserved, but this was
erected by one of the latest abbats, in the reign of Henry VIII And there is an ancient ruin which seems
to have been the east entrance to the abbey It is a strong portal, whose arch is ornamented with the
figures of bishops or abbats, whose heads are gone See Tindal's Hist of Evesham Abbey, p 40, 133

(3) The monkish story of this foundation is given in Fuller, p 96, in Spelman's Councils, p 210,
and at large in Tindal's History and Antiquities of Evesham Abbey, ch. i. p 2, and ch. ii. p 8.

(4) Flor. Wig   (5) Council Brit vol. I

paying any taxes, except to the building of forts and bridges. (1) This bishop died 775, (2) and was succeeded by

WEREMUND, A. D. 775, who sat but three years, and died in 778; succeeded by

TILHERE, A D 778, abbat of Berkley, who was consecrated in 779. This bishop in 780 made a great feast for King Offa at Fladbury, where, among other gifts, the king presented to the church of Worcester a very choice Bible, with two clasps of pure gold. (3) He died in the beginning of the year 781, and was succeeded by

EATHORED, A D 782 He presided in this see seventeen years. He died 798, and was succeeded by

DENEBERT, who was at the famous synod of Clovesho, in the year 803, in the reign of Cenwulf, King of the Mercians; where Litchfield was declared no longer an archbishopric, and Canterbury was restored to its ancient rights (4) He was also at the council of Celchyth, 816, where Cenwulf presided with Archbishop Wulfred, and where, amongst other things, it was ordained, that no bishop, abbat, or abbess, should grant away any of their lands without consent of their families, or for more than one life. and that, for the future, the year of our Lord should be put to their deeds, as well as their names subscribed Denebert, after having sat in this see twenty four years, died in the year 822; and was succeeded by

EADBERT, or Heabert, who was consecrated by Wilfred, Archbishop of Canterbury, to whom he swore canonical obedience. (5) He died in the year 848, and was succeeded by

ALHUNE. This bishop, anno 868, the year in which peace was concluded at Nottingham between the Mercians and the Danes, built an oratory, or chapel at Kemsey, and dedicated it to St. Andrew. He died in 872, succeeded by one of the priests, trained up in the college at Worcester,

WEREFRID, who was consecrated by Ætheldred, Archbishop of Canterbury, on Whitsunday, in the next year. (6) King Ceolwulf, at the request of Werefrid, in 875, exempted the parochia, or diocese of the Wiccians, from providing food for the king's horses and their leaders (7) When the Danes over-ran Mercia, making every where most horrid devastation, this

(1) Spelm Conc sub A 749   (2) Flor. et Annal Wig   (3) Hem. Chart p 95.
(4) Fuller, p 107, 108   Records of Cant Spelm. Conc p 325
(5) Flor. and Alford Annal   (6) R Hoveden   (7) Hem. Chart.

Z

bishop fled to France About the year 885 King Alfred recalled him, and placed him among the first class of the learned, whom he had invited to his court At the request of this king, he translated, out of Latin into Saxon, the pastoral of St. Gregory; which the king published, with a preface of his own, and sent to every bishop's see in his kingdom a copy of it, with an æstell, or style, worth fifty marks, and with an injunction, that it should not be taken away from the book, nor the book from the church. (1) Many of the clergy were at this time so unqualified in their learning, as not to understand the breviary, which they were obliged daily to recite: some of them could scarcely read it, nor could many of them subscribe the canons of those councils in which they sat as members (2) This bishop died, 915, having sat in this see forty-two years, and was succeeded by

ÆTHELHUN, abbat of Berkley He sat about seven years, during the troublesome times of the Danish depredations; and dying in 922, was succeeded by

WILFRITH, (3) or Wilferth, whose successor was

KINEWOLD He was sent by King Æthelstan, with a present to the monasteries of Germany He arrived at St Gall, Oct. 15, and on the second day after, being the feast of St Gall, he entered the church with an offering of money, part of which he laid on the altar, and gave the remainder to the use of the brethren He died 957 The Benedictines lay claim to him as a monk of their order, he was succeeded by the famous

DUNSTAN, abbat of Glastonbury, whom the monks honoured with the name of Saint, because he was their champion against the secular clergy In his own abbey he set the first example of expelling the old society, and introducing monks of the Benedictine rule in their stead. He had a great ascendant at court in the reign of Edred, whom he governed as a child But his successor King Edwy, would not be tyrannized over by this haughty abbat, he took Elgiva to wife in spite of his invectives; and banished Dunstan for his barbarities, which were monstrous, to that princess. Dunstan passed not many months in exile, before Edwy, by the revolt of the Northumbrians and Mercians, lost half his kingdom. Edgar was set up king of the revolting provinces, and Dunstan was recalled from banishment, and placed in this see, then vacant by the death of Kinewold, and the year following

(1) Asserus, Vit Ælfred Spelm Alford An
( ) Pemberton's Hist Cha V vol I p 21, 22 And note h, p 278   (3) Abing MS

he had the accession of the see of London. Both these he held in conjunction about a twelvemonth; when Edgar, then become master of the whole kingdom, translated him to the see of Canterbury; (1) and set over this church the celebrated.

OSWALD, who was of Danish extraction, and nearly allied to Odo, predecessor of Dunstan in the archbishopric of Canterbury, being his brother's son. In his younger years he was one of the secular canons of Winchester, and afterwards dean of the minster there About the year 952, by the persuasion of his uncle, who himself, when archbishop, had submitted to receive the monastic habit from Fleury on the river Loire, he resigned his preferment at Winchester, and took the vow of Benedict's rule, in that famous French abbey; where he continued, till he was ordered into England by Odo in his last illness. Odo was dead before he arrived; but the credit of the monks was now high. Dunstan, who already governed Edgar's half of the kingdom (Edgar himself being young), had formed the plan for bringing these religieux from their deserts into cities, and enriching them with the endowments of secular colleges. Finding in Oswald both abilities and zeal, he made him his confident, and advanced him to the see of Worcester. His success in converting the priests of his cathedral, and forming their college into a monastery, by the union of it with St Mary's convent, has been spoken of already. Secular clerks had got possession of the abbey of Evesham ; but Oswald restored it to the monks; whom he also replaced at Winchcumb and Derehurst, in Gloucestershire. He reformed the convent at Pershore, which before was collegiate, by settling monks on that

(1) Dunstan was a man of great ingenuity, and excelled in painting, engraving, and music He was an excellent workman also in brass and iron, and according to the monkish accounts, it was when employed at his forge, that the devil had the ill luck to visit him in a female form, for which he got pulled by the nose with a pair of red-hot tongs till he roared out for mercy In Goldsmith's hall, London, there is a painting on canvas of St. Dunstan with his unfortunate devil, over whom the heavenly host are exulting, to see him in the power of the saint Mr Pennant remarks on this picture, that " it would seem Dunstan was " conversant in works of gold as well as of iron, and in a place where the *irritamenta malorum* so much " abounded, it was not strange to find the devil at hand "* There is more foundation for the truth of this remark, than might have been known to the learned gentleman who made it. In the British Museum is a MS Tract by Bishop Dunstan, written in 25 duodecimo pages, on the philosopher's stone The work is entitled, " The Entrance into the King's Palace " On the back " Tracts on Alchymy, No 3757 " Plut XVII A Hail Coll This however can only be considered as a transcript left imperfect The end has this incorrect note, viz " St. Dunstan lived and was Archbishop of Canterbury in the reigne of King Edgar, in the yeare 1017 "

* Pennant's London, 2 Ed p 215—389.

Z 2

foundation. He was a benefactor to the abbey of Ramsey, in Huntingdon-shire, which Earl Ailwin founded in 968 Oswald himself may be esteemed (with King Edgar's assistance) the founder of Westbury, in Gloucester-shire, which had, indeed, been an ancient monastery, but had long been impropriated and annexed to the lands of the cathedral of Worcester These reformations endeared him to Dunstan, and gained him great favour with Edgar, who granted at his request considerable privileges to the manors possessed by the bishop and church of Worcester, uniting them all (viz. 300 hides of land, (1) and for the most part lying contiguous) in one hundred, whose court was appointed to be held under the bishop, at a place about four miles to the east of Worcester, called, in memory of the bishop, Os-waldes Lawe, (2) or Oswald's mount This was creating a small palatinate in the county, exempt from all jurisdiction of the civil magistrate. Out of these three hundred hides of land, Oswald granted away no less than one hundred and ninety to his friends, relations, thanes, artificers, and servants, generally for three lives, and with slight services reserved In 971 the ar-chiepiscopal see of York became a second time vacant in the same year, Oskittell lately deceased, and Athelwold who abdicated, made room for Oswald, who was raised to that dignity, but held his bishopric in com-mendam with it, and spent most of his time at Worcester. He died sud-denly there, on Monday, Feb. 28th, in the year 992, having sat 32 years in the Wiccian see, and near 20 in that of York, of which he was the 19th archbishop He was buried in his cathedral which he had built at Worces-ter (3) He invited learned men from abroad to settle in the monasteries that he favoured His meekness and most exemplary piety, above all his zeal for the monastic rule, and the miracles ascribed to his relics, have raised

(1) It is a common mistake, that King Edgar gave these three hundred hides to the see and monastery of Worcester Dr. Thomas, who must have known otherwise, having filled many pages with accounts of the original donors of these lands, seems yet, in p 48, of his account of the bishops, to slide into this error These villages and farms were, partly impropriations out of the estates of old abbies, suppressed long before Edgar's time, and partly the free grants of various kings of Mercia, and other Saxon princes, for the emolument of their souls A meadow beyond the Severn appears to be all the land given by Ed-gar to the church of Worcester, and yet the monks of it had reason to call him their founder

(2) Considerable antiquaries have mistaken the situation of this place, which was not between Spetch ley and Worcester, but between Spetchley and Wolverton, and near the boundaries of the last mentioned village [Hemingus, Chartul p 359] The most part of what is now called the hundred of Worcester was anciently included in that of Oswald's Law.

(3) Le Neve's Fasti Godwin, p 435, 568 Isaacson ex Malmsb.

him into the rank of monkish saints. A solemn day is accordingly appointed in commemoration of him in the English calendar, viz. Oct. 10th. (1)

ADULF, Abbat of Peterburgh, succeeded him in both his sees. This prelate obtained the abbey of Evesham of Ethelred, brother of Edward the Martyr, and deprived it of its liberties, besides which its possessions were much wasted and embezzled, every one depriving it of something. (2)

This prelate, April 15, 1002, in the 24th year of King Ethelred's reign, attended by a great assembly of bishops, abbats, priests, and monks, translated the bones of St. Oswald from his tomb to a shrine which he had prepared for it; (3) and died himself on the 6th day of May, anno 1002, and was buried in the cathedral of St Mary (4) He was succeeded in the archbishopric of York, and in the see of Worcester, by

WOLSTAN, nick-named the Reprobate. The cause for this ignominious name is not certainly known (5) for little can be gathered from that rhyming verse in the register of the priory —nam nimis erravit dum rebus nos spoliavit; i e "for too much he erred, when he spoiled us of our possessions." If the meaning be, that he granted the church lands to favourites upon military service, Oswald and Adulf, his predecessors, were guilty of the same abuse of power; but they being monks and saints, the imputation of injustice fell on Wolstan alone. But though he stands in the monkish list of reprobates, we have no reason to think worse of him, than of many of their saints. According to Mr. Tanner (Pref Not Mon. p. vi.) there was no distinction between the lands of the bishop and the lands of the priory, in any cathedral convent before the Norman conquest. The bishop's reeve or bailiff received all the profits of the estates belonging to the church, and allowed to the monks, out of its revenue, for their sustenance and clothing, what the bishop thought necessary, but what the monks perhaps might not think sufficient. Hence clamour and obloquy might naturally arise, especially at Worcester, whose monks had some estates originally belonging to their church (St. Mary's) before it was made a cathedral. The year in which Wolstan be-

---

(1) Vita ejus, en les Vies des Saints, par Baillet Drake's Ebor p 410 See also Oswald's Life by Fridmer, in Angl Sic (2) Grose's Antiq. vol IV in Worcestershire (3) Flor Wig (4) Annal Wig
(5) The reason conjecturally assigned by Mr Whiston, in Anglia Sac 1. p 473, for this reproachful epithet is by no means satisfactory For no contentions about the proper possessions of each see could easily arise, while one person possessed both Worcester and York When they were separated in 1062, a contest did arise, and ended in the restoration of some manors to Worcester church, which Archbishop Aldred had detained.

came Bishop of Worcester is memorable for the Danish massacre which took place by the order of King Ethelred on the 13th of September. To purchase peace at the hands of those barbarians, whom Swein their king brought with him to revenge the deaths of their countrymen, almost all the plate and ornaments of this church, the tables of its altars, both of gold and silver, the clasps of their books, their chalices and crucifixes were melted down, and their lands heavily taxed to raise their share of the second tribute levied by the Danes in 1012 (1) Nor did they suffer less under the oppressions of his son Cnut.

This bishop died at York on the 28th of May, 1023, (2) and was carried to Ely to be interred (3) At his death the sees of York and Worcester were divided. (4) He was succeeded in that of York by Alfrick Puttoe, provost of Winchester, (who also would have held this of Worcester in commendam, as his predecessors had done, but the Wiccians would not accept of him) and in the see of Worcester by

LEOFFIUS, or Leoferth, abbat of Thorney. He sat therein ten years and three months, dying on the 19th of August, 1033, at his manor house at Kempsey, and was buried in his cathedral at Worcester. in which see he was succeeded by

BRIHTEGUS, or Brihteage, abbat of Pershore ; he was born in Berkshire. About this time many parish and rural churches began to be erected ; the few that were in being when the Danes came into England having been destroyed by them. King Canute (the Danish usurper of the English throne), on his return from visiting the sepulchres of St. Peter and St. Paul at Rome, a pilgrimage that he took as an expiation of his guilt in the depredations he had committed, sent this bishop with his daughter Gunnilda into Germany, to give her in marriage to the Emperor Conrad, by some said to his son Henry He died the 20th of December, 1038 (5) Upon his death Harold, surnamed Harefoot, then King of England, gave this bishopric to

LIVINGUS, a nephew of Brithwold, Bishop of St. German, in Cornwall. He was first a monk of Winchester, then abbat of Tavistock ; and as such

---

(1) Hem Chart p 248 Dr Thomas's Account of the Bishops of Worcester, p 58   (2) Flor Wig
(3) Where, Mr Williss says, is yet a painted representation of him against the wall in the north tran-sept of the choir, under the lanthorn   (4) His predecessors, St Dunstan, St Oswald, and Bishop Adulf, share with him the reproach of holding, the first the bishoprics of Worcester and London, and the two others York and Worcester, as an excess of church power. [Fuller, p 130]
(5) Flor Wig

acompanied King Canute to Rome, who, on his return, made him Bishop of Crediton, or Kirton, in Devonshire, an. 1032 : (1) and, on the death of his uncle, had the bishopric of St German given him When promoted to this see, he held all in commendam with Worcester, contrary to the canons. For which Malmsbury asperses him as an ambitious, arrogant, wanton trampler on ecclesiastical laws, studying nothing more than the gratification of his own will. In the year 1040, upon Hardicnute's coming to the crown, he was accused to him as accessary to the death of Alfred, King Ethelred's eldest son, for which the king divested him of his sees, and gave the care of this to Alfrick, Archbishop of York : but, on paying the king a large fine, they were again restored to him. (2) He, with Earl Godwin, was the chief instrument in raising Edward the Confessor to the throne of his ancestors. This Livingus, Bishop of Wiccia, Devonshire, and Cornwall, died March 23, 1046, and was buried at Tavistock, to which monastery he had been a great benefactor He was succeeded in this see by

ALDRED, or Ealdred, first a monk of Winchester, and afterwards Abbat of Tavistock. In 1049, Griffin, King of South Wales, joining with the force of thirty-six sail of Irish pirates, burnt the town of Dymenham, near the river Wye, Aldred, Bishop of Worcester, at the head of the men of Gloucester and Worcestershire, attacked the pirates, but were repulsed by the Welch, and put to flight (3) In 1055, he was sent by the king to the emperor's court, to negotiate the return of Prince Edward from Hungary. In 1056, he was preferred to the bishopric of Hereford, which he held with this till the latter end of 1060. In 1058, he dedicated the abbey church of Gloucester, which he had rebuilt from the ground, something distant from the place where it first stood, and more to the outside of the town, (4) and with the permission of King Edward the Confessor, constituted Wilstan, a monk of the church of Worcester, to be its abbat. (5) In 1060, he was promoted to the archbishopric of York, and resigned the see of Hereford, with an

---

(1) Goodwin Alf. An sub Anno. W Malm p 145.   (2) Whilst Alfrick held this see during the deprivation of Livingus, the citizens of Worcester refusing to pay the tax called the Danegeld, imposed on the kingdom by Hardicnute, in 1041, in revenge for their disobedience, and for the loss of the lives of two of the Housecarles, sent to gather it, the city was given up to fire and plunder for five days, and the inhabitants forced to abandon it, to preserve their lives Alfrick is said to have instigated Hardicnute to this severity, because the citizens had refused to choose him for their bishop. [W Malmsb. lib. III Hollingshed, p 276]   (3) Lambarde, p 100   (4) Dugdale's Monast. Angl. vol. I. p 994 —Epit. p 118   (5) Leland, vol. VIII. p 64 An Wig Flor Wig.

intent to hold this of Worcester in commendam with York. (1)   But on his going to Rome to receive his archiepiscopal pall, in company with Walter Bishop elect of Hereford, Giso, the elect of Wells, and Tosti, Earl of Northumberland, in 1061, at a synod called there against clerks guilty of simony, by his own confession being found guilty, he was, by Pope Nicholas, divested of all his honours   Aldred, under this disgrace, in company with the others, was returning to England, but fortunately for him, falling into the hands of robbers, who stripped them of all but their clothes, they were through necessity obliged to return to Rome; where, by the remonstrances of Earl Tosti, and others, the pope was persuaded to let him have the archbishopric and his pall; which he granted, on condition that he should resign the see of Worcester (2)   But, on his return, before he quitted it, he is said to have persuaded King Edward to subject it to the see of York. (3)   During the prelacy of Aldred, Urso d'Abitot, sheriff of the county, built a castle on the south side of the cathedral, which encroached too much on the sanctuary of the monks.   Aldred, to whom complaint was made as protector of the bishopric, remonstrated with Urso on his trespass, but without effect. (4)   Aldred died the 11th of September, 1069, and was buried at York.   Mr Willis rather supposes him buried in his own church at Gloucester, where he says is a monument for him (5) On his resignation of this see, he was herein succeeded by

WOLSTAN, or Wulstan II surnamed the Saint; born at Long Ichington, in Warwickshire   His father's name was *Ælfstan*, and his mother's name *Ulgeva*, from whence he had his own name, *Wulstan*, compounded of both theirs   They separated by consent; the husband putting on the religious habit in the monastery at Worcester, and the wife took the veil in the religious house in the same city (6)   He took the habit and order of a monk

---

(1) Flor Wig   (2) Malms p 154   Bromton, p 952   Collier's Eccl Hist vol I p 224
(3) The only proof of this is a charter of privilege to Aldred, dated Dec 31, 1062, anno 21 Edwardi R inserted by Dr Thomas in his Append p 1   This charter, if genuine, was dated above three months after Wulstan's consecration   But it is evidently spurious   It alleges the example of Pope Formosus, who, in Oswald's time, when Oswald sued to him at Rome for the pall, had made the see of Worcester subordinate and vicarious to that of York   It complains, that Formosus's bull had perished in the conflagration of York minster, during the invasion of the Danes   The ignorant monk, who forged this instrument, did not know that Pope Formosus had been dead more than seventy-six years before Oswald was archbishop   Nay, he blunders in his mention of the English king, who conferred on Oswald the archiepiscopal see   (4) W Malms p 154   (5) See vol I p 637, Cath. and his Survey of York Cathedral   (6) Dugdale, p 230

of this church from Bishop Brihteage, by whom he was also ordained both deacon and priest. (1)   His first preferment was that of being master and guardian of the children ; next chanter; then cyrcward, or keeper of the church treasure: at length prior, by the favour of Bishop Aldred ; on whose advancement to the see of York, he was, by the general consent of the clergy and laity, chosen to succeed him. (2)   He was accordingly consecrated at York by Archbishop Aldred, on the 8th of September, 1062, in the 21st year of the reign of Edward the Confessor.   Notwithstanding he was consecrated by the Archbishop of York, he swore canonical obedience to the see of Canterbury. (3)   He was present at the dedication of St Peter's church at Westminster, built and endowed by King Edward the Confessor.   He, with Aldred, Archbishop of York, and many other nobles, after William the Conqueror had gained the battle of Hastings, submitted themselves to him, and attended on his coronation, the Christmas day following.   Wulstan, in common with other bishops, soon witnessed the protection the Conqueror gave to the church ; who, in 1069, being informed that several persons had lodged their money and plate in the monasteries, thence took occasion, under pretence that it belonged to his enemies, to order a general search of the religious houses, and carried off immense spoils, not sparing even the shrines of the saints, nor the consecrated vessels of their altars (4)   From the church of Worcester, as appears by a Saxon note in Heming's Chartulary, p. 393, the following articles were taken, viz. " From off the *Æscene* or *brygile* buc x pounds, off xv roods vi marks, and " off their crucifixes and chalices xi marks, off the long shrine viii pounds, " and off the three horns (5) iii marks, and off the candlesticks x pounds,

(1) Floren Wigorn   (2) Heming, p 404.   (3) Sim Dunelm, p 190, 191
The reason why he was consecrated by Aldred, and not by Stigand, Archbishop of Canterbury, Florence tells us, was, because Stigand was at that time under suspension.

(4) Chr Brompton, p. 967 1 46   Rad de diceto, 482. l 41   Sim. Dunelm, p 199   Dr Thomas, Acc of the Bishops of Worcester, p 77.   (5) These horns were doubtless of that sort by which lands and possessions of various kinds were held by the church, the grants of former kings and other benefactors, as charters or instruments of conveyance.   Of their history as such, a very entertaining and curious account is furnished in the third volume of Archæologia   They are described to be of four sorts; drinking horns, hunting horns, horns for summoning the people, and others of a mixed kind   The mountings and embellishments of these were often very costly, in gold and silver   The belts, feet, tips, and operculums, or covers, were richly ornamented, and curiously engraved   See the vol cited, from p 1, to p 29, in which engravings of six of those charter horns, with their respective garnishings, are introduced

" and off the *Hæcce* XXXIII marks; to which was added XL marks, and VI
" half marks of gold." (1)   In 1084, he began building the present cathedral.   Three years afterwards, he, with Lanfranc, Archbishop, of Canterbury, crowned William Rufus at Westminster, (2) and in 1088 opened his
new cathedral, which was finished.   In the year 1092, he held a synod
here; the acts of which are as follows:

" I Wulstan, by the grace of God, Bishop of Wigorne, decreed to hold a
synod in the monastery of St. Mary, in the vaulted iles, (3) (or chapels)
which I have built from the ground, and by the mercy of God have dedicated   This synod was held in the year 1092, indiction 15   Invited to
this synod, came all the wisest men from the three shires in our diocese,
Wigracestre, Gloucestre, and Warwicce.   Forasmuch as being full of days,
sensible of the weakness of my body, and knowing the end of my life to
draw near, I desired canonically to treat of the ecclesiastical affairs committed to our charge, and by their wise council to correct and amend whatever is to be amended   Wherefore our humility presiding in this synod,
there arose a question between two presbyters, Alfnoth, priest of St Helen's,
and Alam, priest of St. Alban's, concerning the parishes and the customs of
their churches.   The controversy of those priests detained the synod a long
time: I, desiring canonically to determine the same, commanded the old
men, and those who were best acquainted with the antiquities of the
churches or parishes of Wigracestre, to declare the truth concerning the
institutions and parishes, not only of the two forementioned churches, but
of all the churches in the said city.   And because the monks in the midst
of these disputes asserted, that they should suffer loss of their rents, justly
due to them from the church of St Helen's, by reason of the long discord

---

(1) A transcript of this note is in the Cotton library, Plut 464—35—V B Mus Brit   This spoil
must have been made in the ancient church of St Peter   St Oswald's cathedral, which had been destroyed by the Danes in 1041, was in ruins, and the present cathedral was not begun building till fifteen
years after this event, viz 1084   (2) Fuller, Cent xi p 10

(3) " In cryptis quas ego a fundamentis edificavi "   Such is the reading in Wharton's, Hearne's, and
Wilkins's edition of the acts of this synod   So that there is no pretence of inferring hence, as some
do, that this minster was anciently entitled, S Mariæ in Cryptis, unless the reading in this charter had
been, quod ego, &c   When vaulted iles were first introduced, the monks called them in Latin, criptæ
Hence we read of the consecration of several altars in the crypts of the abbey church of Evesham, particularly St Mary's altar, which was daily served with incense, and had no less than twenty-four wax
candles lighted on it at mass time every day, was in one of the crypts of that church; not surely in a sub-
terraneou vault, but in one of the side iles [Stevens's Monast Append p 141, 146]

between the two priests, I commanded, that together with the institutions of the other churches, they would also give an account of the rights of this the mother church. To make this scrutiny, by my order were chosen Thomas, the prior, Alfere, secretary, Godric Pirl, chamberlain, Uhtred, chanter, Agelric, archdeacon, Edwine, his brother, Frederic, Ægelmar, priests, with many others. All these having consulted together, returned to the holy synod, and affirmed, that there was no parish in the whole city of Wigracestre, but that of the mother church, to which St Helen's had been a vicarage, from the time of King Ethelred, and Theodore, Archbishop of Canterbury, when this see was founded, and Bosel made first bishop thereof, in the year of our Lord's incarnation 680, indiction 7. This institution was kept inviolable by the clerks serving therein, from the time of the aforesaid Bosel, through the times of all the succeeding bishops, to that of Oswald, archbishop; who, with the help of King Edgar, and the authority of holy father Dunstan, Archbishop of Canterbury, transferred and changed the society of this church from clerks of irregular conversation to monks of regular conversation and habit, in the year of our Lord's incarnation 969, indiction 12. Winsius, priest of St. Helen's, was then vicar of this the holy mother church; who, leaving the world, took the religious habit upon him, as did the other clerks, upon the admonitions of St. Oswald; and he surrendered up the keys of this church, of which, as vicar, he had been the keeper, with its lands, tythes, and other rents, to the common use of the monks. So that Winsy becoming thus a monk with the rest, who had freely chose to be converted with him, as well the foresaid church as the rest of the churches, which they enjoy to this day, with the lands, tythes, rights of sepulture, and all other customs and dignities ecclesiastical, which were heretofore the property of the clerks, passed in right to them, and were settled to their common use, with the assent of King Edgar, and of the blessed Dunstan, and St. Oswald, archbishops. In the third year after his conversion, blessed Oswald, with the said king's consent, made this Winsy prior over the monks of this church; and likewise granted to him, and to the priors his successors, that they should be deans over all their churches and priests, so that no dean or archdeacon should intermeddle with the churches or clerks of the monks, but by leave from the prior All ecclesiastical dues for these churches he was to pay to the bishop, whose chief dean he was. Of these things, as we have learnt them from our predecessors, and have seen them observed in our times, under your predecessor Aldred and yourself, we are witnesses. Therefore I Wulstan, approving this true testimony, have put an end to the controversy of the priests, and have corroborated the same with the testimony of this holy synod, and our hand and seal : cautiously providing, that no dissension or scandal shall hereafter arise about these matters, in this holy mother church, between the monks or any other persons whatsoever," &c (1)

Great encomiums are given of Wulstan by the monks his admirers, especially by William of Malmsbury, who wrote a book of his life and miracles. (2) He was, doubtless, an extraordinary man : a persuasive and powerful preacher, though his attainments in literature were mean remarkably humble, in an age when the prelatic character was haughtiness : meek and patient, yet, on proper occasions, he wanted not spirit · unversed in the arts of courtiers, unable to put off the austerity of the monk, unsuspecting and generous himself, he was no match for Ægelwig, the sly Abbat of Evesham, who tricked the good bishop out of several manors : but this simplicity was, on the whole, his chief protection ; it saved him, when the jealousy of the Conqueror disturbed and ejected all the other English bishops from their sees   Even Wulstan was not intended to be spared. At a synod, said to be held at Westminster, Lanfranc the Norman, who had been made Archbishop of Canterbury, was encouraged to bring charges of insufficiency against him ; among which one was, that he could not speak French. Wul-

(1) Ang Sac. P I p 542, 543   (2) A great article of commerce among the Anglo-Saxons was slaves it continued to the time of the Confessor Gilb, wife to Godwin, Earl of Kent, was famous for her dealings in this barbarous traffic, by which she accumulated great wealth The people of Bristol, we are told, continued this shocking custom, till they were prevailed on by the advice and entreaties of Wulstan, Bishop of Worcester, to abandon it, • this was in the time of the Norman conquest

The wearing of long hair during the reign of Edward the Confessor was so common, that Wulstan not only boldly inveighed against the custom, and severely reproached the people for their effeminacy, but when any one bowed down their head to receive his blessing, before he gave it, he cut off a lock of their hair with a little sharp knife that he carried about him, and commanded, by way of penance, that they should cut the rest of their hair in the same manner, denouncing dreadful judgments against such as disobeyed that injunction †   The clergy of his time were as much addicted to finery in their clothing as the laity, wearing the richest furs in their dresses, Wulstan often rebuked them for this excess " believe " me," said the good bishop, " I never heard chanted Cattus Dei, but Agnus Dei " ‡

• Hollingshed Vita Wulstani apud Anglia Sacra, tom II p 256. Malmsb lib i c 3 Strutt's Chron vol II chap v p 227, 228 Ibid Manners and Customs, vol I p 73   † Vita Wulstani, Angl Sacra, t II p 254. Strutt's Chron vol II p 239, in notes   ‡ Ibid p 259 —p 242, and Dr Thomas's Acc of the Bishops of Worc p 97

stan had a short time allowed for preparing his defence; and spent that time, not in consultation, but in chanting the breviary with his attendants. By the agreement of the council, Wulstan, who refused to resign his see to any other than the prince who placed him in it, laid his pastoral staff upon the tomb of his benefactor, Edward the Confessor, in token of his resignation, and received it again from thence in the presence of King William, Lanfranc, and many others, as from present governing authority. (1) This gratitude to his dead patron, and the sanctity and simplicity of his manners, as a prelate, procured him favour, made even his enemies revere him, and effected his peaceable confirmation in his bishopric. At the synod of Pedredton, not long before, (in 1071) he had been no less successful against the advocates of the see of York; who, to justify Aldred's detention of twelve manors from the church of Worcester, which the new archbishop, Thomas of Baieux, was desirous of keeping) pretended, that by papal provision, the bishop of Worcester was no more than a suffragan of York But Wulstan boldly supported the rights of his see, and justice was done him; so that the church of Worcester was now quite disencumbered from the encroachments of York, and had all the privileges and liberties granted by the Saxon kings confirmed to it And, though the new metropolitan of York made appeal to the Pope, it was without effect; and the independency of Bishop Wulstan and his successors, against the claim of that archbishop, was finally determined by the king and his nobles at Windlesore, (Windsor) in 1072. The monk, Hemingus, (often cited in these pages) was a great admirer of Bishop Wulstan, and relates several anecdotes that he had learned from his mouth By fraternal agreements subsisting between the convents of Worcester, Evesham, Pershore, &c masses were to be said in all those religious houses for every monk that should die in any of them; and for the soul of an abbat, or a prior, still more of these commendatory services were claimed. Now it happened, that Ægelwin, the intriguing Abbat of Evesham, died of the gout Wulstan, at the head of the brotherhood of Worcester, began the obitual intercessions there, for the repose of his soul, but in attending the solemnities, was himself seized with a severe attack of that distemper. In vain were physicians called in: the gout was stubborn Night, however, produced a vision, wherein it was revealed to the bishop, that this gout was

(1) Matt Paris Ailred Rieval, de Vit Edw p 408. Su H Spelm Ld 1723 p. 119, 120.

inflicted on him, in punishment for his praying for such a wretch's soul; and that he must desist from the charitable office, if he expected any cure. He communicated this revelation to his clerks: a stop was put to the commemoration of the unworthy abbat; and the bishop soon recovered. (1) This little anecdote, which is transmitted to us from his own mouth, shews, that even Wulstan was not quite destitute of art   He died the 19th of January, 1095, aged about 87; having sat in this see thirty-two years, and somewhat more than four months. The miracles pretended to be wrought at his shrine in this cathedral raised him afterwards to the class of saints   Pope Innocent III canonized him in the year 1203   He was the last of the Saxon bishops of Worcester, and had for his successor

SAMPSON, a noble Norman, canon of Baieux in his native country, custos or dean of the collegiate church of Wulverhampton in this, and brother of that Thomas, Archbishop of York, who is mentioned in the former article. He was elected to this see and consecrated in 1096   He conferred on the prior and monks of Worcester his rich church of Wulfrunhampton, with all its territories; of which, however, after his death, Roger, Bishop of Salisbury, dispossessed them   But he disobliged the whole monastic order by his regulations at Westbury; where he replaced secular canons, annulling the constitution of Oswald, who had settled monks in that ancient college. In the year 1100, he, with Gundulph, Bishop of Rochester, and Harvey, Bishop of Bangor, dedicated the great church of Gloucester, which the Abbat Serlo had built from the foundation. (2)   He died at Westbury, May 5, 1112, and was buried before the rood loft in his cathedral of Worcester (3)   He was succeeded by

THEULF, Thewold, or Theulphus, a prebendary also of Baieux, and chaplain to the king   He was elected Dec. 28, 1113, but not consecrated till June 27, 1115   In 1121, he, with the Bishops of Hereford, Glamorgan, and Dublin, consecrated the great church at Tewkesbury. (4)   He died at his manor of Hampton, Oct. 20, 1123, and was interred by his predecessor. (5) In the beginning of the year 1125, the king, then in Normandy, gave this bishopric to

SIMON, chaplain or chancellor, or (as by some said) both, to his second

(1) Mr Tindal has retained this story in his " History and Antiquities of Evesham Abbey," p. 16, 17.
(2) Flor Wig p 469   (3) Ibid   (4) Flor Wig. sub Anno.
(5) Angl Sac P I p 475

queen, Adeleide of Louvain. (1)   In 1130, on Rogation Sunday, he was at the dedication of the new church at Canterbury, with the king and many of his nobles.   In 1136, he, with Robert, Bishop of Hereford, consecrated the church at Lanthony, near Gloucester (2)   In 1139, he went in company with Theobald, Archbishop of Canterbury, and others, being summoned to a council at Rome. (3)   He restored Westbury to the monks, and was a very considerable patron to the church of Worcester, by restoring to it many lands and effects, of which it had been deprived. He died, 20 March, 1149-50   To him succeeded

JOHN DE PAGEHAM, or Pagham, chaplain to Theobald, Archbishop of Canterbury , and by him consecrated to this see, March 4, 1151. He died at Rome, 1158, (4) and was succeeded by

ALURED, or Alfred, King Henry the First's chaplain, enthroned April 13, 1158   It is uncertain how long he sat in this see, the accounts of his death vary so much. (5)   But his successor was

ROGER, son of Robert, Earl of Gloucester, natural son of King Henry I. who was chosen in March, 1163, being then but a youth, and consecrated 23 August, 1164.   He, and Bartholomew Bishop of Exeter, were held in great esteem by Pope Alexander III. who called them the two lights of England, and delegated to them most of the causes of this kingdom that came before him (6) Both of them were firmly attached to Thomas Becket, Archbishop of Canterbury, as appears by several of that prelate's letters. After whose murder, Roger, with others, was sent by King Henry II. anno 1171, on an embassy to Pope Alexander, to assure him of the king's innocence. He was present at the Lateran council at Rome in 1178, and in his return died at Tours, in France, August the 9th, 1179, and was there buried. He was remarkable for many virtues, and much esteemed for his regular life and strict execution of church discipline. That he was of an undaunted spirit, is evident, from what happened to him in St Peter's church, Gloucester   as he was celebrating mass at the high altar, one of the great towers

---

(1) I lor Godwin   (2) Angl Sac P II. p 321, 322.   (3) Flor Wig.   (4) Wharton. Angl Sac P I p 475

(5) According to Mr Wharton, he died 1160, Alford, 1161 but the Worcester Annals say he sat four years, and that he consecrated Fromund, Abbat of Tewkesbury, at Worcester, in 1162, and that he then visited that convent [Angl Sac. P I. p. 476.] And Mr. Abingdon has placed him (by name only) between *Simon* and *John de Pageham.* [See his Account of the Bishops of Worcester, p. 98.]

(6) Angl Sac P II p 425

at the west end of the church fell down with such a terrible noise and dust, that the multitude got out as fast as they could ; but he, with one or two monks that did not forsake him, went on performing divine service un-moved. (1) He was succeeded by

BALDWIN, born of mean parentage at Exeter, where he was schoolmaster some time. Upon his entering into holy orders, he was presented to an archdeaconry, which he resigned ; and taking upon him the habit of a Cistercian monk, was chosen Abbat of Ford, in Devonshire ; and, in a few years, was from thence promoted to the see of Worcester, to which he was consecrated at Lambeth, August 10, 1180; and December 18, 1184, was translated from hence to the archbishopric of Canterbury ; (2) being the first monk of that order that ever was made archbishop there   In the same year the rebuilding of the present cathedral of Canterbury was completed, having been ten years in restoring, after it had been destroyed by fire in 1174 (3) In accompanying King Richard to the Holy Land, he died there, at the siege of Acon, A D 1191. (4) He was succeeded in the chair of Worcester by

WILLIAM DE NORHALE, prebendary of St Paul's, London, and archdeacon of Gloucester. He was consecrated in St Catherine's chapel, Westminster. (5) He died May 3, 1190.

ROBERT FITZ-RALPH, a prebendary of Lincoln, and archdeacon of Nottingham, was next elected. He obtained a mandate from Pope Clement, that he might be consecrated by William, Bishop of Ely, his legate, at Westminster ; but the monks of Canterbury insisted on the performance of this solemnity in their church ; and there accordingly he was consecrated, May 5, anno 1191, by the legate at Canterbury   He died in June, 1193, and was succeeded by

HENRY DE SOILLI, Prior of Bermondsey, and afterwards Abbat of Glastonbury, elected Dec 3, consecrated at Canterbury Dec 12, and enthroned Jan 6, following   He died Oct 25, 1195; succeeded by

JOHN DE CONSTANTIIS, or de Coustances, archdeacon of Oxford, dean of Roan, in Normandy, and nephew to Walter, Archbishop of that city   He was consecrated at Stratford, near London, by Hubert, Archbishop of Can-

(1) Angl Sac P II p 428   (2) Ibid P I p 47,   Godwin Ant Brit   (3) Gervase See Duncombe's Description of Cant Cath p 148, in Appendix   (4) Godwin Antiq Brit
(5) Ann Wig and Le Neve, p 295

terbury, Oct. 20, and dying Sept. 24, 1198, was interred in this cathedral, and succeeded in the bishopric by

MAUGER, or Malger, archdeacon of Evreux, in Normandy, physician to King Richard I. and dean of York His election was rejected by the archbishop, because he was not lawfully begotten; upon which he went to Rome, where Pope Innocent, admiring the elegance of his person, confirmed and consecrated him. In 1204, Bishop Mauger replaced the bones of the blessed Wulstan in the same grave from whence they had been irreverently removed by his predecessor. (1) In 1208, after having laid the kingdom under an interdict by command of the pope, he, with the bishops of London and Ely, his associates, fled into France, where he died, July 1, 1212, at Ponthieu (2)

The monks of Worcester chose RANDULPH, their prior, to be their bishop, on the death of Mauger; but at the instance of Nicholas, the pope's legate, he receded from the election, and was made Abbat of Evesham. Upon which succeeded (3)

WALTER DE GREY, then chancellor of England He was of the family of the Greys, which afterwards was ennobled, and greatly distinguished in the English peerage He had been chosen Bishop of Litchfield by the canons of that church, in opposition to Josbert, whom the monks of Coventry had elected. But both of their elections were annulled by the Pope's legate; and he was made Bishop of Worcester, 20 January, 1214 In 1215, he was translated from hence to the see of York, which had been vacant four years. Simon de Langton, brother to Stephen Langton, Archbishop of Canterbury, had found means to get himself elected by the chapter. To this election King John objected, and set it aside, alleging the danger to the state, to have the whole church of England governed by two brothers. The Pope, then on good terms with the king, annulled Langton's election, and knowing it was his desire to have Walter de Grey become archbishop, he was accordingly appointed. When presented to his holiness for his approbation, the orator, among his other good qualities, thought fit to mention his extraordinary *" chastity, never having known woman from his cradle " " By* " *St Peter,"* exclaimed the Pope, *" chastity is a very great virtue, and there-* " *fore you shall have him."* (4)

(1) An Wig.   (2) Ibid   (3) Lib Alb Episc. Wigorn p 92.
(4) Drake's York, p 425.

B b

SILVESTER DE EVESHAM, first a monk, and in 1215 Prior of this church, succeeded Walter de Grey in the bishopric, April, 1216, and was consecrated thereto by Pope Innocent III at Perugia in Italy, the 3d of July, the same year, where he attended at the Lateran council. The year following, King John died at Newark, and was brought hither for interment In 1218, in the presence of King Henry III and many bishops and nobles, he solemnly consecrated this church, which had been now repaired, after the injuries it sustained by fire in 1202, and dedicated it anew to St Mary, St Peter, St Oswald, and St Wulstan On 16 July following he died at Ramsey, and was brought hither for interment. He was succeeded by

WILLIAM DE BLOIS, archdeacon of Buckingham, who was consecrated to the bishopric Oct. 7, 1218 In 1220, he consecrated the bells which had been newly cast for the use of the cathedral, and put up in the leaden steeple adjoining to it (1) In 1224, he laid the foundation stone of a new front or nave to the church (2) In the same year, he built the chapel of the charnel house, (3) (Capella Carnaria) between the cathedral church and his palace. He died at Allchurch, Aug 18, 1236, and was buried in this church; succeeded by

WALTER DE CANTELUPE, son of Lord Cantelupe, consecrated by the Pope in 1237, and enthroned Oct 13 following, in the presence of the king and queen of England, the queen of Scotland, the pope's legate, the archbishop of Canterbury, and many other peers of the realm He was a man of spirit, and proved himself a strenuous advocate for the liberties of the English church, against the overbearing power of the see of Rome ; especially in the synod of 1255, when, from the example of his intrepidity, the other prelates took heart, and made a noble stand with him against papal oppression (4) In the year 1240, he held, in St Mary's at Worcester, a synod of his clergy ; in which he made fifty-nine constitutions, to be observed in his diocese (5) In the year 1241, he with the legate and others, went to Rome, and, in 1245, made another visit to that metropolis He founded the nunnery of the White Ladies, and on the second of the ides of July, 1255, dedicated its church to St Mary Magdalen. (6) He augmented the chapel of the charnel house, founded by his predecessor ; and ordained,

---

(1) See Sect IV p 43   (2) Ibid p 44   (3) Ibid p 54   (4) Mat Paris, p 448.
Collier's Eccles Hist vol I p 438 439   (5) Labbe's Councils, t II P 1 p 275
(6) Tanner, 623 Gough's Add to Camden, in Worcestershire, and Dr. Nash, vol I. p 209, 210

that there should be resident continually therein four chaplains, one of which to be a perpetual master; that they should say mass daily for the dead, teach in the schools, eat and sleep together in one house. About 1263 he began to fortify the manor house at Hartlebury, but left the work unfinished. He joined the barons in their wars against King Henry III. and for his activity in that cause was, with three other bishops, excommunicated in 1265 by the Pope's legate. He died at Blockley in February of the next year, and was buried in this cathedral; and succeeded in this see by

NICHOLAS, archdeacon of Ely, chancellor and treasurer of England. He was one of the twelve persons appointed by the king and nobles at Kenelworth to settle the peace of the kingdom. He gave by will sixty marks for the re-edifying the tower of this cathedral (1) He sat not quite two years in the government of this diocese, being translated to Winchester in 1268, and succeeded here by

GODFREY DE GIFFARD, lord chancellor of England, brother of Walter Giffard, Archbishop of York; (2) elected to this see in 1268. King Henry granted him leave to carry on the castle of Hartlebury, as begun by his predecessor Walter de Cantelupe (3) This bishop finished it: he made several churches of the patronage of his cathedral prebendal to Westbury in Gloucestershire, where a college for a dean and canons was founded, A D 1288 He was strongly, but ineffectually, opposed in this measure by his chapter (4) He seems to have been a man of a high spirit, overbearing and litigious; was involved in tedious contests with the priory of Worcester; and made his visitations very burdensome, by the great number of horse (not less than a hundred) that formed his retinue He died January 26th, 1301-2, and lies buried in this cathedral.

Upon his death King Edward I granted his licence to the monks of Worcester, which bears date 15th Feb. 1301-2, to choose their bishop. (5) In pursuance whereof they appointed seven of their body as a committee to

---

(1) He died 1280, his body was buried at Waverley, and his heart in the cathedral of Winchester. [Annals Waverl p 223, 224 —Gale's Hist Winchester Cath. p 99]

(2) The Giffards of Weston in Gloucestershire, to testify their descent from this bishop, give the arms of the bishopric of Worcester, being, argent charged with ten torteauxes, signifying the eucharist. Among other legacies, his will directs a ring of not less than 40 or 50 shillings value to be given to every bishop in England   (3) Dr Thomas's Append No 41, p 37

(4) Gough's Additions to Camden, in Gloucestershire, vol 1 p 274, 275

(5) Dr Thomas's Append. No 7, p 82

elect a bishop in the name of the rest, and by whose suffrage they should be determined. This committee unanimously chose John de Sancto Germano, one of their own number, and the election was confirmed by the king (1) But the Archbishop of Canterbury found evasions for delaying his consecration: upon this, the bishop elect applied to the court of Rome, with letters recommendatory from the king, and the prior and convent, (2) but to no purpose, he being there obliged to renounce his right to the bishopric for want of money · and, Oct 22d, the Pope promoted to this see, in succession to Godfrey Giffard,

WILLIAM DE GAYNESBERUWE, or Gainsborough, a Franciscan friar, and who had been lecturer of that order in Oxford ; then reader of divinity in the Pope's palace After he had been consecrated by his holiness, he left Rome and came to London, 1302-3 The king exasperated at his obtaining the bishopric in this manner, withheld his temporalities from him some time; and on his granting them, obliged him to renounce in writing, that clause of the Pope's bull, wherein the Pontiff assumes to himself the right of disposing of the temporalities or spiritualities of this see. (3) On his arrival near Worcester, he was received at Red-hill by a numerous procession of clergy, with some abbats and bishops at their head ; and at the door of St. Wulstan's hospital by the minor or grey friars there he alighted, and to gain the people by a shew of humility, walked barefoot to St. Michael's church, where he was robed ; thence proceeding up the choir of St. Mary's, he was with the usual solemnity enthroned (4) In 1307, he was sent by the king into France, to treat about a marriage between Prince Edward his eldest son, and Isabel, King Philip's daughter ; which he accomplished to his liking ; and on his return died at Beauvais, September 17th, 1307, and was buried the following day He was succeeded by

WALTER REGINALD, or Reynold, canon of St. Paul's. He was chaplain to Edward I and preceptor to the prince, afterwards Edward II and although made chancellor and treasurer of England by him, he basely aided the queen and Mortimer against him, and went into all the popular and vio-

---

(1) Dr Thomas's Append No 71   (2) Ibid, No 72, 73, p 83.

(3) This introduced the custom, which continued to the Reformation, for bishops, when they received the temporalities of their sees, to make renunciation in writing, of all claim to them in virtue of papal provision, declaring their acceptance of them solely from the grant of the king

(4) Dr. Thomas's Append No 76, p 85, 86

lent measures which finally brought that unhappy monarch to his grave. (1)
In 1313 he was translated from this to the see of Canterbury. He is said
to have been a baker's son of Windsor. In the bishopric of Worcester he
was succeeded by

WALTER DE MAYDENSTON, also a canon of St Paul's, and one of the
king's agents at the Pope's court. He had his consecration from the Pontiff,
and received the temporalities of this see Feb. 3d, 1313. Dr. Thomas has
very laudably and successfully taken pains to rescue the character of this
prelate from the aspersions of some of his enemies, among whom Adam de
Murymouth, a professor of civil law, is named, as having in his history given
an unfavourable report of him, but upon very suspicious grounds. (2) He
died beyond sea, 28th March, 1317 ; succeeded by

THOMAS COBHAM, prebendary of St Paul's, archdeacon of Lewes, and
chancellor of the university of Cambridge : a man of eminent learning, and
adorned with many amiable virtues, insomuch that he was commonly distinguished by the name of the good, or the honest clerk. In 1313, he had
the honour of being chosen Archbishop of Canterbury, by the unanimous
suffrage of the chapter there : but that election was over-ruled by the Pope,
at the instance of King Edward II. (3) To make Cobham some amends,
the see of Worcester was then offered him, which at that time he refused :
but upon Maydenston's death, he accepted of this bishopric, and was consecrated thereto at Avignon, 1317 He began a library over the old congregation house at Oxford, about the year 1320, but did not live to finish it,
dying at Hartlebury, August 27, 1327 He, however, left money enough to
complete it, and gave many books to the university, to furnish it when
erected (4) He vaulted the roof of the north ile of the nave of this cathedral at his own expence, and close to the wall of that ile was his tomb. See
Appendix, No. VIII p xxxi

(1) Weever's Fun Mon p. 23, 24 —Duncomb's Cint Cath. p 93.
(2) See Account of the Bishops of Worcester, p 160 to 165
(3) Willis says he refused to accept this offer from his great humility, and chose rather to content himself with this. [Cathedrals, vol 1 p 640]
(4) In his will he bequeathed very liberal donations for the service of this cathedral Among others
were his great missal, an image of the blessed Virgin, given him by the abbat of St Augustin, Bristol ;
his fine mitre given him by the Archbishop of Canterbury, a long carpet of various work, to put under
the bishop's feet, and a jewel set in gold to hang at the high altar [Dr. Thomas's Account of the Bishops of Worcester, p 168, and in Appendix, No. 89, p 103]

Upon his death the monks of Worcester chose Wolstan de Braunsford, their prior, to succeed him . whose election was confirmed by the young king, Edward III It is said the archbishop confirmed it likewise, but durst not consecrate him ; nor, after the archbishop's death, durst the prior and convent of Canterbury, in obedience to the king's command, call together any of the suffragan bishops of the province to do it, being afraid of the Pope ; who, by virtue of his reservation of this bishopric, had given it to

ADAM DE ORLTON, or Horleton, Bishop of Hereford, and a native of that city ; 4 cal Oct. 1324. He was enthroned 19th June, 1329. (1) This bishop seems to have raised himself by actions wholly unbecoming his sacred function Treachery and villainy never cast a more shocking gloom, than when appearing under the robes of a guardian of virtue, and superintendant of religion In the contest between Edward II and Isabel his queen, he joined with her and her followers in their rebellion, and preached against the king at Oxford ; and was thought (2) to be too much concerned in his murder. (3) After this he obtained of the Pope a translation from this to the see of Winchester, in 1333, without the young king's knowledge, which so enraged him, that he ordered an appeal to be prosecuted in the Roman court. His accusation consisted of three articles. 1 That he caused Robert Baldock, clerk chancellor to the king, to be apprehended and imprisoned in Newgate, where he died of his ill usage 2 That he preached publicly at Oxford, in the presence of the queen and prince, and several noblemen, that King Edward was a tyrant, and thereby stirred up his subjects to imprison and depose him. 3, and lastly, That by his persuasion and advice, the queen had departed from her husband. To all which

---

(1) MS Add by B Willis, in Cath vol I p 640

(2) Justice ought to be done even to the infamous Almost all our chronicles relate, that Bishop Adam sent to the governors of Berkley castle, where the king was confined, this ambiguous note " Edvardum occidere nolite timere bonum est "* which at first sight, exhorts to the murder , but admits of a contrary sense, if you place the colon, or stop, after nolite. But of this heinous charge I must pronounce the bishop innocent For he left England in 1327, to solicit the Pope's dispensation in order to the marriage of the young king with his cousin Philippa of Hainault , and was at Avignon with the Pope in September, when the Pontiff promoted him to the see of Worcester Consequently he was beyond sea all the time of the unfortunate king's confinement in Berkley castle, who was brought thither April 3d, and was murdered September 21st, in the same year, 1327   (3) Speed's Chron p 578.

* Camden, in Gloucestershire, vol I p. 262, Mr. Gough's edition.

he returned shuffling and evasive answers; and craftily insinuating himself into the king's favour again, he obtained the possession of his new bishopric the same year; being the first of all the English bishops (if we except Stigandus and Ricardus Pauper) who was translated from a second to a third bishopric (1) He was succeeded in this see by

SIMON DE MONTEACUTO, or Montagu, another bishop put in by the Pope, whose chaplain he was, in subdeacon's orders, and archdeacon of Canterbury. He was advanced to this bishopric at the request of King Edward II who speaks of him as his kinsman (*consanguineus noster*) in a letter to the Pope (2) In 1336 he restored to the prior and convent the manor of Croule, which had been formerly taken from them, and was then held of him in *capite*; for which they made him partaker of all their prayers; and ordered that the day of his death should be inserted in their martyrology, and his anniversary to be kept with mass and chant in their choir (3)

In 1337 he was by Pope Benedict XII translated from hence to the see of Ely; and was in this succeeded by

THOMAS HEMENHALE, or Emenhale, whose name was taken from the place of his birth, a village near Norwich, in which city he was a monk; and upon the death of William Ayremin their bishop, he was, by his fellow monks, chosen to succeed him; and applied personally to the court of Rome for his confirmation therein; instead of which, the Pope promoted him to this of Worcester, having reserved that of Norwich for Anthony de Beck. He sat here but a short time, dying at Hartlebury castle in December, 1338, and was buried in his cathedral here This see having been supplied with bishops by the Pope's provision for the last seven successions, (Reginald's election excepted) the monks resumed their right of choosing their diocesan; and having obtained the king's permission so to do, they elected for bishop, a second time,

(1) The reason for his thus changing about is described in the following sarcastic verses, alluding to the tutelar saints of the respective cathedrals in which he had governed as bishop.

" Thomam * despexit, Wolstanum † non bene rexit,
" Swithanum ‡ maluit Cur? quia, plus valuit "

(2) Bentham, p 159, ex Rymer's Foedera, vol III p 743
(3) Mont. Regis vol II f 19, 20 —Dr. Thomas's Acc of the Bishops of Worcester, p 174.

* Hereford † Worcester ‡ Winchester [Willis's Cathedrals, vol I p 640 —Angl.
Sa P I. p. 553] He died blind, A.D 1345. [Abing MS p 41.—Gale's Hist. Wm. Cath. p 101]

WOLSTAN DE BRAUNSFORD, their prior, (1) then old and infirm. He was consecrated at Canterbury March 28th, 1339. (2) He died at Hartlebury, Aug. 6, 1349. He was succeeded by

JOHN DE THORESBY, or Thursby, in preference to the then prior, John de Evesham, chosen by the monks of Worcester. He was translated by Pope Clement from the see of St David's hither, by virtue of his bull, dated 4th September, 1349 He had been master of the rolls ; and in 1350 was made high chancellor of England. In 1352 he was from hence preferred to the archbishopric of York, to which he was elected by the chapter of that church, as a postulation to the Pope, who thought proper to confirm it, without noticing the measure of the chapter (3) He was succeeded here, by virtue of papal provision, by

REGINALD BRIAN, who had before succeeded him in St David's   This prelate was honoured with the personal regard and friendship of that flower of English chivalry, the renowned and valiant Edward the Black Prince, and was one of the persons to whom he dispatched the first account and particulars of the famous battle at Poitiers, in a letter, written in French, remarkable for its piety, modesty, and politeness, dated at Bourdeaux, Oct 20, 1356, and addressed to Bishop Brian, at Alvechurch. (4)   In 1361, he

(1) Whilst he was prior, he built the guesten hall, at present called the audit house, adjoining to the prior's lodgings, (now the deanry) anno 1320. He is also said to have built a bridge at Braunsford, near Worcester, the place of his nativity, over the river Tame [Lel Itin vol VIII p 127]

(2) Browne Willis's MS p 641, in vol I Cath

(3) This prelate had the credit of ending a dispute which had subsisted between the two archiepiscopal sees for near two hundred years, about the privilege of having each their cross borne up before them in the province of the other   This famous controversy was brought to a crisis in 1315 The superiority and precedency of the see of Canterbury over that of York had been allowed and confirmed by several popes, and kings of England, down to that period, when Greenfield, Archbishop of York, in passing through the diocese of Worcester, presumed to have his cross borne before him, and to give his benediction to the people Walter Reginald, then Archbishop of Canterbury, in which province this diocese is, sent forthwith two mandates to Maydenston, then Bishop of Worcester, commanding him to excommunicate the Archbishop of York, and all his adherents , which was accordingly done at the priory of Lanthony, near Gloucester, and also in the archdeaconry of Worcester • In confirmation of the concordat now acceded to by the two archbishops, Pope Innocent VI to gratify both the parties, invented that nice distinction of *Primate of England,* and *Primate of all England,* which last was given to Simon Islip, then Archbishop of Canterbury †

(4) The original letter is now in the archives of the Dean and Chapter of Worcester [Regist Reginaldi Brien, Wigorn Episcopi, fol 113] A copy of it was communicated by Dr Lyttelton, dean of

• Muyd Regis f 30, 31   Dr Thomas's Account of the Bishops of Worcester, p 162, 163. and in Appendix, No 81, p 93   † Angl Sac. Drake's York, p. 434, 435.

was advanced from this to the see of Ely, by Pope Innocent VI. But he died of the plague at Alvechurch, in December that year, before he could take possession of it; and was buried in this cathedral. He was succeeded here by

JOHN BARNET, in virtue of the Pope's provisory bull. He was chaplain to Thomas de L'Isle, Bishop of Ely, residentiary canon of St. Paul's, archdeacon of London, and then of Essex; from whence he was promoted to this see In 1362, he was constituted treasurer of England, and the year following was translated to the see of Bath and Wells, and from thence to Ely, 1366. He was succeeded at Worcester by

WILLIAM WITTLESEY, translated hither from the bishopric of Rochester, by the Pope's authority, March 6, 1363; to which translation he consented, 6 April, 1364 (1) He was sister's son of Simon Islip, Archbishop of Canterbury; educated at Cambridge, and was master of Peter-house college there, to which, at his death, he left his library. He was also archdeacon of Huntingdon. From the university he was sent by his uncle to the court of Rome, as his proctor In 1368, he was translated hence to the see of Canterbury, in succession to his uncle; and was succeeded in this by

WILLIAM LYNN, then Bishop of Chichester, translated to Worcester by Pope Urban V. 1368 He died Nov. 18, 1373, having been taken with an apoplectic fit as he was mounting his horse to go to parliament. He was succeeded by

HENRY WAKEFIELD, Archdeacon of Canterbury, whom Pope Gregory XI put into this see, in preference to Walter Leigh, Prior, chosen by the prior and convent of Worcester, with the approbation of the king. Two years before his appointment to this see, he had been unsuccessful in his interest to obtain that of Ely; and his receiving this, is said to have been in consequence of that failure, and to make him amends. He was consecrated Bishop of Worcester, Oct. 28, 1375 In 1377, he was constituted high treasurer of England. In the year 1380, he finished the addition of the two Saxon arches to the west end of the cathedral; and, in the year 1386, the great porch or north entrance of it. (2) He died at Blockley,

Exeter, and rector of Alvechurch, to the Society of Antiquaries, before whom it was read, Jan. 24, 1754. [See Archæologia, vol I Art XLIV p 213 and a translation of it in Dr. Nash, vol. l. p. 34]

(1) Hist and Antiq Rochester, p 148   (2) He had a controversy with his prior, John Green, about the use of the mitre, ring, gloves, pastoral staff, tunic, and dalmatic, which episcopal ornaments had been first granted by Pope Clement VI 1350-1, Jan 8, to Prior John de Evesham, and confirmed

C c

11 March, 1394-5, and lies buried between the two lowermost pillars at the west end of the nave of this cathedral. (1)   His successor was

TIDEMAN DE WINCHCOMB, Bishop of Landaff. He had been physician to the king, and Abbat of Beaulieu, a house of Cistertians, in Hampshire. Merks, Bishop of Carlisle, and Tideman, Bishop of Worcester, are said before their promotion to have been of the nocturnal parties, all the year round, in which Richard II indulged himself so excessively, as to have sullied his character living and dead. Tideman was, however, a firm adherent to him, and opposed with all his influence the usurpation of Henry IV. (2)   He died, June 13, 1401, and was buried in this cathedral, being the last bishop interred here before Queen Elizabeth's time (3)

RICHARD CLIFFORD, dean of York, archdeacon of Canterbury, and chaplain to King Richard II bishop elect of Bath and Wells, was elected also by the monks of Worcester to this see, and to which he was confirmed by Pope Boniface, 1401. In 1396, he was made master of Hastings college, which he resigned in 1398. He was canon of St Stephen's, Westminster, and keeper of the privy seal of Henry. (4)   He was sent by the king into Germany, to treat with the emperor about a marriage between his son and Lady Blanch, the king's eldest daughter .(5)   During the prelacy of this bishop, in a synod held at Worcester, A D 1404, temp Hen. IV. by Arundel, Archbishop of Canterbury, one of the acts constituted, that the obsequies of every English bishop deceased should be celebrated in all the cathedrals of the kingdom (6) In 1407, he was translated to the see of London. His successor in this was

THOMAS PEVERELL, descended of an honourable family in Suffolk, bred

by Urban V in 1363, and now enlarged by Pope Boniface , but which Bishop Wakefield would not admit of. The archbishop however intervening, and exhorting the prior to submit, it was thus decreed, 13 Nov 1391 " That the prior might wear in the presence of the bishop his mitre fringed with gold, but without gems and precious stones , also his ring, but no pastoral staff In his absence, for the honour of God, the blessed Virgin Mary, and the church of Worcester, the prior might wear his mitre adorned with precious stones, his ring, gloves, tunic, and dalmatic, and give his blessing at mass and at table He might also carry his pastoral staff, upon condition that it should be much shorter than his, painted with only two colours, white and blue, without any gold colour, or set with any gems or pearls " •

(1) See the Plan, ref No 51   (2) Gough's Sep Mon p 165   (3) Willis's Cath vol I p 642   (4) Willis's MS note, p 642 , in his Cath. vol I. Drake's York, p 564   (5) Hall's Chron p 19   (6) Fuller, Book iv. p 159

• Lib Pens f 51 a   Lib Alb f 412. Wakefield, f. 94   Dr Thomas, Bishops, p. 186. Ibid. Append. No. 110, 111 p. 125, 126.

at Oxford, and became a Carmelite friar In 1398, he was made Bishop of Ossory, in Ireland, by King Richard II. In 1399, removed from thence to Landaff, in Wales; and, in 1407, advanced to this see by Pope Gregory XII. He died at his manor of Hembury, in Gloucestershire, March 2, 1418-19, and was buried in the Carmelite's church, juxta Universitatem Oxon ; for so it is expressly said in the prior and convent's instrument of their election, and notifying the same to Pope Martin V. (1)   The prior and convent of Worcester, April 24, 1419, chose to succeed him

PHILIP MORGAN, LL. D. an eminent civilian, and chancellor of Normandy; during his continuance in which province, King Henry V to whom he had been chaplain, deputed him to treat with the ambassador of Lewis, the dauphin of France, at Alençon, about a peace. Among the six bishops appointed to form part of the privy council during the minority of Henry VI. this bishop received that honour from the parliament. (2)   In 1425, Pope Martin V. translated him from this to the see of Ely, and at the same time conferred this on

THOMAS POLTON, Bishop of Chichester. Whilst he was prebend of Sarum, he assisted at the council of Constance, in 1418 (3)   In 1420, he was made Bishop of Hereford, where he sat but fifteen months before he was removed to Chichester, and from thence to Worcester In 1432, he, with the prior of Norwich, was sent by the king to the council of Basil, where he died, in August, 1433, and was there buried, and not at Rome, as by some is reported. (4)   In his will, in Registro Chicheley, at Lambeth, fol. 438, 439, he directed to be buried in the priory of Bustleham, co Berks, of the order of St. Austin, of which he stiles himself a brother ; and bequeathed his mitre to the cathedral of Worcester (5)

After his death, Pope Eugenius conferred this see on Thomas Brown, dean of Salisbury, who was then at the council of Basil : whilst the monks at Worcester (with the permission of the king, who afterwards prevailed on the Pope to withdraw his nomination of Brown) chose to this see

THOMAS BOURGCHIER, or Bourchier, commonly called Bowser; (6) he was dean of St Martin's, London, son of William, Earl of Ewe, in Normandy, by Ann, daughter of Thomas de Woodstock, Duke of Gloucester ;

---

(1) Dr Thomas's Account of the Bishops of Worcester, p 191.   (2) Fuller's Ch. Hist Book iv. P 170   (3) B Willis's MS in Cath vol I p 643   (4) Reg Sed Vac f 260
(5) Willis's Cath vol I p 643   (6) Synonymous with Burser, of a college, or church.

C c 2

which Thomas was a son of King Edward III He was bred in Oxford, of which university he was, about this time, made chancellor Being as yet under the age which the canons require for episcopal orders, he was not consecrated till April, 1435 In 1436, he was chosen to the vacant see of Ely, by the monks there, and confirmed by the Pope ; but the king refusing his consent, Bourchier, apprehensive of incurring a premunire, durst not accept of it. But on the death of the Cardinal Lewis de Luxemburg, Bishop of Ely, in 1443, the king permitted him to take it From whence he was afterwards translated to Canterbury, in 1454, by Pope Nicholas V In 1455, 33 Henry VI. he was constituted lord chancellor of England, and, in 1464, was created cardinal, by the title of *S Cyriacus in Thermis.* (1)

Though this bishop owed all his promotions to Henry VI yet, by appointment, or *ex officio*, he crowned his successor, Edward IV on whose death, in 1483, the great and privy seal, with the royal signet, or seal ring, were committed to his custody ; and in the year following he crowned his successor and brother, Richard III , and what is yet more extraordinary, he crowned Henry VII. and soon after married him to his queen, Elizabeth of York, daughter of Edward IV (2) He died at his palace at Knoll, in Kent, March 30, 1486, and was buried, according to his will, on the north side of the choir of his metropolitan church, near the high altar, under a very magnificent tomb, which is still remaining (3) He was succeeded in this bishopric by

JOHN CARPENTER, D. D He was rector of Beaconsfield from about 1430 to 1435, and in 1421, was presented to St Mildred's church, in Oxford, (4) of which university he was afterwards chancellor, and provost of Oriel college, in which he was bred, and in which he founded a fellowship for a native of the diocese of Worcester ; (5) he was also master of St Anthony's, London, and was promoted to this see by the bull of Pope Eugenius IV

---

(1) Godwin, p 129 (2) Antiq Brit Eccl p 443 Sandford, p 465 (3) Bishop Godwin remarks, [De Præsul Angl p 129] that Cardinal Bourchier was a bishop above 51 years, 32 years of which he was an archbishop, a longer time than any he had met with among the English bishops He built anew the stately house of Knoll, the seat of his Grace the Duke of Dorset By his will, of which Battelev has printed an extract, he made a bequest of an image of the blessed Virgin, of silver gilt, valued at £69 5s to the cathedral church of Worcester [Weever's Fun Mon p 31, 117 Bentham's Ely, p 174, 175, 176] The memory of Archbishop Bourchier is to be respected, because he was the principal instrument of introducing the inestimable art of printing into England, temp Edward IV

(4) B Willis's MS in p 643, Cath (5) Angl Sac P 1 p 538 Wood's Antiq Oxon I p 104

He erected a handsome gatehouse to his palace at Hartlebury, which was ruined in the civil wars. In 1461, he set up a library in the charnel house at Worcester, and endowed it with £10. per annum, for a librarian (1) He died at Northwyke, near Worcester, from whence he was taken to West-bury upon Trin, his native village, near Bristol, to be interred, where, as Sir Robert Atkyns tells us, was a plain altar monument erected to his me-mory (2)   He retained a fondness for that place, in which he was reve-renced as a saint, and affected to stile himself Bishop of Worcester and Westbury (3) He joined with Sir William Cannings,(4) who was dean there, in rebuilding the college of Westbury; to which he added a stately gate, and augmented the endowment. He was also a great benefactor to St. Mary's hall, Oxford. To him succeeded

JOHN ALCOCK, Bishop of Rochester, translated hither 1476 (5) He was born at Beverley, in Yorkshire, and educated at Cambridge   He had been dean of the royal chapel of St Stephen, Westminster, keeper of the great seal, 1473: president of Wales in the first year of Edward IV and in the next year master of the rolls   In the two ordinances of Edward IV. on committing the care of Prince Edward to Earl Rivers and the Bishop of Worcester, Alcock was the prelate appointed to that honour (6) About the year 1481, he rebuilt the church of Little Malvern, and dedicated it to St. Mary, St. Giles, and St. John the Evangelist (7) He also built a chapel at Beverley, and a chantry for the souls of his parents (8) In 1484, he founded a chapel, (9) or chantry, on the south side of Trinity church, at

(1) Godwin   Abingdon's MS. Fuller, B iv p 104. Willis, vol I p 643 Cath   Leland

(2) " This monument [says B Willis, in his MS note, p 643 vol I of his Cath] seems never to have had any inscription   It is an altar tomb, with only his skeleton lying on it   I saw it myself, and went on purpose to Westbury   His effigies is in painted glass, in the east window of the north ile " The tomb is in the south-west corner of the chancel [Sir R Atkyns's Gloucestershire, p 422]

(3) Bishops anciently appear to have had authority to alter their stile   It was also an ancient custom, that clergymen should take their surname from the place where they were born, and among monks and friars it continued till the suppression of their abbies [Gibbons's MS Plut 30. v A. Harl Col. Mus Brit]   (4) He built Ratcliff church, Bristol, of which city he was thrice mayor growing in years, he took orders, and became dean of the collegiate church of Westbury [C rp v 11 t 39   Dr Tho-mas, p 198]   (5) For the ceremonial of his installation, which took place Dec 8th, 1476, see Appendix to this Section, No IX. p xxxiv, xxxv.   (6) See p 7, Sir John Doderidge's MS Bibl Sloan No 3479. Plut. XXII G Mus Brit.   (7) Godwin.   (8) Osborne's Cat, Bib Harl. vol III. 389   (9) In this chapel he was buried A D 1500 [See Biographia Britannica]

This must be erroneous   he lies buried in the middle of a sumptuous chapel which he had built for himself at the east end of the north ile of the presbytery of his cathedral church   His tomb, with his

Kingston upon Hull. He turned St. Radegund's old polluted nunnery at Cambridge into a new foundation, called Jesus' college (1) He was translated hence to the see of Ely, by Pope Innocent VIII. anno 1486, and the same year made lord chancellor of England In the same year also it appears, in the "manner and order taken for the christening of the hyghe and mighty Prince Arthur, son to our soveraigne lord King Henry VII. that Master Alcoke, Bishop of Worcester, did hallowe the fonte, and christned the prince in pontificalibus," (at Winchester) (2) He was succeeded in this bishopric by

ROBERT MORTON, Archdeacon of York, Gloucester, and Winchester, promoted by the Pope, at the same time that he removed Alcock He was nephew to John Morton, Archbishop of Canterbury In 1479, he was made master of the rolls He obtained a charter of pardon from King Henry VII in 1496-7, of all treasons, misprisions, &c. that he might possibly be taxed with. (3) This indeed was but a necessary security against the odious proceedings of the harpies of that reign, who marked out the old servants of the crown for victims of their avarice, and worried them with frivolous indictments, enforced with outlawries and confiscations. This grant releases the bishop from suffering any penalties for his acceptance of the Pope's provisory bull. He died the beginning of May following, and was buried in the nave of St Paul's church, London; though in his will, in which he gave twenty marks to this cathedral, he directed to be interred in the cemetery where he should die (4) His memory is revered in history, on account

effigies thereon, much defaced, is placed on the north side of the chapel, under an arch of stone [See Plate XXI in Bentham's Ely, and his account of the chapel, p 183]

(1) Osborne's Cat Bib Harl vol III p. 390. In the master's lodgings of that college is still to be seen his picture from the life He was also represented in painted glass, in the east window of Little Malvern church, Worcestershire, with his patron, Edw IV his queen, and family , none of which now remain, but those of Prince Edward and the Princesses, Elizabeth, afterwards queen of Henry VII Cecilie, afterwards Viscountess Wells, and Anne, the third daughter, afterwards Duchess of Norfolk. [Ab. MS p. 60 See also an account of the window, in Dr Nash's Worcestershire, vol II. p 142 ; and of the portraits, in Acta Historica Reginarum Angliæ, art Elizabeth, Queen Dowager of Edward IV. sub an 1483, p. 24, 26 by the Author]   (2) Antiq Repert vol IV p 194, 195 This prelate was not only a considerable writer, but an excellent architect. and, as such, was appointed comptroller of the royal works and buildings under King Henry VII • His own chapel at Ely is a noble specimen of his architectural skill, though at present it lies sadly mangled   (3) See Dr Thomas's Appendix, No. CXXIX. p. 152, 153   (4) Willis's Cath. vol. I p. 643

• Parker's Hist of Camb. p. 119

of his having been instrumental in forming the union of the houses of York and Lancaster. (1)   He was succeeded by

JOHN GIGLES, or de Liliis, LL. D. an Italian, of the country of Lucca, the Pope's questor, or collector for the apostolic chamber in England. He was rector of Swaffham in Norfolk, St. Michael, Crooked lane, London, and of Laneham in Suffolk, prebendary of London and Wells, (2) archdeacon of London and Gloucester, the king's solicitor in the court of Rome, and dean of Wells, 1478. He was advanced to this see by Pope Alexander. (3) He had an extraordinary commission from Pope Innocent VIII. authorizing him to pardon the most heinous offences; whoredom, adultery, robbery, murder, usury, simony, theft, and all sorts of crimes; and to dispense with the non-restitution of goods acquired by any sort of fraud and cozenage, on condition, that part of such gain should be given to the Pope's commissaries, or their deputies (4) Nor can we suppose him negligent in applying this power to his own as well as his master's emolument. He died 1498, and lies buried in the English college at Rome

SYLVESTER GIGLES, his brother's son, had also the merit of being collector of the apostolic chamber, and for his usefulness in that employment was by the Pope advanced to this see. (5)   In 1512, he was sent by King Henry VIII. to the Lateran council, and died at Rome, anno 1521. In St. Michael's church, at Lucca, there is a monument to his memory. He was succeeded by

JULIUS DE MEDICIS, or Julio di Medici, a Florentine, promoted to this bishopric by Pope Leo X. to whom he was nearly related, being his brother's son; whom, from a soldier of the order of St John of Jerusalem, he had raised to be a cardinal priest, and vice-chancellor of the Roman church, administrator thereof both in spirituals and temporals; archbishop of Narbon and of Florence He held this see but one year; for, upon the death of his uncle, Pope Leo, fearing that Adrian, the new pontiff, (who was an Englishman) should think him too great a pluralist, he resigned the mitre of Worcester in September, 1522. He was chosen Pope after the death of Adrian VI. and took upon him the name of Clement VII. (6) and died 1534. He was succeeded in this see by

(1) Batteley's Pref to the second part of Cant. Sac   (2) B Willis, MS. in Cath vol. I. p. 643.
(3) Wharton, Angl Sac   (4) Ibid P I p 538   (5) Dr Thomas's Append. No CXXXI p 155.
(6) This pontiff tried in vain the effect of his Vatican thunder upon Henry VIII. who stood unmoved.

JEROME DE GHINUCCIIS, or de Nugutiis, an Italian, as were three of his predecessors; nor was an Englishman promoted to this see till the Pope's authority was abolished; to such a height was the power of the see of Rome advanced over the English church. In Pope Adrian's bull of provision he is said to be Bishop of Asculum, auditor general of the apostolical chamber, and domestic chaplain to the Pope.

This bishop being employed as envoy by King Henry VIII in foreign parts, was of eminent service to him, in procuring the judgment of the Italian and Spanish divines against his marriage with Queen Catharine, for which, in the year 1533, upon the intercession of this king, and Francis King of France, Pope Clement VII (his predecessor in this see) raised him to the dignity of a cardinal. After the papal supremacy had been abrogated in England, this bishop, because he did not reside in his diocese, was deprived by act of parliament, in the year 1534-5. He was succeeded by

HUGH LATIMER, son of Hugh Latimer, of Thirkesson, in Leicestershire, a reputable husbandman. He was born about 1470, educated in Christ's college, Cambridge, and was cross keeper to that university, where he took orders, and was at first a zealous papist, but afterwards a more zealous protestant In 1529, by Lord Cromwell's interest, he was made vicar of West Kingston, in Wiltshire In 1534, he became chaplain to Queen Anne Bullen, by whose favour he was promoted to this bishopric, and received the temporalities of the king, Oct 5, 1535 (1) He governed this see about four years. His injunctions to his clergy of this diocese sufficiently shew his opinion of the then state of the church, the gross ignorance and negligence which pervaded the whole clergy, and how necessary a reformation was become; of which the first of the series may serve as ample evidence, viz " Item, That ye and every one of you provyde to have of youre owne a Hole Byble yf ye can convenyently, or at the leaste a New Testament, both in Latin and Englishe " (2) In 1539, when, through the prevalence of the popish party, the six articles were imposed as terms of communion; unable to subscribe them, he resigned his bishopric, and retired to a private, but not an obscure or indolent life; for he went on to preach with greater

(1) Angl Sac   (2) These injunctions were given in his visitation in 1537, 29 Henry VII and after the Scriptures were appointed to be read in English •

• Abingdon's Hist of the Cath in Appendix, p 157

liberty and courage than before, and laboured to stem the tide of superstition and oppression, and to establish religion in its native purity. Thus he continued in advancing the protestant faith, till on the death of King Edward VI. he was apprehended and imprisoned, with Archbishop Cranmer, and Bishop Ridley, at Oxford, where, with the latter, he was burnt, October 16th, 1555 (1) In the reign of King Henry VIII. upon his resignation, succeeded

John Bell, a Worcestershire man, who was educated in Baliol college, Oxford, and spent some time in Cambridge ; to both which places he was a benefactor, particularly to the former, endowing it for the maintenance of two scholars, born in the diocese of Worcester. (2) He was rector of Weston Sub-ege, near Campden, archdeacon of Gloucester, prebendary of Lincoln and Litchfield, warden of the collegiate church of Stratford upon Avon, and vicar-general of the bishop of Worcester, from 1518 to 1526. On his recommendation to King Henry VIII. he made him his envoy to foreign princes, and one of his council ; and as a reward for his singular service in defence of his divorce from Queen Catharine, he gave him this bishopric, anno 1539, which he enjoyed not long ; for he resigned it in 1543, (3) but for what cause is unknown, and retired to a private life at Clerkenwell, where he died, 1556, and was interred in St. James's church there. Upon his resignation succeeded

Nicholas Heath, Bishop of Rochester, archdeacon of Stafford, and chief almoner to the king, who had given leave to the dean and chapter to choose him. He was the first prelate on the new foundation in the see of Rochester, to which he was consecrated April 4th, 1540. He held the archdeaconry of Stafford, and the rectories of Shoreham and Cliff in Kent, in commendam with his bishopric ; he likewise had a licence to enjoy the same privilege for five years after his translation to the more valuable see of Worcester (4) In 1549-50, refusing to subscribe the book for the making of bishops and priests, and disobeying the king's orders for discontinuing the

---

(1) See his life in Fox's Book of Martyrs, vol III p 375, &c See also a life of this bishop by Mr. Gilpin, 1755 it is an entertaining piece of biography. Of the famous relic of the blood of *Hales,* Hugh (Latimer) Bishop of Worcester certified to (Lord) Cromwell, on the evidence of the prior of Hales, and three more, that they found it to be " an unctuowse gum colouryd, which beinge in the glasse, appeared red like blood, but out of it glistering yellow like amber." [Gough's Brit Topogr. in Gloucestershire, p 177, 1st edit }   (2) Fuller, B iii p 68

(3) Dr Thomas's Append No 136. p 161, 162   (4) Hist and Antiq Rochester, p 155

mass, (1) he thereby incurred Edward's displeasure ; w as committed prisoner to the Fleet, and by royal authority deprived of his office ; not by the power of an ecclesiastical court, but by secular delegates, three of whom were civilians, and three common lawyers. (2) Upon his deprivation, the king promoted

JOHN HOPER, or Hooper, Bishop of Gloucester, to this see by his letters patent, 1552, and at the same time suppressed that bishopric, and made it an archdeaconry, dependent on Worcester, as it formerly had been but this suppression giving some offence, in order to put a stop to it, Hooper formally resigned, and new letters patent of episcopacy were granted him, like the former, with this difference only, that now the two sees were to be united ; the revenues of Gloucester being but small, the two cities near each other, and the dioceses not so extensive as to require two pastors, they should for the future be united, under the title of the Bishopric or see of Worcester and Gloucester, as are the sees of Litchfield and Coventry, and of Bath and Wells ; and to this end, the bishop was enjoined to spend one half year in one diocese, and the other half in the other (3) In pursuance of this grant, he was rechosen, and confirmed in the united sees as Bishop of Worcester and Gloucester.

Bishop Hooper was bred in Oxford, and travelled into Switzerland, one of the first Nonconformists On his being appointed Bishop of Gloucester, he refused to wear the episcopal habit, and, as generallys upposed, the oath of canonical obedience to the archbishop ; but at length submitted to both, and was consecrated Bishop of Gloucester (4) This bishop, in the next reign, fell a sacrifice to the madness of the times, and died for the protestant doc-

---

(1) Collier's Eccl Hist vol II p 312

(2) Hist Ref P II B 1 As soon as King Edward VI came to the crown, all bishops were commanded to take out commissions to exercise both temporal and spiritual jurisdiction within their dioceses, as Bonner had done, 31 Henry VIII 1539 whereby they all acknowledged that they held their bishoprics only during the king's pleasure, and exercised jurisdiction in them as his delegates, in his name, and by his authority only In December, 1546, an act was passed in parliament to confirm the same, and that for the future, the choosing of bishops by conge d'elire, being tedious and expensive, and only the shadow of election in it, they should be made by the king's letters patent, that courts ecclesiastical should be kept in his name, and they to act by no other authority than his, as the supreme head of the church all offenders to suffer imprisonment at his majesty's will By virtue of which act Heath was imprisoned as above Bishop Heath's commission bears date 26th Feb 1546 [See Dr Thomas's Appendix, No 137, p 163, 164]

(3) Dr Thomas's Appendix, No 138, p 165, &c to 172.   (4) Fuller, Book vii. p 402, 403

trine with a martyr's fortitude: a man of eminent learning, exemplary
piety, unblemished morals, and of most extensive charity (1) Upon the
accession of Queen Mary to the throne, she restored this see to

NICHOLAS HEATH, who was happy enough to be in great favour with her.
She made him president of Wales, and soon after translated him to the see of
York; and upon the death of Gardiner, made him chancellor of England.
The bull of Pope Paul IV. which confirmed his election to the archbishopric
of York, bears date 11 kal. Julii, anno 1555, and is the last instrument of
that kind acknowledged in that see. (2) He was succeeded in this chair by

RICHARD PATES, an Oxfordshire man, and bred in that university. He
was archdeacon of Winchester, and afterwards of Lincoln. he had been
employed in several embassies by King Henry, particularly to the emperor,
1534 and 1540; but in 1542, was attainted of high treason, and deprived of
his archdeaconry. Queen Mary preferred him to this see, in which he
continued till Queen Elizabeth's accession to the throne, when he was deprived, and imprisoned for some little time; and when released, he went

(1) See Fox's Book of Martyrs, vol III f 119 Bishop Blandford in his MS. says, "In the year
" 1551, June 21st, he (Bishop Hooper) came to Worcester with his wife and daughter, he wore a long
" beard" In his person he was tall, and was much afflicted with sciatic pains. He was burnt at Gloucester, opposite the college of priests, Friday, Feb 9th, 1555. When he was chained to the stake, a pardon, on condition of his recantation, was placed on a stool before him, but he was inflexible, and bore
his torments with invincible patience. The following " Order for his burning at Gloucester, in the
time of Queen Mary," is taken from No 464, in the Cotton lib Brit. Mus Cleopatra, E. V. p 380.

" Wheras, John Hooper, who of late was called Bushope of Worcestere and Glocestere, is by due
ordere of the lawes ecclesyastyque condempned and judged for a moste obstynate, false detestyble here-
tycke, and comytted to our seculere poure to be burned accordinge to the holsome and good lawes of o'
realme in that case p'videde, for asmuche as in thos cittyes and diocyes therof he hathe in tymes paste
preached and taughte most pestelente herrecies and doctryne to o' subiects theare. wee have therfore
geven ordere that the sayd Hooper, who yet p'sistethe obstynate, and hath refused mercye when it was gra-
tyously offerede, shall be put to executyone in the sayd cyttye of Glocestere, for the example and terrore
of otheres, suche as he hathe theare seduced and mistaughte, and because he hathe done moste harme
theare And woll that yo're callynge unto yo'' some of reputacone dwellynge in the sheere, such as yee
thinke beste, shall repayre unto o' sayd cittye, and be at the sayd executyone, assystynge our mayre and
sherifes of the same cyttye in his behalfe; and for asmuche also as the sayd Hooper is, as heretickes be, a
vayngloryous p'son, and delytethe in his tonge, and havinge lybertye maye use his sayd tonge to p'swade
suche as he hathe seduced to p'syste in the myserable opynyone that he hathe sowne amongeste them,
our pleasure is thearfor, and wee require yo'' to take ordere that the sayde Hooper be nether at the tyme
of his executyone, nor in goinge to the place thearof, sufferede to speake at large, but thether to be lede
quietly, and in sylence, for eschuenge of further infectyon, and suche inconvenyencye as maye otherwise
insue in this p'te Wherrof fayle yo'' not, as ye tendere our pleasure."

(2) Godwin, Torr. p 473 —Drake, p 453

Dd 2

abroad, and sat in the council of Trent, and died at Louvain, Nov. 22d, 1565, a zealous Romanist, but not of persecuting principles. (1)   On his deprivation succeeded

EDWIN SANDYS, D. D descended from an ancient family of the Sandyses of Bees, in Cumberland ; he was son of William Sandys of Eastwaite Furness, (2) in Lancashire, a justice of the peace, and king's receiver of that county ; educated at Cambridge, and promoted to be master of Catherine hall, and vice-chancellor of that university.   When the Duke of Northumberland came there to oppose Queen Mary, in defence of Queen Jane's right to the crown, he commanded the vice-chancellor (Sandys) to assert the justice of her cause in a sermon, which he did, but in such decent terms, that, notwithstanding they were both seized and imprisoned, and the duke in the event lost his life, Dr Sandys was discharged, after twenty-nine weeks imprisonment, and fled with his wife into Germany ; but was deprived of his offices in the university, and likewise divested of his prebends in the churches of Carlisle and Peterborough. (3)   On the death of Queen Mary he returned to England, and was greatly assisting in preparing the book of Common Prayer, in the translation of the Bible, and in the reformation of the church under Queen Elizabeth, who soon promoted him to this see   He sat here with great reputation   (4)   In 1570 he was translated from hence to the see of London, which he would willingly have avoided, being easy at Worcester And from thence was advanced to the see of York in 1576 ; in both which sees he was successor to Grindal   He died at Southwell, July 10th, 1588, in which collegiate church he lies buried, in the north corner of the choir, under a handsome monument, on which his effigy is laid ; and his children are

(1) Strype's Hist Ref p 146 —B Willis, vol II p 646

(2) Hawkeshead, the fourth market-town in Furness, is the birth-place of Archbishop Sandys, who founded there a grammar school, and made the church parochial, in which his father and mother have a tomb   [Gough's Additions to Camden, in Lancashire, vol III. p 143]

(3) Strype's Annals of the Ref. vol II p 422

(4) Sir John Bourne of Batenhale, near Worcester, who had been one of the principal secretaries of state in Queen Mary's reign, and looked with an evil eye on the Reformation, took an envious pleasure in disturbing the quiet of this bishop   His turbulent behaviour drew on him the displeasure of the lords of the privy council, who committed him to the Marshalsea, but released him on his humble submission [See Strype's Annals of the Ref vol I p 386—403] Fuller remarks, [Book ix p 197] it is hard to say whether Archbishop Sandys was more eminent in his own virtues, or more happy in his flourishing posterity   In 1562, during his prelacy at Worcester, the corn rent was restored to the college   [Bishop Blandford's Ms]

represented kneeling. (1) Upon his removal to London, the queen nominated

Dr JAMES CALFHILL, canon of Christchurch, Oxford, dean of Bocking in Essex, and archdeacon of Colchester, to succeed him, but he dying in August that year, before his consecration,

NICHOLAS BULLINGHAM, Bishop of Lincoln, was translated hither. He was a native of Worcester, and educated in All Souls college, Oxford, where he took a degree in law in 1536 He was afterwards archdeacon of Lincoln, and became that bishop's vicar-general When Queen Mary began her reign, he absconded, and applied himself to the study of divinity ; and on Queen Elizabeth's accession, he became doctor of his faculty at Cambridge, and was appointed a judge ecclesiastical in the court of the Archbishop of Canterbury. In 1559 he was promoted to the see of Lincoln , and in 1570 was translated from thence to Worcester (2) He died here, much respected, anno 1576, and lies interred on the north side of the high altar in this cathedral. To him succeeded

JOHN WHITGIFT, D D. master of Trinity college, Cambridge, nominated 1576 to this bishopric, and confirmed 1577. He was descended of the family of the Whitgifts of Whitgift, a village in Marshland, Yorkshire, (3) born at Great Grimsby in Lincolnshire, and educated in Pembroke hall, Cambridge, under the tuition of the famous martyr John Bradford When young, he was appointed Margaret's professor of divinity at Cambridge, distinguished himself greatly in that chair, and made the way by his merit into higher preferments, and amongst these had the deanry of Lincoln conferred upon him in 1571. His writings were in great esteem · he supported the controversy against the puritans with great spirit. The year after his episcopal consecration, the queen made him vice-president of the Marches of Wales and from a confidence in his well known integrity, she gave him commission to visit the cathedral churches of Litchfield and Hereford, and regulate some disorders in them, of which complaint had been made to her, and which were by him reformed (4) She farther honoured him with a grant of collating to all the prebends in his own cathedral. And in September, 1583,

---

(1) See the Plate, Drake's York, p 456. See also Torr Willis, vol I p 48, 49, and 646
(2) Wood, Athen Oxon vol I p 702   (3) Camden in W Rid Yorkshire, p 35, Gough's ed.
(4) Sir G Paul's Life of Whitgift, p 30, &c

translated him from hence to Canterbury. This see remained void from that time till October in the year following, when

EDMUND FREAKE, D. D. then Bishop of Norwich, was nominated to it. He was a native of Essex, had his education in Cambridge, was great almoner to Queen Elizabeth, and had passed through several ecclesiastical dignities, among which he was archdeacon of Canterbury in 1564, before he came to the deanry of Salisbury; to which was added the bishopric of Rochester, being consecrated thereto on the 13th, and enthroned in person on the 22d of March, 1571; (1) whence he was translated to Norwich, 1575, and from Norwich hither, where he died, 1591; and lies buried in the south ile of the body of this cathedral (2) He approved himself a zealous assertor of the church discipline, and bore the character of a pious and well qualified divine The see again lay void till January, 1592-3, when the dean and chapter, pursuant to the queen's congé, elected

RICHARD FLETCHER, then Bishop of Bristol. He was bred at Benet college, Cambridge In 1583 he was made dean of Peterborough; and in 1586-7, was present with Mary Queen of Scots, when she suffered death in Fotheringay castle, in Northamptonshire (3) In 1589, he was made Bishop of Bristol, and about the same time almoner to the queen · from thence he was promoted to this see, where he continued till January, 1594-5, when he was translated to the bishopric of London, where he died suddenly, 1596, and was buried in St George's chapel in St Paul's, as it stood before the conflagration, 1666 This see remained vacant almost two years, when it was filled by

THOMAS BILSON, D D a native of Winchester, great grandson of Arnold Bilson, a German, whose wife is said to have been daughter of a duke of Bavaria He was educated at New college, Oxford; and 1565 admitted fellow on that foundation From being master of the school at Winchester, he rose to be warden of the college there June 13th, 1596, he was consecrated for the see of Worcester, in which he sat but a short time, being next year trans-

---

(1) Hist of Rochester, p 159   (2) See a description of his tomb, p 88

(3) See his teazing speech to her on the scaffold, in Strype's Annals of Queen Elizabeth, vol III p 385 As soon as her majesty's head had fallen from the block, he cried out, " So may all the enemies of Queen Elizabeth perish!" The contrast between Fletcher's conduct on this occasion, and that of Feckenham, dean of St Paul's, on a similar duty at the death of Lady Jane Grey, is both striking and affecting, and the humanity of the protestant divine stands much lessened in the comparison.

lated to that of Winchester. His merit ranks him with the most eminent of the bishops of Queen Elizabeth's time. he was a master in civil as well as ecclesiastical literature, and wrote in a more clear and elegant stile than any of the divines his cotemporaries. The care of revising and putting the last hand to our present version of the Bible was, in the next reign, committed to this learned prelate, and Dr Miles Smith He died in 1616, and was buried on the south side of Westminster abbey, near the monument of King Richard II not far from the entrance of St Edmund's chapel. (1) His successor in this see was the then Bishop of Exeter,

GERVASE BABINGTON, D. D descended of the family of the Babingtons, in Nottinghamshire He had been fellow of Trinity college, Cambridge, domestic chaplain to Henry Earl of Pembroke, whose countess he was supposed to have assisted in her translation of the Psalms. By the earl's interest, in 1591, he was promoted to the see of Landaff, and four years after to that of Exeter; whence he was translated to Worcester. His life was exemplary; his preaching pathetic; but his theological writings are now in little esteem; as they abound with quibbles, quaint turns, and jingles on words; agreeable to the bad taste which then began to prevail (2) He died of the jaundice at the palace of Worcester, 1610, and was buried in the cathedral without any monument. (3) His collection of books he bequeathed to the library here He was succeeded by

HENRY PARRY, D D. a native of Herefordshire; educated at Corpus Christi college in Oxford; translated to this see from that of Gloucester, where he had sat three years He had been dean of Chester he died of a palsy at Worcester, Dec. 12th, 1616, and was buried in the cathedral. To him succeeded,

JOHN THORNBOROUGH, Bishop of Bristol he was born at Salisbury, educated at Magdalen college, Oxford, he obtained a chaplainship at court, and in 1589, the deanry of York. In 1593 he was consecrated bishop in Ireland for the see of Limerick; ten years after, was removed to that of Bristol, with leave to keep the deanry of York in commendam He was a great adept in chemistry, and wrote a tract about the philosopher's stone. Death

(1) Gale's Hist. Winchester Cath p 105. (2) Godwin de Præsul Angl See his death and character in Fuller, B x. p 56 (3) It is remarked that this bishop's paternal coat of arms was exactly the same with that of his bishopric

was in him the effect of extreme old age, in 1641. He lies interred in this cathedral His successor in this see was

JOHN PRIDEAUX, regius professor of divinity, and rector of Exeter college, in Oxford. (1) He was in great esteem for his abilities in the professor's chair ; and his controversial tracts in Latin had spread his fame into foreign countries He had lately been appointed one of the sub-committee for religion, which was convened by the house of lords, and empowered to inquire into abuses and innovations, and to consult about the regulating and settling the church. (2) But nothing was effected by their deliberations ; for when the bill against deans and chapters came to be agitated in parliament, the assembly broke up. He was a Devonshire man, of low extraction. In his youth, his highest ambition was to be promoted to the clerkship of a country parish : he laudably aspired, but met with a sore repulse ; for a competitor outsung him (3) To make him amends for this loss, a charitable lady supplied him with the means of qualifying himself for the pulpit ; (4) and those talents, which could not enable him to vie with rustics in psalmody, opened him a way to the highest honours, both in the university and in the church He was consecrated to the episcopal office, Dec 19, 1641, in most unhappy times, when the very office was going to be suppressed , for, before the end of that month, the bishops lost their seats in parliament · and the sequestration of their revenues following within two years after, this high preferment proved of little advantage, and rather was a detriment to him. He was disrelished by the warm churchmen, but not less zealous in his attachment to the king than they , as appears from one exercise of his episcopal power, his pronouncing all those of his diocese, who took up arms against the king, excommunicate This exposed him to be plundered ; and he was at last reduced to such difficulties, as to sell his library for the support of his family He ended his days at Breedon, in this county, July 29, 1650 : and, probably had not died much poorer, had he lived and died clerk of the parish of Ugborow (5)

The see lay vacant till the Restoration , when it was designed for Dr. Hammond, who, dying a month before the king's arrival,

---

(1) Fuller, B iv. p 102.   (2) Collier's Eccl Hist.   (3) Prince's Worthies of Devon.

(4) In his highest elevation he forgot not this incident . and used to say, " If I could have been clerk of Ugborow, I should not have been bishop of Worcester " Prince, ibid

(5) Dr Nash observes, that the inscription on the flat gravestone under which he lies buried in the church of Breedon, seems to contradict the accounts which biographers give of his extreme poverty, and

GEORGE MORLEY, D. D. was nominated to the chapter, and consecrated bishop, Oct. 28, 1660. He was born in London, son of Francis Morley, Esq. educated at Christchurch, Oxford, and retained many years as chaplain in the family of Robert Earl of Carnarvon. In 1641, he was promoted from a studentship to a canonry, and afterwards to the deanry of Christchurch, though reputed at that time a favourer of Calvinism. It is certain, that he was unacceptable to the partizans of Archbishop Laud One of his innocent jests was not easily forgiven at court. When he was asked, by a grave country gentleman, (seriously inquisitive about the tenets of different parties) " What the Arminians held?" he answered, pleasantly, that " they held all the best bishoprics and deanries in England." (1) In the beginning of 1648, he was deprived of his preferments by the then prevailing power He continued as long with King Charles I as any of his chaplains were permitted to attend him he attended Lord Capel on the scaffold in 1649; and then left England to follow the fortunes of the exiled king. During his stay abroad, he passed some years at the Hague, as chaplain to the Queen of Bohemia ; and some years at Antwerp, in the family of Sir Edward Hyde, afterwards Lord Clarendon. Upon the Restoration, he was first made dean of Christchurch, and then bishop of Worcester; and, in the space of two years, was translated to Winchester His generous and public spirit was so well known, that when the king gave him the last mentioned bishopric, he said facetiously, but with truth, that " Morley would never be the richer for it " (2) Burnet says, he was extremely passionate, but otherwise of very exemplary life . Lord Clarendon represents him as a man of remarkable temper, and prudence in conversation. He lived to a great age. He was succeeded in the see of Worcester by

JOHN GAUDEN, D. D who, in the year of the Restoration, had been made Bishop of Exeter. He was born in Essex , studied in both universities ; and in the time of the civil war, was dean of Bocking. The merit he claimed at court now, was the being author of Icon Basilike , a work, of which good

of his being employed in the servile offices in the kitchen of Exeter college, Oxford, for a support In the civil wars, his bishopric was sequestered, and he retired to Breedon, to his son-in-law Webb In this distress, which he always bore with cheerfulness and good humour, he was obliged to sell his books and furniture in order to procure the necessaries of life [Dr Nash's Worcestershire, vol I. p. 132. Art. " Breedon " in which an engraving of the bishop's portrait is introduced)

(1) Life of Lord Clarendon by himself, 8vo I. p. 50 (2) Wood Athen Oxon.

critics have thought him incapable (1) He was but four months in the possession of this see, a disease putting an end to his days, Sept 20, 1662, at
the palace in Worcester   Whereupon

JOHN EARLE, D D Dean of Westminster, and clerk of the closet, was nominated bishop, and consecrated in November the same year   As he continued not a full year in this see, I shall speak very briefly of him, though he
ranks with the illustrious of his order   He was a native of York, had been
fellow of Merton college, Oxford, and was placed near the person of the
prince, afterwards Charles II as his chaplain and sub-preceptor   He attended
that prince in his exile , who, prompt as he was to suspect piety in others,
revered it always in Dr Earle   Lord Falkland and Lord Clarendon, eminent
for their discernment of men, valued and caressed him   The character,
which one of those noble writers has left us of him, is truly amiable (2)
He was translated from this see to Sarum   He died in University college,
Oxford, Nov 17, 1665, and lies buried near the high altar in the church of
Merton college (3)   Succeeded here by

ROBERT SKINNER, D D Bishop of Oxford before the usurpation, and one

(1) The attempt to deprive the deceased monarch of the credit of having written this book, so reputable
to his talents, was carried to the greatest lengths by his enemies, whose malice pursued him beyond the
grave, and the pen of the immortal Milton was employed to that unworthy purpose   but his Eikonoklastes,
printed in 1649, in answer to Icon Basilike, totally failed in its purpose, even at the time of its appearance,
to persuade the world that it was not written by King Charles I but by some royalist, to gain respect to his
memory, and less partial posterity, having exercised their judgment upon its motives, have consigned the
unfounded calumny to oblivion   Above twenty editions of the Icon were printed within a year after the
king's death   The original MS was nearly half completed before the king left Oxford to join the Scots
it was found in his cabinet, which fell into the hands of the parliament's army at Navesby fight, and was
restored to him after he was brought to Hampton court, by the hand of Major Huntington, through the
favour of General Fairfax, of whom he obtained it   It had been seen and read by Mr Herbert, (afterwards created a baronet by Charles II) and Mr Levet, a page of the back stairs, who both attended the
king in the Isle of Wight, and had seen him from time to time employed in adding to it, under its first title
of " Suspiria Regalia " From this place, by the king's own orders, it was consigned to the press, through
the hands of Dr Bryan Duppa, then bishop of Salisbury, from whom the Rev Edward Simmons delivered
it, 23d December, to Mr Richard Royston, a bookseller in Ivy Lane, London, to whom his majesty had
before sent to prepare all things ready to print some papers, which were shortly to be conveyed to him, and
which was this copy   Royston made such speed with the printing, that it was finished before the death of
the king, the 30th of January following   The learned Mr Wigstaff has finally, by a multitude of unex-
ceptionable testimonies, proved, beyond a possibility of doubt, his majesty's being the true author of the
Icon, and put an end to the controversy for ever. [See Carte's Hist of Eng vol IV p 606   Dugdale's
View of the late Trouble in Eng p 380, 381   See also Walton's Life of Dr Sanderson , Grey's Hudi
bras, Neal's Hist of the Puritans , Warburton and others

(2) See the Life of Lord Clarendon   (3) Drake's York, p 379   Willis's Cath vol I p 625

of the few prelates of the last reign who lived to be re-established in their former sees. He was born in Northamptonshire; educated at Trinity college, in Oxford, where he became an eminent tutor; consecrated the first bishop for the see of Bristol 1636, and, in 1641, removed to that of Oxford. He joined with eleven of his brethren in a protest against the proceedings of the parliament; for which they were all arraigned of high treason, and ten of them committed to the Tower He was confined there seventeen months His sufferings taught him to temporize for, when deprived of his bishopric, he complied with the new ordinances so far, as to preserve his rectory of Launton, in Oxfordshire, till episcopacy itself was restored. He died at the age of fourscore, and was buried in this cathedral (1) Whereupon another bishop of Oxford,

WALTER BLANDFORD, D D. was translated to this see He had been warden of Wadham college, in which he kept his fellowship during the whole time of the usurpation; was chaplain to lord Clarendon; vice-chancellor of the university; and, in 1665, was promoted to the bishopric of Oxford He died unmarried, at the palace in Worcester, July 9, 1675, aged 59, and was succeeded by

JAMES FLEETWOOD, D D at that time provost of King's college, Cambridge He was born in Buckinghamshire, descended from a genteel family in Lancashire, and nearly related to the colonel of that name, one of the judges who presided at the trial of Charles I. and who commanded under Oliver Cromwell at the battle of Worcester He was educated at Eton school, and the abovementioned college, and was first preferred to the vicarage of Prees, in Shropshire; whence being driven, by a republican garrison in that neighbourhood, he accepted of a chaplainship to one of the king's regiments; and, in the battle of Edge-hill, performed grateful service, by carrying off the young princes to a place of safety For this mark of loyal attention, he was, by the special command of the king, honoured with the degree of doctor of divinity, appointed chaplain to Charles Prince of Wales, and presented to the rectory of Sutton Colfield, in Warwickshire, which was given him immediately after, but which the violence of the times soon forced from him He employed himself till the Restoration as private tutor to young noblemen at that period, he was advanced to the provostship of King's college He had the care of the education of the young Earls of Litchfield,

(1) Matthew, the eldest son of bishop Skinner, had an estate in Oxfordshire, and was returned, in 1660, to be one of the gentlemen qualified for knights of the royal oak

Kildare, and Stirling ; and was afterwards tutor to Esme, Duke of Richmond and Lenox, and to Charles, who succeeded to those ducal honours ; with the former of those dukes he retired into France, and returned at the Restoration, when King Charles II in reward for his sufferings, gave him many preferments, and ultimately the bishopric of Worcester; on his advancement to which, he resigned the provostship of King's college (1) The remainder of his days he spent chiefly in his diocese, both doing himself and exhorting others to do good.   He died in his 81st year, July 17, 1683, and lies buried in this cathedral   His successor was

WILLIAM THOMAS, D D Bishop of St David's and Dean of Worcester. (2) He was born at Bristol ; educated at Jesus' college, Oxford ; had a vicarage before the civil war , and, upon the sequestration of it, subsisted by teaching a school in Caermarthenshire. On the restoration of the royal family, he was appointed one of the chaplains to the Duke of York.   In 1665, he was installed dean of this church , and, in 1678, consecrated bishop of St. David's, with permission to hold the deanry in commendam. He quitted these preferments for the bishopric of Worcester ; a station, in which he conducted himself in difficult times with great reputation of integrity. His steadiness in the protestant cause withdrew from him the favour of King James : and his affection to his old master brought him under difficulties at the Revolution.   On his refusing the oaths to King William, he was suspended ; but died, June 25, 1689, before deprivation, which otherwise must have ensued. (3)   Upon this vacancy

EDWARD STILLINGFLLE1, D D was called to this see ; a divine of great renown   He was descended of an ancient family   Dorsetshire has the honour of his birth ; the college of St John's, in Cambridge, of his education. His first preferment was the rectory of Sutton, conferred on him 1657, by Sir Roger Burgoine, in Bedfordshire   But his best patron was his own pen; which gained him early fame, numerous friends, and rotation of preferments   We find him preacher at the Rolls, rector of St Andrew's, Holborn, lecturer at the Temple, chaplain in ordinary to the king, prebendary of Canterbury, residentiary of St Paul's, and, in the year 1678, dean of that cathedral   He was well versed in all branches of antiquity ; had no equal

(1) Noble' Memoir of the Cromwell House, vol II p 350, 351   Vid Cott MSS vol XV p 93
(2) Cott MSS vol X p 130   (3) See Dr Nash, vol II in Appendix, p 158 an interesting
account of the life of this excellent bishop

in ecclesiastical learning ; an elegant preacher ; a masterly disputant ; exercised in several controversies of note, and with high reputation of advantage ; a vigorous combatant with papists, dissenters, and socinians ; and no unequal opponent to the great Mr. Locke He may be accounted the Bellarmine of the church of England. This extraordinary man was consecrated Bishop of Worcester, Oct 13, 1689. His application to his studies impaired his health so much, as to render him unfit for the metropolitan see, to which Queen Mary was desirous of advancing him, upon the death of Archbishop Tillotson. He died, March 27, 1699, at his house in Westminster, in his 64th year, and was buried in this cathedral I have spoken already of his monument ; but his books, especially his Origines Sacræ, are his noblest and most lasting memorial (1) His successor at Worcester was

WILLIAM LLOYD, D D Bishop of Litchfield and Coventry. He was of Welch parentage , the son of Richard Lloyd, B D vicar of Sunning, and rector of Tylehurst, in Berkshire ; first commoner of Oriel college, Oxford ; afterwards of Jesus' college, where he became scholar and fellow ; B.A. 1642 ; M A 1646 He began to distinguish himself in 1667, by the first of his writings against popery ; and was successively prebendary of Ripon, rector of St Martin's, Reading ; archdeacon of Merioneth, 1668 ; dean of Bangor 1673 ; then residentiary of Sarum ; next, called to a more important pastoral care, that of St. Martin's in the fields, Westminster In this station his sermons were much celebrated He was made bishop of St. Asaph, 1680 ; committed, with six other prelates, to the Tower, by King James, in 1688 ; tried in Westminster-hall for the pretended offence, and gloriously discharged King William and Queen Mary made him their lord almoner ; and translated him to the see of Litchfield and Coventry, 1692 , from which Worcester received him (2) He died at Hartlebury, Aug. 30, 1717, aged 90, and was buried in the church of Fladbury, of which his only son was rector. (3) He was the most eminent chronologer of his time.

(1) See his many excellent works, and his life in the Biographia Britannica

(2) In the election for the county, in 1702, the bishop and his son, Mr Lloyd, opposing the interest of Sir John Pakington, by an interference that was voted in the house of commons, " a malicious, unchristian, and arbitrary proceeding, in high violation of the liberties and privileges of the commons of England " On their address to the throne, the bishop was removed from his place of almoner to Queen Anne, and the Attorney General was ordered to prosecute Mr Lloyd, after his privilege as a member of the lower house of convocation was expired [See State Trials, vol VIII p 82 Law of Elections, p 193, 194 and Dr Nash, vol I p. 450]

(3) Two contemporary bishops of the same name, William Lloyd, have, by several writers, been mis-

Marshal's Chronological Tables being entirely extracted from his manuscript, ought rather to be called Bishop Lloyd's Tables   Burnet represents
him as a holy, humble, and patient man, ever ready to do good when he saw
an opportunity, even his love of study not diverting him from this His successor in the see of Litchfield was also his successor at Worcester, the famous
JOHN HOUGH, a bishop after the primitive model   In his younger years
he was educated at Warsal school, in Staffordshire, admitted fellow of
Magdalen college, Oxford, chaplain to the old Duke of Ormond, and collated to a prebend in the church of Worcester, before the memorable election of him to the presidentship of his own college   At his first entrance
into the world, he distinguished himself by a zeal for the liberty of his country, and had a considerable share in bringing on the Revolution that preserved it.   His ejection from his college, and the deprivation of twenty-six
of its fellows, who adhered to him, were among the violences of a despotic
reign   The Revolution replaced him in the government of his college; to
which King William, A. D. 1690, added the bishopric of Oxford, allowing
him to hold them together, and translated him, A D 1717, to Litchfield:
whence, in 1699, King George I. removed him to Worcester   But his principles never altered by his preferment   He never prostituted his pen, nor
debased his character by party disputes, or blind compliance   Though
warmly serious in the belief of his religion, he was moderate to all who dif-
fered from him   he knew no distinction of party, but extended his good offices alike to Whig and Tory, a friend to virtue under any denomination;
an enemy to vice under any colours   His health and old age were the effects of a temperate life, and a quiet conscience   The mild and amiable character of this prelate cannot be too much admired, or too much extolled
His conversation, as well as his familiar letters, at the close of his life, (1)

taken for the same person William Lloyd, born 1637, at Langower, in the county of Merioneth (where
his father was minister), admitted, 1654, from Ruthin school to St John's college, Cambridge, M A
1662, S T P per literas regias, 1670, vicar of Battersea, chaplain to Lord Treasurer Clifford, Bishop of
Landaff, 1675, Peterborough, 1679, Norwich, 1685 deprived Feb 1, 1690-91, for not taking the
oaths to King William and Queen Mary, died in retirement at Hammersmith, Jan 1, 1709 10, aged 72

(1) Every relic of the good and just is venerable with posterity   The following letter, if not really the
last, must be nearly so, of which the world is in possession from the pen of this most excellent man   It
was written to Lord Digby, April 13th 1743 three weeks before the death of the bishop

  " My Lord,
  " I think myself very much obliged to your lordship's nephew for his kind visit, whereby I have a
more authentic account of your lordship' health than is usuall, brought me by report, and an opportu-

had the cheerfulness and spirit of youth   During his last years he confined himself chiefly to his diocese, and laid out his large revenues in hospitality and charity, yet without ostentation   He was a genuine patriot ; the
delight of the church ; a thorn in the side of oppression ; a pillar of religion ;
a father of the indigent ; and a friend to all   He died universally beloved
and universally lamented, May 8, 1743, in the 93d year of his age, and lies
interred in our Lady's chapel, in this cathedral   This worthy prelate, whom,
as the ideal Persian (1) says, nobody ever thought lived too long, unless
it was out of an impatience to succeed him, has exceeded all others of the
English bishops in the years of his consecration, which, at the time of his
death, was the fifty-third, being two years more than that of Archbishop
Bourchier, already noticed.   He was succeeded by

ISAAC MADOX, D. D Bishop of St Asaph.   He was born in London : had
his academical education first in Scotland, afterwards at Queen's college,
Oxford ; was admitted chaplain to Dr. Waddington, bishop of Chichester;
promoted to the rectory of St Vedast, in Foster-lane, London ; and appointed, by Queen Caroline, to be clerk of her closet   In 1734, he was made
dean of Wells ; in 1736, bishop of St Asaph ; and in November, 1743, was
translated to the see of Worcester   His tract, wherein he vindicates the
spirit and plan of the great conductors of the Reformation, under Queen Elizabeth, against the injurious reflections of Mr Neal, is a lasting monument
of his diligence and discernment (2)   But we injure his character, if we

unity of informing myself in many particulars relating to your noble house, and the good family at Wood-
cote , which I hear, with uncommon pleasure, by one who hath been no stranger to them

" Mr Cotes is blessed in his children, all whose sons are not only deserving, but prosperous and I
am glad to see one of them devoted to the service of God , he may not, perhaps, have chosen the most
likely employment to thrive by , but he depends on a master who never fails to recompence them that
trust in him above their hopes

" The young gentleman will account to your lordship for Hartlebury But I fancy you will expect me
to say something of myself, and therefore presume to tell you, my hearing hath long since failed   I am
weak and forgetful , having as little inclination to business is ability to perform it   In other respects I
have ease, if it may not be more properly called indolence, to a degree beyond what I durst have thought
on when years began to multiply upon me   I wait continually for a deliverance out of this life into a
better, in humble confidence that, by the mercy of God, through the merits of his Son, I shall stand at
the resurrection on his right hand   And when you, my lord, have ended those days that are to come,
which, I pray, may be many and prosperous, and as innocent and exemplary as those that are past, I
doubt not of our meeting in that state where the joys are renewable, and will always endure   I am
your lordship's most obedient and ever affectionate servant,   J WORCESTER."

(1) Lord Littleton, Persian Letters, No LVII   (2) Published

consider him only as an advocate for our establishment · he was an ornament to it. In his retirement, he was condescending, hospitable, open-hearted; in his public station, a patron of merit, and a warm friend to every scheme of useful charity   The infirmary of Worcester acknowledges in him its father. Several of the London hospitals were indebted to him for more than his contributions—his zealous services   He is said to have spent more than 1200l. in adorning his chapel at Hartlebury (1) Happy in the veneration and love of clergy and laity, he presided here sixteen years ; and dying at Hartlebury, Sept. 27, 1759, had interment in the cathedral in our Lady's chapel.   He was succeeded by

JAMES JOHNSON, D D son of the Rev. James Johnson, rector of Milford, Suffolk ; and grandson of George Johnson, Esq. of Bowden Park, Wilts, member of parliament for the Devises.   He was of Westminster school, and from thence elected to a studentship of Christchurch.   Some years after, he was appointed second master of that distinguished seminary, in which he had received his classical education.   In the year 1748, he had the honour of attending King George II to Hanover, as his chaplain, and the same year was made canon residentiary of St. Paul's   He attended the king a second time to Hanover, 1752 ; and in the course of that year, was promoted to the see of Gloucester; and from thence was translated to Worcester, Nov. 9, 1759.   He greatly improved and embellished the episcopal house at Hartlebury, and made some valuable additions to that of Worcester, at an expence exceeding 5000l   He also added to the patronage of his successors the rectory of Ricard's castle, in the diocese of Hereford.   He was remarkable for an uniform sweetness of temper, which constantly displayed itself in placid and cheerful affability, and in condescending acts of benevolence.   He died at Bath (very much lamented) in consequence of a fall from his horse, 1774, and was buried with his ancestors at Laycock, in Wiltshire ; but an elegant monument has been erected to his memory in the cathedral church of Worcester, by his only surviving sister, Mrs Sarah Johnson (2)   The next in episcopal succession was

(1) It ought to be recorded, to the honour of this worthy prelate, that in the year 1758, he informed his clergy, by the archdeacon, that he would every year, as long as he should live, assign 200l to the improvement of small livings within the diocese , a benefaction which would entitle every poor incumbent who should receive it, to 200l more from the governors of Queen Anne's bounty   But death deprived the clergy of his liberality after his benefaction had been once bestowed, and the concomitant addition procured   (2, See the Plate, sect VII and ref. No 41 in the Plan of the Cathedral.

The honourable BROWNLOW NORTH, LL D. half brother to the deceased Frederick, late Earl of Guilford, first lord of the treasury, and chancellor of the exchequer   He was educated at Eton school, and Trinity college, Oxford; from whence he was elected to a fellowship of All Souls college. He was afterwards preferred to a canonry of Christchurch ; and in the year 1770, was advanced to the deanry of Canterbury, and 1771, to the bishopric of Litchfield and Coventry   He was translated and confirmed in the see of Worcester 30th December, 1774; and removed to that of Winchester, 1781.   In the year 1778, his lordship promoted an institution for the benefit of the widows and orphans of poor clergymen belonging to this diocese, in aid of the charity derived to them from the music meetings ;(1) and also for the relief of aged and infirm incumbents of small livings, and of curates with large families, an institution which annually administers to the comfort of many He was succeeded here by his successor at Litchfield and Coventry,

RICHARD HURD, D D confirmed in this see June 30, 1781, to the general and heartfelt satisfaction of the whole county and diocese.   Penkford, in Staffordshire, has the distinction of his birth.   After becoming fellow of Emanuel college, Cambridge, he was appointed archdeacon of Gloucester ; assistant preacher at the Rolls chapel, with bishop Warburton ; clerk of the closet, and, whilst bishop of Litchfield, had the honour of being tutor to his Royal Highness the Prince of Wales. Of this excellent and highly venerated prelate, it only becomes us at present to add, that his eminent learning, his critical, moral, and theological works, have gained him the esteem and the applause of all men of true taste and virtue ; and his benevolence, politeness, and charity, have peculiarly endeared him to the diocese over which he so exemplarily presides   Hartlebury castle, for many centuries past the ancient residence of his predecessors, owes to his lordship's munificence and refined taste, the most valuable ornament it could receive—a noble and elegant library,—which he is furnishing with a select and well chosen collection of books (among which is the principal part of Mr Pope's, and of the late Bishop Warburton's) for the use and benefit of the future bishops of the see of Worcester.   Such is the venerable successor to a long series of prelates, illustrious by their station, and many of them yet more so by the brightness of their characters

(1) See Sect XX

F f

SECT. IX.

A CATALOGUE OF THE PRIORS, TO THE DISSOLUTION OF ST MARY's MONASTERY

THE church of Worcester, was originally founded, as has been shewn, (1) for a bishop and his clerical family, or college of domestic priests; over whom he placed a provost. These conducted the cathedral service from the time the bishop's see was first placed here by King Ethelred, A. D. 680, till St Oswald, afterwards brought in Benedictine monks in their room, under the government of a prior. When the administration of the church, and its revenues, were thus transferred from secular hands to those of regulars, and, in lieu of a college, a monastery had been annexed to the cathedral, it received for its first prior,

WINSY, Winsige, or Winsinus, (2) a secular clerk of the old college, and priest of St. Helen's in this city (3) Bishop Oswald sent him to the monastery of Ramsey, in Huntingdonshire, to perform his noviciate, and be instructed in monastic discipline, whence he recalled him in three years, and instated him in the priorship He died before 987, and was succeeded by

ÆTHELSTAN, 986, who died between 992 and 996.

ÆTHELSINUS, or Æthelsige

ÆTHELSIN II.

GODWIN

ÆTHELWIN, or Agelwin, who was living in 1051

ST WULSTAN, who was made prior by Bishop Aldred He was much encouraged by the beneficence of Earl Leofric, and his lady Godiva; and among other works for the benefit of the church of Worcester, built a tower for the bells (4) He was made bishop in 1062, under which title he is spoken of in the account of the bishops of this see

1062, ÆLISIAN, brother of St Wulstan He improved the revenues

1 See Sect III p 22   (2) He and his successors are, in ancient writings, not always stiled Prior but sometimes Prai Prapositus, or dean   (3) Angl Sac 546, 472.

' It may thave been the base of the leaden spire or clochium, already treated of in Sect IV p 42.

(4) Wair Abbe, vol I p 366

of the church by the purchase of the manors of Lene, Bunhamsted, and Peceslea. (1)

ÆGELRED, sub-prior and chantor in the church of Canterbury.

THOMAS, prior of Westbury. He subscribes as prior of Worcester, the first witness to St. Wulstan's grant of Alvestune to this monastery, A. D. 1084.

1113 NICHOLAS, made prior by bishop Theobald.

1124 GUARIN ; William of Malmsbury says this prior wrote the life of St Wulstan, about the year 1140.

1143 RALPH, who died the same year.

1143 DAVID He was deposed.

1145 OSBERT, or Osbern.

1146. RALPH DE BEDEFORD ; of whom this is remarkable ; that, during his priorship, he elected and presented to the archbishop to be consecrated, five successive bishops of Worcester, viz John de Pageham, 1150. Alured, 1158. Roger, 1163. Baldwin, 1180. And William de Norhale, 1185. He was succeeded by

SENATUS, precentor of this convent, in 1189, who voluntarily resigned his priorship.

1196 PETER, a monk of this church He was deposed.

1203 RANDULF DE EVESHAM, who, in 1213, was chosen bishop of Worcester ; but being obliged by Nicholas, the Pope's legate, to decline that high trust, was soon after made abbat of Evesham ; (2) and was succeeded in his priorship by

SYLVESTER DE EVESHAM, 1215, who was made bishop of Worcester.

1216 SIMON. He was deposed by bishop William de Blois, and excommunicated ; on which he appealed to the Pope, but died before the cause was ended

1222 WILLIAM NORMAN, Prior of Malvern, whose nomination by the bishop, without the consent of the convent, was the occasion of a controversy of two years continuance between them, which ended in the deposition of Norman ; but, in lieu of his priorship, he had, by the unanimous consent of the arbitrators to whom this cause was referred, the manor of Clive for his life, exclusive of tithes to be paid to the convent. And, with respect to future elections, it was resolved, that the convent, upon the vacancy of the priorship, should present to the bishop seven of their own

---

(1) Angl Sac p 547   (2) Tindal's Hist of Evesham Abbey, p 23

monks, out of whom he was to choose one for their prior, and such his choice should be absolute (1)   On this plan were nominated the succeeding priors

1224 WILLIAM DE BEDEFORD, originally a monk of St. Alban's, and afterwards prior of Tinmouth.   He built, in 1225, a new house, with offices adjacent, for the residence of the priors (2)

1242 RICHARD GUNDICOTE, sacrist of this church; who had a dispute with the abbat of Evesham, about common of pasture in certain lordships; which was at length determined at Evesham, to this effect; the abbat and his tenants to enjoy it from Christmas to Michaelmas yearly, and the prior and convent the other part yearly   His successor was

THOMAS, in 1252, who had been sub-prior thirty-two years.   He was succeeded on his death by

RICHARD DUMBLETON, 1260.   In his time the chapter of Worcester compounded with Boniface, Archbishop of Canterbury, about the exercise of the bishop's jurisdiction, when the see of Worcester should happen to be vacant (3)   This prior dying in 1272, was buried in the cloisters, near his predecessors.   His successor was

WILLIAM of Cirencester, 1272, before sacrist of the church.

1274 RICHARD FECKENHAM, chamberlain of this church.

1287. PHILIP AUBIN, sub-prior

1296 SIMON DE WIRE, or Wircestre, sub-prior, who resigned.

1301 JOHN DE LA WYKE, sub-prior   His successor was

WOLSTAN DE BRAUNSFORD   He is said to have built a bridge over the Teme at Braunsford, near Worcester, the place of his nativity   He was chosen by the monks of this church to succeed Thomas Cobham in this see, 1327, but was not consecrated till he was rechosen for Bishop Hemenhale's successor, 1339, under which head I have spoken of him   He was succeeded by

SIMON DE BOTILER, 1339, who died the same year.

1339. SIMON CROMPE.

1340 JOHN DE EVESHAM, bachelor of divinity   He obtained a bull of Pope Clement VI dated 8 Jan 1351, for himself and his successors to be allowed the use of the mitre and pastoral staff; and another of Pope Urban V dated 4th Feb 1363, to the same effect   He died March 27, 1370, and

(1) See Sect IV p 120   (2) Ann. Wig   (3) See Sect IV p 120

was buried in the north ile of the choir of this church (1) His successor was

WALTER LEIGH, 1370, almoner of this church In 1373, on the death of William Lynne, Bishop of Worcester, he was elected his successor by the convent, with the king's consent; but being set aside by the Pope, the see remained vacant for two years, during which the famous John Wicliff attempted to obtain it, but being disappointed, it gave occasion for him to write against the Pope, and to lay the foundation of his new doctrines in the church (2)

1388 JOHN GREEN (3)

1395 JOHN of MALVERN, sacrist He was one of the English divines who were sent to the council of Constance, 1416 (4) He died before the year 1423, succeeded by

JOHN FORDHAM

1438. THOMAS LEDBURY He died 1443, and was buried in this cathedral.

1444 JOHN HERTILBURY

1456 THOMAS MUSARD

1469 ROBERT MULTON, cellarer of this monastery

1492. WILLIAM WENLOKE, sacrist

1499 THOMAS MILDENHAM, sacrist

1507 JOHN WEDDESBURY

WILLIAM MOORE, sub-prior, chosen 1518, and, 1535, on the foresight of the ruin of the monastic orders, resigned it, and had the manors of Crowle and Grimley settled on him for life.

HENRY HOLBECH, alias Randes, D. D was the last elected prior of Worcester, to which dignity he was raised by the king's licence 13th March, 1535.

---

(1) See an account of his tomb in the Appendix, p xxxi   (2) Angl Sac p 805, in Addenda Abingdon's Hist of the Cath p 123, 124 Willis's Cath vol I p. 642 Ibid Abbies, vol I p 309

(3) This prior, according to Walsingham, was chosen successor to Bishop Wakefield in this see, by the monks of Worcester, but Walsingham's authority stands unsupported here

(4) Holingshed, anno 2 Henry V.

SECT. X.

THE SUCCESSION OF THE DEANS OF WORCESTER TO THE PRESENT TIME.

HENRY HOLBECH, who had presided as prior over the seminary of black monks in Cambridge, became first dean of Worcester His election was enjoined by letters to the convent from King Henry VIII In March, 1538, he was consecrated suffragan to the see of Worcester, by the title of Bishop of Bristol, and held this dignity with his priorship Priories were now at their period. By his surrender of this convent and all its appertenances to the king, Jan 18, 1540, monks were displaced from the church of Worcester, of which they had been possessed near 570 years, and the king settled in it prebendaries or secular canons in their stead; over whom Holbech, changing his title, presided as the first dean (1) In 1544, he was made bishop of Rochester, where he was the successor of Bishop Heath, on his advancement to this see; and held the rectory of Bromsgrove, with the chapel of Norton, in commendam with that preferment. He was translated to Lincoln, 1547, (2) where he died A. D. 1551 He was succeeded in this deanry by

JOHN BARLOW, M A installed 1544, but was deprived, when Queen Mary came to the crown, for being a protestant, on which

PHILIP HAWFORD, alias Ballard, who, when very young, was made abbat of Evesham, on purpose to make a surrender of the abbey, and all its lordships, to the king, which service he performed in Nov 1539, and was rewarded with a pension of 240l per annum, and the rectory of Elmeley Lovet Queen Mary gave him the deanry of Worcester in lieu of that pension (3) He died 1557, and lies buried in the Dean's chapel in this cathedral. (4) To him succeeded

(1) Le Neve, fol 301   (2) Hist of Roch Cath p 155
(3) He was the fifty sixth and last abbat of Evesham in succession to Clement Litchfield, who resigned, and supposed soon after to have died of grief for the dissolution and destruction of his abbey, to which he had but just added the beautiful tower, now standing as a portal to the churchyards of All Saints and St Laurence at Evesham [See Tindal's History of that abbey, p 41]
(4) See Ref 2), in the Plan of the Cath to an account of his stone coffin, in Sect VII p 153

SETH HOLLAND, 1557, chaplain to Cardinal Pole, (1) warden of All Souls college, Oxford, he was rector of Fladbury, which he resigned on his appointment to that of Cleeve Episcopi, co Gloucester ; he was also a prebendary in the second stall in this cathedral On Queen Mary's death he was deprived of this deanry, 1st of Elizabeth, and died in the Marshalsea.

JOHN PEDOR, 1559, who, in Queen Mary's reign, had been in exile in Frankfort, was, by patent, advanced to this deanry, the revenues of which were much improved by his care He died April 5th, 1571, and was interred (as I suppose) in the Dean's chapel in this cathedral, in which was a monument placed to his memory, but since gone (2) He was succeeded by

THOMAS WILSON, D D educated in Trinity college Cambridge. He also had been an exile at Frankfort On the accession of Queen Elizabeth he returned to his native country, and was appointed a prebendary in the seventh stall of this church, and chaplain to Bishop Sandys ; who had been in exile at the same time in Frankfort. In the famous synod assembled at Westminster, January, 1562-3, to complete the restoration of the reformed church of England, he was chosen by the dean and chapter of Worcester as one of their proctors On the 4th of May, 1571, the queen appointed him dean of Worcester ; in which station he died July, 20th, 1586, and lies buried in the Dean's chapel (3)

FRANCIS WILLIS, 1586, president of St John's college, Oxford, a native and canon of Bristol. (4) He also lies interred in the above chapel. His successor was

RICHARD EEDES, S. T P 1596, canon of Christchurch, Oxford, chaplain to Queen Elizabeth, and King James. He was much admired for his preaching, and eminent for his learning and virtue He died at Worcester, and lies buried in our Lady's chapel

JAMES MOUNTAGUE, S T P master of Sydney college Cambridge, succeeded him, 1604, and soon after his advancement to this deanry, was appointed dean of the king's chapel, bishop of Bath and Wells in 1608, and translated from thence to Winchester 1616 ; and dying 1618, was buried in the abbey church, Bath (5) His successor in this deanry was

(1) See Life of Pole, Part II p 213   (2) See Appendix to Sect VII No VIII p xxxi
(3) See Dr Nash, Vol II Worc inter p 318, 319
(4) The celebrated Brown Willis supposed himself related to this dean [See his Cath Vol 1 p 658]
(5) Dr Hopkins's MS in the Cott lib. Cleopatra E V p 120.

ARTHUR LAKE, 1608, brother to Sir Thomas Lake, Knt. principal secretary of state to King James. He was fellow of New college Oxford, master of St Cross, near Winchester, and archdeacon of Surrey. In 1616, he was translated to the bishopric of Bath and Wells. He was eminent for his learning, and esteemed one of the best textuaries of his time. He died 1626. Whilst he was dean of Worcester, he accomplished what was designed by Dean Eedes, the redemption of the Meadows (1). His successor in this deanry was

JOSEPH HALL, D D 1616, archdeacon of Nottingham, and well known by his excellent writings, who being promoted to the see of Exeter, 1627, this deanry was given to

DR. WILLIAM JUXON, president of St John's college Oxford, and clerk of the closet to Charles I. In 1633, he was made bishop of Hereford, and afterwards bishop of London; he was sworn of the privy council, and constituted lord treasurer, 1635. King Charles, from the high regard he had for this prelate, chose him to attend him in his last moments on the scaffold. That painful duty performed, he retired to his seat at Little Compton in Gloucestershire, where he continued till the Restoration. He was made Archbishop of Canterbury by Charles II A D 1660, in reward of his virtues and his services. His moderation and amiable deportment gained him the esteem of all parties. He died at Lambeth, 4th of June, 1663, at the age of 81, and was buried in St John's college, Oxford (2). His successor in this deanry was

ROGER MANWARING, 1633, educated at the college school at Worcester, under Mr Henry Bright. He was one of the most abject tools of power; he not only preached at court, but published two sermons, wherein he maintained, that " the king is not bound to observe the laws of the realm, relating " to the rights and liberties of the subjects; but that his royal will and com- " mand, imposing on them loans and taxes, without common consent in par- " liament, doth oblige the conscience of the subjects, on pain of eternal " damnation." It was the general desire of the nation to see such an apostle of slavery punished. He was arrested by order of the house of lords; and sentenced to make his submission at the bar of the houses, to pay a fine of 1000 to be suspended from preaching for three years; and incapacitated from holding any preferment. But the king granted him a full pardon, remitted the fine, and immediately preferred him to a rich benefice in Essex ; and, but a few years after, to the deanry of Worcester : and, as if all this was not sufficient for a service so meritorious, he advanced him, in 1635, to the see of St David's He died in privacy at Carmarthen, 1653, and was buried at Brecknock His successor in this deanry was

CHRISTOPHER POTTER, D D. 1636, who while fellow of Queen's college, Oxford, joined the puritans, and lectured at Abingdon in the Calvinistic way. when made provost of that college, he went over to the court divines, was appointed the king's chaplain in ordinary, and afterwards promoted to this deanry He executed, at a very troublesome time, (in 1640) the office of vice-chancellor of the university. Upon the breaking out of the rebellion, he sent all the plate belonging to his college to the king, declaring, that like Diogenes, he would drink from the hollow of his hand, rather than his majesty should want In the course of the war, he suffered much for the king's cause , who, in recompence, conferred on him, in 1646, the deanry of Durham ; of which he never had possession, for he died at Oxford within two months after his nomination. He was a man of distinguished learning and exemplary life but as he lived not to feel sequestration, or to struggle with want, is by no means entitled to the rank of a semi-martyr, in which he has been placed (1) His successor,

RICHARD HOLDSWORTH, D D 1646, suffered a worse fate in those tempestuous times He had been scholar and fellow of St. John's college Cambridge, master of Emanuel, and, in 1640, vice-chancellor of that university. He had other preferments, but was dispossessed of them all, by the prevalent usurpers, shut up more than once in prison ; and greatly harassed. Soon after the execution of his majesty, being deeply affected at that blow, he died .(2) He never received any profits from this deanry, and was not even installed. After a vacancy of eleven years,

DR JOHN OLIVER, 1660, president of Magdalen college, Oxford, was promoted to this deanry He was originally of Merton college, but re-

(1) See Mag Brit vol VI page 307, 316 His monument is in Queen's college chapel, with a long inscription He wrote against Knot, the Jesuit, whose reply produced Chillingworth's excellent book, " The Religion of the Protestants," &c

(2) His death happened August 22d, 1649, and he was buried in St Peter's Poor church, London. He is ranked among the semi-martyrs of these times See Mag Brit vol VI p 307,—316

moving to Magdalen, was there demy and fellow, and at length president
The Earl of Clarendon, famous as an historian, and not less famous for the
part he bears in history, was his pupil at Magdalen   He was deprived of his
preferments for opposing the visitors of the university, and thereby reduced
to the lowest ebb of fortune   About a fortnight before the king's restoration, he was reinstated in his college, by authority of the parliament;
and soon after, through the interest of Lord Clarendon, was raised to this
deanry, which he enjoyed not long , strangely desirous to leave this world,
though few had greater inducements to stay in it, his desires were by providence granted him, Oct 27, 1661.   He was buried in Magdalen college
chapel, Oxford, and had for his successor

THOMAS WARMESTRY, D. D 1661, a native of Worcester, son of Gervas
Warmestry, registrary of this church.   He was educated in Christchurch,
Oxford.   He represented the clergy of this country in two convocations,
in one of which he made a speech, which he published, against images,
altars, crosses, and the new canons.   In the national combustion which
broke out soon after, he retired to the king at Oxford, whence he removed
to London ; having, after all his moderation, which had gotten him the
name of a puritan, been deprived of his preferments.   But the Restoration
of the king was also the restoration of his fortune ; he being then advanced
to a prebend of Gloucester, and afterwards to the deanry of Worcester.
He died 1665, (1) and was succeeded by

DR WILLIAM THOMAS, 1665 ; who, when promoted in 1678, to the bishopric of St David's, held this deanry in commendam, but resigned it
1683, when made bishop of this see   I have already taken notice of him
among the bishops of Worcester   His successor in the deanry was

GEORGE HICKES, D. D installed 13th October, 1683   He was born in
Yorkshire, educated at Oxford, and chosen there fellow of Lincoln college ;
whence he was called to be chaplain to the Duke of Lauderdale, and afterwards to the king; prebendary, and then dean of Worcester.   He applied
himself with success to the study of Gothic antiquities.   His Thesaurus of
the old northern literature, in folio, is celebrated by the learned both abroad
and at home   During his government of this church, some useful regulations were made ; as, the bringing copyholders to a regular way of fining;

(1) He lies buried in the body of the cathedral, in the middle ile, opposite the fifth pillar from
the belfry

the fixing, in concurrence with the bishop, stated terms of residence for the prebendaries ; and some constitutions for the better ordering of the king's school. Other improvements, which this dean had designed, the Revolution prevented ; at which time, refusing the oaths, and all concurrence in measures then taken for securing the church and state, he was deprived of his preferments, Feb 1, 1691, (1) and would have been more severely persecuted, if he had not been sheltered by the patronage of Lord Somers.

WILLIAM TALBOT, A M. was installed in this deanry, April 23, 1691, which Dr. Hickes opposed in vain by his protest, affixed to the great door of the choir ; wherein he maintained his claim of right to that dignity against Mr Talbot, and all other persons whomsoever. This was called at court Dr Hickes's Manifesto against the government ; and reduced him to the necessity of absconding, till Lord Somers obtained his pardon. Dean Talbot was born at Stourton castle, in Staffordshire, descended from the noble family of the Earls of Shrewsbury. in 1699, he was advanced to the b‍ic of Oxford, with leave to hold this deanry in commendam; which he signed, in 1715, on his translation from the see of Oxford to that of Salisbury, in which he succeeded the celebrated Gilbert Burnet. He died, in 1730, bishop of Durham —England will always boast of the lord chancellor, his son. The bishop's grandson, the right honourable Earl Talbot, presided over the royal household of his present Majesty till his death.

DR FRANCIS HARE, fellow of Eton college, and canon-residentiary of St Paul's, London, was installed dean of this church, in Bishop Talbot's room, April 27th, 1715. He had been chaplain general to the army in Flanders, under the victorious John Duke of Marlborough. He was promoted from hence to the deanry of St. Paul's ; and afterwards, filled successively the sees of St Asaph and Chichester. His edition of the Hebrew Psalms, with notes, has raised him a lasting name in the learned world. On his removal from this church,

DR JAMES STILLINGFLEET, a prebendary of it, and son of the late learned bishop, succeeded him. He was installed dean, 16 December, 1726, and presided in that station near twenty years, a man of strict honour and

---

(1) Dr Hickes lived twenty-five years after in obscurity and les buried near the west end of St Margaret's churchyard, Westminster, under a flat gravestone, the inscription on which is yet legible He died 15th December, 1715, aged 74 [Willis's Cath. p 661, vol 1]

integrity, a sincere friend, an hospitable neighbour, and a worthy country gentleman On his death, in September, 1746, he was succeeded by

Dr EDMUND MARTIN, of Twickenham, canon of Windsor, who was installed here, 24 April, 1747 He enjoyed the deanry but a short time, dying in 1751 . he was succeeded by

JOHN WAUGH, LL D son of the bishop of Carlisle, of which diocese he was chancellor He was installed dean of Worcester, 14 Nov 1751 His knowledge of the civil and common law was extensive , and very assisting to Dr. Burn in his useful publication on the Administration of Justice. During the siege of Carlisle, in 1745, Dr Waugh was eminently useful to the king's forces ; on which account he was preferred to this deanry, where he died, and was interred in the Lady's chapel, 1765 He was succeeded by

Sir RICHARD WROTTESLEY, Bart. LL.D. who was installed May 30th, 1765 This gentleman went late into the clerical order, having been a member of the house of commons, and held a place at the board of green cloth He was father to the present Duchess of Grafton. He died 1769, and was succeeded by

WILLIAM DIGBY, LL D who was installed dean of this church Sept 8, 1769. On his promotion to the deanry of Durham, his successor in this was

ROBERT FOLEY, D D brother of the late Thomas, Lord Foley. He enjoyed this dignity but little more than four years, having been installed Jan. 31, 1778, and having died 1783 He was succeeded by

The late honourable and reverend ST ANDREW ST. JOHN, D D. second son of John, tenth Lord St John of Bletsoe, and brother to the present Countess of Coventry; he was installed in this deanry 29th March, 1783; and died 23d March, 1795 He lies interred beneath the great east window of the Lady's chapel in this cathedral (1) (See Appendix, No VIII. p 25.) His successor is

The reverend ARTHUR ONSLOW, D. D. archdeacon of Berks, canon of Christchurch, and fellow of All Souls, Oxford ; vicar of White Waltham in the diocese of Salisbury , installed 16th May, 1795 He is the youngest son of General Onslow, whose elder brother, the right hon Arthur Onslow, was speaker of the house of commons above thirty years. The speaker was nephew of Sir Richard Onslow, created Baron Onslow, 1716 The speaker's son now inherits the title

(1) See Ref No 67 in the Plan of the Cath to the account of his monument, in Sect VII

SECT. XI.

A CATALOGUE OF THE PREBENDARIES OF WORCESTER.

Concerning the institution of the prebendaries, Chancellor Price says, he believes the omission of it might arise in the reign of James I ; for from the first year of his reign to the third of Charles I reversions of them were granted when they next should become vacant ; and he supposes, that, on a vacancy, the dean and chapter installed the person to whom it had been granted, and thus they became collations regals ; but since the year 1688, they have been regularly instituted by the bishop of the diocese. (1) Of the ten prebends of this church, nine of them are in his Majesty's royal patronage, and one (the sixth) is annexed to the Margaret professorship of divinity in the university of Oxford, by act of parliament These, with the deanry, pay, in lieu of first-fruits and tenths 193*l* 1*s* 8*d*. (2)

FIRST STALL

Thomas Baggard, LL D appointed by the foundation charter, Jan 24, 1541
1544 Robert Johnson, LL B.
1558 William Norfolk, M. A.
1561 Thomas Herle, M A.
1586 William Tovie, B. D
1596 Richard Potter, B D
1628 Richard Steward.
1638 William Smith, D D.
1660 John Bretton.
1675 William Hopkins, B. D
1700 Miles Stapledon, D D.
1731 Philip Smallridge, M. A chancellor of Worcester
1751 Lewis Crusius, D D

SECOND STALL

1541 Richard Browne, M. A.
1546 John Compton, alias Theale, B D chancellor of Hereford.
1555 Seth Holland, M A   He was, A D 1557, made dean of Worcester.
1457 Leonard Lingham, or Linghan, M A.
1568 Richard Longworth, D D afterwards dean of Chester
1579 John Longworth, D D.
1613 John Hammer, D. D.
1629 Giles Thornborough, M. A.
1664 William Owen, M A.
1672 Henry Greisley, M A
1678 Joseph Glanville, M. A

---

(1) Dr Nash, in Introd p 38 vol. I   (2) Bacon's Liber Regis, p. 963

1680 Ralph Battell, M. A

1713 William Bramston, D D

1735 Bernard Wilson, D D

THIRD STALL

1541 Richard Ever, B D

1558 Ralph Cockley.

1558 Thomas Arden.

1560 Lybbeus Byard.

1570 John Bullingham, afterwards
bishop of Gloucester.

1581 Godfrey Goldsborough. He
was also made bishop of Gloucester

1604 William Barksdale, M. A

1628 Stephen Boughton, M A

1660 Barnabas Oley, M. A.

1685 John Hough, M A. afterwards
bishop of Worcester.

1690 Joseph Merill, M. A.

1700 William Galloway, M A

1715 William Worth, D. D. archdeacon of Worcester.

1742 Rice Williams, D. D

1767 Philip Duval, LL B

1772 Gregory Parry, M A.

1785 William Langford, D D

FOURTH STALL

1541 Henry Jolliff, B D ; also dean
of Bristol

1559 Sir Thomas Windebank, a
layman

1607 John Archbold, D D

1627 Francis Chartlet, M A.

1660 William Dowdswell, LL D.

1671 George Benson, D. D. afterwards dean of Hereford.

1692 Richard Bentley, M A. the
famous master of Trinity college,
Cambridge.

1700 John Laughton, M A

1714 William Lloyd, D. D. chancellor of this diocese

1719 George Lavington, LL.B. afterwards bishop of Exeter

1731 Samuel Green, M A

1747 Robert Eden, B D.

1756 Benjamin Newcome, D D.

1767 William Stockwood, M. A.

1768 William Arden, M. A.

1768 John Young, D D

FIFTH STALL.

1541 Gilbert Pourne, D D afterwards bishop of Bath and Wells.

1558 Edmund Daniel , also dean of
Hereford.

1559 Robert Avis, M A

1581 Gilbert Backhouse, LL B

1597 Thos Fenman, or Ferryman.

1619 Henry Bright, M A the famous master of the King's school
at Worcester

1627 Nathaniel Giles, D. D.

1660 Edward Reynolds, M. A

1698 Sir William Dawes, Bart D D
afterwards archbishop of York

1708 Robert Brabant, D D

1722 Benjamin Woodroof, M. A

1726 Thomas Inett, M A.

1748 John Dalton, D. D.

1763 William Jennings, B D.
1788 Thomas Hughes, M. A.

SIXTH STALL

1541 Roger Neckham, D D. a monk of this church
1557 William Turnbull, LL D who quitted it for the tenth prebend
1558 Robert Shaw, B. D.
1560 Thomas Norley, M A
1577 John Ellis, M. A ; also dean of Hereford
1576 Richard Harris, M A
1616 Eustache Moor, B D
1628 Samuel Fell, D. D. afterwards dean of Christchurch, Oxon. (1)
1637 Thomas Laurence, D D
1660 Thomas Barlow, D D. afterwards bishop of Lincoln
1676 John Hall, D D. afterwards bishop of Bristol
1691 Henry Maurice, D. D
1691 Thomas Sykes, S T D.
1705 John Wynne, B D. afterwards bishop of St. Asaph.
1714 William Delaune, D. D.
1728 Thomas Jenner, D. D
1768 Thomas Randolph, D. D.

SEVENTH STALL.

1541 James Lawerne, B. D a monk of this church.

1551 Richard Vernon.
1557 Richard Hall, M A
1560 Thomas Wilson, afterwards dean of Worcester.
1571 Griffith Lewis, D. D. also dean of Gloucester
1607 John Chartlet, D. D
1641 Herbert Croft, D D. afterwards bishop of Hereford.
1661 Joseph Crowther, D. D.
1680 Jonathan Blagrave, M. A.
1698 James Stillingfleet, M. A. who resigned it for the deanry of Worcester.
1726 John Downes, M. A
1737 Edward Stillingfleet, M. A.

EIGHTH STALL.

1541 Roger Sandford, B D. a monk of this church
1550 John Standish, D D
1554 Leonard Pollard, B. D.
1557 Thomas Bastarde, B. D.
1584 William Thornhill, M A.
1626 Robert White, B D.
1660 William Thornborough.
1680 George Hicks, D D afterwards dean of Worcester
1683 John Jephcot, D. D.
1706 Edward Chandler, D D afterwards successively bishop of Litchfield and Durham

(1) In his time, by letters patent, dated July 5, 1628, anno 3 Caroli, this prebend was annexed to the office of Margaret professor of divinity, in the university of Oxford since which time it hath continued on the same footing and all professors, as soon as elected by the university, have, without any presentation from the crown, been instated in this dignity.

1717 Richard Laughton, M A
1723 John Holland, D D.
1735 Richard Meadowcourt, M A
1760 Samuel Wolley, M A.
1764 The honourable Wm Harley, M A
1769 John James Majendie, D D

NINTH STALL.

1541 Humphry Webbely, B D a monk of this church
1551 John Harley, afterwards bishop of Hereford.
1575 Arthur Dudley, alias Sutton
1576 Gerv Carrington, LL D
1611 Richard Thornton, D D
1614 Robert Pritchard, M A
1631 Anthony Tyringham, M A
1660 George Glenn.

1669 Thomas Lamplugh, B D afterwards archbishop of York
1674 William Hore, B D
1687 John Cartwright, M A.
1708 Josiah Sanby, M A.
1743 Edwin Sandys, LL B

TENTH STALL

1541 Richard Lisle, a monk of this church (1)
1558 Wm Turnbull, LL D from the sixth prebend
1573 Thomas Thornton, D D
1629 Nathaniel Tomkins, B D
1681 John Conant, D. D
1694 George Walls, D D
1727 William Byrche, LL D. chancellor of this diocese
1741 Samuel Holcombe, M. A.

MEMBERS OF THE ECCLESIASTICAL COURT OF WORCESTER

The most rev. Dr John Moore, Lord Archbishop of Canterbury, primate of all England, and metropolitan

The right rev Richard Hurd, D D lord bishop of this diocese, ordinary, or judge

The worshipful Sir William Burrell, Bart LL.D chancellor, or vicar general in spirituals, and official principal

Surrogates
Rev Richard Baty, M A
Rev John Griffin, M A
Principal Registers
Rev James Stillingfleet, M. A
Richard Hurd, Gent
Proctors
James Palmore   George Holyoake
John Clifton, deputy register of the diocese
Henry Martin.

(1) The first prebendary of each stall was at the same time appointed by the new charter

MEMBERS OF THE CATHEDRAL CHURCH OF WORCESTFR.

The right rev. Richard Hurd, D. D. Lord Bishop, 1781.

The rev Arthur Onslow, D. D. dean, 1795

The rev Thomas Evans, D. D. archdeacon, 1787.

Sir William Burrell, Bart LL D. chancellor, 1764

PREBENDARIES, OR CANONS

1st. Stall The rev. Jas. Torkington, D D 1775, master of St Oswald's hospital

2d James Stillingfleet, M A 1772, rector of Knightwick and Doddenham, and principal register of this diocese.

3d John Plumptre, M. A 1787, vicar of Stone and Wichenford

4th Richard Kilvert, M A 1786, vicar of Hallow and Grimley, and rector of Alvechurch.

5th Charles Peter Layard, D D 1793, F R S and F A S chaplain in ordinary to their Majesties, and vicar of Newstoke and Worle, Somerset

6th Timothy Neve, D D 1783, Margaret professor of divinity in the university of Oxford

7th John Carver, LL.B. 1777, archdeacon of Surry, and rector of Hartlebury

8th. Thomas Fountaine, M. A 1774, chaplain in ordinary to their Majesties, and vicar of Bromsgrove.

9th. Thomas Evans, D D. 1764, archdeacon of Worcester, rector of Severn Stoke, and vicar of Wolverly.

10th. Matthew Lambe, D. D. 1775, rector of Harvington.

MINOR CANONS.

Rev William Hughes, M. A.

Rev Digby Smith, M A. chantor and precentor, and chaplain to St. Oswald's hospital

Rev Thomas Clarke, M. A sacrist, vicar of Stoke Prior, and minister of St. Michael's

Rev. Evan Griffiths, M. A. vicar of St John's

Rev Jeremiah Roberts, M A rector of Sedgberrow, and curate of St. Martin's.

Rev. George Shelton, M. A. vicar of Overbury

Rev Thomas Heynes, B A rector of St. Andrew's, and minister of Norton.

Rev. John William Harrison, B. A. rector of St. Clement's.

Organist, and Master of the Choristers,
Thomas Pitt.
Lay-clerks, or Singing-men.

Charles Radcliffe	John Southall.
John Radcliffe.	Sam. Dangerfield
Joseph Shelton.	Thomas Pitt
John Griffiths	Sam Symmans.

Ten Choristers
Two School-masters.
Head Master, rev. John Griffin, M A.

Under Master, *vacant.*
Forty King's Scholars.
Two Sextons.
Edward Jeal, Francis Stafford.
Two Vergers
William Bishop, Thomas Knelms,
Two Butlers. One Manciple.
Two Cooks. Ten Beadesmen
Two Porters.

A LIST OF THE ARCHDEACONS OF WORCESTER.

The title of Archdeacon is of no less antiquity than the primitive times of Christianity. They were formerly elected by the deacons from among themselves : and in the time of Henry VIII their revenue arose from pro-curations, synodals, Peter pence, or pentecostals, pensions or indemnities, fines of testaments, vacations of benefices, installations of abbats. (Dugd. in Coventry)

Agelric is mentioned to have been archdeacon here, 1088 and 1094 He is the second subscribing witness to bishop Wulstan's grant of Alvestune to the monastery, and which is dated M LXXXVIII. He signs himself Agelri-cus Archidiacon.

Hugh held it 1120, and died possessed of it March 21, 1125

William Comyn, about 1130. (1)

Gervas, about 1134

Thomas Fitzharding, 1147

Godfrey succeeded, about 1148, and died 1167

Simon Limes succeeded 1167 ; and dying 1189, was succeeded by

Peter de Arche, 1189 ; he died about 1196

John de Cornubia, mentioned as archdeacon in 1197 and 1198.

John de Branastre, 1201, he died 1218

William de Scot, alias Stickhill, in December 1218. In 1225, he was

(1) Neither Comyn nor his successor are in the List of Dr. Thomas's edition of Dugdale

made bishop of Durham, but refused it. (B. Willis MS. p. 662.) He died 1242.

Vincent Bergavenny, resigned the archdeaconry in 1256.

Robert de Asthall, or Escall, canon of St. Paul's, London.

Hugh de Evesham, 1275, of which place he was either a native or a monk. He was proctor for the archbishop of York at Rome, 1280. He was the greatest proficient in physic of his age, on which account Pope Martin IV. created him cardinal of St. Laurence, in Lucina. He died, as is said, of poison, in 1287, and was buried in his church at Rome (1)

Ralph de Hengham, collated 17 Cal. Nov. 1287. He died 1311, canon of St Paul's, London When he had been archdeacon here but one year, he resigned, or rather was dispossessed by

Francis de Sancta Lucia Cardinal, intruded by the Pope. He was installed by proxy, Jan. 8, 1288. He died 1311.

Henry Fitz-Dauphin, of Vienne, collated by the Pope on the nones of September, 1312, and was in possession 1315.

John Brucy is mentioned 1320 He died the following year.

Adam de Champneys de Sandwich, July 20, 1321.

John de Orleton succeeded him, collated thereto by Bishop Orleton, Oct. 17, 1329. He exchanged it for the rectory of Meanstock, in the county of Southampton, to be near Bishop Orleton, who was translated to Winchester, with

Robert of Wirecester, LL D. 7 ides of April, 1337.

John Severle, chancellor of this diocese, collated May 12, 1349. He exchanged this archdeaconry for the rectory of Buxsted, in the county of Sussex, March 6, 1352, with

John de Harewell, who was, anno 1366, made bishop of Bath and Wells.

Simon Clemens succeeded him in the archdeaconry, which he exchanged for the rectory of Elyndon, in the county of Wilts, May 4, 1371, with

John Blanchard He died, anno 1383; succeeded by

William Malpas, collated Dec 4, 1383 He was made treasurer of Chichester about 1400, and seems to have resigned his archdeaconry, for we find

William Rowcomb possessed of it 1401 He died, anno 1412.

John Ixworth, collated Oct 28, 1412. He resigned, anno 1431.

(1) Tanner, Bibl. Brit p. 418. ex. Leland Willis, p. 662. Dr. Nash, vol. I. p 415.

John Burdet, LL.B. collated May 31, 1431.   He quitted it for the arch-deaconry of Chester, when

William Hende was collated in his room, May 5, 1433.   He exchanged it for Breedon rectory, with

John Verney, Nov. 13, 1438.   He was dean of Litchfield   In 1452, he resigned this archdeaconry to

William Vause, LL. B. collated Oct. 19, 1452.   He resigned this dignity long before his death to

Thomas Hawkins, collated Nov. 12, 1467.   On his resignation

Robert Inkbarrow was collated, May 4, 1472 ; but soon quitted this post, for we find

Thomas Hawkins again instated in it, May 14, the same year   His successor was

John Burton, collated July 26, 1476, who resigned to

Richard Burton, LL.B. collated Nov. 14, 1479.   He likewise resigned, and had for his successor

Thomas Alcock, collated Aug 4, 1483   He was living in 1527, being also archdeacon of Ely   We find not the time of his vacating this dignity, but his successor was the famous

Stephen Gardiner, LL D. 1500 ; who, in 1531, was made bishop of Winchester.

William Clayburgh, or Cleburg, succeeded April 4, 1531.   On his death

Peter Vannes, or Vaynor, was collated to the archdeaconry, May 12, 1534   He was also dean of Salisbury   His successor in this dignity was

Thomas Powell, LL.D. collated July 2, 1563   He resigned, anno 1579.

Godfrey Goldsborough, B. D succeeded July 15, the same year ; and was promoted to the see of Gloucester, anno 1598.   He was succeeded in this archdeaconry by

John Johnson, D. D. Nov. 24, 1598 ; who, in 1610, resigned it, and had for his successor

William Swaddon, D D who died possessed of this dignity August 4, 1623, and is buried in this cathedral

Hugh Lloyd, D D admitted 18 August following, on the option of the archbishop of Canterbury.

Edward Thornborough, M. A. son of Bishop Thornborough, collated August 3, 1629

William Hodges, B. D. collated May 30, 1645. He died anno 1676.

John Fleetwood, M. A. his successor, was collated September 4, the same year; he died 1705. His successor was

William Worth, B. D. a prebendary in the third stall of this cathedral, collated December 14, 1705; died in the year 1742, and was succeeded in this dignity by

John Tottie, D. D. canon of Christchurch, Oxford; he died November 21, 1774, a few days before the death of Bishop Johnson, who not having collated to it, the vacant turn devolved to the crown; when this dignity, by virtue of the royal prerogative, was conferred on

John Warren, LL.D. nephew of Bishop Johnson, and prebendary of Gloucester, who was installed April 22, 1775. He died March 9, 1787, when the present bishop collated

The Rev. Thomas Evans, D. D prebendary of the ninth stall of this church, March 21, 1787; and who was installed archdeacon of this diocese, April 5 following (1)

SECT. XII.

OF THE RELIGIOUS HOUSES, ANCIENTLY ENDOWED, AND LONG SINCE SUPPRESSED, IN THIS CITY.

Ancient hospitals were principally intended for the accommodation of pilgrims and poorer travellers on their journies; and, with this view, were built by the sides of great roads, and near the entrance of towns: a few poor

(1) The archdeaconry pays tenths,* and 6l. 6s. 8d. annually for synodals to the bishop of Worcester In the King's books it is rated at 58l 10s The office is supposed to have been erected A D 1088, but I believe it to have been much earlier The survey of this monastery was taken A. D. 1535 while Peter Vannes was archdeacon. The rectory of Claverdon, in the county of Warwick, is appropriated to the archdeaconry, to which, with the chapel of Norton Lindsey, the archdeacon presents

* The tenths became vested in such bishops, and their successors, in exchange for manors and lands which had been alienated from their bishoprics to the crown, wherein an allowance of yearly tenths has been made a part of the whole of the consideration upon such exchange These alienations from the church to the crown, have been restrained by an act in 1603, 1 Jac. cap 3. [Mr Bacon's Pref. to his Liber Regis, p 7]

men were stationed in each, to do the offices of hospitality, and were handsomely paid out of the revenues of their foundation.

ST. WULSTAN'S.

An ancient hospital, built on the south-east side of the city, of which that good bishop was the founder. Its original establishment was for a master, a chaplain, and four poor brethren (1) They were religious, of the order of St. Augustin, and professed the three spiritual vows of chastity, poverty, and obedience. It was to be always in the patronage of the Bishop of Worcester, and his successors, and the preceptor or master, removable by them at pleasure. They had an infirmary, in which, A. D. 1294, were twenty-two persons. In 1268 William de Beauchamp, among the legacies he bequeathed in favour of other religious foundations in this city, left one mark to this hospital (2) William de Molendinis, clerk, was a considerable benefactor to this hospital, as well as to St. Oswald's. In 1294, he gave sixty marks, and ten pounds sterling, by which he ensured to himself and his house, the prayers and devotional services of the brethren of the foundation, and the celebration of his anniversary on the conversion of St Paul, with some degree of ceremony. (3) In 1414, when Bishop Bourchier made his visitation of this society, he made an addition to its members. He ordered, that there should be two chaplains, each to be allowed four marks yearly, a gown, a chamber, diet at the master's table, and, in his absence, ten pence a week for providing for themselves He settled five poor brethren and two sisters in this house, each to have seven pence a week. But, lest complaints should arise of its revenue being unequal to such an additional burden, he forbade the granting of any corrodies (4) for the future. Hitherto the masters had been laymen, as the appellation of Commander, assumed only by lay superiors, sufficiently implies ; but this bishop insisted, that the master should be in priest's orders (5) It had usually the name of the Com-

---

(1) Davies's MS in Stow Leland, who says it was situate in the suburb, without Sudbury gate, adds, " some say it was the foundation of a queen " (2) Dugdale's Bar. vol. I. p 227.

(3) Caligula, A. p 190 M Bibl Cott (4) The founders of hospitals and monasteries reserved a right to their heirs, of quartering, if I may so speak, their old and decayed servants on the religious houses they had so founded. The set allowances of meat, drink, and clothing, which the convent was obliged to find to these eleemosynaries imposed upon it, was called *corredium*, and in English corrody (5) Dr. Thomas's Account of the Bishops of Worc p 195, 196 Walter, the master of this hospital temp Edw I gave the brotherhood a *regular* habit, instead of a *secular* they had before.

mandery, from the title which its masters assumed; who, in imitation of the superiors in military convents, stiled themselves *præceptores*, or commanders This has led some late retailers in geography into a gross mistake; who have ventured to assert, upon no authority but the name of Commandery, which the site of this hospital still retains, that it was formerly a house of the knights of St John . whereas, it is certain that those knights had no possession in Worcester or its neighbourhood. (1) About the end of the thirteenth century, the prior took the title of Preceptor, or commander And, in a patent of Henry VIII. the site of it is granted to Morysine, by the name of *situs præceptoriæ, sive, prioratus S Wulstani, Wigorn.* In May, 1300, Hugh le Despenser, then chief justice of the forest, (afterwards the favourite and principal minister of Edward II.) attended by all the foresters of Feckenham, held his court in this hospital, for imposing fines on the destroyers of the king's game. August 21, 1524, Cardinal Wolsey had a bull from the Pope, authorizing him to suppress this hospital, with several other small religious houses, and with the lands and revenues thereof to endow his two colleges, at Ipswich, and Oxford; but he lived not to see it take effect; the king upon his disgrace having seized them all into his own hands. It continued in the patronage of the Bishop of Worcester till the dissolution, when it was valued, 26 Henry VIII at 79*l*. 12*s*. 6*d*. per ann. in gross, 63*l* 18*s*. 10*d*. clear, as returned by the commissioners. It was granted, 32 Henry VIII. by deed bearing date 15th March, to Sir Richard Morysine, who exchanged it again with that king; and then it became part of the endowment of the cathedral church of Christ in Oxford, of which it was held by lease, till on the 19th of May, in the 36th of the same reign, it was conveyed, in consideration of the sum of 498*l*. to Thomas Wylde, of the city of Worcester, clothier, the lessee; in whose family it remained till a few years since, when it was purchased by John Dunbridge Esq. of Worcester. (2) A moiety of the manor of Pirie, more anciently called Pirian, is mentioned among the estates of this hospital (3) In this

(1) Tour through Great Britain, II p 291.   (2) In the original valor of Worcester diocese, in the first-fruits office, it appears that the chapel of this hospital was dedicated to St Godwald, and offerings were made to his image, &c. " hospitale Sti. Wulstani juxta civitat Wigorn. valet per ann. in oblationibus ad imagines Sti. Godwaldi, et aliorum imaginum in capella hospitalis, 20s." On the margin is written, " Capella Sti. Godwaldi •   (3) Patent 8 45 Ed III.

• In Leland's Itinerary, vol. V f. 184, 6, we read, " There is in this suburbe a chappell of St. Godwald."

manor lies Perry Wood, famous for Cromwell's encampment ; and not less
so, for being named as the scene of his interview with the infernal monarch;
a tale that tarnishes Mr. Echard's History. (1)

ST OSWALD'S.

In the north suburb of this city was another hospital, and was dedicated
to St Oswald   Its original endowment was for a master, a chaplain, and
four poor brethren.   This hospital was originally an infirmary, founded
for leprous monks of Worcester priory   The small-pox, when first brought
by the crusaders into Europe, seems to have been confounded with the leprosy , which was also, from the same conveyance, at that time epidemic in
the West. (2)   There is mention of other establishments for lepers, in various parts of England, and of France especially; which were afterwards
converted into hospitals, *i e*, inns for the pilgrims and the poor, as was this
of St Oswald ; the master of which was nominated, anciently, by the precentor of St Mary's priory   It was in being before A. D. 1268 ; in which
year William de Beauchamp, by will, left it ten shillings (3) Leland has
given a short detail of its state and appearance at his time in his Itinerary.
In several old deeds the chapel belonging to the hospital is said to have been
a parish church ; and Bishop Littleton collected, from the manuscripts in the
library of Jesus' college, Oxford, that there was formerly a church dedicated
to St Oswald, (4) in the hamlet of Whiston, within the parish of Claines.
The patronage was vested in the prior and convent of Worcester, and the
master was appointed by the sacrist of that church   Dugdale and Speed
say it was valued at 13*l* 14*s*. 4*d*. clear per ann   In a manuscript valuation
of Archbishop Sancroft, cited by Tanner, it is stated at 14*l* 14*s* 4*d* in the
whole and upon a new valuation, 4 Edw. VI. at 15*l*. 18*s*.   This house

(1) The Commandery is an edifice constructed of wood, the framing of which is filled with brick and
stone intermixed   The refectory, or great hall, is the principal of its remains , it is nearly a square,
roofed on the plan of Westminster-hall, with Irish oak, but not so ornamented.   The original door and
staircase still remain   The windows, which are lofty and spacious, are filled with small panes of glass,
on which are painted birds, flowers, and other decorations , but the principal part of them are charged
with a scroll inscribed *Emanuel*   The modern additions to this house have made it a very eligible and
desirable residence   (2) Davies, one of Stow's manuscript authors, reports St Oswald to
have been the founder of this hospital himself.   But the leprosy was not known in England till long
after Oswald's time   (3) Dugdale's Baron I p 227   (4) It was to this
church William de Molendinis had began to build its east end in 1296, but died before he had completed
it, as mentioned in the Worcester Annals

was not dissolved, but given by the king to the dean and chapter ; in whose patronage it has remained ever since, except in the reign of James I. (1)

WHITSTANE, OR WISTAN,

A nunnery of seven or eight white nuns, of the Benedictine order, and called White Ladies from the colour of their habit ; situated, says Leland, on the north side of the cemetery of St. Oswald, in the north suburb of this city ; said to be founded by a bishop of Worcester. It was built upon ground that had belonged to the cathedral convent. The site of their house, and the donations which had been made to them, were confirmed by the prior and convent of Worcester, in July, A. D. 1255 ; at which time also, their church was dedicated. Bishop Godfrey Giffard, in the year 1269, gave to this nunnery the manor and patronage of Eston, from whence that village is still called White Lady Aston, or Eston (2) He ordered the prior of Worcester to provide a priest to officiate there, for which he had a maintenance He also gave them, 1271, a portion of tithes and oblations in Claines ; and made interest with Raymond de Nogeriis, the Pope's nuncio, to free them from their tenths. In the reign of Henry IV. a patent passed the seal, for appropriating to them the church of Weston super Avon. There is a tenement, about a mile to the east of Worcester, which was part of the possessions of this religious house, and still bears the name of the Nunnery farm. Their revenue was valued, at the dissolution, 26 Henry VIII. at 53l 3s. 7d. per ann. ; and granted, 35 Henry VIII. to one Richard Callowhill. The site of the nunnery still retains the name of the White Ladies, and is held under the governors of a charity, founded soon after the Reformation by Queen Elizabeth, for the support of a Bluecoat school in Worcester. Richard Blurton, Esq purchased the renewable lease ; from whom it has descended to Richard Ingram, Esq. the present proprietor, who resides on the premises. The refectory remains nearly in its primitive state, a spacious and handsome apartment. The chapel was ruinated on the dispersion of the nuns ; its outer walls, still remaining, ascertain its extent ; the position of its altar, (3) and several of its windows are

(1) The estate of the hospital was formerly esteemed a manor, and was rated at the valuation for tenths, 26 Hen. VIII. [See Dr. Nash, vol. I p. 224.] Of its new foundation on the protestant plan, see Sect. XX. (2) Mr Abingdon. Dr Thomas's Bishops of Worc p. 143
(3) On this altar is placed the monument of Mr. Richard Blurton, formerly the proprietor of this

still visible. Beneath the present flooring is a crypt, probably a place for the interment of its prioresses. Tradition has reported, that subterraneous passages led from this vault to St. Mary's monastery on the one side, and to Henlip house on the other. On a view of the place, no indication of such openings could any where be traced, to authorize the conjecture. The cemetery on the north of the building is now an orchard, where the remains of some of its original inhabitants have been occasionally discovered. This house appears to have been a religious establishment as early as the Norman conquest, and the only nunnery ever founded at Worcester. According to William of Malmsbury, Ulgeva, the mother of St. Wulstan, took the veil in this society. It seems not, however, to have had the support of an ample revenue, and but for the assistance of adventitious benefactors, could not have subsisted. Its founder is unknown. A stone structure, of Saxon origin, and probably sepulchral, which had stood on this spot, and called the White Stane, gave name to the ancient manor of Whitstone, of which the adjoining estate of Sansom-fields forms a considerable part. That estate is held by lease for lives absolute, under the lord bishop of this diocese, which, with several freehold lands contiguous to it, and the improvements made upon the joint property by the present worthy possessor and proprietor, Sir Charles Trubshaw Withers, Knight, (1) forms a pleasing villa, with abundance of rural advantages facing its principal front, and whilst it receives the benefit of being in the neighbourhood of an opulent and populous city, it repays that benefit, by being a real ornament to it.

GRIY, OR MINOR TRIARS,

Otherwise called Franciscans (2) Their house, according to Leland, was " of the foundation of the Beauchamps Earls of Warwick" It was in being

estate; it was removed hither from the old church of St Nicholas when that structure was taken down, in which Mr Blurton was buried. The inscription upon it is supposed to have been written by Lord Somers, when very young. [See Dr Nash, vol II. in Appendix, p cxxxviii.]

(1) By the taste and liberality of this gentleman, a very extensive and pleasurable line of footway traversing a great portion of the pasture grounds of his premises to the east of this part of the town, has been laid open to public accommodation. Parallel with the Foregate street is the principal promenade of the beau monde, bearing the name of Sansom-fields walk, from whence the surrounding eminences, that form the distances in the view represented in the annexed Plate, and which bound the east side of the city, are seen to the greatest advantage. This beautiful assemblage of rural scenery has procured to this spot the most general resort of the inhabitants of this city, for the exercise of walking.

(2) From St Francis of Assisi, their founder, an Italian, who was born A. D. 1182. Entertaining a

Monument of JOSEPH WITHERS ESQ. in St Swithin's Church

SANSOME FIELDS near WORCESTER

before the year 1266. The site of their house extended from Friar-street eastward to the town walls. The church of this society stood without the walls, at the bottom of St. Laurence-lane, (a name that has given place to Friars-gate, leading to the Blockhouse-fields,) and was dedicated to that saint. (1) They had several benefactors in the neighbouring gentry, whose arms are still remaining in the great window of their hall. (2)

The refectory is a spacious and handsome room. The wainscoting, which is of Irish oak, is ornamented above with carvings, in which the instruments of the Passion are represented, inscribed B V. and on some J H S.; whilst others have the plume of feathers, the badge of the Prince of Wales, between the initials E. P., shewing thereby this part of its fitting up, if not also of the erection of the building, to have been subsequent to the date of the event that gave origin to this mark of distinction, which the valour of that prince has conferred on the eldest sons of our kings. It must, however, have been nearly coeval with that period, and most probably in his lifetime, and may consequently rank among the earliest testimonies of respect shewn to the memory of that illustrious character. This building is the most entire remains of an ancient religious house of any in the city; not a room has been changed · and those apartments which once held the religieux to their devotions, now hold the debtor and the criminal to their recollection and repentance It is encompassed (1788) by the ancient wall of the city to the east, and the wall of the Blockhouse to the south. Many human bones have been dug out of its present garden, originally its burying ground In the remains of the city walls the embrasures were stopt up, but were every where discernible ; and being judged insufficient to hold the pri-

fancy that Christian perfection consisted in possessing nothing, he undertook to live the poorest of all men This head had his followers, and those followers have the reputation of being the most obnoxious of all the religious orders ever established [Emilhanne's Hist of Monastic Orders, p. 158.] Their first appearance in England was about the year 1224 They were divided into seven districts or custodies, each governed by a provincial or custos One of these is said to have been fixed at Worcester, and that the custos had the care of the priories of Lincolter, Preston, Chester, Stafford, Shrewsbury, Bridgnorth, Litchfield, and Coventry Affecting uncommon humility both in their name and garb, they stiled themselves Minores Fratres, and went barefooted, with cords for their girdles From the colour of their habit, they had also the name of Grey Friars (1) Abing MS

(2) In a MS in the British Museum, entitled, Donations Brevia, temp Ed V et Ric III Plut 10, 11 C No 433 Art 151 p 28 is the following grant "To I rere Thomas Jonys, of the Freres Minours of Worcestre, the meadow called Digley, lieing under the castell there, during the king's (Rich III,) pleasure, without any thing therefore yeldinge."

soners in safety, have lately been repaired, and rendered more secure. After its suppression, it was granted, 31 Hen. VIII. to the bailiffs and citizens of Worcester, they paying an yearly rent to the crown It is now used as the city gaol. There was formerly, in the eastern wall of this city, a small gate, called Friars gate, opening directly upon this religious house Part of its cemetery, or burial ground, is now a skinner's yard, at the entrance of the Blockhouse-fields.

DOMINICANS

Preaching, or Black friars. (1) Leland says, their house at Worcester was situated in the north part of the city, and was of the foundation of the Beauchamps of Powick 21 Edward III. these black or preaching friars had a grant of a piece of ground within the walls, called Belasses, for building their house upon it (2) In 43 of the same king, they had a legacy of 20l. left them by Catherine, daughter of Roger Mortimer, Earl of March, and wife of Thomas Beauchamp, Earl of Warwick. (3) A new chapel was ordered to be built on the north side of the choir of this friary, for the burial of Sir John Beauchamp, A. D. 1475, who had willed his body to be buried here, and to which he gave, among other bequests, an organ of his own. His lady, who outlived him about two years, bequeathed also her body to be buried near her husband. She willed that a tablet of alabaster should be made, of the birth of our Lord, and the three kings of Coleyn, (Cologne) to be set in the wall over her body. Likewise an image of alabaster of St John the Evangelist, three quarters of a yard long, with the chalice in his hand, to be set over her likewise (4) It was granted, 31 Henry VIII. to the bailiffs and citizens of Worcester.

(1) Dominic, their founder, was born in Spain, A D 1170 They came into England temp Henry III., but when they settled at Worcester is not known They had the name of Black friars from the colour of their cloaks and hoods, which they wore over white cassocks, and of Preaching friars, from their rambling over the country to preach, in which they have been successfully imitated by modern itinerants, as noisily religious, but under neither order or vow They were mendicants, and had no revenues They formerly were called Brothers of the Virgin Mary, from the worship they paid her, and to whom they consecrated wholly their Saturdays Dominic is said to have persuaded Pope Honorius III to establish the office of the master of the sacred palace at Rome, to whom was committed the interpretation of the Scriptures, and the *censure of books*, an office first filled by himself, and afterwards, successively conferred upon a religieux of the same order [Emill Hist Monast Ord. p 149, 150]—Quære, Whether as a *lord chamberlain*, or as a *reviewer*, in England?

(2) It was situated at the back of the Broad-street, and extended to the north wall of the city on one side, and to Angel-lane on the east A set of new houses, called Black Friars, is built on part of its site, and the other part is now covered with gardens (3) Dugd Bar I 1 p 234 (4) Ib. I 1. p 249, 250

PENITENTS.

A convent of fratres de pænitentia Jesu Christi, or Friars of the Sack, (1) made a settlement here in the latter end of the reign of King Henry III. (2)

TRINITY GYLD (3)

The chantry of the chapel of the Holy Trinity, (4) in the parish of St. Nicholas, within the city of Worcester, was founded by Richard Norton and others, by virtue of the king's letters 18 Feb. 45 Edward III to find a priest to sing mass perpetually for the soul of the founder, Richard, and all Christian souls   The gyld, or brotherhood, was established and confirmed by King Henry IV. 1404, in the church or chapel of the Trinity there, by his letters patent, having authority by the same to establish a certain perpetual chantry of three priests or chaplains, to sing mass perpetually for the said king.   The said service, founded partly by the bequest of several persons, and partly purchased by devout persons, for and towards the sustentation of one priest, not only to say mass within the said chapel, but also to help the parson and curate in time of need in the parish church, because it doth abound of houseling people.   The priest is removable   The value of the revenues, according to the book of first-fruits and tenths, is 11l. 3s. 7d. per ann   The yearly value, according to the survey, 10l 2s ; out of which are deductions. (5)   This chantry, with divers houses and lands, both within the city of Worcester and without, belonging thereto, came to the king's hands by

(1) These friars were so called from the sack-cloth habit they wore   They appeared in England, A D 1257   Their order was but short-lived, for they were suppressed by the council of Lyons, in 1307

(2) Bp Tanner's Notitia Monastic fol p 625, 626, 627 , and in Pref p. xxiii. where he says, they had eight houses in England   Mr Pegge, in his Memoir on that order, has enumerated ten, and states, that they were settled in Worcester before A D 1272. [Archæologia, vol. III No XVIII p 130]

(3) Taken by Mr Abingdon, from the account delivered in to the king's commissioners at the dissolution   Gelds, or gilds, were founded either for the purposes of charity, (those were usually called after the name of some saint) religion, or merchandize.   Their feasts and anniversaries, called Gilden, were held at their common charge   [Dugdale, in Coventry]

(4) The order of Trinitaries, or Mathurines, for the redemption of Christian captives from the Infidels, was founded by John of Matha, born in Provence, in France, in the year 1154   Many monasteries were founded of this order, and filled with devotees, under the rule of St Austin, which was finally confirmed A D 1207, under the name of the "Order of the Holy Trinity for the Redemption of Captives"   It was brought into England in 1357, where it was called the Order of Ingham, probably from the place in which they first settled [Helluianne's Hist of Monast Orders   Dugd Warw p 498 Ld Thomas]

(5) See Dr. Nash, vol. II. p cxl in Appendix, ex. Regist Silv. Gigles, f 199 6.

act of parliament, temp. Edward VI. which was granted by his Majesty, in the second year of his reign, to Sir Edward Warriner, Knight, and Richard Catelin, Gent ; who the same year granted it to John Keyme and Richard Keyme. These grants, after passing through several hands, on the 17th Sept. 9 Jac. R Mr. Robert Rowland, alias Steyner, heir to Mr. Robert Yowle, gave to the corporation of weavers, walkers, and clothiers of Worcester, the Trinity-hall, which his grandfather, Mr. Yowle, before intended, and to his power then performed." We have no account of its revenues, or how many brethren the society consisted of it was, however, a fraternity much sought after, from the plenitude of indulgences they possessed, and which they managed to good account with their followers.

The site of their friary is said by Dr Nash, (vol. II. p cxxxix. in the Appendix) to have been " towards the bottom of the Angel-lane, between that and the Broad-street." I am, however, still disposed to think, that the present Trinity-hall is a part of its remains, and that it was there the house of those friars stood Since the dissolution it has a charity upon a new foundation (1)

SECT. XIII.

OF THE CASTLE, AND ITS HEREDITARY CONSTABLES.

THAT there was a fortress of the Romans here, afterwards turned into a citadel by the Saxons, and honoured by the residence of the viceroys of the Wiccii, is sufficiently credible, though history affords no direct and positive proof of it (2) The first castle here, of which any mention occurs, is that which Urso d'Abitot built. (3) The area, which is now called the College green, was in the Norman times the *outer ward* of the castle, behind which to the south was the inner, or fortress itself. The houses in the outer ward were held under the king whereas the inner was part of the fief of the sheriff hereditary of Worcestershire. This appears in the grant made of the

(1) See Sect XX (2) See Sect I and II (3) He signs as the fourth witness to St Wulstan's grant of Alvestune, A D 1088, thus " Urso Vicecomes cu omnib militab' viccecomitit ejus " In Leland's time there was of the Abitots, a man of 20 li land in Worcester towne [Itin vol. VIII p 128]

former to the prior and convent, on the day of King John's interment, by the Pope's legate and the Earl of Pembroke.

I think that the building erected by D'Abitot must have been in this outer ward; for his moat for securing it cut away part of the cemetery or burial ground of the monks This invasion of St Mary's land gave them great disturbance; and they never rested, till they got it restored; which they afterwards did, with interest The inner ward, it may well be supposed, was the older Saxon citadel.

Urso de Abitot, a Norman captain, on whom William the Conqueror had bestowed forty hides of land in this county, with two manors in Warwickshire, and another in Gloucestershire, had, under that king, and Rufus his son, the chief civil and military trusts in the county of Worcester; being constituted sheriff, and constable of the royal castle here, with the very honourable appointment, that these offices should descend hereditarily in his family. He is sometimes called Urso de Wirecestre; I suppose from his residence here. He and his brother Rodbert, who was the king's steward, (1) were troublesome neighbours to the convent of St. Mary's, and found pretences for dispossessing the monks of several of their manors (2) Urso, especially, was greedy in grasping whatever lands he could reach, and sufficiently tenacious of his prey (3) Yet he was no enemy of the monastic institute. This robber of the church was pleased to be the founder of a hermitage, that at Great Malvern; which Bishop Wulstan improved, and, by the aid of considerable benefactions, converted into a priory of monks (4) Urso carried on the buildings and moat of the castle nearer to the cathedral church than the convent could well brook. They appear to have complained to their old prelate and patron, Aldred, Archbishop of York; who meeting with the sheriff, as William of Malmsbury relates, played off his artillery of imprecations, pointed, in the manner of devotive charms, with rhyme·

" Highest thou Urse ?   Have thou God's curse,

" And mine, and that of all holy men, unless thou remove thy castle; and " know assuredly, that thy posterity shall not inherit the patrimony of St. " Mary " This curse, says Malmsbury, seemed to take effect; for Ursus died soon after.

(1) Otherwise called Robert Despenser   (2) Ridmerly, Clopton, Acton, Waresleah, and part of Bengworth, &c seized by Urso Lawern, Elmley, and a moiety of Chorlton, by his brother [Heming. Chartul]   (3) Heming p 257.   (4) Dugdale's Baronage Tanner's Notitia

Roger, the son of Urso, succeeded him, but fell under the displeasure of King Henry I and was deprived of his patrimony, for ordering the execution of one of the king's officers, in the height of his passion, and was forced to fly his country (1)

Walter de Beauchamp, steward to this king, who had married Emeline, the only daughter of Urso, was next instated in the sheriffalty of Worcestershire, with the custody of the castle, as well as in the possession of all the lands of Roger de Worcester, his brother-in-law. According to Leland, he was related to the Conqueror. Elmeley was his capital seat.

William de Beauchamp, his son, succeeded both in the office of steward to the king, and in those of sheriff of the county, and constable of the castle of Worcester. In 1139, he was appointed lord high constable of England; a post of the highest power that any subject could enjoy. His adherence to the Empress Maude, in the war about the succession to the crown, which was kindled immediately after, drew upon him the enmity of King Stephen, who deprived him of his hereditary trusts, gave the government of Worcester, and its castle, to Waleran, Count of Meulant, and constituted him Earl of Worcester. Of this Waleran, who was sufficiently active, soon after the breaking out of that war, in parties of military execution, at the head of his garrison of Worcester, I shall speak in the following section. But the great success of the empress reducing a great part of the kingdom to her subjection, she restored to William de Beauchamp the castle of Worcester, with its outer ward, the sheriffalty of the county, the keeping of the forests, and whatever else did, by right of inheritance, pertain to a sheriff of Worcestershire, and castellan of Worcester; on the condition of his being her liegeman against all persons, especially against Waleran, Count of Meulant, and of his paying to the crown the like yearly rent, as Walter his father had paid. In these possessions he was confirmed by her son, King Henry II with whom he stood in great favour, and had the honour to execute various high offices in his reign He died in 1170, and was buried near the door of the chapter-house of Worcester priory. (2)

William de Beauchamp II his son and successor, died in the beginning of King John's reign whose son, another

Walter de Beauchamp, was made by that king governor of Hanley castle, in this county He took part with the barons against that unhappy

(1) William Malmsbury. Drake's York, p. 413   (2) Ann. Wig 1170.

prince : upon which his lands were seized and confiscated, and himself laid
under the sentence of excommunication This was a fortunate incident for
the church of Worcester, and prevented his opposition to the grant, which,
in 1217, was made to the monks, of a moiety of his castle here, by the Earl
of Pembroke, then guardian of the young king, and by Gualo, the Pope's
legate (1) The moiety then surrendered to the convent, upon the bishop's
representation and complaint, was the outer ward ; but not till a jury of
knights had been impannelled, twelve out of Worcestershire, and two from
Gloucestershire, to inquire concerning the right of the sheriff hereditary
and of the church in the premises, and to make their report to William Earl
of Pembroke. (2) The tenour of their report may be conjectured from the
words of the king's charter in confirmation of this grant ; which distinguishes the northern part of the castle as his own fief, and the southern as
Walter de Beauchamp's ; and grants the former, in which were situate the
king's houses, to the prior and convent, for the enlargement of their close
or court.

After this time it is not probable, that any of the governors had residence
in this castle, except in times of public disturbance ; no convenient offices
being reserved for the reception of a large retinue ; only the main fortress,
of no great extent, including the keep and its moat, (3) being left.

On the death of Walter, in 1235, his son, William de Beauchamp III.
succeeded. This baron aggrandized the family by his marrying Isabella,
sister and afterwards heiress of William de Mauduit, Earl of Warwick. By
his last will, in 1269, he ordered his body to be interred in the church of
the friars minors, without the city of Worcester, founded by this earl or
his ancestors. (4) There is reason to think, that, notwithstanding his own

(1) At this time Walter was a supplicant to the legate, and glad to compound for his absolution. Till
he had given security for his future fidelity, his paternal castle of Elmeley was with-held from him: but
upon security being obtained, restitution was made to him of the castle of Worcester also, (i e its remaining moiety) and of the sheriffalty of this county, yet only for a time, until the king should accom-
plish the age of fourteen years   In the 20th year of Henry III he had a fresh grant of the sheriffalty
as his acknowledged inheritance   (2) Dugdale   (3) Castrum Wigorn nobis redditum
est tanquam jus nostrum, usque ad motam turris [Annal Wigorn sub anno 1217] This grant was
only promised at the funeral of King John it passed the seal on Eastei-eve, 1217, signed by the guardian
of the young king , who, in the sixteenth year of his reign, 1232, confirmed it under his own hand.

(4) See the preceding Sect. Dugd Warw His contests with the bishop of Worcester about his
right to the wreck of barges, &c and the execution of sheriffs' warrants in Oswaldslow hundred, are
too tedious to be here particularized Consult Dr Thomas.

K k

appointment, the monks of Worcester priory obtained the benefit of his sepulture.

William de Beauchamp IV. his eldest son, succeeded; who, in the year before, had been admitted to the earldom of Warwick, in right of Isabella his mother. Hitherto Elmeley castle was the chief seat of this family, but from this period, the castle of Warwick.

A rumour, maliciously propagated, that his father's body had been thrown out of his sepulchre, hurried the earl to Worcester in 1276, when the grave or tomb being opened, in the presence of this nobleman, and his brothers, (1) the body of the old Lord of Elmeley, distinguishable by certain signs, was recognized, and left to its rest. This had never been entered in the annals of Worcester convent, if the honour of the convent had not been concerned in the scrutiny.

In the reign of King Edward I. we find this earl frequently employed in awing the Welch, against whom he had successful campaigns; especially in the year 1295, when he made great slaughter of them, in a battle near Montgomery. Next year he had a command in Scotland, and, by a most bloody victory that he obtained there, compelled the surrender of the fortress of Dunbar. He died in June, 1298, and was prevailed upon by a friar minor, who drew up his will, to order his interment, not at the cathedral, where his ancestors lay, but in the choir of those friars at Worcester. In that will he bequeaths to them two great horses, which at his funeral should carry his armour; and for the solemnizing of his interment, he left 200l. (2) On the 27th of June, these Franciscan brethren, as though on purpose to mortify the monks of the cathedral, made a procession, as it were in triumph, (3) carrying the body of this great man through the streets and lanes

(1) This earl had three younger brothers, Walter, Lord of Powyk and Alcester, Sir John, Lord of Holt, and Sir James, who died in 1296, distinguished by the annalist as the friend of Worcester church. The two last were buried in the cathedral.

(2) Among the various other legacies he bequeathed by that will, the following are found relating to Worcester.—To a priest, to sing mass daily in his chapel, without the city of Worcester, near the house of the friars minors, for the health of his soul, and the souls of Isabell his wife, and Isabell de Mortimer, and all the faithful, he gave all the rent of the fee of Richard Bruh, in Wiche and Winchester. To Joan, his daughter, a kind of canopy, sometime belonging to St. Wulstan. To the friars minors of Worcester, xls. To the hospital of St. Wulstan, at Worcester, 1 mark. To the hospital of St. Oswald, there, x sol. To the church and nuns (the White Ladies) without Worcester, 1 mark. To every anchorite in Worcester, and the parts adjacent, iv s. [Dugdale, p. 312. Ld. 1656 Lond.]

(3) Quasi victores capta præda. Ann. Wig. The cemetery, wherein an earl of Warwick, and a lord

of the city, and then deposited it, says the splenetic annalist, in ground, " wherein, during the winter season, it may rather be said to be drowned " than interred; in a spot whereon I have seen vile kitchen-herbs grow." (1)

His son, Guy de Beauchamp, Earl of Warwick, was his successor; and signalizing himself greatly by his valour in the war of Scotland, received, as his reward, a vast accession of domains, which had belonged to the royal house of Baliol, in the bishopric of Durham. He was one of the nobles whom King Edward I charged, on his death-bed, not to suffer Piers Gaviston to return to England, and be employed about the person of his son. But Edward II. could not live without his favourite. Piers was king in effect; till he was seized by an association of the nobility, of whom Earl Guy was the most active, being particularly piqued at the nickname of Black Dog of Arden, (2) which this haughty favourite, in allusion to Guy's swarthiness of complexion, had too contemptuously given him; and for which he paid by his life; for Guy, without ceremony, cut off the prime minister's head, on Blacklow hill, near Warwick. for which fact, however atrocious, he was too powerful to be brought to punishment; and, in 1314, extorted the king's pardon of the murder. But he died himself the next year, August 12th, in his castle at Warwick, as some insinuate, of poison, aged about forty-four, and was buried in the abbey of Bordesley, in Worcestershire; to which he had been a considerable benefactor. (3) He founded the college or chantry of priests at Elmeley. His son

Thomas, Earl of Warwick, was at that time an infant. The king gave to Hugh le Despenser, another of his favourites, the custody of the castles and all the great patrimony of this minor; and, after Hugh's fall, Roger, Lord Mortimer, the favourite of Queen Isabella, obtained the right of this custody in his room. But as soon as the young earl had attained the age of seventeen, King Edward III. gave him possession of his father's lands; and, in the next year, admitted him (though still under age) to the sheriffalty of Worcestershire, and the post of chamberlain in the exchequer, with

treasurer of England (John Lord Beauchamp of Powyk), and others of this illustrious family were buried, is now full of pits for the dressing of sheep skins. See Sect XII

(1) They had, about eight years before, a quarrel, similar both in its nature and result, with the monastery about the interment of one H Poche, who had willed himself to be buried at the friars minors, but whose body, on his decease, was obtained by the sacrist, and buried in the cemetery of the cathedral [Dr Thomas's Account of Bishops of Worcester, p 146. and Append No 64. p. 55.]

(2) Arden forest, in Warwickshire See Sect I p 9, 12.   (3) Dugd p. 315.

K k 2

power of delegating to whomsoever he pleased, the execution of these hereditary offices, after the example of his ancestors. He was one of those noble warriors who contributed to raise the glory of England in the days of Edward III   In the battle of Cressy he commanded the van of the English army   in the field of Poitiers he galled his hand, (less tender, we must presume, than the hands of modern heroes,) by the long and forcible exercise of his sword and poll-axe ; and among his prisoners there, took William de Melleun, the Archbishop of Seinz, for whose redemption he received eight thousand pounds.   But the account of his military exploits, his expedition at the head of a retinue of three hundred horse, to war with the Infidels in the Levant, &c. comes not properly within the plan of this work.   It is sufficient to observe, that he was chosen one of the knights of the garter, at the first institution of that noble order ; that he was appointed earl marshal of England in 1344 ; and that he died near Calais, of the plague, 13th of November, 1369, at a time when he was meditating conquests. (1) His son,

Thomas II. Earl of Warwick, succeeded him ; to whom, in the third year of King Richard II. 1380, the house of commons committed the care of the young king's education   He also was a knight of the order of the garter. His close connections with the king's uncles were his ruin.   In 1387, he raised forces with the Duke of Gloucester and other confederate lords, who, marching to London, gave law to the throne.   This violence was pardoned ; but in 1397, the king's jealousy broke out, and could be allayed by no less a sacrifice than the lives of that duke and his principal adherents.   The ambitious Gloucester was assassinated ; this earl impeached of high treason, and condemned   Proud and haughty hitherto, he stooped now to beg poorly for his life, which was granted him ; but with the sentence of perpetual banishment to the Isle of Man ; from whence, within a year, he was remanded back to the Tower of London   At this time the office of hereditary sheriff of the county, and the keeper of the castle of Worcester, was suppressed, and annexed to the crown   The castle of Warwick, with several lordships in that county, and the manors of Packingham, Salewarp, Wadbergh, Scelton, and Beoley, in Worcestershire ; and Haselore, in

(1) He lies interred in the midst of the choir of the collegiate church at Warwick, with Katherine, his countess, daughter of Roger Mortimer, created first Earl of March   Their effigies, in white marble, are placed on the tomb erected over them   This countess left, by will, to the convent of Friars Preachers in Worcester, xx li [Dugd Warw p 319 Ed. 1656]

Warwickshire: part of the Beauchamp inheritance was conferred by the king on Thomas Holland, Earl of Kent and Duke of Surry, of this family (1) Some other lands in this county, forfeited by the attainder of the Earl of Warwick, were probably given to Sir Thomas Percy, who at this time was advanced to the long dormant honour of Earl of Worcester.

Thomas, the unfortunate Earl of Warwick, survived his troubles ; and, in the beginning of the next reign, was restored to the enjoyment of his liberty, honour, and the greatest part of his possessions (2) But the custody of Worcester castle was no longer a fief of this family. Sheriffs have since that period been appointed annually ; and, during their offices, have the charge of the castle.

A gaol, for the reception of the prisoners of the exterior county, is all the structure now seen on the spot where kings of England have kept their courts There is a steep artificial mount, whose area at the top is not more than six yards in diameter ; on which, it is probable, the donjon, (3) or keep of this fortress, anciently stood. The rampire to the south of it, extending from the river almost as far as Edgar's tower, is not yet levelled ; and the ditch on the outside may be easily traced.

(1) Dugdale, Baron. II p. 76   I find, however, the city of Worcester mentioned among the possessions of his grand-daughter, Anne, Countess of Warwick, which, by feoffment, Dec 13th, anno 3 Hen. VII she settled on the king and his issue male   [Ibid I. p 307]

(2) He died April 8th, 1401, and with Margaret his countess, daughter to William Lord Ferrers, of Groby, lies buried under a costly monument on the south side of the collegiate church of St. Mary, in Warwick, the choir of which, begun by his father, he finished, and entirely built the body of the church as it now stands   [Dugd p 323.]

(3) The donjon was the highest and strongest tower of the castle, in which prisoners were kept. (Johnson's Dict)   The modern word dungeon conveys a very different idea, that of a dark and subterraneous prison.   The ancient tower, built, A D 914, by Lady Ethelfleda, at Tamworth, was placed on an artificial mount, called the *Dungeon,* upon which mount the castle now stands   [Toldervy, p 411 Octavo Lond 1762]   The tower in the hospital meadow, at Norwich, called the *Dungeon,* served as a prison for the jurisdiction of the cathedral   [Parkyns's Hist of Norwich, p 271]   The *Dungeon-hill,* at Canterbury, is supposed to have been a work of the Danes.   [Gough's Additions to Camden, in Kent, vol I p 237]

SECT. XIV.

OF THE EARLS AND MARQUISES OF WORCESTER.

THE title of Earl gives nothing now but rank, and a seat above barons and viscounts in the house of lords But anciently considerable power and jurisdiction was annexed to the honour.   Earls, by the Saxons, were called Ealdormen, and was the highest magistrate in the county that gave him title.   He had the government of the chief city or town and castle of his territory.   It was not a title or degree of dignity, but the office and judicature in some city or portion of the county, circumscribed anciently by the bounds of the bishopric of the diocese ; for that the bishop and the earl presided together in one court, and heard jointly the causes of the church and the commonwealth, as they now do in parliament. (1)   The military command of the shire was vested in him ; and he presided as judge in the county courts, where the titles of lands, and the causes of freeholders, were tried and decided.   The sheriff, or vicecomes, was a subordinate officer, whose more immediate jurisdiction was over the king's demesnes ; and with whom was also intrusted the execution of the king's mandates, and the collection of his rents, fines, reliefs, customs, &c throughout the whole county.   Earldoms were, at first, offices during the pleasure of the king, and but for life only : they were made hereditary, feudal, and patrimonial, by William the Conqueror.   The earl had a revenue for the support of his dignity, namely, the third part of all mulcts, forfeitures, and profits accruing to the exchequer from the county. (2)   For this third part the sheriff stood responsible to the earl ; and for the other two parts to the king ; (3) except in the city of Worcester, where, as we have already seen, Ethelred, Duke of Mercia, and the Princess Ethelfleda, with the allowance of her father, King Alfred, had given to the bishop one half of the king's profits (4)   This particular constitution of the revenue at Worcester, is taken notice of in Domesday book , wherein it is said, that " in King Edward's time, the bishop had the third

(1) Sir H Spelman's Works, (Feuds and Tenures) c 6 p 13 Part II
(2) Dr Brady's Hist vol I p 82   (3) Madox, Hist Exc chap 23 Sect 2.   A certain sum is now annually paid them out of the exchequer in lieu of the third penny.
(4) See Sect II p 18

" penny in the borough, and still has it, as well as the king and the earl. (1)
" The bishop's profit of the third penny amounted, in that king's time, to
" six pounds; and now (*i e* in the time of William I.) amounts to eight
" pounds" (2) (annual income) (3)

As there was at that time no earl of Worcester, the sheriff (vicecomes), who was his proper substitute, received the third penny in lieu of the earl. There is no mention of any earl of Worcester till the reign of King Stephen The highest officer, before the year 1139, resident in this county, was the sheriff; for which reason, the county itself was frequently distinguished, in those days, by the name of *vicecomitatus de Wirecestre.*

Waleran de Beaumont, younger son of Robert Count of Meulant and Earl of Leicester, received, by the grant of King Stephen, the earldom of Worcester, with the custody of the castle annexed to it As a soldier, he had variety of fortunes, especially in the wars of Normandy ; in which province he had large possessions As a scholar, he distinguished himself, in 1119, at Gisors, when King Henry I and the Pope had an interview there : our young count and his brother engaged the cardinals in a dispute, and so dexterously entangled them in the forms and subtleties of logic, that their eminencies, with all their skill, could not evade nor break through the argument.

The city of Worcester was, in the beginning of November, 1139, plundered and set on fire by the troops of Milo, Earl of Hereford, who was one of the most zealous adherents of the Empress Maude Waleran, the new

(1) Mr. Graves's Extracts from Domesday , published in Hearne's Chartul Wigorn

(2) Eight pounds in coin, at that time, was equivalent to one hundred and eighty pounds sterling, at the present rate of money

(3) The Norman kings soon found it their interest to pull down the power of hereditary earls Their whole jurisdiction was transferred to sheriffs, assisted in their courts by the king's justiciaries But they retained their third penny for some longer time In the dialogue concerning the exchequer, written in the time of Richard I an earl is thus oddly defined, " An earl," says the old writer, " is one who re-" ceives a third part of the fines in each county " The Empress Maude created an earl in the following form I Matilda, daughter of King Henry, and Queen of England, give and grant to Jeofrey de Magna-ville, for his services, and to his heirs after him by inheritance, that he shall be Earl of Essex, and have the third penny of the pleas in the sheriff's court, as the earl ought to have, for the support of his earldom in all things " [From the original instrument in Camden's possession, the oldest charter of creation he had seen] The same provision is made by Henry II for Hugh Bigod, Earl of Norfolk, which the old register of Battle abbey thus explains " It was an ancient custom that prevailed all over England, for the earls to have the third pennies of counties, whence they are called Comites " [Gough's edit of Camden, vol I Orders in England, p 137]

Earl of Worcester, came, on the 30th of November, to take possession of the castle here, which had held out for King Stephen ; and, marching out at the head of the Worcester men, made most severe reprisals upon the tenants and adherents of Milo ; took Sudley castle, in Gloucestershire, and ravaged the whole country round it, returning with droves of cattle and of prisoners to Worcester.   In 1140, he attended King Stephen to Worcester ; and while the king marched forwards to Hereford, Waleran fell upon Tewkesbury, and took immense spoils, sparing only the goods of the abbey church ; but setting fire to the magnificent seat of the Earl of Gloucester, and pillaging or laying in ashes all the houses, till he approached the city of Gloucester, within the distance of a mile (1)   On his return with his party to Worcester, he protested, with an inhuman glee of triumph, that " neither in Nor-" mandy nor in England had he ever burnt more villages and houses in one " excursion "   In the next year Waleran had the command of a wing of King Stephen's army in the battle of Lincoln   In 1146, he took upon him the cross, and performed a pilgrimage to Jerusalem   After his return to Normandy, we find him among the partizans of the empress and her son. King Stephen, in resentment of his desertion, (2) made an attempt, in 1150, on the castle of Worcester, but not being able to carry it, wreaked his fury on the city, which he abandoned to flames (3)   In the following year he made another assault, but with no better success ; the garrison made a gallant defence . the king raising the siege, contented himself with blocking up the castle by two forts, which were soon after taken by Robert, Earl of Leicester, the elder brother of Waleran, Earl of Worcester and Meulant.   When Henry II son of the Empress Maude, came to the crown, one of his first acts was, the depriving the pseudo-earls (those who had been instated by the usurper King Stephen) of their dignities   But Waleran, though no longer an English earl, continued a count in France , where, in 1166, he ended his days, a monk in the abbey of Preaux, in Normandy, so easy was the transition in those days, from the fierce warrior to the trembling devotee   Trophies in a camp and beads in a cloister were successively amusements for the grandee

(1) Contin Flor Wig sub anno 1140   (2) I have followed here Mr Carte's account But it is more probable that William de Beauchamp had before this time seized Worcester for the empress, and was the governor who so bravely maintained the castle against King Stephen   [See the last Sect]   It may be questioned whether Earl Waleran was ever resident in England after his return from the Holy Land.   (3) Hollingshed, p 384

After him, there was no earl of Worcester for above 200 years. In 1397 (at which time earls had nothing from their counties but a title) Sir Thomas Percy, admiral of the fleet, vice-chamberlain and steward of the royal household, was, by King Richard II created Earl of Worcester, Sept. 29. He was younger brother of Henry, the rough and boisterous Earl of Northumberland. In January following he was made governor of Calais. Henry IV on his accession to the crown, sent him ambassador to France, in conjunction with Walter Skirlow, Bishop of Durham; (1) and in 1402, made him his lord lieutenant throughout Wales, for the subduing of the rebels under Glendowr. In 1403, he hurried from his honourable station at court to join the Percies in their unfortunate rebellion. In the bloody battle fought, July 2, near Shrewsbury, his nephew Hotspur fell, and the eorl himself was taken prisoner, and, by the king's order, beheaded at Shrewsbury (2) He had no issue. In an age that abounded with brave commanders, his valour was acknowledged and admired.

The title of Worcester was dormant for a few years. King Henry V. in the 7th year of his reign, conferred it upon Richard Beauchamp, Lord Bergavenny, son of William de Beauchamp, Lord of Abergavenny, nephew of Thomas, Earl of Warwick, the last hereditary sheriff and castellan of Worcester (3) He had rendered, in the war of France, very important services to that monarch , who, in recompence, gave him this dignity , and, for the support of it, made him large grants of land in Normandy, and other provinces of France. (4) He had but short enjoyment of these marks of royal favour, being wounded, but a few years after, at the siege of Meaux, in France, March 18, 1422, by a stone from a sling; of which wound he languished, till death relieved him, 5 Hen V. (5) He left an only daughter, born at Hanley castle, in Worcestershire, who carried his estate and the barony of Bergavenny to her husband, Sir Edward Nevill, and his descendants. The title of Worcester was in him extinct. Earl Richard was buried at Tewkesbury abbey, where the ancestors of his wife Isabel, Lady Despenser, had been usually interred. She erected over his sepulchre, on the north side of the choir, a very elegant chapel, dedicated to Mary Mag-

(1) Hollingshed, p 1125   Hall's Chron p 16   (2) Speed's Chron p 629   Collier's
Led Hist vol 1 p 619, 620   (3) Willis's Notitia Parliamentaria, p 154
(4) Biograph Britann 1 p 608   (5) Dugd 1 p 242   Camden, in Monmouth-
shire, Gough's ed p 479

L l

dalen, wherein his and her anniversary might be celebrated   The chapel still remains.

King Henry VI in the 27th year of his reign, on the marriage of Sir John Tiptot, Lord Tiptot and Powys, with Cecily, relict of Henry de Beauchamp, Duke of Warwick, (1) revived, in favour of this accomplished nobleman, the title of Earl of Worcester. This lord was born at Everdon, in Bedford-shire; was educated at Baliol college, Oxford, and signalized himself early by his military services, and by a taste for literature, very extraordinary in that age.   He passed through a series of the highest posts; justice of North Wales, steward of the household, twice treasurer of the exchequer, twice en-trusted with the government of Ireland, twice lord high constable of Eng-land; honoured with the order of the garter   His vehemence in support of the house of York had raised him to intoxicating greatness : and the insta-bility of that family on the throne was his ruin.   In 1470, the reign of Ed-ward IV was suddenly interrupted by the restoration of Henry VI. who was called out of prison to his last scene of royalty   This revolution was stained with no blood, but that of the Earl of Worcester ; who, endeavouring to elude the search made for him, was discovered in his place of concealment at the top of a high tree, was brought to London, and beheaded on Tower-hill, Oct 18 (2)   Caxton, who published a translation of Cicero on friendship, and other tracts, the work of this ingenious nobleman, laments his fall, and celebrates his virtue.   " At his deth every man that was there might lern to " dye, and take his deth paciently "—And again, " The noble famous erle " of Wurcestre in his tyme flowred in vertue and cunnyng; to whom I " knew none lyke emonge the lordes of the temporalitie in science and mo-" ral vertue."   Learning, indeed, had a patron in him ; but true honour and virtue will scarcely allow him a seat in their temple   History brands him with venality and avarice, and, what is worse, with cruelty all his love for the sciences could not soften in him the ferocious temper of the unhappy times in which he lived, of which, his destroying two infant sons of Lord Desmond ; and his hanging and empaling, in virtue of his authority as lord

(1) This Henry Duke of Warwick, was great grandson of Thomas de Beauchamp II Earl of Warwick, with whose history and attainder the last Section concluded

(2) Biograph Britan II p 1239   He had deserted the cause of Henry, and suffered by order of the great Earl of Warwick, who had just before thought proper to abandon that of Edward   He is buried in the cathedral of Ely, where, on a very handsome tomb in the south ile of the choir, his effigy is laid between those of his two wives   [See Bentham's Ely, Plate xxxviii]

high constable, twenty gentlemen taken on ship-board, in the service of Henry VI. are mentioned as flagrant instances. (1).

Edward Tiptot, the son of this lord, was restored in blood to his father's title, as soon as King Edward IV. regained the throne. But died before he came to age, in 1485, the last earl of Worcester of this family.

The honour lay dormant near thirty years. Henry VIII. renewed it in the person of his chamberlain, Charles Somerset, who was made knight of the garter, and lord chamberlain of the household by Henry VII. ; and in the beginning of his reign, was summoned to parliament as Lord Herbert of Gower and Chepstow, and created, in 1514, earl of Worcester and baron of Ragland. This Charles was a natural son of Henry Beaufort, Duke of Somerset, who was beheaded at Hexham, 1464 It does not appear that he had any connection either with the city, castle, or county of Worcester. He died in 1526, and lies buried at Windsor, under a stately tomb (2) As the history of his noble descendants may be found in every account of the present peerage of England, I shall content myself with subjoining little more than their names, in the order and with the dates of their succession

1526 Henry Somerset, son of Charles abovementioned, was Earl of Worcester after him. He died 1549, and was buried in the church of Chepstow, in Gloucestershire, under a handsome monument On his death,

1551 William, his son succeeded He was one of the peers that sat on the trial of Mary Queen of Scots. In 1573, this earl was sent into France with a font of pure gold, to be present as surety or godfather, in the name of Queen Elizabeth, with the procurators of Mary the Empress, and of the Duke of Savoy, at the baptizing of the French king's daughter. (3) He died, A D 1588, and was buried at Ragland.

1588. Edward Somerset succeeded his father in his title, and in the ho-

---

(1) See the Hon Mr Walpole's character of him, in his List of Noble Authors, vol I p 63 Le land, in his New Year's Gift to Henry VIII as translated by Bale in his fourth division of the Literati of this Kingdom, down to his own time, has honoured this earl with a place among them His town residence, called Worcester Place, was near the water side, a little to the west of Vintner's hall [Pennant's London, p 340 2 Ed] The earls of Worcester had a very large house between Durham Place (now the Adelphi) and the Savoy, with gardens to the water side It was pulled down by their descendant, the Duke of Beaufort, and the present Beaufort-buildings rose on its site Ibid p 145

(2) Atkyns's Hist of Glouc. p. 127 Sandford's Gen Hist. p 338

(3) Camden's Life of Q Eliz. p 168. Hollingshed's Chron. p. 1865. Sandford. p 347

nours of public service.   During his youth, he was one of the finest gentlemen, and one of the best horsemen and tilters of his time ; which, together
with his being of royal blood, recommended him to Queen Elizabeth, who,
to the promotion she bestowed on him, added the honour of making him her
ambassador to Scotland to James VI on his marriage with Anne of Denmark.   He died at Worcester house, in the Strand, 1627   " He was so
fruitful of issue, (says Camden, in whose time he lived,) that he had more
sexes than, of late, all the earls of England had," viz. eight sons, and seven
daughters, by Elizabeth, daughter of Francis Hastings, second Earl of
Huntingdon.

1627. Henry Somerset, his second son, succeeded his father as Earl of
Worcester   He had been created a peer in his father's lifetime, by the title
of Lord Herbert   He was reputed once the wealthiest of the peers of his
time   He sacrificed all his riches to the service of Charles I. who created
him Marquis of Worcester, 1642, in return for his loyalty, and the ruin of
his fortune   He defended his castle of Ragland with the intrepidity of a
hero ; and had the honour to find himself the last opposer of the enemies of
his king, and his castle the last that surrendered to their power   He died
at the age of 84, and was buried at Windsor, 1646 (1)

1646. Edward, his son, known in his father's time by the title of Earl of
Glamorgan : a man of a most extraordinary genius, in mechanics a famous, but rather too fanciful, projector. (2)

1667. Henry, his son, the third Marquis of Worcester, was made lord
president of Wales, 1672, installed knight of the garter, and admitted
privy counsellor the same year   He was also lord lieutenant of the counties
of Gloucester, Monmouth, Hereford, all Wales, and Bristol, which city he
defended in Monmouth's rebellion with great reputation   He was created
duke of Beaufort, in 1682, 34 Charles II.   He died 1699, and lies buried at
Windsor, near his ancestor Charles Somerset, first earl of Worcester of this
noble family (3)

(1) Sandford, p 354   Sir Robert Atkyns's Hist of Glouc p 127   In the Antiquarian Repertory,
vol III No V p 150 to 155, is " an account how the earl of Worcester (Henry) lived at Ragland
castle before the civil wars began, in 1641 "   It exhibits a very curious instance of the hospitality of our
ancient nobility , and leaves little for modern refinement to boast of on the score of costly abundance.

(2) See his " Century of the Names and Scantlings of such Inventions as he had tried and perfected "
Publ. hed in 1655 and dedicated to Charles II , republished by I Payne, in 1746 [See Appendix !

(3) Sandford, p 364,   Atkyns's Glouc p. 127   Dugd Bar II p 295.

1700. Henry Somerset, his grandson, Duke of Beaufort and Marquis of Worcester Appointed, in 1710, captain of the band of pensioners.

1714 Henry, his son, then a minor.

1745. Charles Noel Somerset, brother to the last duke; whose abilities and oratory distinguished him in both houses of parliament.

1756. Henry Somerset, his son, the present Duke of Beaufort, Marquis and Earl of Worcester , a nobleman of great accomplishments.

SECT. XV.

BATTLES, SIEGES, TUMULTS, AND OTHER REMARKABLE OCCURRENCES RELATING TO THE CITY OF WORCESTER.

LAMBARDE, a celebrated antiquary and historian, who wrote cotemporary with Mr Camden, makes this remark in his short account of this city, (1) that he never met with a place that had so great experience in the calamities of the intestine broils of the kingdom, and other casual disasters, as the city of Worcester.   If, as he hath observed, it then stood foremost in the list of misfortune, how much more so does it since that time, in which a desolating pestilence, the scourge of two sieges, the terrors of a fierce battle, and the ruin of a destructive plunder, to which it was on each occasion consequently abandoned, are to be added to the catalogue of its miseries : these have indeed confirmed its claim as having had a larger portion of the bitter draught of general affliction, than has fallen to the lot of any of the inland cities of the kingdom   .

About the year 894, Ethelred and Ethelfleda rebuilt this city, which had been ruined by the Danes ; and, with leave of King Alfred and his nobility, they gave to the church of St. Peter, and to Bishop Werferth, (Werefrid) half of all that belonged to the king, whether in the market or in the street, for their better support and maintenance ; upon which the bishop ordered, that at morning, evening, and undersong, should be said for them the psalm *De Profundis,* as long as they lived , and, after their death,

(1) See his Alphabetical Description of England Quarto.

Laudate Deum; and, every Saturday, in St. Peter's church, thirty psalms with masses (1)

1041, May 4. A tumult happened at Worcester, in the collecting a tax that was deemed exorbitant (2) Thurstane and Feader, two of the hus-carles (*i. e* domestic servants) of King Hardicnute attended as receivers. The multitude rose upon them They endeavoured to shelter themselves in the tower, (probably that which is called Edgar's,) but, in their flight thither, were intercepted and slain The king, highly incensed at this riot, sent a large body of forces to be executioners of his vengeance ; who entered the city, Nov 12, without resistance ; the inhabitants having prudently abandoned it, to fortify themselves in an island of the Severn, called Bevere, within two miles distance from it, toward the north ; where they determined either to purchase their freedom, or sell their lives in a brave defence. The rifling of the city was a work of four days. Avarice was at length glutted ; but cruelty not so, till the streets themselves were set in flames. The vindictive army marched then, laden with its plunder, to the attack of the entrenchments at Bevere ; but were there so warmly received, that, after several unsuccessful assaults, the royal generals were obliged to grant an honourable capitulation to the besieged . who, returning to their city, rebuilt it.

1074. When a conspiracy was formed against William the Conqueror, by some noble Normans, viz. Roger Earl of Hereford, his brother-in-law Ralf de Gauder, Earl of the East Angles, and other lords, who had invited succours from Denmark, but, by the king's vigilance, were hurried to take the field before those could arrive ; the junction of the forces of the conspirators was prevented by the activity of the king's friends in Worcestershire Bishop Wulstan, Urso, the sheriff, and Agelwy, abbat of Evesham, assisted by Walter de Lacy, a powerful baron in Herefordshire, assembled a sufficient body of troops for guarding the passes of the Severn, whereby the Earl of Hereford's march was stopped, his whole design frustrated, and the rebellion easily quashed (3)

(1) Hicks's Thes p 624 &c. Sept. Gram Ang Sax p. 78
(2) A tribute called *Danegelt*, imposed on the people to repel the ravages of the Danes on their first coming among us I thelred has the reputation of raising this tax, and it is stated as the first ever laid by any king of England • [See Flor Wig p 403 Sim Dunelm p 161. W of Malms II. p 43.
(3) Hollingshed's Chron vol I p 11

• Gibbon's Analecta Hist Polit No 980 Plut 30 V A Brit. Mus

1088 (1 Will II.) Bernard de Neumarché, Lord of Brecknoch, Osbern Fitz-Richard, surnamed Scrope, Roger de Lacy, Ralf de Mortimer, and other potent barons of Shropshire and Herefordshire, came with an armed force against Worcester, which had declared for the reigning king. Bishop Wulstan acted on this occasion the part of a worthy prelate and brave Englishman, by arming his tenants, and animating the citizens; whose wives, children, and moveables, were secured within the walls of the castle; whither the bishop himself retired, and encouraged the garrison to a most vigorous defence. The besiegers over-ran the suburbs, and set them on fire; but being more intent on plunder than conquest, they spread themselves over the adjacent country in quest of pillage, the garrison seized the opportunity, made a sally, came up with the enemy as they were ravaging the bishop's lands at Wick, took or killed five hundred men, put the rest to flight, and freed the city from its blockade (1)

1113 June 19, the city of Worcester was consumed by fire, even the buildings in the castle and cathedral not escaping. According to the Worcester annals, one monk, and twenty of the inhabitants perished in the flames. It was, however, suspected, from its nearness to Wales, and from the people there at this time inclining to insurrection, that this fire was one of their first movements in their invading and laying waste the English marches. (2)

In Nov. 1233, great part of the city was again burnt down, by a casual fire, and the cathedral much damaged (3)

1139 On the 7th of November, the forces of the Empress Maude came from Gloucester, and attacked the city. The inhabitants, before their arrival, being apprized of it, had deposited their goods in the cathedral. The clergy, in care for the safety of the church, and what was concealed in it, assembled the choir, who sung in form, preceded by the relics of St Oswald, which were carried before them from one gate to the other, to terrify the besiegers, who attacked a strong fortress, said to be the castle hill, raised at this time, (4) on the south side of the city, but were repulsed (5) In their attack of the north side, they gained admittance into it, and immediately set fire to it in several places; a great part of it was consumed, and

(1) Henry of Huntingdon Hollingshed, vol I p 17 (2) Flor Wig Polidor Hollingshed, vol I p 37 (3) Dr Thomas's Account of Bishops of Worcester, p 107, and Abingdon's MS p 31 (4) Abing MS p 23 (5) Contin. Flor. Wig. f 672, 673. Stow's Chron. p 145

the whole rifled and plundered (1) The narrative of this attack, and the taking of the city, is given in a very descriptive and interesting manner by Florence's continuator, who was an eye witness to the transaction, and a monk of this church, whose danger and distress he very feelingly describes.

1149. King Stephen took and burnt Worcester ; (2) but the castle, against which he raised two strong forts, resisted all his attempts, having been rendered extremely strong. The remains of one of the forts, which was raised on Red hill, near Digley, are still to be seen The other was raised upon Henwick's hill, to command the Welch road from Ludlow (3)

Eustace, his son, afterwards invested the castle of Worcester, then in possession of Count de Meulant; but he met with such a vigorous resistance, that, notwithstanding the two bastilions of timber, which he raised against it, called, in those days, Malevicines, they were both destroyed, the castle saved, and he was compelled to desist : (4) in revenge of which, he set fire to the city

In 1157, Worcester was fortified, by Hugh Mortimer, against King Henry II , but on the approach of the royal forces to dispossess him, he submitted, and was pardoned (5)

1175. The new tower at Worcester fell down. (6) In what part of the city this was situate, we have no account.

In 1189, almost all the city of Worcester was destroyed by fire. (7)

In the fourth night of the Easter week, A D 1202, the cathedral, with its adjacent offices, and great part of the city, were burnt ; but the walls of the cathedral, being of stone, were not thrown down (8)

1216 When Lewis, eldest son of the King of France, was invited to the English throne, by a confederacy of the barons, the leading men in Worcester declared for him, and received William Mareshall, son of the Earl of Pembroke, as governor of the city for the dauphin. On St Kenelm's day,

(1) Dr Brady's Hist Eng p 280
(2) Huntingdon, p 395 In speaking of this king, as to the character he bore in the eyes of the nation, Robert of Gloucester has thus berhymed it, and recorded this event

    " King Stephen his luthenesse withdrew yers a fewe,
    But er V yer wer goo he ganne to wex a shrewe
    For he wende aboute and robbyd the lond, and to grownd broght,
    Then the tounc of Wyrcester he vrent all to nought "   [Weever's Fun Mon p 75]

(3) Dr Nash, vol II p 109, in Appendix   (4) Lambarde, p 407 ex Sim Dunelm
(5) Grafton' Chronicle, p 51   (6) Ann Wig   (7) Angl Sac p 477
Abingdon', Priors of Worc p 119, and Willis's Abbies, vol I p 307   (8) Ann Wigorn

Ranulf, Earl of Chester, came up with a body of king's troops, and meeting with unexpected resistance on the north side of the city, and the utmost resolution in its defence, detached a party to the south, which broke into the castle, (1) by surprise, and through it into the town : the inhabitants were taken captives on their ramparts, and compelled, by exquisite tortures, to discover their treasures. The soldiers of the garrison, who had taken sanctuary in the cathedral, were forced thence, the church and storehouses of the convent plundered; and a fine of three hundred marks imposed on the monks, for the payment of which, they were reduced to melt down the embossments of St Wulstan's shrine. In the same year, King John was buried here. (See Sect IV p. 58)

1218 Bishop Sylvester obtained the grant of a fair, in honour of St. Wulstan, to be held four days before the feast of St Barnabas (2)

Near the end of the year 1222, the two smaller towers were destroyed by a violent storm (3)

1225 A great tournament was made at Worcester, for which Bishop Blois excommunicated all the persons concerned in it. (4)

1263. Robert de Ferrers, Earl of Derby, Peter de Montfort, and Robert, son of Simon de Montfort, Earl of Leicester, with other barons of their confederacy, laid siege to the city of Worcester; and, after several assaults, took it, 28 February The church they spared, but rifled the houses of the citizens, the Jewry especially, in which some of the Jews were put to the sword, and others imprisoned. (5)

1264. Towards the end of the year, King Henry III. was brought to Worcester, by Simon, Earl of Leicester, then his keeper, into whose hands he had fallen at the battle of Lewes.

(1) The new governor had seasonably retired, forewarned, it is said, by his father, who was a steady adherent to King John, had the merit of establishing Henry III his successor, and governed, as regent, during the minority of that prince (2) Ann Wig (3) Abing Antiq Worc. Cath p 3 Willis's Abbies, vol I p 302 (4) Both papal and regal decrees against tournaments were very severe, on account of the fatal consequences of many of them They began about A D 930, and continued to the time of Henry VIII , who himself greatly delighted in them, and had nearly fallen a sacrifice to the custom, by the hands of his favourite, Brandon, Duke of Suffolk * In the Harleian library is a MS containing "Ordinances and Statute Rules (to be observed in Tournaments) made and inacted by John Tiptott, Earl of Worster and constable of England, by the Kynge's commandement at Windsor, the 6th yeare of Kynge Edwarde the fourthe "
, (5) Hollingshed's Chron p. 266, Stow's Chronicle, p 193, and Lel Coll vol I p 457.

* Camden, in Herefordshire Lambarde's Perambulation in Kent, p 448. Strutt's Man. and Cust. vol III p 126, 127

M m

1265. Prince Edward, afterwards King Edward I. who had been taken prisoner by Simon Montfort, was carried with the king, his father, to the castle of Hereford, from whence he found means to escape to Worcester, by stratagem. Here an army was speedily assembled under his banners, which enabled him shortly afterwards to defeat that of the Earl of Leicester, in the famous battle fought at Evesham, on the 4th of August of that year, in which Montfort and many of his principal adherents were slain. By this important victory gained by the prince, the regal power of the kingdom, which had been nearly annihilated, was restored; and the captive Henry, who had been placed in the front of the battle, clad in a suit of Leicester's own armour, miraculously preserved, and ultimately restored to his throne and kingdom. (1)

1281. April 27, Godfrey Giffard, Bishop of Worcester, laid the first stone of the pavement of the town (2)

1299 A street in the suburb of Worcester, leading towards St. John's, was entirely consumed by fire. (3)

1313. The stone bridge was built across the Severn, (4) as appears by the register of the priory. The former bridge was, it is probable, of wood, and had been destroyed by the abovementioned conflagration.

In 1342, April 18, a plague broke out in Worcester, very fatal to the inhabitants.

Another pestilence, in 1349, carried off so many of the citizens of Worcester, as to make it unsafe to admit interments of those who died of it in the cemetery of the cathedral; on which account, Bishop Wolstan de Braunsford granted the citizens leave to have a burying place at St. Oswald's hospital. (See Sect VII p. 145.)

1401 Worcester was burnt and plundered by Owen Glendowr's troops, with their French auxiliaries; from whence Henry IV drove them back into Wales. The king in his return halted at Worcester; where, on the approach of winter, he dispersed his troops, and privately made his way to London. (5).

---

(1) See Tindal's Hist and Antiq of Evesham, ch ix a very interesting detail of this battle See also Lambarde, p 148 M Paris, &c   (2) Ann Wig This was long before the streets of Canterbury and Southampton were paved See Anderson's Chronology Deduction of Commerce

(3) Ann Wig   (4) Willis's Hist of Abbies, II p 262

(5) Monstrelet, c 15 Hall's Chron. p 18, 19 Guthrie and Gough's Additions to Camden in Worcestershire, p 258.

John of Lancaster, Duke of Bedford, constable of England, had that office granted to him by letters patent, dated at Worcester, 10th Sept 1403, 4th of Henry IV. (Sandford's Gen. Hist. p 304)

1471 The defeat of Queen Margaret's forces in the battle of Tewkesbury, together with the murder of the prince her son, raised her indignation and grief to the wildest transports, and her imploring the vengeance of Heaven against Edward by her imprecations and tears, were collected by Lord Stanley, who had been sent to seize her (1) after the battle, and produced by him as new crimes before the king, to whom he presented her at Worcester. Edward was in danger of abusing his power, by making this miserable reason a pretence for taking away her life on the spot; but the reflection of a moment on the unworthiness of the design, made him resolve to send her to London, in order to be tried by the parliament for the crime of high treason. (2)

All our historians mention a most wonderful flood of the Severn, in the year 1484, which was such an inundation as to carry away men, women, and children This was called the Duke of Buckingham's water, because he lay with an army of Welch, ready to march against Richard III. and was stopped by it; being so sudden, as in one night's time to render passage every where impossible. His men, for want of provisions and pay, deserted him This providential deluge seated Richard in his usurped dominion, from which the duke was preparing to dislodge him (3)

1485. This year was Bosworth-field, and then was the city of Worcester seized into the king's (Henry VII.) hands, and men were beheaded at the High-cross and there were paid for the redemption of the city, five hundred marks; whereof three hundred went to the king, and two hundred to the Duke of Bedford (4)

1486 The loyalty of Worcester to King Henry VII was very near drawing upon it the severest calamities. Sir Humphrey Stafford and his brother, and Lord Lovel, having escaped from the sanctuary at Colchester, raised a rebellion; and while Lord Lovel, at the head of three or four thousand men,

---

(1) She was found in a poor religious house not far from Tewkesbury, to which she had retreated on the day of the battle Hollingshed's Chron p 1341 Speed's Chron p 696

(2) Hist Marg. of Anjou, from the French of the Abbe Prevot, vol II. Part IV p 182, 184.

(3) Hall's Chron. fol xv 3 Rich. III. Hollingshed's Chron p 1402

(4) Bishop Blandford's MS.

advanced to surprise York, where the king then was, the two Staffords marched, with what force they could collect, to attack the city of Worcester. Lovel miscarried by his own cowardice   he deserted his camp ; and all his thousands, upon the offer of the king's pardon, made a surrender of their arms, and dispersed   These tidings reached the other body of insurgents, at the time when they were allotting to each man the post he should undertake in the assault upon Worcester.   All their measures were instantly broken. Sir Humphrey Stafford was executed at Tyburn

1534. Sept. 15th, a great earthquake happened at Worcester. (1)

1558. A sore *new* sickness raged in Worcestershire, thought to have been the *sweating* sickness (2)

During the pontificate of Bishop Whitgift, Sir John Russel and Sir Henry Berkley, having a great misunderstanding subsisting between them, came to the sessions at Worcester, with a select number of friends, domestics, and followers armed, with an intent to decide the controversy by dint of sword. But luckily the bishop was timely informed of their design, and found means to frustrate it, by providing a strong guard at the gates of the city, whom he directed to arrest both parties, on their appearance, with their attendants, and caused them, to the number of four or five hundred, to be conducted to his palace ; where he insisted on a surrender of their arms to the custody of his servants.   He then expostulated with the leaders to bring about a reconcilement   By persuasion and threats, as the argument occasionally required, he happily put an end to their differences, and both, in perfect amity, attended him to the town-hall ; where they were more properly engaged in the service of their country (3)

In the beginning of June 1637, a most destructive pestilence broke out in this city, and continued its ravages till April the following year ; during which time it appears that 1551 (4) persons fell sacrifices to its fatal effects. The island of Bevere was, on this afflicting occasion, again an asylum to many of the distressed inhabitants of Worcester, who fled to it as a refuge, from the infection, and as a place where they could be supplied with provisions, till they could return in safety to their desolated city (5)

(1) Bishop Blandford's MS   (2) Ibid   (3) Sir G Paul's Life of Whitgift, p 30 31   (4) See a table of the number of persons who died of the plague in the respective parishes of the city and suburbs, in a late publication from a MS poem of considerable merit, written at the time, by Philip Tinker, Gent entitled, " Worcester's Affliction "

( ) The humanity shown on this melancholy occasion towards the distressed sufferers, who, but for the

SIEGE OF WORCESTER, A D 1642.

Our national history has already so amply developed the political interests of those events that took place at Worcester during the grand rebellion, from the year 1642, when the first blow was struck there, to the year 1651, when the last kindred blood was shed within its walls, and terminated that memorable and important contest; that little is left to be added, except the detail of local circumstances that occurred in those encounters between the contending parties, in and near this city (1)

The loyalty of Worcester became an early object of the jealousy and displeasure of parliament About the middle of September 1642, the inhabitants opened their gates to Sir John Biron at the head of 300 cavaliers, whom they assisted in fortifying the city against the parliament He was joined by Lord Coventry, with some troops of horse, (2) and expected farther supplies of men from the king He was not suffered, however, to remain long inactive in his post · Colonel Fynes, with a force of 1000 dragooners, joined by the trained bands of Gloucestershire, and a body of troops under Lord Say, from Oxford, laid siege to Worcester in favour of the parliament and on the report, that the king, with 1,500 horse and 3000 foot, was approaching to raise the siege, the Earl of Essex, at the head of an army of 14,000 men, had set forward to prevent it (3)

On Wednesday, September 21st, Lord Say, Colonel Fynes, Captain Browne, Captain Seaton, and Captain Thackhouse came to the gate of the city, when Lord Say, having formally demanded entrance, and being as formally denied it by Lord Coventry and Sir William Russell, gave orders to assault, and force a passage into it. Captain Browne had the honour to commence hostilities by striking a hole through the gate with a pickaxe, and firing a musket shot into the town. This attack was immediately answered by the gate being thrown open by the cavaliers, who

assistance of the neighbouring gentry, must have perished through want, is the subject of another poem, written and published by J. Toy, M A master of the College school, entitled, " Worcester's Elegy and Eulogy "   (1) A very extensive collection of diurnals, political pamphlets, newspapers, and other periodical publications of those times, presented by his Majesty to the British Museum, is the source from whence those particulars are principally derived The jet of their politics, is may be naturally expected, is entirely devoted to the service of the then prevailing power of parliament.

(2) Vol No 3 Coule's Perfect Passages, No 15 p 4 16 Sept 1642

(3) Perfect Diurnal, No 15, published by Cook and Wood

rushed out upon the assailants, and in a skirmish killing four or five of them, returned into the city without being followed by any of the besiegers, who, it appears, were ill provided to effect any important service against it, not having a single piece of ordnance to support them (1)

Prince Rupert, with his brother Prince Maurice, and a considerable body of troops, having joined Sir John Biron, on Friday the 23d, with fifteen troops of horse, marched out of Worcester into a green meadow (Pitchcroft) on this side of the city, daring their adversaries to combat. The republican spirit was roused to indignation at this taunting display of heroism, and notwithstanding that, from the dispersion of their force on every side of the town, and on the other side of the Severn, they were not justly enabled from the numbers they could immediately muster, to encounter them, yet Colonel Sandys and Colonel Austine determined to risk an engagement with them: a charge was forthwith made upon them with effect, and, being joined by others of their party, a very spirited action was supported through the whole of the afternoon The prince and his troopers, at length, perceiving a reinforcement of horse approaching to sustain the enemy, who, they conceived, came from the forces which the Earl of Essex was hourly expected to bring to Worcester, retreated into the city, pursued by the parliamentary army, where the fight was continued till towards midnight; when, with his beaten troops, the prince was obliged to abandon the town, and escaping over the bridge, took his route towards Herefordshire in great disorder (2)

(1) Perfect Diurnal, p 8. (2) Leach and Cole's Special and Remarkable Passages in Parliament, No 10 p 4, 5, 6 A manœuvre was practised during this conflict with some success on the part of the royalists A detachment of 1000 horse had been sent from the parliament army to Powick, and about the same number of foot on the side of the city, with a view of surrounding the prince's forces To the detachment at Powick, a spy (who pretended himself chief gentleman to the Earl of Essex) was dispatched with information, that the lord general had entered Worcester, and that if they would advance, the retreat of the royalists might be effectually cut off Following this advice, they arrived on their march at the rising ground, (now occupied by a cherry orchard,) near which an ambuscade of horse and foot was stationed, by whom they were attacked with great fury, and twenty-five of their men were left dead on the field At the same time also another false rumour was dispatched to the regiment on the city side, that Prince Rupert was advancing against them at the head of 10,000 men, on which report, they hastily fell back to the distance of four miles By this stratagem of dividing the attention of those parts of their forces, the prince was enabled to offer battle to the remainder of their army, in which, however, he only experienced a disgraceful defeat •

In the first of these conflicts, Prince Maurice had one of his hands almost struck off, and was danger

• England's Memorable Accidents, p 29, 30 a weekly paper

The Earl of Essex arrived the same night with his army before the town, but thought it not prudent, on suspicion of treachery, to enter it till the morrow, (1) when the parliament forces took full possession of it, and all the horrors of a pillage followed. On the Sunday (Sept. 25th) the soldiers visited the cathedral ; where, after every sort of vulgar abuse and wanton destruction that could be effected on its altar, which they pulled down, and its vestments and furniture, which they destroyed , the vault beneath it was explored, and a considerable treasure of stores and provision was discovered in it, supposed to have been sent thither from the collegians of Oxford, as a depot for the use of the royalists, and consigned to Dr. William Smith, one of the prebendaries, and Dr Potter, then dean of Worcester, both of whom had made their escape (2) The mayor of Worcester, (Edward Soley, Esq.) with alderman Green of the same city, were taken into custody by order of the lord general, for having given up the town to the cavaliers, and were conveyed under a strong guard to London, where, on their arrival, Oct. 19th, they were imprisoned. A waggon load of plate, containing 2200lb. weight, was sent with them , part of which belonged to the mayor, and was intended for the use of the king (3) A gallows was set up in the market-place of Worcester, by order of the lord general, to hang some of the townsmen who had betrayed Col Fynes' troops to the prince; (4) and a commission was appointed by parliament, authorizing Sir Robert Harlow and master serjeant Wilde, to go down to Worcester to examine delinquents, and to secure the city (5) The lord general, as a primary operation of punishment,

ously wounded in the head with a poll-axe , Commissary Wilmot was run through the body with a sword by Col. Sandys in a single rencontre , the Lord John, brother to the Duke of Lenox, was very dangerously wounded about thirty gentlemen of the prince's party, and double that number of the common troopers were slain , about thirty others were made prisoners On the side of the parliament, Major Douglas was slain Colonel Sandys narrowly escaped with his life from having been dragged by his horse about the field, on falling from his saddle Twenty six of their troopers are reported from their own party to have been killed This action, and its consequences, were considered of such importance to the republican cause, that the parliament drew up an order, that public thanks should be given in all churches in London, on the fast day, for this great victory •

(1) Ibid. (2) Remarkable Truths, Octob 4, 1642 (3) Cook and Wood's Perfect Diurnal of Parliament, No 16 See also Vol. No. 4 Cole's Special Passages, Nov 2, 1642.

(4) England's Mem. Accid Octob 12 p 43. (5) Cole's Perfect Relation or Summary, No 2. Upon his information also Edward Soley, John Elmbury, and George Street, aldermen of Worcester, accused upon oath before the committee of both houses of parliament of divers crimes and misdemeanours against the government of the city, were removed, and other aldermen elected in their

• Leach and Cole's Contin of Special Passages, No. 10.

put the city to the ransome of 5000 pounds. About the middle of October, having repaired its fortifications, engaging the citizens to lend 3000l. to the parliament, dividing his army, which now amounted to about 24,000 men, into three brigades of about 8000 each, and dispatching them in different directions to oppose the king's march, which was reported to be intended for London, he left Worcester at the head of one of the brigades himself, and marched towards Shrewsbury in pursuit of the forces headed by the king in person (1)

SIEGE OF WORCESTER, 1646

The loyal spirit of Worcester was not, however, to be broken or subdued by the event of a single defeat; communications were kept open with the royal party, the magistracy of the city were firm in their attachment; and by a series of resolutions in their corporate capacity, they determined to support the royal cause, by holding the city to the king's use, and assisting him by every other means in their power   To that end, " at a chamber meeting, Oct 9th, 1648, the election of Mr. Hacket to the mayoralty was set aside, he being formerly elected sheriff for this year, and as the offices jointly were incompatible , and it being suggested in his majesty's letter, that, in consideration of the troubles then existing, it would be most proper that some able and expert man, who had borne that office before, should be elected ; it was agreed and ordered, that Mr Daniel Tyas (2) should be sworn mayor, and that Mr Hacket should be sworn sheriff, in pursuance of his first election , which was accordingly done." (3)   Additional ordnance was provided by them for their defence, and levies of men to work on the fortifications, and of money to defray the expences, and to remit to the king

stead   [See Chamber Orders, from A D 1602 to 1650 p 211 in the Archives of the corporation of the city of Worcester]

(1) England's Mem Accid Sept 29 p 29, 30 31, 39, 47   (2) Mr Tyas was an apothecary , he had served the office of mayor in 1639, and in consequence of the able discharge of his duty at that time, and his being now called upon to sustain it in a time of danger and difficulty, the king conferred upon him the honour of knighthood   (3) Chamber Orders, p. 210. Sir William Russell, who principally resided amongst them, and who had already distinguished himself as a stanch royalist, had received from them the following honourable distinction for his services " In a chamber meeting, holden July 18th, 1643, a certificate was agreed upon to be presented to the king, expressive of the confidence of the mayor and corporation in the courage and good intentions of Sir William Russell " And at a subsequent meeting he was presented with the freedom of the city. [Chamber Orders, p 216]

for his use, were raised with an alacrity that evinced their earnestness in his cause. Thus preparing themselves for the worst, they met the approaches of a second siege with a resolution and firmness that reflects honour on their constancy and courage.

March 26, 1646, Sir William Brereton, Colonel Morgan, and Colonel Birch, with about 2500 foot and horse, faced the city of Worcester, and sent a trumpeter with a summons demanding its surrender to the parliament. At night, however, they drew off to Droitwich, and some of them went to the siege of Litchfield. The king having escaped from Oxford, in disguise, to Newark, a letter from the garrison of Worcester was sent to him, desiring his particular directions Meantime, May 16th, a letter from General Fairfax, then at Heddington, near Oxford, to Governor Washington, requiring the surrender of the city, had the following spirited answer —

" Sir,
" It is acknowledged by your books, and by report of your own quarters, that the king is in some of your armies; that granted, it may be easy for you to procure his majesty's commands for the disposal of this garrison , till then, I shall make good the trust reposed in me. As for conditions, if I shall be necessitated, I shall make the best I can ; the worst I know, and fear not ; if I had, the profession of a soldier had not been began, or so long continued, by your excellency's humble servant,

HENRY WASHINGTON."

May 25th, Colonel Whalley having encamped on Rainbow, or Wheeler's hill, a sally of four horse from the town alarmed the besiegers, who drew out sixty horse and one hundred foot, and coming within reach of the guns of the city, ten were killed and twelve wounded, without any loss to the garrison.

Upon a review taken, May 29th, the total of soldiers in the garrison of Worcester, including officers, amounted to 1,507, besides the gentlemen and the city bands The force of the besiegers, after the reinforcement had joined them from Ludlow, the castle of which had surrendered on the 27th, was supposed to be 5000 men.

During this siege, many skirmishes took place with various success , among which, the most remarkable was that which occurred on the 12th of June, at St. John's. The parliament forces, consisting of eight colours of foot, and 200 horse, drew to St. John's, which they lined with musquetry,

N n

and quartered the rest of their foot behind the tower, to block up the city on the west side of the river   At eleven o'clock that night, a strong sally was made from the town upon their quarters, with 500 foot and 200 horse, with a view to dislodge them, and to burn that part called Cripplegate, which hindered a sight of the town and street. This attack was made with such re-solution, that, notwithstanding the parliament troops had strongly barricaded all the avenues, the assailants, some by highways, and others by the back parts of the houses, entered the passages, and drove them out, though some of them took refuge in the church. In this sally, 100 of the parliament forces were killed, and 10 taken prisoners   three colours and one drum were also taken   Of the royalists, Capt Chapman and five gentlemen were killed, and fifteen wounded (1)

Whilst these operations were carrying on, four expresses had been dis-patched to the king from Worcester to know his pleasure respecting it, who never returned. A female messenger was sent, but no instruction was ob-tained. It was now near the middle of July, and a want of discipline was prevailing among the royal troops, and great disorder pervaded the whole

(1) *Notices respecting the Siege of Worcester.*
June 2, a great iron culverin burst at St Martin's gate, and wounded the best engineer and a matross 11th, a cannon ball struck the bishop's palace , 13th, one of the four pieces of ordnance fired into the town that day, killed a poor man and his wife, who were in bed in the Trinity   14th, Sir Rowland Berkley's house in the corn market, was much damaged by the ordnance   15th, Captain Hodgkins, an officer of horse, called " Wicked Will," for his desperateness and valour, sallied out with 16 horse, in a drunken exploit, and attacked the besiegers court of guard in St John's, killed one, and returned safe, though so drunk that he fell twice by the way, and was carried over the Severn in a boat half asleep   On the same day, the cannon at the key played at that guard, and killed five men at the back of the Swan inn, St John's   24th, An iron saker broke at the Blockhouse, one piece, 160lb weight, fell upon the Rose and Crown inn, near St Helen's church, and some in Broad-street , it wounded four persons   The cessation of arms, which had taken place on the 27th, ending on the 29th, the first cannon was fired at the be-siegers by the governor himself, and did execution   The cannon at the Castle-hill shot the steeple at St John's   One of the culverins at the Severn hit the great cannon at Rogers's hill   July 4th, a ball from Barnshill went over the college, and fell in Broad-street   5th, A smart skirmish took place, begun by the besieged, in which the governor assisted , it lasted near an hour, although one man only was wounded   This skirmish is indeed more remarkable for the needless risk the governor ran of being either killed or captured, and the town consequently endangered, than for any importance it was of to either party , his own horse, and that of Colonel Walsh, were wounded   6th, Capt Wicked Will made a second sally, behaved most gallantly, and brought in seven prisoners   10th, A shot from the top of Perry-wood hill, towards the Red hill cross, hit the priory gate, being a long mile distant from the works   11th, Two brass sling pieces were carried to the top of the tower, which commands Windmill hill   12th, A ball fired from Rogers's hill, struck the town hall, and rolled from thence to the Earl's post, a distance of forty yard

city. Provisions began to fail; and ammunition was so far exhausted, that the garrison had not powder to sustain an hour's contest, should the town be stormed No reinforcement of troops had arrived, or could now be hoped for from the king, either to strengthen the garrison or to attempt the raising of the siege : on the contrary, General Fairfax's army, consisting of 10,000 foot, and 5000 horse, being, on the surrender of Oxford, at liberty to act where occasion might require, were daily expected in aid of the besiegers : these combined circumstances, and a variety of other considerations not less important, induced the governor to hearken to the repeated solicitations made to him to enter into a treaty with Colonel Whalley, for the surrender of the city. Meantime an order had been communicated by the king to both houses of parliament, dated from Newcastle the 10th of June, for the surrender of all towns, castles, and forts, and to disband all the forces in his service throughout the kingdom.

On the credit of the printed copy of that order, a treaty was accordingly opened with Colonel Whalley , but it was strongly objected to by some, who contended, that " their orders from the king were to hold out till they heard from his majesty " Much division arose among the gentlemen who had been called to a council held at the bishop's palace, in which the prelate acted as a temperate moderator, whether to treat or not , this question, after a long and stormy debate, was at length carried, unanimously, in the affirmative.

About the 10th of July, Major-general Reynesborough succeeded Col. Whalley in the command of the besieging army ; and, according to their own accounts, having made his approaches so near to the city as to terrify the inhabitants, they, in a kind of mutinous manner, pressed the governor to hasten the surrender Thus critically circumstanced, he felt himself warranted to address the following letter

" To Major-general Rainsbourow, Commander in Chief of the forces before this city of Worcester

    " Sir,

" This city was first summoned by your General (Fairfax) upon promise of honourable terms, and hath been since invited to a treaty by Colonel Whalley In order to which (upon assurance of the rendition of Oxford, and credence of his majesty's printed letter) we of this city offered propositions, with the reservation, that if any demands on our parts might seem too high, or any denial on yours, to trench too much upon our honours, neither side should so insist upon their own sense, as not to submit to better reason, which was mutually assented unto On this foot we left them, being assured, upon the word and honour of your commissioners, we should receive an account of them within a few days; if that resolution be altered, we shall desire to have a clear and perfect answer, that the world may be the judge between us, upon whose score the effusion of so much innocent blood shall rest; since, in conformity to his majesty's command, we do not decline the rendering of this city upon honourable and equal conditions So I remain, Sir, your humble servant,

Worcester, 16 July, 1646   HENRY WASHINGTON." (1)

A parley commenced immediately, and was carried on by the gentlemen who had been chosen on each side to conduct the treaty with much gallantry and prudence, and the result produced the articles on which Worcester was surrendered, and which were signed by the governor and Major-general Reynesborough, 19th July, 1646 (2)

(1) Coe's Perfect Occurrences, 30th week, July 1646   (2) See the articles of the surrender in Dr. Nash, vol II p cm in Append from a MS of Mr Townshend, of Elmley Lovet, who was in the city during the whole siege, and kept a regular diary of the most material occurrences The seventh article of that account stipulates, " that the garrisons of Worcester, Evesham, Strensham, Hartlebury, and Maddresfield be disgarrisoned, and the Bishop of Worcester, Sir William Russell, and Colonel Lygon be restored to their houses and estates " This, however, we may suppose was not agreed to, from its not appearing in any of the articles of the surrender published by the parliament, of which none of their accounts state more than the six first articles   [Ibid   Coe's Perfe t Occurrences]

The last of those six articles, which stipulates, " That Sir Wm Russell, now resident within the city of Worcester, be exempted from any benefit by these articles," was strongly opposed and protested against by most of the gentlemen of the city and garrison, who thought it extremely dishonourable to deliver up any gentleman who had so faithfully served his majesty, into the hands of his enemies, alleging, " it was as much as consenting to his murder, if he should be put to death, and, as one of the prince's commanders, that he ought to have soldiers' conditions upon surrender, as well as any one else " But Sir William himself carried this matter with a gallant and gentlemanly resolution, declaring, " he would tender himself to General Reynesborough for their good " He modestly also refused the general intention of an intercession in his behalf to Sir Thomas Fairfax The honour of the noblemen and gentlemen was not, however, to be satisfied without an exertion to ward off the danger that awaited this brave royalist, and a letter was prepared by them for that purpose to General Fairfax, from whom, before it had been sent off, assurances were received, that Sir William Russell should be used like a gentleman, and that Major-general Reynesborough should have him as his prisoner

" The house, upon some special informations, ordered, that the late Bishop of Worcester, Sir William Russell, and the late mayor of Worcester, shall be sent for up into safe custody, to answer such thing as shall be against them objected " [Cole's and Blakelock's Perfect Diurnal Monday, Dec 7th, 1646 p 1405

On Thursday the 23d, the garrison of Worcester, with a great number of persons (1) to whom passes and protections were delivered, marched out, and General Reynesborough entered the city On the morrow he commanded all the citizens to bring in their arms upon pain of death ; and on the 25th, says the journalist, " they begin to inventory men's estates ; demand great arrears of contribution, 25 per cent. of every man's estate ; then make him a delinquent, and squeeze him, so that he cannot recover in an age. Thus this ancient city was delivered up into the hands of the parliament ; being the first of cities that declared for the crown, and the last which held in defence thereof."

BATTLE OF WORCESTER, 1651.

A respite of five years only from the horrors of civil commotion, during which interval the death, or rather as they saw it, the murder of Charles I. had taken place, the city of Worcester, for the third time within the space of nine years, was again the scene of slaughter of kindred subjects, in a cause now arrived at its last crisis, and to which its citizens, who had been subdued, but not conquered, still attached a truly Roman firmness of support.

(1) The following persons marched out of Worcester on its surrender, Thursday, July 23d, 1646, viz. The Earl of Shrewsbury, Lord Talbot, Lord Brereton. Sir Edward Littleton, Sir Ralph Clare, Sir Rowland Berkley, Sir John Winford, Sir Edward Watson, Sir Thomas Edwards, Sir Robert Lowe, Sir William Bridges, Sir Martin Sandys, Sir Jo le Hunt, Sir Tho Dabridgcourt, Sir Cha. Lloyd, Sir John Knotsford, Sir John Crosland, Sir William Russell,• Sir Barnaby Scudamore, Knights.

Henry Townsend, Henry Bromley, Ralph Godwin, William Dansy, Anth. Langstone, Ed Pennel, James Ingram, Joseph Walsh, Walter Hanford, Robert Peckham, Jo Culpepper, J Hanbury, William Massey, Will Babington, Edward Bysden, Edw Evans, Joseph Cox, Tho Hornyold, Will Sheldon, Tho Russell, Edw Sheldon, Tho Acton, Will Childe, Daniel Sparrey, James Eastland, Geo Manwaring, Cha Paulet, Rich Robbins, Wallop Brabaston, Thomas Winfield, Fran. Wye, Will. Brereton, Edmund Pershal, Andrew White, Samuel Holland, Cyprian Moore, Will Bade, Will. Flare, Edm. Downey, Humphrey Weld, Geo. Weld, Tho Savage, Tho. Connisby, Jo Bromley, Esquires Colonels 10. Lieutenant Colonels 8, majors 16, captains 70, lieutenants 49, cornets 24, ensigns 40, one bishop ; many doctors, parsons, vicars, and curates ladies not a few

There were found in the town 3000 soldiers, whereof townsmen near 2000, 3000 stand of arms, 28 cannon, drakes 6, and sling-pieces, powder about 30 barrels, match 6000, corn and malt for six months, [Cole's and Blaikelock's Perfect Diurnal, No 157, p 1256, 1257] There were killed during this siege on the side of the royalists, 1 officer, and 16 privates, wounded 17 privates. On the side of the parliament, 2 officers, and 147 privates were killed, and 54 privates wounded.

* A very good portrait of Sir William Russell, Bart from whom the late Lady Withers was descended, is now in the possession of Sir Charles Trubshaw Withers, Knt at Worcester

On Friday morning, 22d of August 1651, King Charles the Second with his army from Stirling in Scotland, commanded under him by the Dukes of Hamilton and Buckingham, the Earls of Lauderdale and Middleton, David Lesley, Montgomery, Wilmot, Wentworth, and other leading men of both nations, arrived at, and possessed themselves of, Worcester, after a slight opposition from the parliament forces who were in possession of it (1) The common council of the city had directed the gates, which the soldiery had shut, to be thrown open to the king on his approach, or to burn them down.   The order was obeyed

At the entrance of the king into Worcester, Thomas Lysons, Esq the then mayor, carried the sword before his majesty ; and on Saturday the 23d he was proclaimed with great solemnity King of Great Britain, France, and Ireland, by the mayor, the sheriff, and the whole magistracy of the city. On the same day the king published his manifesto or declaration, thereby inferring his wrongs, and withal exhorting the people to assist in establishing him in his rights to the throne of his ancestors.   At the rendezvous held in consequence of this general summons, on the 26th, in Pitchcroft, there appeared Francis Lord Talbot (afterwards Earl of Shrewsbury), Sir John Pakington, Sir Walter Blount, Sir Ralph Clare, Sir Rowland Berkley, Sir John Winford, and some others, with a reinforcement of about 2000 men, which added to the king's army, amounted to about 12,000, and those not the most completely equipped for a field of battle   The Earl of Derby, with 1500 men had been intercepted and defeated at Wigan, in Lancashire, in his way to join the king, and himself wounded in the mouth. (2)   He, how-

(1) In the beginning of the narrative declaring the grounds and reasons for setting apart Friday, the 24th day of October, 1651, for a day of public thanksgiving, the reasons supposed to have influenced the king in selecting Worcester as the place best suited for him to commence his operations in England against the republican army, are thus summarily stated   " The 22d of August, with 500 horse and dragoons, about noon, he (the king) entered Worcester, than which, no place seemed more to answer all his ends, it being a city seated on the Severn, within 12 miles of five counties, near unto Gloucester, the forest of Dean and South Wales where Massey (who was a little before called off from the E. of Derby to serve this design) pretended his greatest interest to be, and by gaining that place, the enemy well knew he should be master of all the passes upon Severn from Shrewsbury to Gloucester (and there not being 100 of the parliament's forces within 20 miles of him) he might be the more secure for refreshing his wearied men, employ his interest to get what additional strength he could from those parts, or at least might make it a winter war, and thereby gain time for forrain assistance, and better opportunity for his agents to stir up tumults in England, and for raising a new army in Scotland under the Earle of Leven (whom he had left gen there for that purpose), to come also into England " [Ibbitson's Proceedings in Parliament, No 105, p 1622]   (2) Carte's Hist. of Eng vol. IV. p. 637, 638.

ever, effected his escape to Worcester, where he tendered his personal service to the king, which was accepted. (1)

Cromwell, who had suspected the king of a design of getting into England, on the first favourable occasion, soon prepared to follow him   He accordingly began his march from St Johnstone's, to which he had laid siege on the 3d of August, and on the 28th appeared with an army of 17,000 men on Red-hill, a mile to the east of Worcester, a route of near 300 miles, and fixed his head quarters at Spetchley, at the house of Judge Berkley   This force, added to those already arrived under the Generals Fleetwood, Lambert, and Harrison, augmented by the Suffolk and Essex forces that joined them on the 31st, under Sir Thomas Honiwood and Colonel Cooke, formed an army of upwards of 30,000 men, chiefly cavalry

The day of the Lord General's arrival was marked by the commencement of hostilities. The quarters of the royal army then lay very large on the western side of the Severn, reaching nearly as far as Malvern hills, and on the river as low as Upton, the bridge of which was broken, and Major-general Massey, with a detachment of five hundred horse, and a few dragoons, was posted there to defend the pass of the Severn. On the morning of that day Major-general Lambert, with a regiment of horse and three troops of dragoons from Evesham, joined by some horse from the main army, about 10 o'clock arrived at the pass, not so much with a view of attacking, as of reconnoitering it. Perceiving, however, a slender guard upon duty, he ordered a few dragoons to get possession of the church, the situation of which commanded the pass, a service they performed with little annoyance   The time occupied before Massey's troops could assemble to oppose them, allowed a strong party of Lambert's horse to cross the river about pistol-shot below the bridge, in support of the detachment who had now taken possession of the church ; but not before Massey's troops had began to attack them, by ineffectually firing their pistols, and thrusting their swords in at the windows ; whilst the party within, more secure and deliberate in their defence, returned their fire, and killing three or four of the besiegers, with eight or nine of their horses, threw them into disorder, which now became augmented by the approach of the troops that had made good their landing in aid of the besieged   The confusion they were thrown into was not to be overcome ; it terminated in a complete route of the whole detach-

(1) Hist. of the Revolutions in England under the Stuarts, p 153

ment, which retreated into Worcester. In this attack Major-general Massey was dangerously wounded : his enemies, however, have done justice to his personal bravery, in their report of the dislodgement of his troops, by saying, " indeed Massey brought up their rear when they turned about very stoutly ; at least 40 carbines were shot at him within half pistol shot, and he was for certain shot through the hand, and through the thigh." (1) His horse was killed under him.

This important achievement gave infinite advantage to the Oliverian troops : the bridge was repaired, and a force of upwards of 10,000 men immediately posted there to preserve the pass. The royal army, upon this defeat, thought it necessary to contract their quarters on that side of the Severn to within two miles of the city, which was now fiercely bombarded by the Lord General. The fort royal had been repaired, and in turn fired on the enemy, " as if " (according to their remark) " they feared never to want powder or bullets."

The king in council determined on the following night to have an abrupt interview with his foe To that end a select party of horse and foot was chosen, to the number of 1500 men, part of whom were directed to attack a post about two miles out of the city, guarded by about 200 musqueteers , and the other to make an attack on the enemy's camp; but the scheme was frustrated by treachery The parliament's army being apprized of their design, defeated them at the out-post, killing eleven of their men, who were found in the morning dead on the highway Of the other party, who gallantly made a full charge on Colonel Fairfax's regiment, three of the privates were killed. One who had been supposed by the enemy to have been a lieutenant-colonel by his dress, " coming very boldly up, and leaping over a hedge, rushed upon a stand of pikes, and so (as his victors termed it) lost his life in a vapour."(2) This officer proved to be Major Knox.

Between five and six in the morning of the 3d of September, Lieutenant-general Fleetwood had orders to advance with his brigade, together with

(1) Ibbitson's Proceedings in Parliament, p 1559

(2) Ibid p 1560   In a letter from Spetchley, dated 31st August, it is said, this sally had been rendered abortive by the villainy of one Guyes a tailor in Worcester, who had betrayed their signals to the enemy, which was, wearing their shirts over their armour , for this service he received his reward , he was hanged the day following   " Thursday, Sept 9th, 1651, the parliament voted that Mrs. Guyes, whose husband was executed by the King of Scots at Worcester, for giving our forces intelligence of the enemy's signal, should have £ 200 in money, and £ 200. per annum   [Clowes's Perfect Passages, No. 57 p 376 No. 54]

the troops under Major-general Deane, and the Colonels Ingoldsby, Goff, and Gibbons, from Upton to Powyck ; a bridge was thrown over the Teme, and another over the Severn was forming near the conflux of those rivers, to open a communication with the army on the east of the city, with the forces now entering upon service on the west of the Severn. This eventful scene had been anxiously beheld in its progress from the top of the cathedral tower, by a council of war convened there by the king ; and the firing which 'had begun between Fleetwood's detachment and those of the king's party that lined the hedges between Upton and Powyck, was clearly discerned. It was on this discovery that the king in person set forward to give orders to Major-general Robert Montgomery, who, with Colonel George Keyth had the command of a royal brigade of horse and foot at Powyck bridge, to maintain that pass with the utmost of their power, and to detach a party to oppose the finishing of the bridge of boats over the Severn, and after giving those directions, his majesty returned to the city, where his whole force, who had been ordered to arms, were now in readiness for action. But the king's instructions were rendered ineffectual by the enemy ; the bridge over the Severn was completed ; the detachment from Upton cleared its way by scouring the hedges and defiles that obstructed them ; whilst the force that now made way over the Severn, drove in those troops that were sent to oppose them   The right wing of the brigade under General Fleetwood having crossed the Teme, and the left arrived at Powyck bridge, they drove in the foot of the royalists " to their main body of horse and foot which was drawn up in Wikefield, near Powyck bridge, being the same field wherein the late king first engaged the forces of the parliament, in the same month of September, 1642. The republican horse and foot marched up with great resolution to their enemies body, and came to push of pike with them, and after a contest of nearly two hours, drove them back, and wholly routed them, killing many upon the place, and pursuing the rest to the drawbridge and gate of the city " (1) In this action Colonel Keyth was left a prisoner, and Montgomery was severely wounded. Cromwell himself was the first that landed on the west side of the Severn, over the

(1) From the detailed particulars of the battle of Worcester, officially drawn up, and published by the authority of the parliament, preceding the declaration of the " grounds and reasons for setting apart Friday, the 24th day of October, 1651, for a day of public thanksgiving " [Ibbitson's Proceedings in Parliament, No 105, p 1622]

bridge of boats, and acted on foot against his enemy, who lined the hedges in his way to the scene of action ; and from whence, having witnessed the complete success of the enterprize, he returned to his main army to prepare them for the approaching battle.

The principal part of his force was settled in an advantageous position at Perry wood, at the south end of which a strong breast-work was raised ; and a battery of great guns was also opened against the fort royal.

It was drawing towards evening when the king, with the Dukes of Buck-ingham and Hamilton, Lord Grandison, Sir Alexander Forbes, and many others of the English nobility, marched the main body of the royal army, horse and foot, out at Sidbury gate, to make the grand attack on that part of the Cromwellian forces that remained on that side of the town, under the persuasion, that most of their troops had been drawn over to the other side of the Severn, and that, by being thus divided, they were consequently weakened The principal part of them, however, were found on their post, awaiting the approach of their adversary, with Cromwell at their head.

No sooner had the royal army taken their ground and formed, than by the command and encouragement of the king, a general charge was given. The contest was eager, fierce, and resolute, and prosecuted with equal bravery on both sides for three or four hours The scale of victory turned first in favour of the royalists, before whom their enemy retreated in disor-der, and left them in the actual possession of their great guns. (1) At this juncture, however, new supplies arriving from the other side of the Severn in considerable numbers, joining and supporting the parliament army, and the main body of the Scottish horse not coming timely up from the town to the king's aid, after sustaining a very unequal conflict for a considerable time, fighting with the but-ends of their muskets after expending all their ammunition, and giving every proof of undaunted valour, the royalists were at length overpowered, and the king, with his worn-out troops, forced to retreat, in great disorder, back again through Sidbury gate into the city (2)

(1) The honour of this achievement appears to belong to the Duke of Hamilton's regiment, which, after passing the line, the hedges of which were lined with two bodies of foot that greatly annoyed them, they made good the pass, routed a troop of horse and foot stationed near the battery, and made themselves master of the guns [Burnet's Mem of the Dukes of Hamilton, p 428   (2) The king would certainly have been taken by Cromwell's cavalry, who were close at his heels, had not one of the inhabitants drawn a load of hay into the gateway, which blocked up the passage, so that no horse could enter   The king was obliged to dismount and creeping under the hay, entered the city on foot A cry being made to remount the king,

He now perceived many of the Scottish foot to throw down their arms, and decline the battle. This, indeed was no more than what Lesley had before intimated to him, by saying, that as well as they appeared they would not fight. He now experienced it fully. Nor was he so ill a judge of probabilities, as to imagine they were able to oppose a veteran army, flushed with success, and masters of the treasures of the nation. Notwithstanding which, he used every argument to persuade them, riding up and down amongst them, with his hat in his hand, exhorting them to stand to their arms, and fight like men, urging and alleging the justice of the cause they fought in. But finding all his entreaties in vain, he exclaimed, " I had rather you " would shoot me, than keep me alive to see the sad consequences of this " day."

During this engagement, Lambert's party, on the other side of the river, possessed themselves of St John's; the brigade of his majesty's foot, commanded there by Major-general Daliel, after a slight resistance surrendered.

The Earl of Rothes, Sir William Hamilton, and Colonel Drummond, with a party of Scots, defended the Castle hill with great bravery and integrity, till terms of capitulation were agreed upon.

The enemy having carried the fort royal by storm, put all the troops found in it to the sword, because they had refused to surrender on the first summons. (1) Its guns were now pointed at and fired into the town, and the dismay and consternation, which had now become general, was heightened by the entrance of the victors, who, having borne down every obstacle, poured into the city on all sides with irresistible impetuosity. The king, not unmindful of his unhappy condition, sought means of safety, by making his escape with Lord Wilmot, the back way of the house where he quartered, narrowly avoiding the close pursuit of Colonel Cobbet, who entered the foreway of the house, at the same time, in quest of him (2)

Mr William Bagnal, a loyal gentleman who then lived in Sidbury, turned out his horse ready saddled, upon this horse his majesty (after the fate of the battle had been decided,) escaped from Worcester. This anecdote was transcribed by Dr Nash from the papers of Bishop Thomas, whose eldest daughter was married to a son of Mr Bagnal. [See Vol II p cvi in Appendix]

(1) It is probable this exploit was performed by the Essex troops, whose colours the lord general commanded to be set up in the fort. [Ibbitson's Proceedings in Parliament, No 102 p 1566, 1567.]

(2) In a letter from Paris, Oct 31st, 1651, it is said, " The Scots king told them it the Louvre, (the queen his mother, and the court) how he slipped out of Worcester, and how near he was taking there, first in the fort, and after in his chamber " [Ibbitson's Proceedings, No 109 p 1690]

O o 2

The Earl of Cleveland, Sir James Hamilton, the Colonels Wogan, Carlis, and Slaughter, the Captains Hornyold, Giffard, Astley, and Kemble, Mr Peter Blount, and others, rallied what forces they could, and again charged the enemy in Sidbury and the High-street, which though unsuccessful with respect to victory, was yet of singular service to the unfortunate king, by diverting the attention of the Oliverians, whilst he made his escape through St Martin's gate, who, otherwise, had been taken prisoner in the city

At the town-hall the royalists made their last stand, no less unsuccessful than any of their former   In this dispute, Mr. Coningsby Colles and several others were slain, Sir James Hamilton and Capt Kemble (1) desperately wounded, and many were taken prisoners

The parliament army, now masters of the city, gave way to the most atrocious acts of outrage that the meanness of rapacity could stimulate in the dark mind of a sanguinary puritan   and although ostensible authority for a general pillage was not absolutely given by Cromwell, it is as certain that not the least restraint was put upon the brutal violence of his ruffian troops, who fell to ravaging and plundering without mercy, few or none of the devoted citizens escaping their cruelty

The chief persons slain in the course of this battle were, the Duke of Hamilton, whose horse was also killed under him, Captain William Erwyne, Major Knox, Sir John Douglas, and Mr Coningsby Colles; about 3000 private men were also killed   The chief prisoners were the Earls of Derby and Lauderdale, taken in pursuit by Colonel Lilburn; the Earls of Cleveland and Shrewsbury, Lord Wentworth, and others, taken also in flight; as

---

The house at the corner of the north end of New street, on its east side, is said to have been the king's quarters whilst at Worcester   The tradition is handed down in strong and direct terms by the oldest inhabitants of the city, and by the relatives of the proprietors and possessors of the house at that time, whose names were Durant   The room in which the king slept faces the corn-market   Over the entrance of the house is this inscription, " LOVE GOD [W B 1577 R D] HONOR THE KING "   It is the largest of the old houses in the city •   Mr Cooksey has, however, stated strong evidence also that the king's " secret quarters" were at the White Ladies †   But, unless we allow that he had both public and private quarters, the one within and the other without the wall, we can hardly suppose he would have taken up his residence at such a distance from the town, in which his presence was every moment required

(1) He was captain lieutenant to the Earl of Talbot   He received eleven wounds   Living in 1675

• Supplement to the Gentleman's Magazine for 1790, p 1191
† Cooksey, Essay on the Lives of Lord Somers, and the Earl of Hardwicke, p 4, 5.

were Major-general Massey, (1) Lieutenant-general David Lesley, and Lieu-tenant-general Middleton. Sir Alexander Forbes, commander of the fort royal, was shot through both the calves of his legs, lay in Perry wood all night, and was next day brought prisoner to Worcester. Robert Earl of Carnwarth, Alexander Earl of Kelly, John Lord St Clare, Lord Grandison, Sir John Pakington, the Major-generals Montgomery and Piscotty, Colonel Keyth, Mr. Richard Fanshaw, (2) the king's secretary, the general of the ord-nance, adjutant-general of foot, marshal-general, six colonels of horse, 13 of foot, 9 lieutenant-colonels of horse, 8 of foot, 6 majors of horse, 13 of foot, 37 captains of horse, 72 of foot, with a great number of inferior officers, were also taken prisoners · 158 colours, the king's standard, his collar of S S his coach and horses, and other things of great value, fell into the hands of the victors

This memorable battle was the decision of the controversy so long subsist-ing between the king and parliament, during that horrid din of despotism and usurpation, and the last of any consequence fought on that account; the fortune of which gave to the latter the entire government of the three kingdoms

The king having escaped the dangers of the field, and the snares of treach-ery, was conducted from Worcester to Boscobel, where he was hospitably entertained, and carefully concealed from those keen hunters of royal blood, by Mr Richard Pendrill, and from thence safely conveyed on his way to France (3)

---

(1) Having reached Leicestershire, and unable to proceed farther from the badness of his wounds, Mas-sey surrendered himself prisoner to the Countess of Stamford, who caused his wounds to be carefully dressed, and sending information to parliament of the occurrence, he was ordered up to London, and sent to the Tower to await his trial [Ludlow's Memoirs, Vol I. p 363 and Ibbitson's Proceedings, No 103, p 1584]   (2) He was made a baronet after the Restoration, and sent Ambassador to Spain Cromwell had a great respect for him, and would have bought him off to his ser-vice at any rate. His health being impaired by his confinement, Cromwell obtained his enlargement upon 4000l bail, notwithstanding it was strongly objected to by Sir Henry Vane, by saying, " he would be instrumental for all he knew to hang them all who sat there (at the council) if ever he had opportunity " [From MS Memoirs by Lady Fanshaw, addressed to her son]   (3) Mrs Wyndham's Bosco-bel During his continuance there, he was some time concealed in the boughs of a large oak, in Bosco-bel wood, from whence it acquired the dignified appellation of the Royal Oak At the time when this singular occurrence took place, this oak was in its fullest growth, and its boughs much covered with ivy. The curiosity of travellers had nearly cut its trunk in two, when Basil Fitz Herbert, Esq fenced its re-mains round with a handsome brick wall, and placed a suitable inscription over its gate, in gold letters, which remained till 1784, when the stone was broken and the wall thrown down. [See Gough's Add. to

NOTICES RESPECTING THE BATTLE OF WORCESTER, 1651.

In Leach's " Diurnal of the Proceedings of the Army," No. 91. p 1287, the first account of this victory received by the parliament, is given in a letter, written by Cromwell, dated the 4th of Sept 1651, in which he states the royal army to have been about 16,000 men ; that the battle was long, and very near at hand , often at push of pike , and that his own loss did not exceed 200 men   And in another, written by Colonel Robert Stapylton, dated the 3d of September, in which he says, " this day hath been a very glorious day ; this day twelvemonth was glorious at Dunbar ; the word then was, " *The Lord of Hosts,*" and so it was now.   The same signal we had now as then, which was *to have no white about us* "   He also says, their quarter-master-general (Mosley) and Captain Jones were slain, and Captain Howard, of the life guard, was wounded   But the following letter from Cromwell, written the night of the battle, and comprehending the substance of those letters, excepting the foregoing extracted particulars, will give the most faithful view of the event, as beheld in its first state by the victor himself

" A Letter from the Lord Generall, for the Honourable William Lenthall, Esquire, Speaker of the Parliament

   " SIR,

" Being so weary, and scarce able to write, yet I thought it my duty to let

Camden, Vol. II. in Shropshire, p 419] At his Restoration the king graciously rewarded Mr Pendrill for his services, confirming to him and his heirs, perpetually, an annuity of 100l per ann   Among the MSS presented by Mr Pepys to Magdalen college, Cambridge, is one entitled " An account of his Majesty's escape from Worcester, dictated to Mr Pepys by the king himself."   It appears to have been written at Newmarket, and is dated, Sunday, Oct 3d and Tuesday, Oct 5th, 1680   The following passage in the king's narrative, does the brotherhood of the Pendrill's the highest honour   " There were six brothers of the Pendrills, who all of them knew the secret" (of his concealment and disguise) " and (as I have since learned from one of them) the man in whose house I changed my clothes, came to one of them about two days after, and asking him where I was, told him that they might get 1000l if they would tell, because there was that sum laid upon my head , but this Pendrill was so honest, that, though he at that time knew where I was, he bade him have a care what he did, for that I, being gone out of all reach, if they should now discover I had ever been there, they would get nothing but hanging for their pains " p 9, 10, 11   A descendant of the Pendrills, of the name of John, is now living in Worcester   His pretension to the inheritance of the reward promised, have been approved by many who have inquired into and examined them   The preservers of kings in another nation are proscribed characters   It is pity, however, that in any kingdom those who had deserved so well should be forgotten, " or that their seed should be neglected "   Qu —Who last enjoyed this pension ?

you know thus much. That upon this day, being the third of September, (remarkable for a mercy vouchsafed to your forces on this day twelvemonth in Scotland) we built a bridge over Severn, between it and Thame, about half a mile from Worcester, and another over Thame within pistol shot of the other bridge. Lieut. generall Fleetwood, (1) and Major generall Deane, marched from Upton, on the south-west side of the Severn, up to Powick, a town which was a passe the enemy kept. We past over some horse and foot, and were in conjunction with the lieutenant-generall's forces. We beat the enemy from hedge to hedge, till we beat them into Worcester. The enemy then drew all his forces on the other side of the town, all but what he lost, and made a very considerable fight with us for *three* hours space; but in the end we beate them totally, and pursued him to his royal fort, which we tooke, and indeed have beaten his whole army

" When we took this fort, we turned his owne guns upon him The enemy hath had a great losse, and certainly is scattered and run severall wayes: we are in pursuite of him, and have laid forces in severall places, that we hope will gather him up

" Indeed this hath been a very glorious mercy, and as stiffe a contest for *four* or *five* houres, as ever I have seen both your old forces and those new raised, have behaved themselves with very great courage, and he that made them come out, made them willing to fight for you. The Lord God Almighty frame our hearts to reall thankfulnesse, for this which is alone his doing I hope I shall within a day or two, give you a more perfect account; in the mean time I hope you will pardon, Sir, your most humble servant,

Near Worcester, 3 Sept (3) 1651, 10 *at night.*   O. CROMWELL." (2)

---

(1) Son in law to Cromwell, he and General Lambert so won the regard of Oliver in this battle, that it was with difficulty he was prevented from knighting them. [Noble's Memoirs of the Protectoral House of Cromwell, vol II p 355]   (2) Ibbitson's Proceedings in Parliament, No. 102 p 1565.

(3) Friday, Sept 5, 1651 In parliament, " Resolved upon the question, that an act be brought in to appoint an annual observation of the third day of September,• in commemoration of this wonderful mercy " [Ibid p 1571]

• This may certainly be ranked as a singularly eventful day in the annals of those times The battles of Dunbar, 1650, and of Worcester, 1651, so fatal to the cause of royalty, were signally propitious to Republicanism and to Cromwell The instrument framed to be the foundation of his government, provided as its second head, " that the first parliament should assemble on the 3d Sept 1654." [Noble's Memoirs of the Protectoral House of Cromwell, vol 1 p 119 Ld. 2] It was also the day that terminated his greatness in his death, Sept 3, 1658

The following cant is in the true spirit of the times. "Mr Peters (1) (after the fight, and when there was an opportunity to draw the militia regiments together) gave them five observations, to meditate upon as they went home.

"1. To think better of God than ever they had done, and go home with their faces *shining*, having spoken with *him* on the *mount*

"2. To think aright of our army, whom they saw so willing to do the work

"3 To study themselves, as unworthy and unlikely to be preserved, and yet made the monuments of mercy; not to go home boasting, but humble and wondering

"4 To mind the enemy, who was very strong and cruel

"5. To think well of the *present government,* who was so watchful for the whole

"Lastly, when their wives and children should ask them where they had been, and what news, they should say they had been at Worcester, where England's sorrows began, and where they were happily ended."(2)

In the accounts received from Worcester, Sept. 6, "things were there in great confusion. Lords, knights, and gentlemen, were then plucking out of holes, by the soldiers; the common prisoners they were driving into the cathedral; and what with the dead bodies of men, and the dead horses of the enemy filling the streets, there was such nastiness that a man could hardly abide in the town; yet the lord general had his quarters in Worcester, the walls whereof he hath ordered to be pulled down to the ground, and the dykes filled up. (3)

The prisoners of rank taken at Worcester, in the custody of the marshal general, were thus disposed of to await their fate. In the Tower, the Earls of Cleveland, Rothes, Kelly, and Corneway, the Lords Sinclair, Spany, and Grandison, Major-generals Massey, Piscotty, and Deal.

At Windsor castle, Major General James White, Lieut. General James Weymis. Colonels Sir George and Sir William Keyth, Sir Thomas Thompson, with other general officers and colonels; and in various parts of Westminster; at the Artillery ground, and Chelsea, nearly five hundred others of inferior rank, with many of their sick and wounded at Hicks's hall. At Worcester, Major General Montgomery, Sir James Hamilton, Sir Alexander Forbes, (4) and Sir John Douglas, remained under cure. The mayor

---

(1) A bigotted puritan preacher   (2) Leach's Diurnal, No 93. p 1292.   (3) Ibid.
(4) The first knight made by the king in Scotland

and sheriff of Worcester, were ordered to be tried at Stafford or Chester, (1) in which last place the Earls of Derby and Lauderdale, and the Generals Lesley and Middleton were prisoners, of whom, in a letter from thence, dated Sept 16, the following curious accounts are given.

" The Earl of Derby is very insinuating ; he hath as many fetches as a jesuite, some *camera* he would faine imagine to juggle withall, as he did in his treaty not long since, holding in suspense a seeming pretension to have surrendered the Isle of Man, when indeed nothing was lesse intended But that season wherein he might have done his country and himself good, he let slip, and hath now wilfully brought himself under the lash of justice

" The Lord Lauderdale is in a terrible vexation, and exceeding sad and vext, he seems to be a man of a pestilent nature, and dangerous to be conversed with ; and yet he keeps his flesh as fat as ever he was ; but blessed be God, his insolent spirit is now overawed

" Lieut gen Leshley, drinks and roares when he can get it, and takes not much care which way things go ; he is vext he cannot ramble as he would ; he hath fury enough, but short hornes ; and pretends all his designe to have been as a souldier to his king, and builds upon that confidence.

" And Lieut gen. Middleton is as melancholy as Leshley is mad ; crying out against his misfortune in every designe he undertakes It is well if God give him grace to repent truly, and turn to God. He hath ill requited this commonwealth for all the favour they formerly shewed to him."(2).

The return of the Lord General to London after this important conquest, which he termed " a crowning victory," was marked by every token of respect by all ranks of people.

It is certain, that after this event, Cromwell took upon himself a more stately behaviour, and chose new friends, and instead of acknowledging the services of those who came from all parts to assist him, he frowned upon them, and the very next day after the fight, dismissed and sent them home (3) It appears, however, he was determined that not only the army,

(1) In a letter from Coventry, (Monday, Nov 24, 1651) it is said, " the mayor and sheriff of Worcester, are to be conveyed by Major Knight's troop from Warwick castle to London, for their trial, where when they arrived, they were sent prisoners to the Tower " [Leach's Diurnal, No 103 p 1469]

(2) Ibbitson's Proceedings.   (3) Ludlow's Memoirs, vol 1 p 363 In Symond's Historic Notes, No 991 Plut 30 V A p. 90. Harl Coll Mus Brit is the following curious note " When the king (Charles 1) was beheaded, and the body and head put in a coffin, and set in the Banqueting House, Oliver Cromwell came, with one Bowtell of Suff, near Framingham, and tryed to open

but also that the navy should have this notable service in perpetual remembrance " Thursday, Sept. 18, 1651, this day his excellency the Lord General
Cromwell, with many officers of the army, was at Woollidge at the launch-
ing of a gallant new frigot of the States, carrying three score peeces of ordnance, and called her name WORCESTER " (1)   From this date, the English
navy hath had a ship of the line of that name, which originated in this memorable event

As a proof that the arts were not wholly neglected in these times of confusion, Mr Turnor of Panton, in Lincolnshire, has a very good portrait of
his ancestor, Sir Edmund Turnor, painted when he was a prisoner of war in
Worcester, 1651.

1672, Dec. 23.   A great flood happened on the Severn, the rise of which
is marked by a plate still remaining in the wall, by the side of the river
near the water-gate.

The society of broad-cloth makers of Worcester, was incorporated 2 Hen
VI (2) from which time, till the end of the last century, that trade was
here, the most considerable of any in England.   It appears from Bell's Oration (3) before Queen Elizabeth when she visited this city, that, within memory, 380 great looms, which gave maintenance to 8000 persons, had been
employed in Worcester ; that number, however, was then reduced to 160
looms, and 5000 persons were thence thrown out of work   The queen, upon
petition, in the 32d year of her reign, A. D. 1590, with a view of reviving
the falling credit of the trade, granted her charter (4) to the clothiers ; and
its spirit was in consequence so effectually restored, that at one time shortly
afterwards, six thousand persons were employed in the trade in Worcester,
and above twice that number in carding, spinning, &c. in the neighbouring
towns and villages.   But, from the nefarious practices of the manufacturers,
its ruin soon afterwards became inevitable , by overstretching their cloths
so much, when they came to Blackwell hall, they were found wanting in
their measure , this, added to the obstinacy of the workmen themselves, who

the lid with his staffe, but could not , then he took Bowtell's sword, and with the pummel knockt up the
lid, and looked upon the king, shewing him to Bowtell   Then at that time this Bowtell askt him, *What
government wee should have?* He said, *the same that as now.* This Bowtell told Col Rolston, who
at first was his (the king's) great enemy and persecutor, but afterwards left the service " Col Rolston

(1) Leach s Diurnal, No 93 p 1322   (2) Dr. Nash, in Appendix, Vol II p cxvi
(3) See Appendix to Sect XVI p xliv No XII   (4) Ibid No XVI p lxxi

persisted in making a thick heavy cloth, instead of a light and spongy, which took a better dye, their best customers, the Turks, (who preferred the cloths of the last description,) from these united causes of complaint with-held their orders; and thus dwindled away by degrees one of the most valuable branches of the commerce of this kingdom, which had distinguished Worcester through every quarter of the globe to which Britain had then extended her trade.

1723 The summer assizes of this year were the first held in the present Guildhall. (1)

1724, June 11th. A severe storm of thunder and lightning here did much damage (2)

In the year 1733, June 5, the steeple of St Andrew's church in this city, was so much fractured by lightning, that it was obliged to be taken down and rebuilt Other damage was done in the city at the same time.

In the spring assizes of the year 1757, a violent west wind blew down a stack of chimneys from the south wing of the Guildhall at Worcester, which fell upon the roof of the Nisi Prius bar, whilst the court was sitting, broke through the ceiling, and killed six men on the spot, who were buried in the ruins; many others were terribly bruised. Sir John Eardley Wilmot, the judge then presiding, with great difficulty escaped unhurt, by making his way close to the wall of the court, round the ruins, and through the hall door. This melancholy catastrophe put a period to the business of the assize

1762, Aug. 11th. By an explosion of three barrels of gunpowder, occasioned by boys indiscreetly setting fire to some scattered grains of it; the warehouse, at which it was unloading in New-street, was blown up, many other buildings were much damaged, and several lives lost.

1768 December 20th two very smart shocks of an earthquake were felt in this city, between five and six o'clock in the evening; its direction was from east to west. In Herefordshire and Gloucestershire it was felt in a very alarming manner, particularly in the city of Gloucester, the cathedral of which was much shaken by it. At Droitwich, and other towns and villages in this county, it was also very sensibly felt. In Worcester no damage was sustained by it

1770 A very great flood on the Severn did considerable damage to the

(1) Worcester Post Man, No 738
(2) See Dr. Beard's account of it in the Philosophical Transactions, No. 394 p 118.

parts of the city bordering on the river, and endangered the lives of many of the inhabitants; fortunately, however, none were lost.   On the city wall at the water-gate is a memorial of this inundation fixed up, with the following inscription; " On the 18th of Nov 1770, the flood rose to the lower edge of this brass plate, being ten inches higher than the flood which happened on Dec 23, 1672 "

1795 The Severn shared the fate of most of the rivers in the kingdom during the uncommon severity and length of time the frost of the last winter continued   We have before seen both that river and the Thames frozen over, but we have never before seen either event recorded in the singularly appropriate manner in which that of the Severn has been entered up   Its novelty has a claim to attention ; and as a curious memorial of a remarkable occurrence attaching to Worcester, it has a legitimate claim to a place in this work (1)

On midsummer day, 1791, and on the 12th of Feb. 1795, two of the highest and most alarming floods of the Severn known since the building of the new bridge, occurred   The first is remarkable from the day on which it happened ; the last from its tremendous appearance and alarming effects, occasioned by the breaking up of the ice on the river, which choked its passage at the bridge   The waters rose precisely to the height of that which happened in 1672, and was three feet above the high water line of the bridge ; which, however, withstood the torrent that foamed round it, and threatened its destruction   The following memorial of this event is fixed on the wall of the parade near the bridge   " On the 12th of February, 1795, the flood rose to the lower edge of this stone. T P C."

On Wednesday night, Nov 18th, 1795, a slight shock of an earthquake was felt in this city, a few minutes before eleven o'clock   It was also felt through all the adjacent country, but providentially without doing any damage.

Such have been the sufferings of Worcester, which, phœnix-like, hath risen from her ashes with added lustre

(1) A paper distributed to the populace assembled on the ice, contained the following notices, and apt quotation, viz   " The art of Printing was invented by Lawrence John Koster, and brought into England, by Caxton and Turner, in the year 1468 "
         " HIS hoary frost, HIS fleecy snow,
            Descend and clothe the ground ,
         The liquid streams forbear to flow,
            In icy letters bound "   " Psalm cxlvii ver 16, 17 "
      ' Worcester, Printed upon the Severn, January 23, 1795 "

SECT XVI.

ROYAL VISITS TO WORCESTER.

THAT our monarchs of old entertained a regard for the city of Worcester may be collected from the following passage, extracted from the annals of the church of Winchester, under the year 1042 " Rex Edwardus (scil 1) instituit et carta confirmavit, ut quoties ipse, vel aliquis successorum suorum Regum Angliæ, diadema portaret Wintoniæ, vel Wigorniæ, vel Westmonasterii ; præcentor loci recipiet de fisco, ipsa die, dimidiam marcam, et conventus centum *simnellos*, et unum modium vini " King Edward hath ordained, and by charter confirmed, that as often as he himself, or any of his successors, kings of England, shall wear the diadem at Winchester, Worcester, or Westminster, the chanter of the place shall, the same day, receive from the exchequer half a mark, and the convent 100 simnels, (1) and an hogshead of wine

According to T. Rudborne, in Angl. Sacra, Vol I. p 259. William the Conqueror was accustomed, in those winters that he passed unmolested, to keep his Christmas at Worcester, his Easter at Winchester, his Pentecost at London ; and at all these solemnities to be crowned. It is probable he may have passed one or more of his Christmas festivities here , but other historians say, that Gloucester was the usual scene of the Conqueror's holding that church celebration of the Nativity.

1129. King Henry I kept his Christmas here (2)

1139. King Stephen came to Worcester in Easter-week, and was received by a solemn procession of the clergy and laity. Stephen was, at this time, on his march to the siege of Ludlow castle , to which place, as an hostage, he was attended by the Prince Royal of Scotland. The king offered at the high altar his ring, as a votive present (3)

1159 King Henry II. and his queen keeping their Christmas at Worcester, were crowned in the cathedral, and after the celebration of mass, made an offering of their crowns at the altar, when Henry made a solemn vow,

(1) See Cowel's Interpreter, vox *Simnell* The simnel (from the Latin *simila*, fine *flour*) is yet made at Worcester, in the season of Lent It is a sort of cake, generally about three inches in thickness , the crust, or shell, of which envelopes a layer of sweetmeats But the simnel bread of our ancestors was merely the purest white bread , " Panis regie mensa aptus qui *simenel* vulgo vocitur. '

(2) Huntingdon, p 384.   (3) Engl. and Wales described, p 246

that he would wear his crown no more   A great assembly of the nation, the usual mode of holding the parliaments, was held here at the same time (1)

1207. King John came to Worcester in September, and performed his devotions at St. Wulstan's tomb; to which, since the year 1201, great resort had been made, on account of the fame of the miracles said to be wrought there   The king gave to the monastery one hundred marks towards the re-building their cloister and offices.

1214 King John kept his Christmas here (2) At that time many of the barons petitioned him for the exercise of their ancient laws; the king promised fair, but instead of performing any thing, he collected an army, and commenced a civil war, that rendered his name and character odious to the nation

1232 King Henry III. kept the festival of the Nativity at Worcester (3) It was at this time that he adopted the bad policy of Peter de la Roche, Bishop of Winchester, who advised the removal of the English nobility from his councils, and supplied their places by needy Normans, of mean condition, and thereby laid the foundation of the great contention that arose between him and his barons (4)

1234. The king kept Whitsuntide at Worcester, and there invested Gilbert Mareshall, the new Earl of Pembroke, (a younger brother of William before-mentioned) with the order of knighthood (5)

Henry III. after the battle of Evesham, came to Worcester, where he employed himself in revoking all such grants and concessions he had been obliged to make and sign, whilst under the control of Leicester, in prejudice of himself and family

King Edward I (who seems to have had a predilection in favour of this city,) after his accession to the throne, made eleven visits to Worcester. The first, in September, 1276. The second, in October, 1278, when Llewellyn, Prince of Wales met him there, and was gratified with the marriage of an English heiress, daughter of Simon de Montfort   His third visit was on Christmas-eve, in 1281. The next year he came to Worcester, May 15, and held a parliament there about a military expedition against that prince. In November, 1283, we find him again at Worcester, and in March, 1289,

---

(1) Dr Nash, Vol 1 note in Introd p xxiv   (2) Collier's Eccl Hist.

(3) Ann Wig   (4) Lambarde, p 410   (5) Ann. Wig.

and November 1291, (not 1292, as is set down by Dr. Thomas, in his Account of the Bishops, p. 151.) In the year 1294, he came twice to pay his devotions to St. Wulstan. In July, 1295, he came hither by water. In April, 1301, he brought his queen with him, then big with child, and took the pleasure of being rowed to Kemsey, along one of the finest rivers in his kingdom

Henry IV. visited Worcester twice in the year 1407. (1)

1459 After the battle of Bloreheath, on the borders of Staffordshire, between the Yorkists and Lancastrians, the success of which favoured the royal party, Henry VI came to Worcester, from whence he sent offers of pardon to the Earl of Warwick's party, which were refused by their leader. (2)

King Henry VII. his queen, Prince Arthur, and the Countess of Richmond, the king's mother, visited Worcester at the same time (3)

1552 Jan. 25th, the Lady (Princess) Mary came to Worcester. She had not then completed the tenth year of her age. (4)

1574, Aug. 13, Queen Elizabeth did the city of Worcester the honour of her presence; at which time, among other benefactions, she made a grant of free-bench to widows whose husbands died seized of freehold-lands within the city, by which they are empowered to enjoy such freehold estate during their lives in preference to any claim that may be made by creditors, or any other claimants whatsoever, in cases of insolvency or otherwise. For a particular detail of this visit, see Appendix, No. XII. p xxxvii.

On Sunday, 31st August, 1645, King Charles I. came with his army from Shipston upon Stour, to Worcester, where they rested till Wednesday the 3d of September, when they removed to Bromwich, in Herefordshire, where his court was, and the army lay in the fields. The guards lay at Claynes while the king was at Worcester. (5)

In 1687, King James II leaving his queen at Bath, arrived at Worcester, in his progress to Cheshire, on the 23d August. Bishop Thomas, who had invited his majesty to make this city in his way, received him at the gate of his palace, attended by his clergy, and in a short Latin speech, congratulated him on his arrival. His way from the gate to the palace was covered with

(1) Montague's Hist of England

(2) Peck's Annals of Stamford, p 48 Art 30   (3) See Bell's Oration before Queen Eliz in Appendix, p. xliv Sect XVI No XII   (4) Bishop Blandford's MS

(5) Symonds's Notes on the marchings and actions of the royal army, from the 17th of August, 1645, his majesty being personally present [No. 944. Plut 30 V A p 23 Mus. Brit]

white broad-cloth, of the manufacture of Worcester, strewed with flowers.
His majesty condescended to honour the prelate with one remark on his
episcopal residence as he passed along · " My lord, this looks like White-
hall." Having refreshed himself after his journey from Gloucester, the
king visited the cathedral, from whence he was conducted by Dr. Hicks,
then dean of Worcester, to the college gate, to take a view of the curiosi-
ties of the town ; among which the fort royal, and the site of the battle between the forces of the late king his brother, and those of Cromwell, were
shewn and explained to him   The next morning, being the feast of St
Bartholomew, the king attended in the cathedral, to gratify such as offered
themselves for healing · and, this ceremony performed, proceeded in great
solemnity to a popish chapel, built at his accession to the throne, on the east
side of the Foregate-street, preceded by the mayor and aldermen, &c   On
their arrival at this oratory, his majesty asked, if they would not go in with
him ? to which the mayor, (Thomas Shewring, Esq.) with becoming firmness, replied, " I THINK WE HAVE ATTENDED YOUR MAJESTY TOO FAR AL-
READY." Depositing the sword, therefore, before the king in the chapel,
and making their reverence to him, they retired, and returned to divine service at the cathedral   When the royal devotions were finished, they were
ready to escort his majesty back to the palace to dinner. An entertainment
suitable to the royal guest, had been provided by the bishop ; but he had the
mortification, at his own table, to see a Romish priest ordered to invoke the
blessing, and his own offer to do that part of his duty rejected by the king,
who said, " he would spare him that trouble, for that he had a chaplain of
his own " Before his majesty's departure, which was immediately after he
dined, he condescended to express his approbation of the attention he had
received from the gentlemen of the county, and his entertainment by the
bishop   The piece of white broad-cloth was an expence to the bishop of 27l.
which the attendants of the king took away with them, as belonging to his
wardrobe (1)

In the year 1788, his present Majesty, having resolved to pass some part of
the summer at Cheltenham, in Gloucestershire, for the benefit of its medici-
nal waters, arrived at that place on the 12th of July, accompanied by the
Queen, the Princess Royal, and the Princesses Augusta and Elizabeth. The

(1) Ludlow was the next place honoured with the royal presence in his progress, which he reached that
day. [Dr Nash, Vol II p clxi in Appendix]

meeting of the three choirs of Worcester, Hereford, and Gloucester, by triennial rotation, was to be celebrated that year at Worcester, in the beginning of the ensuing month, and his Majesty having received information of the nature of the institution, that its object was the relief of the widows and orphans of the clergy of the three dioceses, declared his intention of honouring the meeting with his presence, to the Rev. Dr. Langford, who, with the Hon. Edward Foley, were the stewards of the meeting; and that the orchestra should receive the addition of his private band.

On Saturday, the 2d of August, their Majesties, with the Princesses, and the Duke of York, passed through this city, on a visit to Dr Hurd, Bishop of Worcester, at his palace at Hartlebury; and on the 5th, between seven and eight o'clock in the evening, their Majesties arrived at the episcopal palace in this city. As the royal party approached the palace, the college (cathedral) bells were rung with the greatest glee, and in a few minutes all the steeples in town resounded with joyous peals At half an hour after nine, the whole city was grandly illuminated, many of the houses exhibiting various-coloured lamps, emblematic transparencies with mottos, &c. At ten his Majesty took a view of the illuminations *incog.*

On the 6th, his Majesty, being a very early riser, had surveyed the cathedral and its precincts, and walked to almost every part of the town before seven o'clock. At half after ten, his Majesty had a levee at the palace, when the bishop, attended by the dean, prebendaries, and some of the parochial clergy, addressed the King (with his usual dignity and propriety) in a loyal and dutiful speech; to which his Majesty returned a most gracious answer, delivered with an energy which affected all who heard it His lordship afterwards addressed the Queen in a short speech. They all had the honour of kissing hands. The corporation of the city, (72 in number,) attired in their proper gowns, and attended by their officers, were next introduced The Right Hon. the Earl of Coventry, as recorder, was pleased to accompany them, and address the King in a very elegant speech. His Majesty's answer was great and benignant, and is said to have contained this patriotic and generous sentiment —"The loyalty and affection which I have experienced amongst my subjects in this part of the kingdom, and especially on this occasion, are an ample recompence to me for the *public service* of twenty-eight years" The several members of the corporation had the honour of kissing the King's hand: and then a considerable number of the nobility and gentry, chiefly of this neighbourhood, were introduced, the Earl of Oxford attending as lord in waiting; and the honour of knighthood was conferred on Charles Trubshaw Withers, Esq. a most vigilant and worthy magistrate of the county.

At half past eleven, their Majesties and the Princesses, with their retinue, proceeded from the palace to the cathedral, and were received at the great north entrance by the bishop in his episcopal robes, and the dean and prebendaries in their surplices and hoods, and conducted by them to a magnificent gallery, prepared for their reception, under the great west window. The gallery was spread with a rich Worcester carpet, lined and faced with crimson silk, and shaded with a lofty canopy of the same, terminating in a crown. In a division of the gallery on the right were seated the bishops of Worcester, Gloucester, and Hereford, and the stewards of the meeting; on the left, the dean and prebendaries. In front of the royal gallery, a lower one was prepared for the nobility and persons of distinction; and from the corners of this were extended seats for the mayor, corporation, and their families. The area was benched for the people in general. As soon as their Majesties and the Princesses had taken their places, the music band (consisting of the first vocal and instrumental performers in the kingdom) immediately began the coronation anthem; this was followed by the overture in Esther; after which the Rev Mr. Clarke, a minor canon of the church, began to chant the service, which comprehended the Dettingen Te Deum, and two anthems. The lessons were read by the Rev Mr Fountaine, sub-dean of this cathedral, and chaplain in ordinary to his Majesty; and the sermon preached by the Rev Dr Langford, from 2 Kings, iv 7. " And live thou and thy children of the rest "

On the afternoon of this day, their Majesties and the Princesses, attended by the Countess of Harcourt, the Earls of Harcourt and Oxford, Lord Courtoun, Colonels Goldsworthy and Digby, walked to Messrs Flight and Barr's elegant china shop in High-street, where they remained almost an hour, and greatly admired the beautiful porcelain, manufactured under the direction of those gentlemen, and gave orders for an extensive assortment of it. They then proceeded to the carpet manufactory of Michael and Watkins, in Silver-street, whose productions were likewise honoured with their approbation and orders (1) The zeal of the populace to see their Sovereign, the Queen, and Princesses, and to express their joy at the

(1) Both of the manufactories have received the royal patronage, an honourable distinction their respective merits have most justly deserved

royal presence, was so great, that it was almost impossible to secure a free passage for them on this account the Queen and Princesses remained at the manufactory till a carriage arrived for them ; but the King returned to the palace on foot.

On Thursday, August 7, his Majesty again walked out early to different parts of the town, and in the course of his tour, visited the Rev. Dr. Evans, archdeacon of the diocese, with whom he found the Bishops of Worcester and Gloucester. At half after eleven, the royal party went to the cathedral, with the same state as on the preceding day, to hear a selection of sacred music from the works of Handel. In the evening they drank tea at the Deanry

Friday, August 8, his Majesty having signified his pleasure to pay a visit to the corporation at the town-hall, the mayor, recorder, aldermen, and common council, in their gowns, attended by their proper officers, band of music, and flags of the city companies, repaired to the palace, and conducted his Majesty in procession (the mayor bearing the sword, and four of the senior aldermen the maces) from thence to the hall. His Majesty first viewed the courts of justice, and the pictures on the ground floor, paying particular attention to the portrait of the present recorder. He then walked up to the assembly-room, which he judiciously stiled a handsome gallery. A table was here spread with fruits, biscuits, wine, &c. His Majesty was pleased to accept a glass of Port, and graciously drank, " Prosperity to the city and corporation of Worcester " On his Majesty's commanding them to ask some mark of his royal favour, the recorder, in the name of the body, requested the picture of a Sovereign who had conferred so distinguished an honour on them, to which his Majesty most graciously assented About half after 11, the King, Queen, and Princesses went to the cathedral to hear the oratorio of Messiah, at which near 3000 persons were present an assembly so numerous and brilliant, at this distance from the metropolis, seemed to strike the royal eye with pleasing surprise In the evening the royal family went to the college-hall to hear a miscellaneous concert, which concluded the meeting His Majesty retired from his box under the most exhilarating burst of applause ever heard This spontaneous impulse of joy was raised to the most sublime effect by the full harmony of that favourite national strain of " God save the King," mingling as a grand chorus with the ardent shouts of loyal gratulation, in which all hearts and voices united, formed a close indescribably impressive and affecting, and truly worthy the august splendour of the scene. The same thunder of applause succeeded the departure of the Queen and Princesses, and was continued as long as they were in sight.

On Saturday morning, Aug 9, their Majesties, the Princesses, and several of the nobility, went to the china manufactory, and saw the whole process of making china, at which they expressed great satisfaction, and the King was pleased to leave ten guineas for the workmen At eleven o'clock, the royal family and suit left this city, and returned to Cheltenham.

Their Majesties gave 50l each to be distributed amongst the poor of the city, and the King 200l to the collection for the relief of clergymen's widows and orphans in the three dioceses; and 300l. to liberate debtors of a certain description, (1) besides many private donations. His Majesty also ordered, that his pardon should be extended to such criminal prisoners under sentence of transportation, as, from the regularity of their conduct in the gaol, or other favourable circumstances, might (in the judgment of the county magistrates) appear to deserve it (2)

(1) For an account of the application of the royal bounty to those prisoners, see the Appendix, No XIII p xlviii   (2) See " a Narrative of the late Royal Visit to Worcester," in the Gentleman's Magazine, for September, 1788, p 755.

END OF VOL I

INDEX TO VOL. I.

scribably impressive and affecting, and truly worthy the august splendour of the scene. The same thunder of applause succeeded the departure of the Queen and Princesses, and was continued as long as they were in sight

On Saturday morning, Aug 9, their Majesties, the Princesses, and several of the nobility, went to the china manufactory, and saw the whole process of making china, at which they expressed great satisfaction, and the King was pleased to leave ten guineas for the workmen. At eleven o'clock, the royal family and suit left this city, and returned to Cheltenham.

Their Majesties gave 50*l* each to be distributed amongst the poor of the city; and the King 200*l*. to the collection for the relief of clergymen's widows and orphans in the three dioceses; and 300*l*. to liberate debtors of a certain description, (1) besides many private donations. His Majesty also ordered, that his pardon should be extended to such criminal prisoners under sentence of transportation, as, from the regularity of their conduct in the gaol, or other favourable circumstances, might (in the judgment of the county magistrates) appear to deserve it (2)

(1) For an account of the application of the royal bounty to those prisoners, see the Appendix, No XIII p. xlviii. (2) See " a Narrative of the late Royal Visit to Worcester," in the Gentleman's Magazine, for September, 1788, p. 755

INDEX TO VOL. I.

•

AN

ACCOUNT

OF THE

DISCOVERY OF THE BODY

OF

KING JOHN,

IN THE

CATHEDRAL CHURCH OF WORCESTER,

JULY 17th, 1797,

FROM AUTHENTIC COMMUNICATIONS ; WITH ILLUSTRATIONS AND REMARKS.

By *VALENTINE GREEN*, F. S. A.

AUTHOR OF THE HISTORY AND ANTIQUITIES OF THE CITY
AND SUBURBS OF WORCESTER.

―――――――――――

LONDON:

PUBLISHED BY V. AND R. GREEN, PERCY STREET, BEDFORD SQUARE ; AND F JUKES,
ROWLAND STREET. SOLD BY R. FAULDER, CADELL AND DAVIES, AND THE
OTHER BOOKSELLERS OF LONDON AND WESTMINSTER.

WORCESTER:

PUBLISHED BY JAMES ROSS, ENGRAVER ; AND SOLD BY SMART, TYMBS, HOLL,
ANDREWS, WOOD, AND THE OTHER BOOKSELLERS.

――――――

1797

A N

ACCOUNT

OF THE

DISCOVERY OF THE BODY

OF

KING JOHN.

Among the various circumstances which eventually produced the discovery of the body of King John to have been deposited in the tomb in the choir of the cathedral church of Worcester, the following, as the most prominent, are conceived necessary to be stated.

In the course of my researches into the History of that Cathedral, and a minute examination of its fabric and monumental remains, for the purpose of forming a part of my new edition of " the History and Antiquities of the City and Suburbs of Worcester" published in two volumes, quarto, 1796, I was led to adopt the opinions of the most eminent and learned of our antiquaries who appeared to have joined in a conclusion, that although the original interment of King John had taken place in the Lady's chapel of that cathedral between the sepulchres of the Saints Oswald and Wulstan, before the altar of the blessed Virgin, yet that the effigy of the king, at the time of the reformation was removed from his grave, and laid upon the tomb which had been newly erected in the choir to receive it, and that this was done without removing the body, which was conjectured to have been left in its original state of sepulture in the Lady's chapel.

These conclusions deduced from the accounts and authorities of Leland, Abingdon, Dr. Stukely, Brown Willis, Mr. Garbet, Mr Gough, Dr Nash, and others, had been opposed by Dr. Thomas, and Mr Dougharty,[*] the first affirming the interment of King John to have been in the choir, in the place on which the tomb now stands, and the last that the royal body remained within the tomb. After

---

* See Vol. I. Sect. IV. p. 68, and Sect. VII. p. 156, Hist. and Antiq of Worcester.

A

weighing thofe oppofite opinions with the moft fcrupulous attention, and proving, by actual meafurement the affertion of Dr Thomas " that graves could be made there" to be erroneous ,* and that Mr Dougharty had afferted that which it would feem he had not actually examined , and alfo that what he advanced was invalidated by another refpectable authority, which ftates from what muft have been imagined the refult of careful infpection, " that no bones were found in the fepulchre "

Thus warranted by ancient and modern teftimony, and ftrongly fortified by perfonal inveftigation ; together with a modern altar tomb before me of the precife form and ftile of embellifhment of that of Prince Arthur in the adjacent chapel, and probably the work of the fame artifts, it was felt that without better proof to the contrary, it would have been a prefumption favouring too much of pertinacity, to have afferted that the remains of King John were firft depofited there, or that any other fign of him was to be expected out of his grave in the Virgin's chapel, than the effigy of his perfon cumbent on the cenotaph in the choir.

The principle of thofe opinions had been adopted by me fo early as 1764, and then made public in the firft edition of the Survey of Worcefter, (fee p 40) and in 1788 perfonally difcuffed with the Honourable and Reverend Dr. St Andrew St John, late Dean of Worcefter, who was induced from what then paffed on the fubject, to adopt the refolution of opening the tomb to afcertain the fact, but his death which happened previous to the publication of the fecond edition of the Hiftory of Worcefter, preventing the intended fearch, thofe conjectures, with much auxiliary and concurrent fupport, were again avowed, and have again been publifhed.

In the prefent revifed and enlarged form thofe conjectures are now prefented, they have fallen under the notice of the Reverend Dr. Arthur Onflow, the prefent worthy Dean of Worcefter, to whom, in a converfation on the general repair of the interior of the cathedral, which his judicious tafte had already planned for the improvement and beautifying of it, I again ventured to fuggeft the opening of the royal tomb, and if, upon examination, no veftige of fepulture fhould appear, its removal from thence to the Lady's chapel, and there erecting it over the ancient grave in which King John's remains were fuppofed to lie, would be a meafure fully fanctioned by propriety in refpect of its appropriate defignation, and in which portion of the cathedral it would alfo prove a befitting and dignifying object. As a meafure of expediency, its removal had long been the wifh of many,

* This has been confirmed by the late difcovery. The ftone coffin in which King John's remains are contained is laid *upon*, and not buried *in* or *under* the pavement of the choir The depth of ground between that flooring and the crowns of the arches of the crypt beneath it, being not more than twelve inches, would not poffibly admit of an interment : and the royal tomb ftands precifely upon the centre of the arch at the extreme eaft end of the crypt. See the Plan of the Cathedral, fig. A. Vol. I. Sect. VII. Hift. and Antiq. of Worcefter.

thereby to reſtore the orderly conduct of the devotional ſervices of the church, ſub-jected to much annoyance by the preſent poſition of the tomb, eſpecially in the approach to the altar

The caprices of modern reformation having no ſhare in the projected arrange-ment, much leſs the unneceſſary and indecent diſturbance of royal inhumation. uſeful accommodation and the attainment of decorous order ſuitable to the ſo-felm purpoſes of the place being the ultimate objects in view, on Monday the 17th of July 1797, the taking down of the tomb of King John was proceeded upon in the following order.

On the removal of the royal effigy, and the ſtone ſlab on which it had been laid, and which had been broken in two in ſome former operation about the tomb, the objects firſt preſented to view within it, were two partition walls of brick, raiſed to aſſiſt in the ſupport of the ſuperincumbent covering and figure of the king, and to take an equal bearing of their weight with the ſide and end pannels of the tomb   The ſpaces between thoſe walls, and between them and the ends of the tomb were filled up with the rubbiſh of bricks and mortar.   On taking down the pannel at the head, and one on each ſide, and clearing out the rubbiſh, two ſtrong elm boards originally joined by a batten nailed at each end of them, but which had dropped off and left the boards looſe, were next diſcovered, and upon their re-moval, the ſtone coffin, of which they had formed the covering, containing the entire remains of King John became viſible !

The Dean and Chapter being immediately convened, my friend Mr James Roſs was deſired to attend for the purpoſe of making obſervations on the object, and to tranſmit them to me in London. from thoſe remarks ſo communicated, and more eſpecially from others made by Mr. Sandford, an eminent ſurgeon of Wor-ceſter, obligingly furniſhed at the ſame time, together with the annexed plate exe-cuted by Mr. Roſs, from a drawing taken by him on the ſpot, the following further particulars are extracted and preſented.

THE BODY

was found to have been adjuſted in the ſtone coffin preciſely in the ſame form as the figure on the tomb.   The ſkull, inſtead of being placed with the face in the uſual ſituation, preſented the foramen magnum, the opening through which the ſpinal marrow paſſes down the vertebræ, turned upwards.   The lower part of the os frontis was ſo much periſhed, as to have become nearly of an even ſurface with the bottoms of the ſockets of the eyes.   The whole of the upper jaw was difplaced from the fkull, and found near the right elbow : it contained four teeth in very good prefervation, and free from caries, two of them were dentes molares, and two bicufpides. The lower jaw was alfo feparated from the fkull, the coronoid proceffes were very perfect, as well as the condyles · there were no teeth in this jaw. Some grey hairs were difcernable under the covering of the head. The ulna of the left arm which had been folded on the body was found detached from it, and lying obliquely on the breaft , the ulna of the right arm lay nearly in its proper place, but the radius of neither arm, nor the bones of either hand were vifible. Thofe of the ribs, pelvis, &c, were fo much covered with duft, and the foldings of the decayed robe as not to be clearly diftinguifhable   Part of the tibia of the right leg, in nearly its proper pofition, was expofed   The knee of this limb appeared to have been contracted, not lying fo ftrait down as the left · occafioned probably by other bones or fragments having fallen under it. The bones of the toes were in good prefervation, more particularly thofe of the right foot, on two or three of which the nails were ftill vifible. The reft of the bones, more efpecially of the lower extremites were nearly perfect, and on the whole, appeared to have lain as they might naturally have done in their quiefcent progrefs through the various ftages of decay and diffolution. Some large pieces of, mortar were found on and below the abdomen , and a vaft quantity of the dry fkins of maggots were difperfed over the body ; thefe are fuppofed to have been produced by fome part of it having gone into putrefaction (a circumftance imagined fometimes to have happened notwithftanding the precaution of embalming)* previous to its removal, and the maggots having remained undifturbed, were upon the prefent difcovery feen in fuch great numbers. Or, that fome parts of the drefs being of leather, they might have been produced by the natural putrefaction of that animal fub-ftance. The body meafured five feet, fix inches and a half.

THE DRESS

in which the body of the king was found appears alfo to have been fimilar to that in which his figure is reprefented on the tomb, excepting the gloves on its hands and the crown on its head, which on the fkull in the coffin was found to be the ce-lebrated monk's cowl, in which he is recorded to be buried, as a paffport through the regions of purgatory. This facred envelope appeared to have fitted the head very clofely, and had been tied or buckled under the chin by ftraps, parts of

* The bowels and heart of King John were buried at Croxton Abbey, in Staffordfhire ; the Abbat of which had been his Phyfician, and performed the operation of embalming him. See Holingfhed, p. 606. M. Paris, p. 283.

the body of King John as it appeared on opening his tomb in Worcester Cathedral Monday July 17 1797

The body 5 ft long

London Pub by James Ross Esqr at Bristol 1 and RC Nightingale & F Jones Vaultn In C Street Bath

which remained. The body was covered by a robe reaching from the neck nearly to the feet, it had some of its embroidery still remaining near the right knee. It was apparently of crimson damask, and of strong texture : its colour however was so totally discharged from the effect of time, that it is but conjecturally it can be said to have been of any, but what has now pervaded the whole object, namely, a dusky brown The cuff of the left arm which had been laid on the breast remained. In that hand a sword, in a leather scabbard, had been placed as on the tomb, parts of which much decayed, were found at intervals down the left side of the body, and to the feet, as were also parts of the scabbard, but in a much more perfect state than those of the sword. The legs had on a sort of ornamented covering which was tied round at the ankles, and extended over the feet, where the toes were visible through its decayed parts, the string about the left ankle still remained. The upper part of those coverings could not be traced, and it is undecided whether they should be termed boots, or whether they were a part of the under dress similar to the modern pantaloons. It would have been fortunate had it been determined whether they were of leather, or of what sort of drapery.

THE COFFIN

is of the Higley stone of Worcestershire, white, and chissel-levelled, wholly dissimilar in its kind to either that of the foundation of the tomb, its pannels, covering, or figure of the king Its shape is best exhibited in the annexed plate A very considerable fracture runs through it in an oblique direction, one foot six inches from the left shoulder, to two feet nine inches from the right. The coffin is laid upon the pavement of the choir, without being let into it Its original covering, is that stone out of which the effigy of the king is sculptured, and now lying on the tomb, the shape of which is exactly correspondent with that of the stone coffin, and its extreme dimensions strictly proportionate to its purpose.

MEASURES.

	Feet.	Inches.
Depth of the cavity of the stone coffin in which the body is contained - - - - - -	0	9
Ditto, of the circular part, containing the head -	0	6 ½
Ditto, of the outside of the coffin - - - -	1	—
Thickness of the sides, ends, and bottom - - -	0	3,

	Feet.	Inches.
Length, inside - - - - - - -	5	7
Extreme length, outside - - - - -	6	1
Breadth at the head - - - - - -	2	2
Breadth at the feet - - - - - -	1	0
Length of the original cover, or lid of the stone coffin	6	4
Breadth at the head - - - - - -	2	5
Breadth at the feet - - - - - -	1	2*

REMARKS AND ILLUSTRATIONS.

It hath already been said, that the foregoing discovery of the remains of King John, had resulted from the strong assumptions of conjecture, founded on the opinions of former antiquaries of established character, and supported by those of others of the present times, asserting that the original sepulture and interment of the royal body was in the Lady's chapel of this cathedral; nor has the least circumstance from the recent disclosure of it in the tomb in the choir, arisen to invalidate those opinions and conjectures.

To give farther support to the proofs already adduced, that the ancient graves of the canonized saints, Oswald and Wulstan, are in the Lady's chapel, and that the body of the king first received interment between them, would amount only to a waste of words; to point out the similarity of the construction of this ancient series of royal and ecclesiastical sepulchres, may however be somewhat satisfactory to those who have never seen them, or their actual position

Let then the reader form in his imagination the stone coffin, in which the remains of the king now repose, to be let into the floor of the Lady's chapel, between the figures of the two bishops already laid there, and so deep as to have its top level with the pavement; and let him also suppose the sculptured figure of the King, now lying on the tomb, placed on the coffin as its covering, and which would apparently seem laid on the floor, he will then have the entire ancient sepulchre of King John, as originally constructed in that chapel, fully before his " minds eye "

Those of the two prelates are precisely of the same fashion, laid the same depth in the earth, and in nothing different but the sculptures and the kind of stone of which they are formed †

---

* See Hist and Antiq. of Worcester, Vol I Sect. IV, p 58, Note.

† It is here necessary to observe, that the stone coffins of the two bishops are laid on the sites of the ancient graves of St Oswald and St Wulstan, that to the south containing the remains of Bishop Sylvester, who per-

It is prefumed from the abundant evidences apparent on the view of the royal body and its appendages, that they have unqueftionably undergone a tranflation fince the time of their original interment in this cathedral. The change in the pofi- tion of the fkull, the difplacing of the jaws, the lofs of the bones of the hands, and the radii of both arms; the mutilations of the fword and its fcabbard, and the broken fragments of the mortar upon and below the abdomen, the large fracture, fuppofed to be entirely through the ftone coffin, and laftly, the tomb itfelf of modern conftruction, paired indeed, but not matched with the ancient, form to- gether a teftimonial phalanx of evidence, much too ftrong to be refifted with a view to proving that the place in which the body is now found depofited, was that of its firft burial. And thus, while a lefs dignified tenant may have been ad- mitted to the poffeffion of the royal grave, the king himfelf is proved literally to remain above ground, intombed indeed, but unburied

In the courfe of this curious and interefting inveftigation, we have wit- neffed a no lefs curious refult —Speculative opinions, to which the refearches into the tranfactions of paft ages, muft more or lefs fubject the antiquarian and hiftorian to enter into, having in this inftance elevated into an affumed fact, an event of ancient date of which no record had been made in the archives of the cathedral, a reliance on thofe opinions, and a confequent refort being had to the only practical means of eftablifhing or deftroying them, that effectual ordeal is feen in its operation to have fecured a valuable recompence to pofterity, in the de- ftruction it has wrought on ingenious fpeculation, founded on fpecious poffibilities, out of the ruins of which hath been raifed a pofitive truth, that has for ever clofed the lips of conjecture, and happily placed an ancient fact, beyond the reach of future doubt

Had the fugitive memorandum made by Mr. Dougharty, dated July the 24th, 1754, and inferted as a MS note in p. 35, in his copy of Dr Thomas's Survey of the Cathedral, and now in the poffeffion of Sir Charles Trubfhaw Withers, Knight,* been fortunately entered in its proper place, in the Archives of the

formed the ceremony of interring King John in this cathedral, and died himfelf 16 July, 1219, in the fame year he had difplaced the remains of St Wulftan from his grave, and put them in a new fhrine, in which operation he fawed fome of his bones in funder with his own hands. The remains of St. Ofwald had been firft enfhrined by Bifhop Adulph his fucceffor, A. D 1002, and again by Bifhop Wulftan in 1089, at the opening of the prefent cathedral The grave of St Wulftan to the north, which the author examined in 1796, is occupied by the ftone coffin and remains of William de Blois, fucceffor to Bifhop Sylvefter; he died Auguft the 18th, 1238. See Hiftory and Antiquities of Worcefter, Vol I. Section IV p. 73, 74; Section VII. p 186, and plan of the Ca- thedral, Ref 1, 2, 3 It appears therefore that the three coffins, of the fafhion of that period, were all made and placed there in the courfe of only twenty three years Other inftances of the fame mode of interment in the fame fort of coffins occur in this cathedral, of which that of William de Harcourt, temp. King John, in the Dean's chapel, is one.

* See Hiftory and Antiquities of Worcefter, Vol. I. Sect. IV. p. 70.

Dean and Chapter, it would then have borne the indubitable ftamp of official au-
thenticity upon the face of it, and could have been cited as fuch   It is however
fatisfactory that even in its prefent form, difcovered by mere chance, its veracity
hath been fully proved   But the defcription of the tomb having been opened at
that period, being liable to more than a right reading from its ambiguity, and
ftanding infolated from other fupport, became too fufpicious for decided adoption,
efpecially when it was to be oppofed to fuch odds of direct contrary opinion, and
thence it hath remained to the prefent time, like the prophecies of Caffandra,
difcredited but true.

It is much to be regretted that the impatience of the multitude to view the
royal remains, fo unexpectedly found, fhould have become fo ungovernable, as to
make it neceffary to clofe up the object of their curiofity fo precipitantly, as to
render it extremely difficult to obtain that regular account of a difcovery fo truly
interefting demanded   Under that difadvantage however, ftrict and minute truth
is attached to each particular of the accounts communicated, with a faithfulnefs
of defcription that muft be approved, and the juftice evidently rendered to the
graphic reprefentation of the object will amply demonftrate that it had the peculiar good fortune whilft vifible, to have fallen under the moft judicious and accurate obfervation

On the evening of Tuefday the 18th of July, the day after it had been taken
down, and the royal remains laid open to the view of fome thoufands of fpecta-
tors, who crouded to the cathedral to fee it, the tomb of King John was completely reftored and finally clofed.

F I N I S.

Lightning Source UK Ltd.
Milton Keynes UK
UKOW011931011012

199925UK00004B/99/P